Charles Clifton
of Pierce-Arrow

Charles Clifton of Pierce-Arrow

A Sure Hand and a Fine Automobile

ROGER J. SHERMAN

McFarland & Company, Inc., Publishers
Jefferson, North Carolina

LIBRARY OF CONGRESS CATALOGUING-IN-PUBLICATION DATA

Names: Sherman, Roger J., 1941– author.
Title: Charles Clifton of Pierce-Arrow : a sure hand and a fine automobile / Roger J. Sherman.
Description: Jefferson, North Carolina : McFarland & Company, Inc., 2019 | Includes bibliographical references and index.
Identifiers: LCCN 2019002167 | ISBN 9781476675848 (paperback : acid free paper) ∞
Subjects: LCSH: Clifton, Charles, 1853–1928. | Pierce-Arrow Motor Car Company—History. | Businessmen—United States—Biography. | Automobile industry and trade—United States—History.
Classification: LCC HD9710.U52 S54 2019 | DDC 338.7/629222092 [B] —dc23
LC record available at https://lccn.loc.gov/2019002167

BRITISH LIBRARY CATALOGUING DATA ARE AVAILABLE

ISBN (print) 978-1-4766-7584-8
ISBN (ebook) 978-1-4766-3609-2

© 2019 Roger J. Sherman. All rights reserved

No part of this book may be reproduced or transmitted in any form or by any means, electronic or mechanical, including photocopying or recording, or by any information storage and retrieval system, without permission in writing from the publisher.

Front cover: image oil painting of Charles Clifton (courtesy Michele Clifton); inset, 1916 38-C-4 sedan body for the owner-driver: two doors, seating seven passengers (courtesy Pierce-Arrow Society)

Printed in the United States of America

McFarland & Company, Inc., Publishers
Box 611, Jefferson, North Carolina 28640
www.mcfarlandpub.com

To Bernard J. Weis, long-time editor
of Pierce-Arrow Society publications, who for decades
devotedly preserved historical materials that were
essential to the construction of this narrative

Acknowledgments

To reconstruct a chain of events that took place more than a century ago, obtaining accurate and useful information about them is crucial. For the present narrative such information was gathered during years of looking through contemporaneous documentary accounts written for periodicals that served the automobile industry and those covering the locations where events in the story took place. The specific sources are largely mentioned while telling the story of Charles Clifton. These were mostly found as described above with sources.

Those documents were only modestly useful in providing information about Charles Clifton's family and upbringing, which made the generous contribution of the Colonel's great-granddaughter Michele Clifton and her father Mark Clifton especially important. Without her researches it is doubtful any outsider, as I am, could piece together the histories of the Clifton and Dorsheimer families in America. I wish to express my gratitude to both for their patient help and generous assistance in constructing that part of the story and providing related illustrations.

Likewise, reconstructing the story of a life that took place largely in Buffalo, New York, a place about which I knew little, required some local guidance. This was supplied, thankfully, by my cousin Suzanne Argenio who was born and raised in South Buffalo. She and her mother, Ruth Evelyn Baxter, spent many hours finding ways to facilitate my absorption of information about the city (which has since continued to fascinate me) while also being most hospitable during my visits.

Their work was extended by another native of the city, Henry May IV, great-grandson of the Pierce-Arrow vice-president, and G. Marc Hamburger, a former president of the Pierce-Arrow Society, who both kindly reviewed the manuscript, offering comments and support.

Technical review of the automotive side of the story was provided by the generous attentions of the Pierce-Arrow Society Technical Committee chair, H. Paul Johnson, Jr. Indeed, members of the Pierce-Arrow Society greatly assisted my understanding of the story in uncounted ways, for which I am most grateful.

Despite such kind assistance, errors may well have remained despite my determination to expel them. All of those must be attributed to me.

All through the long research and construction of this story I enjoyed the support and encouragement of my wife Kathleen and my daughters Melissa and Laurel; the latter even generously proofread the completed manuscript for me.

These and many more contributors, some of whose names I never knew, have my deepest gratitude.

Table of Contents

Acknowledgments	vi
Preface	1
Introduction: Spokesman for the Industry Itself	2
1. A Leading Family (1853–1899)	5
2. Our Little Wagon (1900–1904)	15
3. American Cars (1905–1907)	30
4. Showdown Over Selden (1907–1911)	41
5. Conflict and Character (1912–1913)	73
6. Excellence in Every Desirable Particular (1914)	90
7. Unexpected Bonanza (1915–1916)	112
8. War Work (1917–1918)	130
9. Esprit de Corps (Early 1919)	159
10. Finding a Peace Basis (Late 1919)	169
11. Toward Quantity and Profit (1920)	178
12. A Most Difficult Year (1921)	202
13. Searching Out Safety (1922–1923)	217
14. New Horizons (1924–1927)	232
15. Passing (1928)	268
Sources	275
Index	277

A peer conducts himself in a pious, high-minded, grave, dignified and manly kind of way, in his course through life: his last will is very often a remarkable piece which one lingers over. And then you perceive that there was kindness in him as well as rigour, pity for the poor; that he had fine hospitalities, generosities, in fine, that he was throughout much of a noble, good and valiant man.

—Thomas Carlyle, inaugural address at Edinburgh University, 1866

Preface

This book traces the life of a once famous, now largely forgotten pioneer of the American automobile industry. Its genesis was my purchase of a low-mileage Pierce-Arrow car as a young man, along with joining of the Pierce-Arrow Society to obtain background about it and useful service information.

I was, alas, not able to keep the Pierce-Arrow for a lifetime, but my interest in the make has continued. It remains an object of fascination to me as an artifact itself and a splendid illustration of the life of bygone days.

During my long membership in the Pierce-Arrow Society, where I presently hold a position as editor of its quarterly magazine, *The Arrow*, I became increasingly interested in the accomplishments of Col. Charles Clifton (1853–1928), longtime general manager of the Pierce-Arrow Motor Car Company, and nearly a celebrity among early automobile executives. To the best of my knowledge Clifton has never received the attention he deserves among automobile historians, despite a sterling reputation within the industry that matched a high standing in his native city. For nearly a quarter of a century, Clifton was repeatedly elected by his fellow automobile executives as president of industry associations. In fact, upon his retirement in 1927, he was made lifetime honorary president and honorary board member of the National Automobile Chamber of Commerce, later renamed the Motor Vehicle Manufacturers Association. Clifton was a leading participant in the famous Selden patent controversy and also helped negotiate the important cross-licensing agreement among the automobile companies that brought an end to destructive patent fights within the industry. His efforts were important in the whole industry's development.

Meanwhile, the Pierce-Arrow Company of Buffalo thrived under his leadership for years, producing cars of the highest reputation that served even the White House, and are still prized possessions to this day.

While this book contains many details about the Pierce-Arrow cars, it is not a company history, a task taken up previously by such notables as Bernard J. Weis, Marc Ralston, Brooks T. Brierley and the redoubtable Maurice D. Hendry. This is a narrative of the man himself and the history of his efforts for and dedication to the industry and his city along with Pierce-Arrow. Consequently, coverage of these larger stories ends with Colonel Clifton's death in 1928.

Remaining records and the continued efforts of his great-granddaughter, Michele Clifton the family genealogist, furnished the details of this account, and any unwitting mistakes found are the regrettable shortcomings of the author himself.

Introduction
Spokesman for the Industry Itself

For nearly the whole of the first quarter-century in the development of the American automobile industry, Charles Clifton was prominent among its well-known executives in the popular press. He was quoted whenever an important event affecting the industry arose. Each January he penned stories for the automobile pages of the papers describing the trends seen at the New York Automobile Show. Many of the industry's most irascible figures would defer to his judgment as the elected head of important industry trade associations, especially with regard to public relations. Their respect stemmed from his reputation for being a careful listener to all conflicting sides of an issue before taking his eventual strong stand. Clifton was 74 years old when he died on June 21, 1928, but he had been a public figure for only the last thirty of those years. He himself considered his wealth and position a result of happenstance and good fortune, quietly distributing continual gifts to causes and people he considered worthy of support while disdaining showy excesses.

The happenstance that resulted in his good fortune was his being hired in 1897 as assistant treasurer for the George N. Pierce Company in his home city of Buffalo, New York. At that particular moment the hiring seemed more lucky than auspicious. The failure of the Bell, Lewis and Yates Coal Mining Co., of which Clifton was treasurer, had left him jobless with a wife and two young children to support. Even with the new job there were concerns because the Pierce Co. was mired in difficulties at the time. The company had developed over some twenty years in Buffalo's harbor district at the corner of Hanover and Prime from a manufacturer of such household items as iceboxes and birdcages to a respected producer of high-quality bicycles during the height of the bicycle craze in the early 1890s. Pierce had suffered from a reduction of sales as the craze ended, and in 1896 had to seek financial help to stay in business.

Col. Charles Clifton (1853–1928), ca. 1915 (courtesy Pierce-Arrow Society).

The "angel" who gathered the needed capital for its survival was a Buffalo wallpaper tycoon, one George Kingsley Birge, who with two associates stabilized the finances, allowing Pierce to continue. Subsequently, the bicycle company was transformed over time into the producer of one of the most prestigious luxury automobiles ever made in the United States—the Pierce-Arrow. "They were all Buffalo men," the company later wrote about its early owners, "friends and neighbors." When those words were written in 1920, Clifton was described as "the active executive head."

~ 1 ~

A Leading Family
(1853–1899)

> The late Col. Charles Clifton was the company's chief representative before the public. He officiated at state occasions and served in trade associations as Pierce-Arrow's spokesman. He embodied the popular conception of what a wealthy automobile executive looked and acted like. One night he invited five of his cronies of his less affluent days to the Buffalo Club for dinner and under each napkin tucked a $10,000 check.
> —Nat Gorham, in the Buffalo *Evening News*, 1944

After joining the Pierce Company, Charles Clifton's circumstances reached a level of comfort from which they never descended. It was his cousin, writing in the Buffalo *Evening News* some years later, who remarked that Clifton "embodied the popular conception of what a wealthy automobile executive looked and acted like." But the first 45 years of his life found him in situations of ease that alternated with setbacks. As young children, Clifton and his five siblings were accustomed to the early steamship passage necessary to visit their relatives in the canton of Wollstein in western Germany northeast of Stuttgart. This was the region from which their maternal grandfather Philip Dorsheimer had emigrated in 1822 to Pennsylvania and, later, Wayne County New York where he was successful in the grain milling business. Moving to Buffalo, mouth of the new Erie Canal, in 1836, Dorsheimer continued his successful career and expanded it into a widely-admired reputation as an hotelier, capped by an active role in New York State politics.

Charles Clifton was born on September 20, 1853, in room 13 of the Mansion House, his grandfather's famous hotel in Buffalo. His mother was Philip and Sarah Dorsheimer's only daughter, Elizabeth, and his father was Henry Clifton, a native of the British Isles and the hotel manager, distinguished by his polished manners. At that time Buffalo was a thriving center of transportation that would shortly become the largest inland port in the United States. Industries and financial institutions derived from that rapid growth were already being built up. In a later reminiscence, Charles Clifton recalled the Mansion House as "just about the center of things, at least I thought so." Located at a central place, the southeast corner of Main at Exchange Street, the hotel was on the steep edge of Buffalo's "Terrace," only a block away from the railroad station where New York Central trains from Manhattan were "exchanged" with the easternmost of a string of railroads that connected to Chicago. These were later consolidated into the Lake Shore & Michigan Southern. Other lines served

Niagara Falls and Canada. All eventually became part of the New York Central System. This proximity to the traveling public of the Railroad Age made the Mansion House a very profitable property indeed. Perhaps his birthplace was itself formative because Charles Clifton would spend a great deal of time in hotels during his life.

Clifton's first years saw the controversy over slavery sharpen into the break that fractured the United States itself. The Battle of Gettysburg was fought only a few weeks before his tenth birthday. As one of the early members of the Republican Party, Grandfather Dorsheimer was well known and respected far beyond the city of Buffalo. "Originally, he had been a Democrat of a mild type," Charles Clifton later wrote of him, "but when slavery became a political issue and the Republican Party was formed, my grandfather was one of the foremost. This brought him into contact with all the leaders of that party, and when I first remember he was surrounded by the great men of the day, partly by virtue of 'keeping tavern' and partly by a strong personal magnetism and fund of good humored wit."

It is significant that when newly-elected Abraham Lincoln traveled to his presidential inauguration, he stopped in Buffalo and attended services at the First Unitarian Church down on Franklin Street, the Dorsheimers' house of worship. An 11-year-old Charles Clifton may also have been witness to the obsequies for the slain president on April 27, 1865, as the casket containing the body was transported from the special funeral train to St. James Hall for a public viewing before continuing its final journey to Springfield, Illinois.

Politics and public service were also taken up by Philip and Sarah's son William, Charles Clifton's uncle. William Dorsheimer, was regarded by Roy Nagle, a

Top: **Philip Dorsheimer (1797–1868) brought a heritage of grain trading to the United States in 1816, eventually settling in Buffalo, New York, where he became a well-known political figure and hotelier.** *Bottom:* **Sarah Gorgas Dorsheimer (1802–1869) married Philip Dorsheimer in 1821. Two adult children survived them, one of whom was Charles Clifton's mother. No record seems to exist of Charles Clifton's paternal grandparents (courtesy Michele Clifton).**

noted Niagara Frontier historian, as a much-underrated giant of Buffalo's early years. A lawyer by profession, Dorsheimer had to withdraw from Harvard College in 1849 at the end of two years due to ill health. Nonetheless, he was eventually admitted to the bar in 1854. Dorsheimer's political loyalties wavered between Democratic and Republican over the years. His first public position was as U.S. District Attorney for Northern New York, being appointed in 1867 by President Andrew Johnson. Seven years later, in 1874, he was nominated as the candidate for Lieutenant Governor on a ticket with Samuel Tilden, was elected and served in that post until 1880. In 1882 he was elected to Congress from New York's 7 District. He served on the House Judiciary Committee and chaired the committee in charge of the completion of the Washington Monument.

William Dorsheimer (1832–1888) was a prominent Buffalo figure and politician remembered for his impact on the city plan (courtesy Michele Clifton).

Dorsheimer had a continuing interest in architecture and the design of public spaces. It was at his H.H. Richardson-designed home at 434 Delaware Avenue in Buffalo that he and his associates met with landscape architect Fredrick Law Olmstead to shape the park and parkway system that so characterizes the city. Dorsheimer was parks commissioner at the time. He was named by President Grover Cleveland to supervise the "Niagara Reservation" around the falls in 1883. He was also one of the founders of both the Buffalo Fine Arts Academy and the Historical Society.

Charles Clifton remembered his Uncle William, 21 years his senior, as "great fun for us children because he loved to play with us, and he was very strong so we always felt sure in his arms and standing on his shoulders. We all lived together at the Mansion House."

This extended family seems to have lived together for Charles Clifton's whole childhood. One family story told of diva Jenny Lind singing Charles' older sister Jeanie to sleep as a baby in the Mansion House. Their eventual separation was caused, perhaps, by the death of Grandfather Philip Dorsheimer and the hotel's sale in 1868. The family consisted of both of the Dorsheimers' two children, Elizabeth and William. The Clifton branch was made up of Charles' mother and father, along with their children, Jeanie, Charles and, as time passed, an additional two sisters and two brothers. The youngsters' father, a valued principal in the operation of the Mansion House, remains of undisclosed origins.

Henry Clifton gave his six children his last name, but very little else about the man can be ascertained. His birth date was said to have been August 20, 1820, at an unspecified location in England. He was also said to be the youngest child, but no parents are named. His family name at birth is unknown. The 1850 Federal Census for Ward 1, Erie County, New York, lists Henry Clifton (age 30) as a resident at the Mansion House in Buffalo, employed as a "clerk."

On August 13 of that year he married his employer's daughter Elizabeth. By 1861 he was a naturalized U.S. citizen. What Henry had done for the first thirty years of his life is not documented, including how he came to end up at the Mansion House. It has been suggested that he might have emigrated from Canada to Buffalo. He had, purportedly, been employed at the Clifton House in Clifton, Ontario. In fact, that very employment has been speculated as the possible origin of his eventual last name. Mark Clifton, Henry Clifton's great-grandson, speculates that he might have been a "remittance man," a person sent away to live off "remittances" from the family to cover some embarrassing situation. No one has yet found the documented truth. Grandfather Dorsheimer, once deceased, left an estate that was doubtless substantial. His widow, grandmother Sarah Gorgas Dorsheimer, survived him but a year.

The Dorsheimer children set out on new paths. William, now on an upward political course, began the construction of his Delaware Avenue home. The 1870 Federal Census for Ward 7 in Buffalo lists Henry Clifton, 50 years of age, as a "farmer," born in England, owning real estate valued at $20,000 and personal property valued at $5,000. His wife, Elizabeth Clifton, 43, is listed as born in N.Y. State, "keeping house," owning real estate valued at $7,000 and personal property of $2,000. The children are listed as: Jenny [Jeanie] Clifton (19 years old); Charles (17) "attending school"; Alles [Alice] (13); Sarah (11); Philip (4); and Henry (2). The property the family claimed was of significant value at the time.

Then something quite unexpected happened. Henry abruptly left the family or was possibly thrown out by Elizabeth. It is not certain which, but surviving letters to daughter Alice in the possession of her grandson Fredrick Gilbert II show quite a painful separation. They were composed over the years of 1876 and 1877 while Henry was acting as the agent for a Buffalo friend, one James Dormer, at remote Beaver Island on Lake Michigan. He describes his loneliness and bitter winter cold and wind. Elizabeth is never mentioned. He compliments his daughter for "meeting your hard lot the way that you do." He eagerly responds to every scrap of news about his children. No hint, however, is found of the reason for this painful separation from his family. Henry Clifton died on Beaver Island at 2:00 p.m., August 14, 1877, of apoplexy, and is buried there beneath a simple headstone. During this time, a great many people and businesses suffered losses stemming from the financial crisis of September 1873 and the following six-year economic depression. It is likely that the Clifton family was affected by this downturn. Certainly, Charles Clifton was in altered economic circumstances by 1871. In his obituary he is reported to have attended "the Buffalo public schools and the Highland Military Academy of Worcester, Massachusetts." He is, in fact, listed on that school's register for the session ending July 1, 1870. For an editorial published in a Pierce-Arrow company

Henry Clifton (1820–1877), an emigrant from the British Isles, married Philip Dorsheimer's daughter Elizabeth in 1850. Charles Clifton was the second of their six children (courtesy Michele Clifton).

1. A Leading Family (1853–1899)

publication in May 1920, Clifton wrote: "It was a keen disappointment to me that I could not have had a college education, but stern necessity compelled me to become a breadwinner at 17."

For the next 27 years Clifton followed a varied career at local establishments until he was hired by the company he served with exceptional devotion for the rest of his life. The firm that first hired him in late 1870 was Sidney Shepard & Co., a producer and distributor of hardware. His exact position is not known, but Clifton worked there until sometime in 1876, when he took a job as a clerk for the wide-gauged Erie Railroad in Buffalo, a position he appears to have kept for the next

Top: Elizabeth Dorsheimer Clifton (1828–1915) married her father's hotel manager and started a family. *Bottom:* Henry Clifton II stands on the steps of the family home in Buffalo, perhaps the one at 881 Main St., a boy proud of his snow shoveling (courtesy Michele Clifton).

two years or so. This was followed by employment at the Buffalo Grape Sugar Co. for another two years. In the Federal Census of 1880, he is listed as "Head of Household" at 881 Main Street. His age is given as 26, and he is employed as "Clerk in Sugar Works." His mother, Elizabeth, age 51, is "Keeping House" at this location, and sister Sarah (21 years old), brothers Philip (13), and "Harry" [Henry] (12) live with them, along with a "domestic" [servant].

Charles Clifton's star appeared to be on the rise in 1881 when he took a job as general manager for the Colgate and Gilbert Company, a starch manufacturer. This was doubtless made possible because Charles' sister Alice had married Fredrick M. Gilbert in 1879, and Gilbert owned the starch company. The expected stability and advancement inherent in that position did not, however, materialize—quite the reverse in fact. Within two years Clifton and the Gilbert family had split apart, never to reconcile. The patent issue parting them left such hard feelings that one of the Gilberts later referred to the former general manager as "that pirate Charles."

Michele Clifton, Charles Clifton's great-granddaughter, having delved into the obscure matter, states flatly, "I think, unless that whole Gilbert thing is what they are intimating it to be, it was something they were doing. Because we know they were infringing. We know that much. But I don't know whether he was threatening to go to the authorities or whether he was threatening blackmail in exchange for silence.... I don't know."

Whatever the truth is, Clifton was out of a job and the rift between the two branches of the Clifton family has lasted for a century.

At about this same time, in 1881, Charles enlisted in the New York militia or National Guard, where he served until 1903. During his service he eventually attained the rank of colonel on the staff of Brigadier General Peter C. Doyle, 4th Brigade. This title remained attached to Clifton's name and reputation from then until his death. The *Buffalo Directory and Family Guide* for the year 1883 listed Charles Clifton as a member of the City Club. George Gorham was then president, and the membership included G.K. Birge. Both of these gentlemen played notable parts later in Clifton's life.

It was apparently sometime

Alice Clifton Gilbert (1857–1942) with young Colgate Gilbert II (1896–1954). A patent dispute pitted the Gilbert branch of the Clifton family against Charles Clifton (courtesy Michele Clifton).

during these eventful years that Charles Clifton found himself in financial difficulties. At one point an illness brought medical and hospital bills that he was unable to meet, and he never forgot his embarrassment and shame at his failure. His embarrassment was only increased when the First Unitarian Church forced him to give up his accustomed sitting space in a particular pew at Sunday services because he could no longer pay the rent. These difficulties evidently continued for some time, and they had long-term repercussions.

Issues of the *Buffalo Directory and Family Guide* for this period show signs of instability as well. In 1883, he and his mother Elizabeth still lived at 881 Main Street. At that time, Charles is listed as "Quartermaster of the 14th Brigade of N.G.S.N.Y." By the next year their residence changed to 128 Morgan. In 1887 neither mother nor son is listed in this directory. Sister Sarah and brother Philip are reported in 1890 as residing at 178 Pearl Street; Charles and his mother are unlisted that year. For 1892–93 Charles is recorded as living at 39 N. Pearl, while his mother has moved in with Philip.

The *Buffalo Directory* for 1889, however, does include Charles Clifton, who is then employed as treasurer for the Bell, Lewis & Yates Coal Mining Co. at 17–21 Coal & Iron Exchange. His home address is listed as 89 West Genesee Street. Meanwhile, Mrs. Elizabeth Clifton is included at 254 Franklin with Sarah, Philip, who works at the *Buffalo Morning Express*, and Harry, employed as a "clerk." Charles Clifton, according to this source, is now stationed at Fort Porter with rank of "Lt. Colonel, Asst. Adjutant General to Brig. General Peter C. Doyle, Commander." Clifton's two positions clearly show that his life is taking on a bourgeois stability and promise. He had also been admitted as a member of the Buffalo Club on July 21, 1888.

As if in celebration of these ripening achievements, Charles Clifton married Miss Grace Gorham at 7:30 on the evening of January 22, 1891, at Trinity Church, the Rev. Francis Lobdell officiating. This event demonstrates several important strides in Charles Clifton's personal and professional standing. Emily Grace Gorham, 29 years old, was the daughter of George Gorham and his late first wife Emily Augusta Hall Gorham. George Gorham was an esteemed lawyer in Buffalo, and, according to his obituary, a "very loyal son of Harvard and seldom failed to attend Commencement at Cambridge … ever since graduation in 1857." He had been president of the Buffalo Harvard Club, and president of both the lofty Buffalo Club and the City Club of Buffalo. He regularly attended impeccable Trinity Episcopal Church on Delaware Avenue, and served there as one of its wardens as well as a trusted advisor. He had also served on the City Council and as vice-chancellor of the University of Buffalo.

Charles Clifton in his uniform of the New York State Militia (courtesy Michele Clifton).

These are powerful auspices, but they dovetail well with the Dorsheimer family position earlier in the century. In fact, it is hard not to think that the families knew each other years before, since George Gorham as a young man was a clerk at the United States District Court at the time that Charles Clifton's uncle William was district attorney for Northern New York State.

Charles and Grace Clifton presently took up residence at 61 Irving Place, just below North Street in a developing upper middle class residential area away from the increasingly industrialized neighborhood in which he had grown up. This Irving Place address would be their home for the next 20 years or so. Charles also became a parishioner at Trinity Church. His new wife, Grace Gorham Clifton, had been properly schooled to be a genteel lady at Buffalo's School of Practice and Buffalo Female Academy before attending St. Agnes School in Albany and Mrs. Pratt's School in Utica, New York. Clifton had what appeared to be a secure management position in a healthy company. There can be little question of the couple's elevated social standing.

In August of 1892, their first child, Katherine Gould Clifton, was born. This was followed by the birth of a son, Gorham, in November 1893. A third child, Alice Dorsheimer Clifton, would arrive 10 years later in May 1903.

As we have seen, this happy situation was threatened profoundly when the Bell, Lewis & Yates coal company collapsed in the mid–1890s. At length, the George N. Pierce Co. stepped into the breech, hiring Charles Clifton as assistant treasurer. There are no remaining details of his hiring that shed light on the circumstances. It could well be that Mr. Pierce or Mr. Birge

The Charles Clifton residence (1890–1910) at 61 Irving Place in Buffalo in a recent photograph that includes Charles Clifton III to the right (courtesy Michele Clifton).

1. A Leading Family (1853–1899)

knew Clifton earlier, but that is not certain. Clifton's advent was in 1897, a year after the refinancing of the George N. Pierce Company that brought great changes to the management of the firm. Birge, his associate, William H. Gardner, and his attorney, William B. Hoyt, replaced directors previously associated with George N. Pierce. Only Pierce himself and his valued factory chief, Henry May, remained. In addition, William Gardner's son Laurence became company secretary. That same year and into 1898 Charles was the secretary of the Buffalo Club. In 1899 he would be its "3rd Vice-President." His father-in-law, George Gorham, had been president of the Buffalo Club for 1896–1897. After 1890 Clifton was a club director from time to time over the years.

One thing that seems remarkable is the rapid rise of Charles Clifton in the day-to-day management of the Geo. N. Pierce Company, its connections with other similar firms and the public at large. Very soon, Clifton had become treasurer and head of sales.

At the time it seemed that the hastily arranged infusion of outside capital had stabilized the Pierce enterprise. Its business seemed prosperous, and the company offered a number of circulars to the public that kept attention focused on its product while providing useful information. One example is the 97-page booklet it released in 1899 entitled *Buffalo Cycling Tour Book* that offered several descriptions of tours possible in what the book called the "Paradise of Cyclers." This was in reference to the city of Buffalo itself and its surrounding countryside attractions such as Niagara Falls. "With the continued increase in the mileage of smooth pavements," the booklet avers, "the appellation becomes more than ever appropriate." Tours began at 566 Main Street, the George N. Pierce retail outlet in the city.

The Henry Clifton family, with mother Elizabeth (*center front*), includes: (*left back*) Alice Clifton Gilbert (1857–1942), Edward B. Guthrie, Philip D. Clifton (1866–1959), Sarah D. Clifton (1858–1958) and (*in front*) Henry Clifton II (1868–1929), Jean Clifton Guthrie (1851–1901), Mother Clifton, Charles Clifton (1853–1928) and Emily Grace Gorham Clifton (1861–1940) (courtesy Michele Clifton).

The "Tried and True" Pierce bicycle had a reputation as a reliable machine, and it attracted members of the bicycle racing fraternity such as Frank L. Kramer, the American Amateur Champion in 1898 and 1899.

Company directors were starting to think they might consider expanding the product line into an even more promising direction.

~ 2 ~

Our Little Wagon
(1900–1904)

> "'Few persons knew how widespread and how unostentatious were his charities,' said a friend last night. 'He was a gentleman in the real meaning of the word—gentle, kindly, just.'"
> —Buffalo *Courier-Express*, June 22, 1928

In 1900 the George N. Pierce Co. began to evaluate new products that would eventually supplant the bicycle as the company's focus. That year the board of directors was made up of George N. Pierce, president, Henry May, long-time associate and vice-president, Charles Clifton, treasurer, George K. Birge and William H. Gardner. In a later account, the company reported, "Early in 1900, a decision was reached by the Board of Directors to begin experiments with two types of 'horseless carriage' one to use steam the other a gasoline engine." These efforts would take place in its four to five-story factory at 6–22 Hanover Street, near the foot of Buffalo's Main Street.

Such a decision reflected a need to gain greater sales than the bicycle line then offered. It also implied a willingness to attempt much more technological sophistication than the firm had yet demonstrated, although the *Scientific American* for January 20, 1900, had printed a description of the firm's innovative designs for cushion frames on both its chain-driven and shaft-driven bicycles, and a Pierce associate, one Lorenzo B. Somerby, had filed an application for a patent on his shaft-drive for bicycles on September 9, 1899, which would be granted on December 22, 1903.

But the company's enthusiasm for an expanded scope in its business reflected the city of Buffalo's optimism at the time. As the year 1900 began, the city was already clearing some 350 acres to the north of Delaware Park for a great world's fair to be called the Pan-American Exposition, scheduled to open in May of 1901. It would be the grandest public event ever staged at Buffalo, and the city was electric with anticipation.

The George N. Pierce Company was eager to find a profitable new market, and the self-propelled motor carriage looked promising. Alexander Winton, an ambitious bicycle builder in Cleveland, laid claim to the first recorded sale of an American motor car to a private owner in March of 1898, when he sold a one-cylinder model. It was followed by sales of 21 more that year. Winton quickly became an automobile manufacturer.

To oversee the experiments with self-propelled motor vehicles the board chose Percy Pierce, son and heir to George N. Pierce; F.A. Nickerson, who went on to become a Pierce agent in Portland, Maine; and Ephraim N. Bowen. So far as we know, none of these worthies was expert in any aspect of motor car design or construction, although Bowen had made a patent application with the U.S. Patent Office for an improved "binder" for bicycle handlebars and seats on September 9, 1899. The patent, No. 644,573, was granted March 6, 1900. The likelihood is that they were trained mechanics, able to fit pieces successfully and determine what kinds of things needed to be done to make them work together properly.

In later company accounts, the origins of its interest in motor vehicles was credited to George K. Birge, who was accustomed to spending time in France on vacation. At the time, France was the leading motor car producer in the world, and the French company founded by the Compte Albert de Dion with partner Georges Bouton made both steam-powered and gasoline-powered vehicles. Their firm led the French industry in exploitation of gasoline power with its small single-cylinder, high-speed engine incorporating water-cooled head, air-cooled cylinder and advanced electric ignition. This engine was used to power countless De Dion tricycle machines. The driver rode on a

George Kingsley Birge (1849–1918), a noted Buffalo businessman who, with some associates, rescued and then took financial control of the George N. Pierce Co. in 1896 (courtesy Pierce-Arrow Society).

saddle, mounted ahead of the engine, which was connected to the two rear wheels, pedaling to start the engine and assist it when needed to keep up the necessary speed. These engines were also sold to other firms for their own motor vehicles. Birge, so the company reported, had used a three-wheeled Bollée car to tour the "chateau country of France" in 1894, and was so impressed that he encouraged Pierce to look into its merits.

The Pierce efforts were carefully calculated. No one in the firm had any useful experience with such machines, so the plan was to apply the knowledge of others and thus shorten the time required to develop a useful automobile. The fact that the board wanted to investigate both steam and gasoline powered machines shows that the argument about the most successful method to provide power was still unsettled.

This was, after all, the height of the steam era. Seven years before, engineer Charlie Hogan had run the New York Central's crack *Empire State Express* at 112.5 miles per hour over a measured mile on the main line near Batavia, New York, not that far from Buffalo. The Pierce board seemed to feel that steam might be the best bet. They agreed to purchase from the Overman Steam Car Co. of Chicopee Falls, Massachusetts, a set of plans for a steam carriage. These may have been similar to plans for the four-cylinder Victor steam car that Overman offered at the time. Pierce began working with the plans in March of 1900, and by August 21 the mechanics had taken a short ride in the finished product. The machine had many shortcomings. The boiler leaked; air for combustion and fuel were occasionally cut off; sitting near the boiler was uncomfortable; and if the wind pushed from behind, the exhaust was irritating. Ephraim Bowen, who kept a diary of their efforts, wrote of his experiences as

Hanover Street Factory - Birhtplace of Pierce-Arrow

The George N. Pierce Co. factory, 6–22 Hanover St. at the foot of Main Street in Buffalo, New York, around 1900 (courtesy Pierce-Arrow Society).

a driver, "It was hard work for me. The steering is so very stiff and the smallest move of the hand is risky when going fast. Of course, one can get used to it. The roads were very rough, and often a heavy bump would put out our fire...." Their work continued into September and October, and from time to time directors took rides with them. Percy Pierce often drove the car and "Mr. Birge, Mr. Clifton and Mr. William H. Gardner" were recorded as passengers at one time or another. However, frequent failures continued, especially with various supposedly automatic devices meant to keep the machine running safely. All in all, the steam car, known as the "Little Teapot," was a disappointment to its handlers.

Vice-president Henry May, plant manager at Pierce, apparently was the person who discovered the research vehicle for the study of gasoline-powered automobiles. He, of course, knew about Mr. Birge's experiences in France with the Bollée. On a trip to New York City, Mr. May was surprised to see in the show window of John Wanamaker's store "a three wheeled De Dion car of the same type Mr. Birge had ridden in France. He bought it and shipped it to the factory in Buffalo." So went the account printed in a story for the company magazine in 1920. An earlier history from 1918 describes the gasoline vehicle as a "Diamond Quadricycle" that was delivered to the factory on September 28, 1900. There is no record of who manufactured and sold the Diamond Quadricycle, but the specifications show that it was, indeed, based on the De Dion three-wheeled vehicle that was so popular. In any case, evaluation of this machine quickly began. The power plant was a 2¾ HP version of the single-cylinder De Dion motor powering the rear axle. It was steered by tricycle-like handle bars from the driver's seat, or saddle, mounted between the handle bars and the engine. A passenger's seat was attached to the handle bars in front of the driver. The passenger, as the company's account describes, "rode with nothing before him but the world at large, and behind him a poor guarantee of an uninterrupted journey." Henry May rode in the seat one September morning over 28 miles at an average speed of eight miles an hour through the city. The record shows Col. Clifton also rode in that seat for seven miles of Buffalo parkway and seemed satisfied that it had some practical value. It was clearly not perfect, however, even to the unschooled mechanics and executives who were studying it.

Having spent nearly a year with these two vehicles, the company realized that neither was the kind of product that they wanted to offer. They were not reliable or very pleasant to use. If the firm was to have something to show at the Pan-American Exposition the next spring, they would have to rethink what their motor vehicle should be. Consequently, on October 3 Mr. Birge, Mr. Clifton, Mr. May, and Mr. Bowen met to lay down the specifications for a revamped motor car design. To begin with, they decided that it must have four wheels and the passenger and driver should sit side by side as on a good buggy. Over the course of several meetings the committee decided on a wheelbase of 54 inches and a track of 48 inches. The running gear would incorporate a friction clutch, foot brake, side steering on a 35-inch seat, a "skeleton body" and a crank starter for the motor.

The rebuilt machine was finished by November 24 and trials began. An important passenger rode on the first trip: Charles Sheppy, who became a dominant figure in the engineering staff as time went by. This time the results were far less unsatisfactory, but all the men felt that they still had quite a lot of development ahead of them before they would have a truly reliable, comfortable, and practical car. Tests and modifications continued into January of 1901 without a final design being decided upon.

At this point a truly wonderful, and entirely unexpected, event took place at the George N. Pierce Co. Word of its lengthy efforts to design a saleable car evidently had traveled as far as Syracuse, New York, and the E.C. Stearns Company, which employed a technical expert from Great Britain named David Fergusson as an engineer. He had come to the United States in 1899 with a partnership that unsuccessfully promoted the licensing of their patents related to motor vehicles. Fergusson had acted as their chief designer, but left when the partnership broke up and moved to Stearns, then working on motor car designs. Fergusson had a very impressive background, having grown up in the industrial heartland of northeastern England. He was a graduate of the Bradford Technical College in Yorkshire at the age of 19 and was further trained at several companies in that area before joining the patent partnership. He had been an active cyclist for years and had designed several versions of self-propelled vehicles. At Stearns, he worked out a new design for a two-passenger, self-propelled, light, gasoline-powered car but found the other Stearns engineers favored steam. Pierce's troubles with its steam car may have come to his attention, as well. In any event, on January 21, 1901, thirty-one-year-old David Fergusson came to the Pierce factory to have a look at the Pierce experimental car. He also revealed to its interested executives that he had been working on a "car with two-speed and reverse gear, all machinery attached to a bridged rear axle, and folding steering lever that lies on the knees."

On or about February 1, 1901, Fergusson signed a six-month contract to be the George N. Pierce Company's "General Expert in their Automobile Department," where he would design and build his proposed 600-pound car, receiving $38 per week, according to his diary. He immediately began to produce drawings and supervise the purchase, production and assembly of parts into two prototype cars that, with no substantial changes, became the

2. Our Little Wagon (1900–1904)

The first Pierce "Motorette" in an early photograph, carrying its designer, David Fergusson and Percy P. Pierce, son and heir to the founder of the company. While the little car now has fenders, its later dash is not yet applied (courtesy Pierce-Arrow Society).

famous Pierce "Motorette" model, going into production for the 1902 market. The first prototype, with a 2¾ HP De Dion motor but without the projected reverse gear, was first driven on April 30, 1901, the day before the Pan American Exposition opened. After the lengthy development time, the Pierce board had wisely decided that these experimental Motorettes would be severely tested around the country while visiting their bicycle dealers and would not be displayed at the George N. Pierce stand in the Machinery and Transportation Building on the fair grounds. (George K. Birge, a Pierce director and also head of the Exposition's building committee, had made sure Pierce bicycles were used to patrol the fairgrounds.)

That spring of 1901, Charles Clifton mourned the death of his older sister, Jeanie Clifton Guthrie, in Buffalo at age 50.

Tonawanda and Niagara Falls were the locales used for the early tests of the first Motorette prototype. According to David Fergusson's detailed notes about the tests, on May 8 the little car left the factory on Hanover Street at 9:45 a.m. and drove via Delaware Avenue and Humboldt Parkway to Mr. Pierce's house. Arriving at 12:50 p.m., the drivers, Fergusson and Percy Pierce, discovered they needed to repair a loose exhaust pipe (a continuing problem), but by the end of the day the little car had completed 56½ miles, its longest trip so far.

Two days later, Fergusson and a Mr. Winslow drove up to the Pan-American, stayed for 45 minutes or so and then continued on another test drive. The day following, the little car was taken to the King Spring Co. for the installation of mudguards and steps for passengers boarding and de-boarding the machine. Test runs were continual over the summer.

On May 15, an afternoon trip took "Mr. Clifton to the Exhibition." (His invitation to the opening of the Exposition on May 1 is still preserved at the Buffalo and Erie County Historical Society.) Later in the afternoon of the 15th, Mr. Birge rode up to the Pan-American in the prototype. Seventy-one miles were put on the car that day.

The test drivers now began to travel other routes around Buffalo on longer journeys. David Fergusson remembered driving to demonstrate the car at Pierce cycle agents in New York state and Pennsylvania, going as far away as Pittsburgh. Most worrisome on these trips was holding back restless horses alarmed by this unfamiliar machine. The "Knockabout" Motorette had traveled a thousand miles by June 7. The next day Percy Pierce and a "Mr. Goreham" were picked up for rides to the Pan-American. Mr. Goreham may be a misspelling for George Gorham, Col. Clifton's father-in-law. Late in July, "Mr. Goreham" was a passenger again, as was "Master Clifton," very likely Charles Clifton's seven-year-old son Gorham Clifton. Two other passengers were also given rides that day. By that time, a second prototype had been completed, and was possibly used for some of these trips. Charles Sheppy, Percy Pierce, and even Henry May were drivers on prototype runs. Many difficulties with the cars had been remedied, and the design was proving practical. Its lack of a reverse gear was deftly bypassed one time during a demonstration by George N. Pierce himself, who picked up the buggy-like machine by the front and swung it around to face a new direction.

The company had no hesitation about entering the two vehicles in the 500-mile New York to Buffalo Endurance Run in celebration of President William McKinley's visit to the Pan-American. This run began in New York City on September 9 and included two Pierce "Knockabout" models: car number A-7, driven by David Fergusson assisted by Al Keller, and A-8, driven by Percy Pierce assisted by Charles Sheppy. According to David Fergusson's recollections in 1929, these cars were the prototypes themselves, although Pierce was already planning to commence production of these 2¾ HP "Knockabout" Motorettes for 1902. These entries were smaller, lighter, and less powerful than any of the other 80 cars in the run, but the Pierces acquitted themselves well. As *Cycle Age* reported in its September 26 issue, "The wonder of the trip was the PIERCE machine. It is a well-recognized fact that what the PIERCE CO. does, it does well, but no one expected it to take a motor of 2¾ horsepower and build around it a vehicle which could accomplish a feat which overcame vehicles of five times the power and three times the weight."

The death of President McKinley (a victim of an assassin's bullet and misguided medical procedures) on September 14 brought an end to the Endurance Run at Rochester. The Motorettes both made it on to Buffalo that Saturday. They had done well, better than expected, evidently. Charles Clifton wrote a letter criticizing the tone of an article in *The Horseless Age*, which published his response in its September 25 issue. "We desire to inform you," Clifton wrote as treasurer of the Pierce Company, "that your correspondent's fears about these wagons [the Motorettes] lasting through to Buffalo were entirely without warrant inasmuch as they both ran all the way through with a minimum of troubles as compared to even the large machines.... We trust that our little wagon will not be overlooked inasmuch as we believe that there will be a demand in the trade for a useful runabout wagon with good speed and endurance and at a moderate price.... We trust you will do us the justice in your next issue of setting us right. Very truly yours...." This letter suggests that Clifton had been given responsibility for handling publicity and public relations for the "wagons," and perhaps the company itself. His impact on the automobile industry itself had only begun.

The early cars had proved reliable enough to produce, and a demand for them developed as well, as indicated by the following story from C.B. Glasscock's 1937 memoir of the early automobile industry, *The Gasoline Age*. One of the longtime companies in the auto business was Willys Overland. According to Glasscock, its namesake, John N. Willys, was operating a sporting goods store in Elmira, New York, when his path was diverted by seeing one of the Pierce Motorettes sometime during their early tests. Willys had been to Cleveland on business, where he saw his very first automobile on the street. Returning to Elmira the next day he saw a Motorette in his hometown. This unexpected spotting of two horseless carriages in as many days was evidence to Willys of a new and potentially popular product. He quickly left for nearby Buffalo to talk with Charles Clifton about the chances of securing an agency for these cars. "Clifton demurred," Glasscock continues, and

Charles Clifton during his early years at the Pierce company, but already a rising influence in the automobile industry (courtesy Michele Clifton).

explained the machine was not yet fully satisfactory to the company. "That attitude of honesty," Glasscock avers, "coupled with superlative ability, eventually raised Clifton to a position of power and honor in the industry, making him perhaps the most highly respected and generally loved man among automobile makers." All the same, salesman Willys persuaded Clifton to sell him the next car produced. Reportedly, Willys sold two cars in 1901 and four the next year.

The George N. Pierce Company was heading determinedly into the nascent automobile market. On August 1, 1901, David Fergusson had signed a one-year extension of his contract to head the firm's automobile department at a salary of $200 a month, and plans were put together to market the 2¾ HP "Knockabout" Motorette cars through the company's extensive bicycle dealer network. These were sold as 1902 models, as were the 3½ HP "Runabout" models with a reverse gear, introduced shortly after, using a larger DeDion engine. An advertising brochure released by Pierce contained an extensive review of the Endurance Run and some of the press comments about the performance of the two Motorettes. The accompanying slogan proclaimed them to be "Tried and True," like the Pierce bicycles. During 1902, something like 125 of these two models were sold. The overlap of the model years makes exact calendar year figures difficult to ascertain.

By this time automobile manufacturers had already organized the National Association of Automobile Manufacturers (NAAM), which had been one sponsor for the first automobile show at New York's Madison Square Garden in November of 1900. In August of 1902 the *Automobile and Motor Review* reported that Charles Clifton had been added to the NAAM's executive committee. He was also active in the Automobile Club of Buffalo. The importance of the industry was clearly growing, as was Clifton's importance in it.

These satisfying advances in Charles Clifton's career were overshadowed by the illness and eventual death of his and Grace Clifton's first child, 10-year-old Katherine Gould Clifton, on January 30, 1902. Her passing had a deep and lasting effect on the Clifton family. Although a last daughter, Alice Dorsheimer Clifton, was born to them in May 1903, some observers felt the warmth began to drain away from the marriage. Without question the loss of his daughter affected Charles Clifton profoundly, as we will see.

In early 1903, a decisive confrontation that shaped many subsequent interactions within the infant American automobile business took place, and Charles Clifton was among the conspirators who brought it about. Central to this particular confrontation was the Selden Patent. The patent was named for one George B. Selden, a patent attorney in Rochester, New York. As Beverly Rae Kimes noted in *Pioneers, Engineers and Scoundrels*, Selden had early ambitions to become the originator of what came to be called the automobile. He had seen a two-cycle Brayton petroleum engine in action at the 1876 Centennial Exposition in Philadelphia and decided it would offer good power for his conceptual "land carriage." An inveterate reader of technical journals, Selden, by December of the next year, had produced an embryonic improvement on the Brayton that developed two horsepower with less than a third of the Brayton's weight. Selden considered the engine's weight low enough for a road machine, but there were many more details of the vehicle yet to be worked out. Nonetheless, he submitted his application for a patent on the wagon's design on May 8, 1879. The purpose of the patent was to claim for Selden the invention of the whole concept of a gasoline-powered vehicle in America. He used the opportunities provided in the patent law to delay its acceptance until 1895 through continual modification of details. Selden wanted his patent to take effect when the automobile industry actually began to make money.

In late 1899 he could see this happening, and on November 4, George Selden sold an exclusive license to the Electric Vehicle Company, a large enterprise intent on making thousands of electric taxicabs for city use as well as other electric vehicles. Its founder, William Collins Whitney, had been an organizer of the American Tobacco Company and also controlled several profitable metropolitan street railways in the East. Bicycle tycoon Col. Albert Pope agreed to build the vehicles for Whitney's Electric Vehicle Company at his Connecticut factories. Whitney, sensing the possibilities of self-propelled carriages, bought up all the related patents, even if some of them did not apply to electric vehicles. This would both protect his company from patent suits and open up a possible cash flow from licensing arrangements. For his exclusive license Whitney paid Selden $10,000 and agreed to pay a $15 per vehicle royalty as well. The Electric Vehicle Company actually did not believe such gasoline vehicles had much of a future. In their view, the vehicles of the future would be electrics.

By early 1900, their grandiose plans had gone awry. The anticipated thousands of electric vehicles were not produced, and several gasoline-powered competitors had appeared. The Selden Patent license was suddenly seen as a way to bring in some badly needed cash, and the Electric Vehicle Company (EVC) began to send out infringement notices to gasoline car makers, among which was the successful Winton Motor Carriage Co. of Cleveland. Legal maneuverings followed.

Afraid that Winton might cave, Fred Smith, head of Oldsmobile, and Henry Joy of Packard, along with representatives of nine other important gasoline automobile producers met to strategize in Detroit at the start of 1903. Joy was raised in a wealthy family involved with railroad equipment and understood very well how useful an access to patents could be, and the Oldsmobile Company had contributed far more to developing the infant gasoline automobile technology than Selden or his licensees. The two men wanted to take control of the patent and set up an industry body that would shape the patent issue to the makers' own advantage. A representative of the George N. Pierce Co. was present at this meeting, but it is no longer clear exactly who it was. The representatives decided to create a Manufacturers' Mutual Association to contest the patent with Electric Vehicle and reduce the demanded royalties. A $2,500 "fighting fund" assessment from each member was also collected. During that January's automobile show in New York Whitney himself invited five spokesmen from the association to his palatial New York City mansion for discussions. The association had already warned George Day, Electric Vehicle's president, that if their demands were not met the manufacturers would unite with Winton in legal opposition. The validity of the patent was already widely questioned, but the first defendants sued by the EVC had settled in May of 1901 and accepted its validity. It was a welcome precedent for the Electric Vehicle Company and George Selden.

Among the five industry representatives who met with Whitney in his majestic Fifth Avenue drawing room at the beginning of March 1903 was Charles Clifton. Following the plan agreed upon on their way uptown, Elihu Cutler of Knox Automobile Company acted as spokesman for the group. Association demands were simple: They would take over enforcement of the patent from the Electric Vehicle Company, and royalties would be reduced to 1¼ percent, of which the EVC would get ¾ of a percent and the manufacturers association would keep the rest. It was a showdown. Cutler alone spoke, relentlessly repeating the demands each time a question was asked. Eventually, Whitney and his attorney gave in. It must have been high drama to watch—a united front of auto executives had bested one of the "Robber Barons."

The next step was the creation of the Association of Licensed Automobile Manufacturers (ALAM), incorporated on March 3, 1903. Smith was president, Joy secretary-treasurer, Barclay Warburton of Searchmont vice-president and Whitney's George Day general manager. Winton Motor Carriage Company was welcomed as a member and ended its opposition. Their attorneys were put on a $5,000 a year retainer by the EVC who were careful to collect all their opposing evidence. The ALAM executive offices were promptly set up in the Transit Building at 7 East 42nd Street in New York City, just down the street from towering, brownstone Grand Central Station. From that point on, the ALAM decided who would be allowed to join the association and how infringements of the Selden patent would be handled. The ALAM presently ran advertisements warning gasoline car makers that they and their customers were in danger of prosecution for infringing the Selden patent unless they were members of the association. While the association did not have sufficient resources to follow through on all its threats, it assumed they would coerce members to join up. This did, in fact, occur. There were 37 members in the ALAM by 1904. Threats of lawsuits also scared off investors from automobile producers who did not have a license. All the same, some members of the association were still not entirely convinced that the patent was really valid. Many considered their membership merely a precaution.

That summer, the new Ford Motor Company, having checked out the threat with a noted patent authority, took out its own ads declaring it would defend against any infringement suits to itself and its customers. This was a frontal attack the ALAM could not ignore, and it filed a suit of infringement against Ford in October 1903. The Selden Patent also had international implications. Four more such suits followed during the ensuing weeks, some against firms importing Renault and Panhard gasoline cars from France. The New York firm of Betts, Betts, Sheffield & Betts, hired by EVC began to amass the volumes of testimony they and the defendants' attorneys, led by Ralzemond A. Parker of Detroit, would assemble to pursue and defend the suits. Some of the defendants, including Ford, formed a competing American Motor Car Manufacturers Association (AMCMA) in 1905 to match the efforts of the ALAM for its members. The AMCMA general manager was Alfred Reeves, a former newspaperman who would be a notable automobile industry figure until 1940.

Charles Clifton rose within the Association of Licensed Automobile Manufacturers even more rapidly than he had at Pierce. He was elected vice-president in November 1903 at the first ALAM annual meeting and was president a year later. It is not certain how convinced he actually was about the patent's validity. He was also vice-president of the earlier National Association of Automobile Manufacturers, whose members were split over the issue. In any case, this and his other activities on behalf of the automobile business and the Pierce Company in particular were frequently covered in the press.

The George N. Pierce Co. offered no fewer than five models in 1903. David Fergusson had designed an improved 1-cylinder engine, which appeared in three of them, replacing the imported DeDions. As the year progressed, his engine was enlarged, and its power rose from 5 HP to 8 HP. The most powerful engines were mounted in "Stanhopes," four-passenger cars with a fold-out front seat ahead of the driver. They had lever steering and two speeds forward and reverse. Close to 200 of these cars, along with a few "Runabout" Motorettes, were made in 1903.

Added to the line late in the season was a tonneau model, with passenger space on a back seat. It had a two-cylinder DeDion motor and was called the "Arrow." It had the first

The first two-cylinder Pierce car, called the "Arrow," also the first Pierce with tonneau seating and a steering wheel (courtesy Buffalo and Erie County Historical Society).

steering wheel offered on a Pierce car. Its name referred to the graphic arrow used for years by Pierce in its bicycle publicity. Some 50 of these radically different cars were made. They followed the industry trend away from engines mounted under the body to the so-called "Panhard system" with engine in front, driving rear wheels with a shaft. This 1,800 lb. water-cooled prestige car sold for a substantial $2,500, compared to $1,200 for the 1,200 lb. Stanhope.

Three Pierce cars took part in the New York to Pittsburgh endurance test, which ran from October 7 to 15 that year. Fred Nickerson drove a 2-cylinder Arrow as a pilot car. Running in the contest itself were Percy Pierce in an 8 HP Stanhope and Charles Sheppy, driving an early version of a Pierce-made 15 HP 2-cyl. Arrow. Percy Pierce won a second-place gold medal in his car. Sheppy had to content himself with a fourth-place finish.

In the October 24 issue of *The Automobile*, Charles Clifton was described as "highly pleased" by the success. "Yes, we have been most successful," he was quoted as saying "and I am proud of it. Our cars and our boys have come through with flying colors. The boys, I am told, held out a helping hand to all…. I told them to get the cars through without racing and

The 1904 model Arrow participating in the New York to Pittsburgh run in October 1903, Charles Sheppy driving. Henry May's nephew Herman is seen behind Sheppy. An official from the run is seen in the left-hand front seat, and an unknown rider behind him (courtesy Buffalo and Erie County Historical Society).

to do as they would be done by, lend a helping hand and wherever possible make friends. The run has certainly proved American cars to be best for American roads." Clifton's instructions to his team may sound a bit unusual for a competitive event, but this was what it said it was—an *endurance* run. Its purpose was to demonstrate the reliability of the new motor car in ordinary touring, not speed. In the early years these contests served the important purpose of allowing the public to see what ordinary cars could do during ordinary touring.

In 1904, 50-year-old Charles Clifton had three automobile models and several bicycle models to market as Pierce sales manager. He represented the company at the New York Automobile Show in January, accompanied by F.A. Nickerson, Percy P. Pierce, F.S. Dey, W.H. Ellis of Buffalo, and Henry Paulson of Chicago, according to the February 11 issue of *Motor Age*. The Pierce treasurer was also quoted extensively in the January 27 issue of *The Horseless Age*, saying "I have been as busy as could be since it [the show] started, and the rush is still on. You will have to excuse me if I don't talk very long, but every minute is worth money to me just now. Most of the manufacturers have placed a lot of agencies, I guess. We have only closed two new ones as yet. Will see you later. Excuse me. Good day." There is no doubt the man felt some commercial pressure, especially with the company president's son looking on.

Automobile Topics, in an article that season entitled "Getting Ready to Begin Work at Madison Square Garden," had written, "Charles Clifton is as prominent a figure as any in the industry, he being treasurer of the George N. Pierce Company and president of the Association of Licensed Automobile Manufacturers, with all the affiliations and activities those positions imply."

By March of that year, the Pierce Company had representatives in 15 cities, as well as the main salesroom in Buffalo. Available for sale were the Stanhope, with fold-out seat, the Arrow with tonneau seating, now with a Pierce-made two-cylinder engine, and, lastly, a super luxury, $4,000, 4-cylinder touring car called the "Great Arrow." The movement of the model range was clearly upward toward the luxury car. The new Great Arrow had 24 to 28 rated horsepower, a three-speed progressive transmission, a pressed steel frame, and a revolutionary body made of cast aluminum panels. It weighed 2,600 lbs. A canopy top and windshield were available at extra cost. Some 350 cars, mostly Stanhopes, were made by the George N. Pierce Co. that year. This success suggested to the directors that David Fergusson's salary be raised by five dollars a month. The change was ratified in the August 1 contract that year.

At home, Charles Clifton was active in the Buffalo Automobile Club and was on the committee that organized the Buffalo Automobile show at the Convention Hall that March. Away from home in Chicago earlier in 1904 he had been among those at the NAAM who decided on the installation and decoration of the American automobile exhibit at the St. Louis Exposition that summer.

As president, Clifton chaired the meeting of the ALAM on March 26, 1904. Its focus was on the infringements of the Selden Patent evident on various makes displayed at the New York and Chicago shows earlier that year. Hermann Cuntz, general manager and George Day's patent expert, reported that he had found 454 infringements, by "outsiders" [non-members], according to the March 26 issue of *The Automobile*, adding, "Mr. Day said proceedings would be started against a certain proportion of the infringers." With limited funds to pursue infringement, the main target was still Henry Ford. A hoped-for outcome in his case was to pressure Ford to relent and join the ALAM. Charles Clifton was active in that effort.

Clifton traveled a good deal while carrying out his duties with the Pierce Company, the

ALAM and the NAAM, meeting to discuss common concerns with other members of the industry all over the country. *Motor Age* noted in their May 12 issue, "George H. Day, Charles Clifton, E.H. Cutler and L.T. Davis Jr., were a notable quartet at Clason Point, New York on a recent evening."

In June, the ALAM board met in Buffalo. Such meetings in Clifton's home town became a tradition for the automobile associations he headed, as a convenience but also a tribute to the man and his perceived dedication. This was also a pleasant summer meeting site. The 1904 meeting concentrated on the problems agents faced, especially territorial "encroachment" upon dealers by "curbstone agents," according to *The Horseless Age*, but the Selden patent litigation was also discussed. "After the general meeting on Tuesday," they added, "members of the local automobile houses placed 10 cars at the disposal of visitors, who were taken to various points of interest. In the evening, they enjoyed dinner at the Buffalo Club. Charles Clifton acted as toastmaster, and speeches were made by Thomas Henderson of the Winton Company, G.H. Stilwell of the Franklin Company and M.I. Brock of the Autocar Company."

Motor Age in its September 1, 1904, issue had covered product development at the George N. Pierce Co. "Charles Sheppy," they wrote, "who drove the Pierce *Arrow* car entry No. 14 in the New York to Pittsburgh endurance run," would drive a new model 1905 Great Arrow touring car through the White Mountains in New England on test. "The car Sheppy now has may not be exactly like the 1905 model, for the Pierce company intends to make any changes that Sheppy's experience may prove to be necessary."

The writer added: "The oft-repeated announcement that the Pierce people intend to build a high-powered track racer is strongly denied by Charles Clifton, vice president of the company." Although Clifton was still treasurer, not vice-president, his denial was likely accurate. The company never built a track racer, although in later years they did assemble special cars for high-speed endurance runs.

One impressive plan the company had almost completed was the construction of a brand-new salesroom and service garage in Buffalo, "being built specially for the company farther north on Main Street next to the Teck Theatre," *Motor Age* reported in the same issue. It would replace the former salesroom on Main near Chippewa Street. The new establishment at 752–758 Main with a substantial service garage behind on Pearl may well have been the very first structures designed from the ground up for such specific automobile purposes anywhere. It remained, much expanded, Pierce's headquarters until a yet larger facility was erected in 1929 even farther north. For a time, the company's executive offices were also installed here, away from the Hanover Street factory.

The Horseless Age reported in October that "Charles Clifton of the George N. Pierce Company has been authorized [by the ALAM] to appoint a committee to draw up plans for a permanent organization of the automobile engineers." This was called the "Mechanical Branch" and was the seminal event that ultimately produced the Society of Automotive Engineers (SAE).

The ALAM met for its Annual Meeting the week of October 30, 1904, at its headquarters on East 42nd Street. According to the report in *Horseless Age* for November 9, 1904, Clifton was re-elected as president, William Metzger of Detroit, vice-president, L.H. Kittredge of Cleveland, secretary and H.H. Franklin of Syracuse, New York, treasurer. "A report on the litigation over the Selden patent was presented," the magazine noted: "During the last two

The George N. Pierce Co., salesroom at 752–758 Main Street in Buffalo that opened in 1904—a very early purpose-built automobile sales installation (courtesy Pierce-Arrow Society).

months 1,450 pages of testimony have been taken on the [infringement] suit." Expenses for both sides in the dispute continued as depositions from various witnesses were obtained in Federal court sites around the country.

The December 1904 issue of *Cycle and Automobile Trade Journal* published an article by Horace L. Arnold, who wrote under the pen name of Hugh Dolnar, which thoroughly covered the features and construction of the 30 HP four-cylinder 1905 Great Arrow model. He noted that "Of these large and high-priced cars, fifty have been made at the date of this writing, October 25, 1904, and forty-eight have been delivered to purchasers." Arnold was greatly impressed with the car. "This whole Pierce car story," he wrote, "is highly instructive, and shows the value of experience and thorough mechanical training on the part of the car designer." Of all the features of the car he admired, its lubrication system seemed to him the most significant. "Mr. Fergusson, the Pierce chief designer," he explained, "discards all individual bearing lubrication oiling schemes, and also pronounces against splash, and introduces a simple flooding lubrication, on wholly different lines from common practice, either American or European, and this flooded system, coupled with 'mist' cylinder and piston and piston pin oiling, appear to be simpler, cheaper, and surer in action than any previous car-oiling system whatsoever." Treated to a journey from the factory up to Niagara Falls and back with "Mr. Sheppy driving, Mr. Fergusson in the tonneau, and the writer in the left-hand front seat" aboard the "only Pierce 1905 4-cylinder as yet on wheels," Arnold waxed ecstatic. "There is little to say about such a drive," he wrote, "where the action of the car is perfect at all points."

This Great Arrow model would inaugurate the Pierce reputation for greatness.

~ 3 ~

American Cars (1905–1907)

> The office of Sales and Treasurer was filled by a brilliant, charming man whose keen brain helped him to cut to the heart of a problem as directly as a surgeon wielding a scalpel. This was none other than Col. Charles Clifton, known nationally as a prominent figure in the world of business. He was tall and slender, with white hair and short cropped moustache. His bearing was erect and he moved quickly. His manner of speaking was direct and thoughtful. His extensive vocabulary enabled him to express his thoughts with clarity and conviction. Also it enabled him to dress you down in a quiet and decisive manner that did not call for a Thesaurus to enable you to interpret his meaning.
>
> —Herbert M. Dawley, Director, Art Department

The year 1905 would prove to be of great importance to the George N. Pierce Company. Along with the Stanhope (now with a steering wheel) they offered three lines of 4-cylinder cars rated 24–28 HP, 28–32 HP and 40 HP. Touring cars were priced from $3,500 to $4,500, and closed cars for chauffeur-driven use could be had, including some models with bodies by Quinby and Company, the New York City coach building house. These last were priced at a healthy five grand apiece. The company's cars were clearly offered to the so-called carriage trade. "American Cars," as Pierce described them, "for American conditions and American Temperaments." Their mechanical construction was very conventional for the time: water-cooled T-head engine in front, transmission amidships and a bevel-gear rear axle. What was exceptional was the thought taken to make sure engine parts and running gear were sufficiently lubricated and protected from road dirt. This increased operational reliability of the cars, which would be dramatically demonstrated later that year.

Demand for the cars was good, and the company was already considering the need for expanded production space. Vice-president Henry May had to oversee a 75,000 sq. ft. factory on the Buffalo waterfront turning out many bicycle models as well as the passenger cars, some of which were now produced in the hundreds.

Anxious to expand its recognition, the company continued to enter various endurance runs. For July, they planned to enter a newly organized tour of the northeastern states for a 400 oz. silver trophy donated by Jasper Glidden, a wealthy telephone magnate who loved touring. The purpose of the contest was to determine the best touring car available by observing entries on a challenging route through the eastern mountains. Winning the Glidden Tour was a lofty goal.

3. American Cars (1905–1907)

The 1905 Great Arrow 28–32 HP touring car with four cylinders, 104" wheelbase and cast aluminum body construction (courtesy Pierce-Arrow Society).

At the January shows, meanwhile, the ALAM created controversy when it took exclusive option to hold the New York automobile show for 1906 in the Madison Square Garden, thereby giving them the sole power to select participants. Non-members would certainly not be welcome. This did not go over well with those companies. *Motor Age* called the act "A Napoleonic stroke by George H. Day" (the ALAM general manager). Asked to comment, Charles Clifton tried to put the best possible light on the decision, saying the show was getting too crowded for the available space at the Garden. He then warned against the danger to the public of "many small and irresponsible makers, who take this chance to offer to the public cars that have not been properly tested or proven reliable." His remarks, quoted in the January 19 issue of the magazine, went on to suggest "in this way the public is placed in danger to its peril and injury of the American industry." It was the ALAM's prepared defense, and poorly designed and constructed cars were a genuine problem. However, non-members of the ALAM were outraged by the organization's action and stressed that they too could organize an auto show in New York. In the end, that is exactly what happened. For some years New York City had two January auto shows.

The controversy spilled over into the meeting of the NAAM that month. Two slates of officers, one from the licensed manufacturers, which included Charles Clifton, and another of unlicensed manufacturers' representatives, were offered. The licensed candidates won by several votes in every case. Afterwards, *Motor Age* observed, "it is evident that smoldering in the breast of the independents is the desire to find a good soft spot back of the ear of the A.L.A.M. that they might return deftly and with sportsmanlike promptness the coup which the licensed Napoleon handed unto them." Shortly after, a competing American Motor Car Manufacturers Association organized the separate, independent show.

That spring, the George N. Pierce Company announced a contest for artists and designers, offering prizes for designs of both open and limousine Pierce cars and "best color scheme for motor car bodies." A thousand dollars had been set aside for the prizes, and the company offered to send sketches of their current bodies for artists to color. "Men of prominence," they assured the contestants, "will act as judges." The contest ran until June 1. An undated form letter, sent out by the company after the judging was complete, named as the judges "William W. Ogden, President of the J.W. Quinby Company, Newark, NJ; C.L.W Eidlitz, Architect, New York City and C.J. Richter, of the firm of Brewster & Company, New York." It was a blue-ribbon panel.

The ALAM committee for the 1906 New York show met in New York on March 27, with Clifton as chairman and members Col. George Pope of the Pope Manufacturing Co. and Marcus I. Brock of the Autocar Co. At the same time, it was revealed that the Patents Committee, made up of Giles H. Stilwell (Franklin), E.H. Cutler (Knox) and Marcus Brock, would investigate infringement issues.

The summer of 1905 was a busy time for the Pierce Company. In July, Vice-President Henry May, the Pierce factory manager, and Chief Engineer David Fergusson took a trip that lasted over a month to look over motor cars and construction methods in England, France, and Germany. It was a way to compare the Pierce cars with European models and improve the George N. Pierce Co.'s production techniques. In England they visited the Crossley works and also noted that Daimler "test their engines by a rope brake similar to our method." Daimler was seen enlarging their Coventry factory to meet increased demand. In late July, May and Fergusson arrived in Paris, spending the rest of the month looking at such French makers as Panhard & Levassor, Renault and DeDion Bouton. Several suppliers of automobile parts and metals were also investigated. In Germany the two men concentrated on the ways to obtain the best quality steels. At the end of the report, they noted, "Every maker is doing more business than they can attend to and all are greatly enlarging their plants to supply this necessary demand. In nearly all these cases the type of new shops is single story with roof of the saw tooth type." This was useful information because the Pierce Company was increasingly convinced that they needed more factory space.

The most exciting event of 1905 for the George N. Pierce Co., however, was doubtless the Glidden Tour in July. It ran from New York City over 867 miles of primitive roads through the East into New England's mountains and back. Percy Pierce was the company entrant, driving a 28–32 HP touring car, and he took his parents and his fiancée along, as well as mechanic George Ulrich, who ended up going mostly for the ride. Out of 1,000 points, the Pierce entry ended up with 996 and won the trophy for the Automobile Club of Buffalo, making, in the words of the Glidden Committee, "an ideal tour of the trip, fulfilling in spirit as well as in the letter the conditions and purpose of the contest." The win was proof that the Pierce firm made cars that could stand up and perform in very difficult conditions, and its prestige and sales rose in consequence.

On August 5 *Automobile Topics* reported on the ALAM summer session, held in Niagara Falls July 27–28. "As executive sessions ruled," they wrote, "only partial reports of the proceedings have been permitted to filter through the regulation channel of information." The ALAM had decided that "straddling" agents selling both licensed and non-licensed vehicles were "to be proceeded against." And they reported that the ALAM had formed a patents committee to hold various patents which the organization owned. Clifton was among the organizers of the holding company set up in New York State "to take care of all patent interests of the association and its members, with the important exception of the Selden patent."

On Wednesday, November 1, the new ALAM Mechanical Branch met in New York to discuss common problems regarding crankshafts and their bearings. The participants "shared drawings, discussed pressures on bearings, materials of construction, methods of lubrication, etc." The agenda for the December meeting was "best method of testing and inspecting cars before shipping them from the factory." This organization became a vital clearinghouse for communicating improved methods and establishing industry-wide standards.

Sometime during late 1905 or early 1906, the Pierce directors resolved to remedy the problems besetting their production of both automobiles and bicycles in the same plant. The methods used were too dissimilar to avoid complications, and the solution was seen to be the erection of a separate factory for building just automobiles. At length, a plot of land was obtained in the northern section of the city on Elmwood Avenue, just south of the Belt Line Railroad crossing, which would give the facility excellent rail connections. The plot had been part of the Midway at the 1901 Pan-American Exposition. George K. Birge's connection with that event may well have facilitated this purchase. As planning proceeded, the board employed Albert H. Kahn as the lead architect for the production spaces, with the Trussed Steel Concrete Company and the Boston firm of Lockwood, Green and Company assisting. Kahn had recently designed a pace-setting automobile factory building for Packard in Detroit, and he expanded on his ideas with the George N. Pierce Co. structures.

Kahn's plans visualized a series of metal-working, supply intake and automobile shipping buildings built along the belt line railroad, accompanied by a power plant. A machine shop would rise to the south of that, further south, an erection hall, complete with two three-ton overhead cranes to assist assembly, and a body manufacturing building beside the "proposed street" on the southernmost edge of the property. All were to be constructed of reinforced concrete with glass curtain walls and sawtooth roofs to provide an abundance of natural light. These buildings proved to be efficient and adaptable for the next 30 years of the company.

A separate Office Building faced Elmwood Avenue, containing board room and offices for the company executives. The basement included facilities for the plant's work force, such as lockers, wash basins, and even a medical facility in the charge of a physician. A cafeteria seating 800 was located on the top floor. It is generally agreed that Charles Clifton insisted the factory be a pleasant environment for the workers there, and even such things as soap and hand towels were provided for them. This office building, sometimes referred to as the Welfare Building, was designed by a prominent Buffalo architect, George Carey, who, perhaps not coincidentally, was married to Birge's daughter Allithea.

Meanwhile, an increased tempo of production continued on Hanover Street. Company records show that only the 4-cylinder 28–32 HP Model NN and 40–45 HP Model PP cars were in production in 1906. They followed the mechanical specifications of earlier 4-cylinder Pierce cars and carried the cast aluminum bodies as well. Production in 1906 far surpassed the 206 built in 1905. Over 700 cars were made, although the new factory would not be ready until the fall. This suggests that the winning of the Glidden Tour by Percy P. Pierce stimulated sales. Buyers may well have been impressed by the trouble-free operation that the Great Arrow had demonstrated

On March 14, Clifton was appointed with Windsor White and W.R. Innes to serve as a committee on railroad transportation for the NAAM by the president E.H. Cutler. Meanwhile, the American Motor Car Manufacturers Association, the ALAM's great rival, sent its show committee to Buffalo to develop plans setting up an outdoor automobile show. The rancor over the ALAM corralling of the New York show clearly had not ended.

Clifton attended the NAAM executive committee meeting in early April, at which the contest committee reported it was unable to agree on rules for "all possible cars" that might enter the second Glidden Tour to be held in July.

A more successful event was held at about 1:00 p.m. on April 26, when George N. Pierce himself turned over the first spadeful of dirt beginning the excavation of the factory site for the new plant on Elmwood Avenue, near the plants of the American Radiator Co. and the Railway Signal Co. The site measured 600 feet along Elmwood Avenue and 1000 feet along the Belt Line railroad. Plans had by now matured and a thousand workers employed by the Trussed Steel Concrete Co. were set to erect the major production buildings and offices in a time span of 95 days. The ceremony was witnessed by Henry May, George K. Birge and W.H. Gardner of the company building committee. Charles Clifton and E.H. Rounds represented the company itself, along with company attorney W.B. Hoyt. J.L. Costello, represented the contractors along with one George E. Matthews, whose connections to the work are not clear. The *Buffalo Courier* of April 27, 1906, reported, "After the breaking of ground the party was taken in automobiles to the Park Club, where lunch was served and a bumper was drunk to the success of this latest undertaking of one of Buffalo's leading industries."

The 21 men in this slightly damaged glass-plate photograph are at the groundbreaking for the new George N. Pierce Co. factory on Elmwood Avenue, April 26, 1904. No definitive identification of the individuals in the photograph has been found, and what is presented here is an incomplete but likely identification of some of the important participants seen in the print. George N. Pierce stands beside the handle of the shovel he will use to lift the first soil from the excavation. To his left (*viewer's right*) stands Charles Clifton, then Henry May. At Pierce's right are grouped board members William H. Gardner, George K. Birge (in unbuttoned top coat with fancy collar), and, quite possibly, William B. Hoyt, company attorney. Others are hard to identify, although Percy Pierce looks to be the man seen at Henry May's left and Laurence H. Gardner, company secretary, stands just to Percy's left (courtesy Buffalo Pierce-Arrow Museum).

The *Times* newspaper of Buffalo the same day included several additional participants: Laurence B. [*sic*] Gardner, company secretary, E.C. Bull, the manager of the Buffalo sales outlet on Main Street, Percy Pierce, Charles Sheppy, F.S. Dey, a "Mr. Roach" of *Motor World* and Thomas Carey. It was a grand celebration of the projected new factory.

The week of June 5 was eventful for Charles Clifton. He met in New York as a member of the NAAM executive committee. H.A. Lozier of the Lozier Motor Co. and A.L. Garfield of Elyria, Ohio's, Garford Co. were admitted to membership. The Glidden Trophy rules were then worked out by the Contest Committee in conference with A.B. Tucker of the American Automobile Association.

Three days of that same week were taken up with the Semi-Annual Meeting of the ALAM, of which Clifton remained president. Various branches met the first day, while on Wednesday and Thursday the Executive Committee and the Board of Managers held sessions at 7 East 42nd Street. Reports were heard from the Trades Committee on agencies, the Show Committee about the 1907 Madison Square Garden show, the Tire Committee and the Traffic Department. The Mechanical Branch had met in Hartford, Connecticut, so members could see the new laboratory available to them under the charge of Henry Souther. The New York meeting ended with a banquet on Friday evening.

It may be that this was the time that an important addition was made to the creative staff of the George N. Pierce Co. by Col. Clifton. One of the entrants in the body design and decoration contest set up by the company in 1905 was a 26-year-old graduate in mechanical engineering named Herbert Dawley. According to Dawley's recollections in 1968 for the Pierce-Arrow Society, the Colonel wrote him suggesting a conference. Such a meeting was needed not because Dawley had won, but because Dawley's designs were preferred by the company over the winners chosen by the outside judges. Accordingly, having awarded Dawley separate prize money, Clifton asked him if he would consider a position with the company when the new factory was completed. Without hesitation Dawley accepted. He would have a lasting impact on the products the firm produced.

Meanwhile, Percy Pierce had taken a 45 HP Pierce Great Arrow with a cape top to Germany as a competitor in the Herkomer Cup race, and the Prince Henry Trial, a 3,000-mile event similar to the Glidden Tour, with an additional speed trial and a mountain climbing segment. Teams of cars came from all over Western Europe, especially Germany. Percy's Pierce was the only American entry, but he acquitted himself well, finishing with a silver medallion. Percy Pierce always maintained that he should have won outright, but that the organizers scored in such a way that only a German make could win. In any event, he had a flawless run, until he was involved in an accident after the tour while avoiding a horsecart's swerve on a public highway, ending up in jail with his car wrecked.

Interviewed by the Buffalo *Express* upon his arrival back in New York on July 5, Percy remarked that, as he could not use the damaged Great Arrow, he would have to find a replacement to drive in the Glidden Tour that month. The Buffalo *News* reported in its January 6, 1907, issue that another 45 HP touring car was found and repurchased from its owner the day before the Tour began. Fifty-seven entrants left Buffalo on July 12, among them Percy Pierce. They headed for Bretton Woods, New Hampshire, by way of the Adirondacks, and Canada. This year, two other Great Arrows ran the tour as well, a 45 HP and a 32 HP. All three Great Arrows finished the tour with perfect scores, and, since his previous record was not surpassed, the judges ruled that Percy Pierce won the Glidden Trophy for the second year.

Perhaps an even greater accomplishment was the demonstration made by a fourth Great Arrow on the tour, as reported by the Buffalo *News*. This car was not entered in the competition, but was a prototype driven by company test driver F.S. Day. This first Pierce six-cylinder prototype accompanied the tourists and delivered messages, conveyed newsmen, and did other odd jobs. It carried from 9 to 11 passengers and covered nearly double the distance the actual competitors covered. It was a thorough test run, in public no less, and the new six-cylinder had passed with flying colors. In addition, a *Horseless Age* report in the September 26 issue cited a 40–45 HP Great Arrow entered by Frank Botterill as scoring a third-place finish in a Ft. Logan, Colorado, hill climb behind a 20 HP Stanley steam car and a 50 HP Stevens-Duryea. The year 1906 had been a triumphant display of Pierce prowess. The board then gave David Fergusson a contract at a monthly pay of $270.82 for the first year, to be raised to $291.66 the third year, according to the chief engineer's carefully kept diary.

Then things seemed to become somewhat unsettled. The September 7, 1906, issue of the Buffalo *News* reported that Percy Pierce was "through with the automobile business." This unexpected development was part of a reorganization that would not just separate automobile and bicycle production into two factories, but would separate the bicycle business itself from the George N. Pierce Co. A newly organized Pierce Cycle Co. would take over the Hanover Street plant. Papers incorporating the Cycle Company were being sent to Albany. Percy Pierce would be the president, and W.B. Colburn secretary and treasurer. The directors were George N. Pierce, Moses Shire, the Pierce family attorney, and Charles Clifton. The management at the George N. Pierce Co. was, apparently, unchanged. The reason for this split-up has never been explained, but the Pierce Cycle Co. produced bicycles from then until 1918, when it was bought out by the Emblem concern in Angola, New York. They also made 4-cyl. and single cylinder motorcycles from 1909 to 1914.

George N. Pierce remained president of his namesake company, which contemplated moving into its new Elmwood Avenue plant when it was equipped with the necessary production machinery in November. Although Charles Clifton had purchased 200 shares of the cycle company stock, he also remained a director and treasurer of the George N. Pierce Co.

After the Glidden Trophy win, the Bailey Tire Company congratulated the Pierce Company on its triumphs. Clifton responded with this letter:

C.J. Bailey, Esq, (Personal)
22 Boyston St., Boston, Mass.

> My dear Mr. Bailey:—Your esteemed favor of the 30th ult. is at hand and noted. We are very much obliged to you for the congratulations on the records made by the four Pierce cars in the Glidden Tour. While I have no reports from the drivers, I am entirely satisfied that the Bailey treads did perform their part and again justified our faith in them.
>
> > Very truly yours,
> > Charles Clifton

This letter was later used by the Bailey Company in its magazine advertising.

Clifton also wrote a letter to the ALAM Mechanical Branch on September 21, in which he stated, "I have made something of a study of the thirteen cars finishing with so called perfect scores in the Glidden Tour, and observe that all, except one, were cars made by members of the licensed association. As president of that association it seems to me it is fitting to pay a tribute to the mechanical branch, which has been doubtless largely instrumental in bringing about this very desirable result, and I sincerely compliment your branch on the result as I do the individual members whose cars have made such a gratifying showing. I trust the good work may be continued, to the end that all licensed cars be known as sound to the core and safe beyond peradventure."

The annual election of ALAM officers was held on November 7 at the New York headquarters, and Charles Clifton was re-elected president. The board also approved the plans for the ALAM's New York show to be held in Madison Square Garden January 12–19, 1907.

This was perhaps Clifton's last public duty of 1906. *The Automobile* noted in its October 25 issue that "Mr. [Charles] Clifton had been directed to take a European trip by his physicians, and will be absent several months." The conditions that brought on this order are not known, but overwork might well have been a contributing factor, given Clifton's expanding roles in the two Pierce companies and the auto industry as a whole.

The George N. Pierce Company, meanwhile, took possession of its new automobile factory in late 1906, and the transition carried well over into the year 1907. It is not certain on exactly what date the factory management left the old plant and the sales office left the downtown location at 752–758 Main Street. However, in his methodical way, Chief Engineer Fergusson noted, "Started in new plant Nov. 25, 1906." The new facilities would enable an output that was very close to 1,000 cars during a calendar year.

The new year continued a transition away from the Pierce family, which concentrated on bicycles and would soon enter the motorcycle business. At this point it seems certain that George K. Birge was in firm control of the automobile company even though George N. Pierce was still president. While Birge's impact was not always obvious, the undisputed fact was that he had several trusted associates in active management, while the redoubtable Henry May remained in charge of the production spaces he had helped to design.

The company offered in 1907 two four-cylinder Great Arrow models, the 30NN and 45PP, and the first six-cylinder Pierce Great Arrow, the Model 65Q. This last was an out and

The first six-cylinder Pierce Great Arrow 65 HP Touring Car, 135" wheelbase, $6,500 price (courtesy Pierce-Arrow Society).

out luxury car directed at those for whom cost was no consideration. The expanded production space encouraged new directions, and very serious work had already begun to develop and market a successful line of motor trucks under the Pierce name. A prototype version was completed by that March. Large as the new plant already was, it was progressively enlarged for the next decade until it contained one and a half million square feet of productive space on its 16-acre site.

At the Annual Meeting of the Board of Management of the Association of Licensed Automobile Manufacturers on April 2, the *Cycle & Automobile Trade Journal* reported, Charles Clifton was named to the Show Committee in place of Assistant General Manager Marcus Brock, who was finding his managerial duties too great to permit him to remain on the committee.

It was during this spring of 1907 that Herbert Dawley took up the employment Colonel Clifton had offered him the previous autumn. Dawley remembered the occasion well. "You will be in the sales department under my jurisdiction," Clifton explained. "Mr. Birge and I were impressed with your design and feel that you have talent which can, in time, be a valuable asset to the company." Dawley felt the Colonel had welcomed him in such a way as to put him at ease in the "immense factory and magnificent offices" that confronted him.

Dawley's reminiscences are the first extensive account we have of the way that the Pierce Company and its treasurer conducted business. While it was evident that "Mr. Birge" was the final boss, Clifton clearly had Birge's confidence and exercised considerable authority around the executive offices. In Dawley's case, Clifton invited him to study the people and processes around the plant to learn how a motor car was made. "Get acquainted with the department heads," the treasurer told him. "All of them are very much older than you and have been with the company for many years, so I counsel you to treat them with respect, but not just because of their seniority."

Years later, in 1968, Dawley still remembered those department heads very well, providing deft thumbnail sketches of them. He stressed the personalities of the men who "created the sinews and efficiency of the motive power," the factor he called "the *soul* of the organization," which began with the company's owners themselves. "It would be hard to find a more ideal group of contrasting personalities," Dawley remarked. "One might compare them metaphorically to a gourmet's recipe. They had many a donny-brook, but just as iron must go through the fires of the smelter and Bessemer furnaces before it becomes steel, so the Pierce-Arrow emerged from its ordeals."

At the apex was George K. Birge, who would shortly become president of the company when George N. Pierce decided to retire. Birge had inherited control of his father's wallpaper company, which he had first sold, and later repurchased from a national wallpaper trust. Besides being a respected businessman, Birge was an accomplished musician who entertained guests in his lavish home on Buffalo's "Circle" (now Symphony Circle), at the console of its pipe organ. Not surprisingly for a wallpaper tycoon, he was also a patron of the arts and was also fond of extensive European vacations. The Pierce Company, under his leadership, became a leader in merchandising luxury from design to publicity and promotion.

Pierce's vice-president was Henry May, the factory head. It would not be unfair to say that this German boy, who immigrated to Buffalo in 1868 at the age of seven years, with this widowed mother, rose to success through unceasing and thoughtful effort. He obtained a job with Heintz, Pierce, and Munschauer as an errand boy at age 12 and left with George N.

Pierce when he started the George N. Pierce Co. several years later. May worked tirelessly through the Pierce establishment and at business school. He was eventually elevated to a partnership with Pierce, supervising the high standards Pierce demanded in his bicycle plant. Henry May was a no-nonsense administrator with utter focus on the business at hand. The whole staff respected him, and he had a reputation for complete fairness in dealing with conflict. "He was referred to as 'Uncle Henry,'" Dawley wrote. "His home life was simple, unpretentious and happy."

Dawley remembered treasurer Charles Clifton as "a brilliant, charming man, whose keen brain enabled him to cut to the heart of a problem as directly as a surgeon wielding a scalpel." His reminiscences clearly imply that Dawley considered Charles Clifton's guidance and counsel as being above and beyond what was merely necessary to start his new employee, and that his thoughtful training enabled Dawley to move far beyond the point expected. Clifton addressed Dawley as "Son" and seemed to enjoy his protégé's success as much as he appeared disappointed in his own son's growing shortcomings.

Birge's attorney William B. Hoyt worked for the management and remained on the board of directors until his death in 1915. Hoyt had also represented the Vanderbilt railroad system among other important industrial clients. He was a notable trial lawyer as well. Dawley remembered Hoyt as "A handsome man of imposing physique, and the graciousness and savoir-faire of a diplomat, but hard and unyielding where the affairs of the Pierce-Arrow Co. were involved."

A last member of the Pierce board was William H. Gardner, who, according to some sources, "came out of the West." Yet, he was born in Buffalo in 1841 and was educated in the public schools there. His company obituary in 1915 revealed that his early business life was connected with a local tannery, a common business in those days with meat packing in the city. "For thirteen years," the memorial continued, "he was in St. Louis as Vice-President of the Missouri Car & Foundry Company, manufacturers of railroad cars." He later moved back to Buffalo as general manager at the Buffalo Car Manufacturing Company before it was absorbed by the American Car & Foundry Company. At that point Gardner retired. Local directory sources suggest he might have been a member of a

A late photograph of Henry May, vice-president of the Pierce company for many years (courtesy Henry May IV).

Buffalo contractor family. At the time Gardner joined Pierce he lived near George K. Birge and was one of the investors who rescued the George N. Pierce Co. in 1896. W.H. Gardner held no office in the company, but, according to Herbert Dawley, spent a good deal of time at the plant "keeping an eye on doings in and about the factory." Employees referred to Gardner as "The Snooper." Dawley found him a friendly and pleasant man who made useful suggestions. His son Laurence H. Gardner was company secretary

These owners and executives had by late in the century's first decade developed a very profitable organization out of the struggling bicycle manufacturer. In later years, their success carried an almost legendary quality. For years, the company was reportedly the largest employer inside the city of Buffalo. The organization seemed always to have a clear sense of purpose and determination. "The Pierce-Arrow Company fostered a particularly harmonious labor/management relationship," Dawley remembered. "Though not paternalistic in its attitude, yet the welfare of its employees was of paramount importance. Only for the most serious offense was anyone ever fired." Employees carried on at similar tasks for years, honing their skills. Some had careers that stretched back before the Pierce bicycle.

In 1907 they were newly housed in a technically advanced automobile factory with all the latest machine tools, building automobiles for the most discerning market to be found. The reputation was building up that the Pierce Great Arrow was the finest car for touring in the world. The management was determined to take full advantage of that.

~ 4 ~

Showdown Over Selden (1907–1911)

> I went with my mother and brother to visit him for ten days or two weeks in the late 1920's. I was five or six years old. He was a fine, upright person, and I can understand how he commanded such respect. We rode with him in his car—chauffeur-driven—very distinguished, royal-looking.... My grandfather talked to us, but he did not seem to know how to input with children and spoke with them as though it was expected of him rather than from any real feeling for them.... At his house children were to be seen and not heard. My strongest impression was that, after dinner, Grandfather sat by himself to one side of the living room, very taciturn and reserved, playing solitaire, while my mother and Grandmother talked. His room was the library, surrounded by his collections of books and paintings. What seemed important to him was his work, his collections and his church.
>
> —Mark Clifton

Meanwhile, the seemingly endless accumulation of legal evidence in the Selden Patent infringement suit continued, and some unexpected exhibits were prepared for demonstration that summer of 1907. George Selden had stated in his patent application that "The object of my invention is the production of a safe, simple, and cheap road locomotive light in weight, easy to control, and possessed of sufficient power to overcome any ordinary inclination." He had never actually built such a machine. His patent contained drawings and a description of how he imagined the various parts that would accomplish his objective would work together. Questions arose about how the machine described in the application would work—or even *if* it would work. Selden and his two sons assembled a Selden Buggy (Exhibit #89) in Rochester, New York, and the Electric Vehicle Co. built another (#157) in its Hartford, Connecticut, shops to prove the application described a functioning design at the time it was submitted. Both designs worked, after a fashion, although they were not at all reliable, but the important point was that they did run. That would support the application as valid in 1877.

The defendant Ford Motor Company also produced an exhibition model called a Lenoir-Ford that used a different, non-compression gasoline motor, unlike the Brayton compression engine specified in the Selden application. It was the purpose of this vehicle to demonstrate Selden's contention was untrue that this earlier Lenoir-type engine could not successfully power a road carriage. Mounted on an old Ford chassis, this engine seemed to perform very well. The defense asserted that its success proved that the Selden patent did not cover all the gasoline engines that could be used to power a car, and was, therefore, not as broad a patent as Selden assumed.

Further complicating the Selden cause, the Pope Manufacturing Co. failed in August 1907 and the Electric Vehicle Company itself failed that December. The company licensed by Selden was now defunct. It would take some time to straighten out the resulting problems with the 1909 organization of the Columbia Motor Car Co., EVC's successor. In addition, George H. Day, the ALAM general manager, died in November.

As the summer of 1907 progressed the George N. Pierce Co. changed the face of its advertising from lauding the new factory and its facilities in text accompanying a black and white photo or drawing of a typical Pierce Great Arrow model. Suddenly splendid four-color illustrations by noted commercial artists of the day were lavishly incorporated in its ads. As explained by *Automobile Quarterly* magazine in its Third Quarter issue for 1976, this was due to the company employing the New York firm of Calkins & Holden to manage their advertising and publicity. The new advertisements were at the cutting edge of advanced promotion for the day, and they soon set the standard for American luxury-class motor car advertising. The first of these was a late evening illustration of a Great Arrow Suburban car with chauffeur, curbside at a New York theater, painted by Edward Penfield that appeared in the August 15, 1907, issue of *Life*. The entire copy consisted of bold type reading: "The Great Arrow." For the rest of the firm's existence such a style of advertising was frequently employed.

Whether it was the new advertising, a growing reputation or expanded sales efforts, increased sales required that a third story be added to the two-story body buildings of the factory that year.

While there was no Percy P. Pierce to lead Pierce efforts in the 1907 Glidden Tour, the company seemed equally determined to defend the Trophy. According to Marc Ralston in his study *Pierce-Arrow*, not only were four Pierce Great Arrow cars entered in the 1,470-mile competition, but in the spring a 65 HP model had laid out the route that the tour followed later that summer. The two Great Arrows from the Buffalo team successfully defended the Glidden Trophy as desired, and two other Great Arrows finished with perfect scores as well. Perhaps as a direct result, on September 1 David Fergusson signed a three-year agreement to continue as chief engineer for the Pierce Company at the greatly increased annual salary of $5,000.

Regarding the Glidden Tours, Col. Clifton wrote the following letter responding to a request from the editor of *The Horseless Age*, which appeared in the August 31, 1907, issue:

Editor, Horseless Age,

You have kindly suggested that I should look over your marked copy, July 31, page 142 in re the Glidden Tour of another year. Personally, I have always felt that the Glidden run should be a tourist's run and purely of an amateur character. I have not changed my opinion. I believe, however, in competitive tests. I think that by that means alone are builders stimulated to proper endeavor and improvement; and, from that point of view, even the Glidden run as it has been handled for the past three years, has given decided food for reflection to the thoughtful and nothing but disappointment and expense to the thoughtless.

My opinion is, however, in view of all the criticism that has been heaped upon the organization of the A.A.A. in this particular, that it might be well to have an expression of opinion from the users of automobiles as to what general contests they would suggest. I think the critics have had their inning and it is about time that the man who pays the freight should be heard from in this particular.

Charles Clifton
Treasurer, Geo. N. Pierce Company

Clifton was the ALAM representative on the AAA committee meeting that fall to "consider the advisability of sanctioning track races in the future," according to *The Automobile* of September 26. The committee was made up of three members of the Racing Board along with the presidents of the ALAM, the AMCMA. and the Importer's Salon. Clifton had previously been quoted in the January 1907 issue of *MoTor* that the Geo. N. Pierce Co. would not build an Arrow racer "until the weight limit is raised." The committee was expected to report its findings at the AAA director's meeting in November.

The November *Horseless Age* reported that both the NAAM and the ALAM met on November 6, the former at the Hotel Victoria in New York City, and the latter presumably at its East 42nd St. headquarters. At the Automobile Manufacturers meeting, Clifton was among the members re-elected to the executive committee. The others were S.T. Davis, Jr., of Locomobile, S.D. Waldon of Packard, L.H. Kittredge of Peerless, and W.E. Metzger of the E.M.F. Company.

At the Licensed Manufacturers annual meeting Clifton was re-elected president along with Thomas Henderson of the Winton, vice-president; H.H. Franklin, treasurer; and Kittredge secretary. Milton Budlong was elected general manager to replace E.H. Cutler. Clifton also served on the executive committee along with Metzger, Davis, Henderson and George H. Day, the patent specialist.

In the fall of 1907 the U.S. economy began to experience a shortfall of capital, and a full-fledged panic began when the Knickerbocker Trust Co. failed on October 15. The intervention of J. Pierpont Morgan managed to stabilize the situation, but the whole economy was in steep decline by the end of the year.

The ALAM held its New York auto show in early November of 1907, a couple of months ahead of the usual January dates. Despite the economic downturn, attendance was down only slightly, and some evenings had more attending than corresponding dates for the previous January show. As president of the ALAM, Charles Clifton was quoted by the *New York Times* of November 10 that the show was "the best ever held in this country. There was a noticeable lack of crudity in design and finish," he continued, "and the details in construction indicated that our master mechanics are no longer proceeding upon tentative theories but are working upon the lines of the best practice wrought out upon the anvil of their own experience and not upon the expensive experience of the user." Clifton went on to contend that the "American automobile has evolved a perfect combination of chassis and body work both in touring and town cars of the inclosed [*sic*] design."

These remarks reflect the ongoing dispute between the patent-holding ALAM and the resisting AMCMA. The Licensed Association always publicly asserted that they used the patent merely as a guarantee to buyers against shoddy constructors, who, without their valiant efforts, would soon swamp the industry. Although there were many poorly conceived and assembled automobiles around, there is no strong evidence that the ALAM contention was particularly justified. Henry Ford, ever resistant to the Licensed Association, was, at that very time, hard at work developing the Model T, a car that was anything but shoddy and would soon dominate the industry.

As the George N. Pierce Co. remained in a state of transition as the influence of the Pierce family steadily declined, its cars changed little for 1908, although a fourth line—a 40 HP six-cylinder model—was added. In its publicity materials, the Pierce Company boasted at length about the superiority of its engine lubrication system, incorporating a tank of motor oil, mounted above the exhaust manifold, that flooded the main bearings and valve gear with warmed oil, and was conducted through the drilled crankshaft to the rod bearings. The tank was kept full by a scavenging pump in the crankcase

Despite the growing popularity of the selective gear system, Pierce continued to use a progressive three-speed transmission with the gear change on the steering column. Their cast-aluminum bodies were now available in a greater variety of styles, the emphasis unmistakably on their appeal to the "carriage trade." All the same, their production would fall in 1908, due to depressed economic times.

On February 1, *Automobile Topics* noted that Charles Clifton had been named by the newly elected president of the Automobile Club of Buffalo, Frank B. Hower, to the club's executive committee. He also served on the club's board.

The February 13 issue of *The Automobile* revealed that George N. Pierce, "founder of the business has retired from active participation in the [George N. Pierce] company's affairs." Mr. Pierce had "disposed of all his holdings in the company to his associates in order to relieve himself of active business, a step largely brought about by the ill-health of Mrs. Pierce...."

George K. Birge now assumed the office of president of the George N. Pierce Co. Henry May remained vice-president, along with Charles Clifton as treasurer and Laurence Gardner as secretary. Birge, May, and Clifton remained as directors with William H. Gardner and William B. Hoyt. "This is the same organization that has been in control of the company during the past ten years, during which Mr. Hoyt has acted as counsel," the magazine commented.

It is not certain exactly when Charles Clifton became a member of the owning board of the George N. Pierce Company. In September 1903 the capitalization of the firm had been increased from $280,000 to $315,000, and it is possible that Clifton had the means to buy in at that point if he had not done so earlier. George N. Pierce's treatment of Henry May demonstrated that he was of a generous nature with his employees, and Clifton may have benefited from a similar kindness. In addition, Clifton's father-in-law, George Gorham, had died on June 2, 1906, and could have left Mrs. Clifton an inheritance.

The Cycle and Automobile Trade Journal of May 1908 printed "a short resume of the growth of the auto industry, compiled by Charles Clifton of the George N. Pierce Co." Between 1898 and 1908, Clifton found automobile makers had grown in number from 17 to 175. Car production per year stood at 239 in 1898 and 50,000 by 1908. Value of the product had increased nearly 50 times to $106 million. Automobile agencies had numbered 40 in 1898 and totaled 2,150 a decade later. Additional details showed how the growth of the industry had developed a whole profitable network of supplier industries employing additional thousands of workers.

The Pierce Company concentrated a good deal of thought and preparation on the Glidden Tour for 1908, scheduled for July 9–22. It would start from Buffalo and, covering a difficult route, end in Saratoga Springs. Its point of departure was the main Pierce showroom at 752 Main Street near St. Louis Church.

In advance of the tour itself, Teddy Day, a company test driver, left on a preliminary run over the course the morning of June 18. Accompanying Day were John Williams, who was scheduled to drive the car New York dealer Robert D. Garden had entered in the contest, along with a Mr. Law of the Pierce sales force and company photographer and publicity man F. Ed. Spooner. According to the June 20 *Automobile Topics*, "The idea of the supplementary

4. Showdown Over Selden (1907–1911)

trip occurred to Mr. Charles Clifton of the George N. Pierce Co., some time ago. Mr. Clifton was anxious to have his drivers secure at first hand all information regarding the route and its capabilities. Mr. Spooner proposed making the trip to ascertain the actual condition of the roads and also to determine the real schedule of speed which might be placed on each day's run of the tour." Clearly, the company and Clifton took the upcoming Glidden and Hower Tours very seriously.

In the actual Glidden Tour (for large touring cars), Charles Clifton entered two Great Arrow cars and J.W. Maguire, Pierce's Boston agent, another. Two Pierce Great Arrow cars were entered in the Hower Tour (for runabout models), one by Clifton, the other by Robert D. Garden, owner of Harrold's Motor Car Co., the New York City Pierce agency. The Great Arrows successfully defended the Glidden Trophy for yet another year. Pierce also won the Hower Trophy, although it took a runoff trip between Pittsburgh and Bedford Springs to decide the winner. The two competing Stoddard-Daytons withdrew during the runoff with problems that included a broken frame in one case. When the Great Arrows, driven by Edward Retling, another factory test driver, and John Williams from the Harrold's agency finished up at Bedford Springs they were declared the winners. It had been another Pierce triumph, doubtless made even more welcome for Clifton by the fact that Stoddard-Dayton was not an ALAM member company. At about this same time, Pierce's great Buffalo competitor, Thomas Flyer, was determined to be the winner of the famous New York to Paris Race. This must have been a satisfying summer for Buffalo automakers.

The Automobile quoted Col. Clifton extensively in its August 13 issue in an article entitled

Three 60 HP Pierce cars entered in the 1908 Glidden Tour by J.W. Maguire, driving car number 3 on the left, and Charles Clifton. Car number 1 is driven by Teddy Day and car number 2 by Arthur Kumpf. Other occupants are not identified (courtesy University of Michigan Special Collections).

"Distance Tours Are Education." Clifton described great benefit obtained from sending "men from the factory working force" as observers on the Glidden runs. This enabled them to see the effects of much harder service than the car would see in private use or even factory road tests. Consequently, improvements were continually made to the production cars because of what the observers had seen. "We want to make a car that will stand up under anyone who may happen to become a purchaser," the Colonel went on. "From the outset of these tours we have competed for this reason, and the experiences each year have been carefully noted and incorporated in the cars of the next year. Our experiences have enabled us to produce a car which would do as those of this year did, go through two-thousand miles without necessitating the use of one stock equipment [replacement] part in the long journey." Clifton went on to congratulate the E.R. Thomas Co., for its victory in the New York–Paris Race, which meant "the entire world has cause to know that America builds cars capable of such a feat." This one article demonstrates Charles Clifton's energetic efforts for two of his important positions, boosting the Great Arrow as Pierce sales manager and extolling the licensed American industry as president of the ALAM.

Another commitment that characterized Charles Clifton was demonstrated this same year when he paid the remaining $25,000 of the mortgage owed by the First Unitarian Society of Buffalo for their new home on Elmwood Avenue. This had been the traditional church of his family, and his sister Sarah was still an active member of the congregation. His gift, however, carried a stipulation: the pews of the sanctuary would "be forever free." No other member would experience the embarrassment he had when encountering hardship.

Automobile Topics for September 12, described the decorative features planned for the 1909 National Automobile Show scheduled at New York's Madison Square Garden for January 16–23, under the sponsorship of the Association of Licensed Automobile Manufacturers. The Board of Managers had spent the day of September 3 going over the decorative effects for the show drawn up by the ALAM Show Committee, of which Clifton was a member under Chairman Col. George Pope. They included, along with other splendors, "a magnificent triumphal arch." The board also endorsed "an aggressive policy of prohibiting their dealers from handling unlicensed cars."

In the same issue, the magazine reported in its "News Notes" Clifton's defense of Pierce's automobile body construction. The company had developed a unique system that assembled cast aluminum panels into complete bodies with no major wooden structure. This advanced idea originated with James R. Way, Pierce's body engineer and designer, who had been trained at Brewster & Company, New York City carriage and body builder. The George N. Pierce Co. hired 42-year-old Way in 1904. Clifton remarked that many people assumed that the cast aluminum Pierce bodies were "several hundred pounds heavier than competing bodies." Comparing overall weights of seven passenger cars "embodying Pullman seats," he asserted the Pierce body weighed only 40 or 50 pounds more if a wooden body was equally well made. Clifton did not believe the body of metal on a wood frame (what became known as the "composite body") was comparable, either. He insisted that the additional wood reinforcement the sheet metal required gave no great advantage in weight for the metal-paneled body, "but in point of durability and safety to the riders, from the point of liability for personal injury, our body is certainly not to be compared to any other body made anywhere in the world." Observing Pierce bodies involved in accidents showed "the cast aluminum body seems to be of such a character that they do not crush or collapse, and consequently save from serious injury their occupants." The Pierce Company continued to develop its cast aluminum bodies for more than another decade with great success.

The new ALAM *Handbook of Automobiles* was readied for publication at a meeting of the handbook committee on October 8 held at the New York headquarters. The committee consisted of Thomas Henderson of Winton Motor carriage Co., Wm. E. Metzger of the Everett, Metzger, Flanders Co., Charles Clifton and E.P. Chalfant, asst. general manager of the ALAM. Contract for the publication was awarded to Brewer Press of New York. This handbook of facts about cars offered was an important yearly project of the ALAM. The 1908 issue was the sixth edition.

The 40S six-cylinder engine of 1908, intake side. Note copper motor oil tank at the back above the engine that fed oil to bearings by gravity (courtesy Pierce-Arrow Society).

The annual meeting of the ALAM was held at the East 42nd Street headquarters on November 10, and Charles Clifton was re-elected president. Other officers were vice-president Thomas Henderson (Winton), secretary L.H. Kittredge (Peerless) and treasurer George Pope of Pope Mfg. Co.

Another example of Charles Clifton's role as head of the ALAM was mentioned in the November 12 issues of both *Automobile Topics* and *Automobile*. This was a lengthy review, entitled "American Ideas in Construction and Exposition." It described the efforts that the organization pursued on behalf of what Clifton called the "legitimate" manufacturers. "The legitimate manufacturer," he averred, "is typified in an essentially modern man; progressive, or he would not be in the business, alert and full of nervous energy, if he shall succeed and survive." These men made it possible, he believed, for the industry to be among the first to recover "from recent financial conditions." There followed a listing of all the programs and projects that the Licensed Manufacturers had instituted, including standardization of parts and measurements, collection of relevant periodicals of information, improvement of technology through the Mechanical Branch, supervision of road racing, and, finally, the development, organization and production of the Annual Automobile Shows at the Madison Square Garden. This was yet another instance of the claims of superiority the ALAM pressed in the still-unsettled conflict over the Selden Patent.

It had been an eventful year for the industry and for Charles Clifton personally. It is, accordingly, not surprising that in its edition of December 3, 1908, *The Automobile* reported "Charles Clifton, treasurer of the George N. Pierce Company of Buffalo, sailed for Europe last week on *Kronprinzessin Cecille*. While absent he will look over the new models exhibited at the Paris salon by the European manufacturers." Even on vacation it seemed Clifton could find work to do.

The arrival of 1909 did not suggest the high drama that would unfold during the year's passage for Charles Clifton, his employer, and the automobile industry as a whole. The first week was certainly exciting enough, taken up with the New York show sponsored by the American Motor Car Manufacturers Association (AMCMA) at the new Grand Central Palace. Then, two weeks later the Association of Licensed Automobile Manufacturers (ALAM) presented its New York show at the Madison Square Garden. The Pierce offerings were only seen at the latter show, naturally, and they were extensive: two lines of 4-cylinder cars (24 HP and 40 HP) and three sixes (of 36 HP, 48 HP and 60 HP). Nearly a thousand expensive Pierce cars would be built in 1909. Two of them would be the first cars purchased by the White House for presidential use. This was the final year the company would market 4-cylinder cars. All transmissions were now 4-speed selective shift.

At the opening of the lavish Madison Square Garden event a superbly trimmed Model 60QQ show car on the Pierce stand generated great interest. It was a standard Suburban body, meant for motoring in grand style. The chauffeur sat behind a windshield, his seat roofed over but with no side doors or windows. The fully-enclosed tonneau was upholstered in silk, grey stripes alternating with yellow "enhanced with long garlands of roses through the center of the grey stripe," according to a review in *The International Studio* magazine for February. The fittings included golden yellow satinwood trim and gold-plated, specially-designed hardware all done in Louis XVI style. The *New York Times* described it as "the acme of taste in body design and interior and exterior appointment." These details demonstrated some of the skills young Herbert Dawley was providing the company in the art department. The car itself was another among luxury conveyances, such as railroad Pullman cars and Atlantic liners, decorated carefully to an antique style at the time.

The car attracted the attention of the wife of William Howard Taft, the president-elect who was determined to inaugurate the official use of automobiles by the Chief Executive. Helen Taft was just as determined to use motor cars herself. Two six-cylinder Pierce-Arrows were eventually purchased by the government in March 1909 for these purposes. The sale, as uncovered by Michael L. Bromley for his book *William Howard Taft and the First Motoring Presidency*, consisted of a fully-equipped 48 HP Suburban ($6,100 fob. Buffalo), a similar 36 HP Landau ($4,600) and a separate touring car body for the 48 HP, all included at a steeply-discounted price of $4,900 delivered to the White House. The Suburban arrived in time to carry the Tafts to the Inaugural Ball the evening of March 4. Charles Clifton, doubtless with the approval of George K. Birge and the board, was deeply involved in this transaction, the importance of which in prestige was only too obvious. The tradition of the Pierce company leasing current models for White House use would begin in 1910 at $500 a year per car and continue into the Franklin Roosevelt administration. There were even Pierce-Arrow advertisements that discreetly used a White House setting.

During the ALAM show a rumor swept the participants, according to the January 28 issue of *The Automobile*, "that Colonel Clifton and all his associates in the George N. Pierce Company had resigned from that concern." And then, "the smiling Colonel himself" confirmed it!

Actually, a new concern called the Pierce-Arrow Motor Car Co. had been incorporated on January 20, 1909, capitalized at $1.5 million, which then absorbed the "entire assets, goodwill and business of the George N. Pierce Co." Its capitalization had more than quadrupled to "manufacture automobiles, motor cars, motor boats, cars, locomotives and engines of every description, carriages and conveyances of every nature that can be operated or used upon land, water or through the air" according to the Certificate of Incorporation for 50 years duration filed with the State of New York. Shares in the George N. Pierce Co. were duly exchanged for shares of the new Pierce-Arrow Motor Car Company. It is clear that George K. Birge controlled the new firm through his ownership of around half its 15,000 shares of common stock (par value $100 a share). The cars would be known as Pierce-Arrows from then on.

The management was unchanged. The new name became world famous.

Charles Clifton attended the regular monthly meeting of the NAAM in New York on March 3, according to *The Automobile*. S.D. Waldon of the Packard Motor Car Co. occupied the chair for the first time since his election as president. Ten company representatives were present along with S.A. Miles, the general manager. A resolution was passed that declared "Inasmuch as Detroit has become the greatest automobile manufacturing city in the world" it deserved to be the starting place for the annual Glidden endurance contest. Clifton was named to the Audit Committee at this meeting. He would sponsor two Pierce-Arrow entries participating in that Glidden Tour in July and another two in the Hower. His entries successfully defended the previous wins in both events that summer, keeping the winning Pierce sweeps unbroken. This, however, would be the last time the company sponsored an entry into these events. The board decided that the development of the automobile had advanced enough that they no longer needed to participate in events "of this nature."

Clifton was also present in Albany on May 13 to testify before Governor Hughes in support of the Allds-Hamm automobile legislation, a bill to tax cars at a higher rate to pay for road repair and construction, while abolishing speed limits. The hearing unfortunately ended before Clifton could speak.

Early in 1909, the gathering of evidence for and against the suit alleging infringement of the Selden Patent by the Ford Motor Company and others was finally completed. Evidence collection had taken more than five years and was probably lengthened by the way it was conducted because the process allowed a far greater volume of evidence than a more disciplined approach would likely have allowed.

The decision on the case would be made by the judge of the U.S. Circuit Court of the Southern District of New York, who would hear evidence at the Federal Court House in Lower Manhattan. This would not be a jury trial, and it attracted few spectators. Proceedings opened on Friday, May 28, before Judge Charles M. Hough, who had been appointed to the court in 1906 by President Theodore Roosevelt. He was a well-respected, diligent and determined man. His lack of familiarity with patent law and the terminology associated with automobiles meant that the judgment required a considerable effort on his part even to comprehend the issues in the case. All through the court proceedings he demonstrated a yearning to discover the underlying simplicity in this endlessly convoluted controversy. The case was not just a question of infringement of the patent, but would determine if the patent itself was valid, covering all gasoline cars. Having heard the presentations by lawyers on both sides during a week of hearings, Judge Hough then took the mountain of evidence collected to his Rhode Island summer home, vowing to read the entire record while preparing his decision.

When Samuel Betts and William Redding, the ALAM leading attorneys, presented their case they stressed that Selden was a pioneer developing the idea of the self-propelled gasoline-powered car, even declaring that he had commenced to build the vehicle described in the patent, although that had not happened, as we have seen, until 1907. Still, the brief they submitted concentrated on the pioneering aspect of Selden's patent, arguing that he alone was the originator who first combined the particular components needed to make a functioning car, and that the two models built as Exhibits 89 and 157 had proved the patented vehicle could be operated under its own power. Those charged with infringement, they maintained, had no choice but to respect the contract between the patent holder and the U.S. Patent Office that had granted the patent. Claims by Ralzemond Parker and the other defense attorneys that other inventors had successfully driven petroleum-powered vehicles before Selden's application in 1877 were swept away as irrelevant. The simplicity of the plaintiff's argument had a strong appeal to someone not familiar with the complex technology under scrutiny.

By contrast both the brief and the evidence presented by the defense was centered on a mass of detail concerning the technology employed during the long development of automobile vehicles, the timeline of those developments and the inconsistencies in the ALAM case.

Judge Hough's approaching decision had the potential to reorganize the forces within the American automobile industry, an already powerful and rapidly growing part of the U.S. economy. While all producers were welcome in the pioneering National Association of Automobile Manufacturers, the ALAM and the competing AMCMA were outgrowths of the Selden controversy, which limited their membership. One, even while supporting the patent, had members who harbored doubts about its true validity, while the second association had no doubts that the patent was invalid, period. The decision could possibly destabilize the awkward balance inside the industry.

In its May 6, 1909, issue, *The Automobile* published an article by Charles Clifton entitled "Why Auto Industry Does Not Resemble Predecessor." In it he maintained that bicycle making and automobile manufacture did not develop in the same way. Rather, when the popularity of the bicycle began to wane in the late 1890s, "a large amount of capital, energy, producing and selling brains was rendered comparatively idle and consequently those forces were logically attracted to the automobile business, which had alluring prospects and called apparently for the same essential elements." This may well have been Clifton's own observation in the Pierce factory at the time.

Later that year, in the June 24 issue, Clifton authored a discourse called "Logical Plea for Automobile Sanity" covering several controversies involving the industry that included tire wear, various driving styles on the road and "autoists versus farmers." In both features his position as president of the Licensed Association was carefully noted. When the Licensed Association's general manager, E.P. Chalfant, resigned to join the Packard Motor Car Co., the board met June 25 in New York, Clifton presiding, to elect Coker F. Clarkson as his replacement. *The Automobile* reported in its July 1 issue that "Mr. Clarkson has been connected with the association for some years in the mechanical and publicity departments...."

The Pierce-Arrow factory layout and production methods were featured in an article with photos entitled "Many Systems in Pierce Plant" published in the June 10, 1909, issue of *Motor Age*. The writer seemed quite taken with its "order in layout." The general logic of its movement of parts toward assembly was followed and explanations made of wheel construction, close tolerances and the use of overhead cranes in assembly. Considerable detail was devoted to the treatments applied in the "steel room," especially the recording thermometers for the furnaces that made easier the tracing of defects. Inspection procedures were detailed as well as the superior working conditions for employees. The basement of the administration building was described as being devoted exclusively to the comforts of the men. "This complete arrangement for the benefit of the workmen is a suitable introduction to the factory proper and suggests the order, cleanliness and organization that might be expected." The Inspection Department was said to be of particular interest. "It consists," writes the author, "of fifty-four men who do nothing but see that the factory workmen do their work right." This article shows the impact the factory had on progressive production methods. Success at Pierce-Arrow now prompted the board to conclude a five-year contract with David Fergusson on October 1. The chief engineer's yearly salary remained at $5,000, but with a bonus of another $5,000. This agreement was duly recorded in Fergusson's diary.

Judge Hough handed down his patent infringement decision on September 15, 1909, and he agreed with the complainants that the Selden patent had been violated by Ford and the others. Hough found that "after 30 years [since Selden first applied for the patent] no gasoline motor car has been produced that does not depend for success on a selection and organization of parts identical with or equivalent to that made by him in 1879." He further denied that any gasoline vehicles had been built before that which even faintly fulfilled the requirements Selden's design had met. Therefore, any gasoline-powered car design was covered by the patent.

There can be little doubt that all the members of the American Motor Car Manufacturers Association were dismayed by Judge Hough's surprising decision that left no alternative to their obtaining a license from the ALAM, quite possibly in addition having to pay a penalty for their recalcitrance.

It is also impossible to suppose that the members of the Association of Licensed Automobile Manufacturers were all jubilant at the decision, even though they were on the winning side. Selden himself might well have been, as, perhaps, would remnants of the Electric Vehicle Co. as holder of the original license from the patent holder. To those less financially benefited, the ruling meant that they would continue to be beholden to the ALAM, paying royalties until the patent expired on November 5, 1912. Not everyone was entirely convinced the patent holder had earned his royalties, let alone the Licensed Association's power over the industry.

The decision shook the automobile industry to the core. Henry Ford made it clear that he was willing to go broke appealing the case. "I expect," he wrote, "that ultimately the supreme court of the United States will hold that the Selden basic patent is not valid." Others who had allied themselves with him were less confident. The October 7 issue of *Motor Age* reported, in an article titled "Selden Decision Produces Quick Results," that a "conference of great importance, the first of the moves in a new alignment of concerns, was held in Buffalo last Wednesday." Participants included H.O. Smith of Premier, chairman of the AMCMA committee of management, Benjamin Briscoe of Maxwell-Brisco, C.G. Stoddard of Stoddard-Dayton, R.E. Olds of Reo, Charles Lewis of Jackson, and William Mitchell Lewis of Mitchell. Stories in the Detroit *News-Tribune* mentioned "a representative of the A.L.A.M." who was "more or less present." Since Buffalo was his home it would have been easy for Charles Clifton to have attended such meetings, and, certainly, he had an inside view of the Association's attitudes at the time.

Whoever it was made the clear argument that the Association would take "a broad view of the situation, and not attempt anything which might prove detrimental to the industry as a whole." The industry was conscious that "matters of great moment," to use the words of

The Automobile in its October 7 issue, would come before the Association. Charles Clifton had openly expressed support of the "broad view" for some time, according to the magazine, "though he encountered some difficulty convincing others of the wisdom of his course. His advice," they concluded, "is likely to be quite potential [*sic*] at the present time."

The "broad view" policy consisted of both inducement, in the form of reduced license fees, and more restricted competition for established makes. The possible later punishment by punitive assessments for lagging acceptance of the ALAM offers was an unspoken goad, and several of the companies at the meeting relinquished their membership in the AMCMA and signed up with the ALAM. Even Henry Ford seems to have wavered in his determined resistance when the ALAM seemed willing to admit Ford Motor Co. without assessing back royalties. He rejected even this offer when the Association, on advice of counsel, refused to reimburse his court costs.

As if to emphasize its determination, the Association commenced to file suit on imported cars for license royalties in September. The makes included Benz, Daimler, Zust and Otto of Germany, Renault, Ducasse, and Delahaye of France, Italia and Isotta of Italy and the English Daimler. New suits had not been filed against American manufacturers and dealers, but that possibility was openly discussed, as were threats of suits against *users* of infringing cars.

At a meeting on October 6 in New York, the NAAM Executive Committee transferred the membership of the now insolvent Electric Vehicle Company (together with its Selden license) to the Columbia Motor Car Co., according to an October 14 article in *The Automobile*. It duplicated a similar transfer of membership in the ALAM. Even the favorable Selden Patent decision had not been able to preserve its primary license holder.

The ALAM held its annual meeting November 4, and the event was covered in the November 18 issue of *The Automobile*. Charles Clifton was re-elected president, Samuel T. Davis of Locomobile vice-president, L.H. Kittredge of Peerless, secretary, and George Pope of Pope Mfg. Co., treasurer. The membership of the Association was now greatly enlarged by the influx of members due to the Selden patent decision.

Two weeks later Clifton was among the members of the New York Automobile Show committee of the ALAM, meeting under Col. George Pope's gavel in the New York headquarters. The upcoming "Tenth National Automobile Show" would be held in the Madison Square Garden January 8–15, 1910. An extensive writeup in the November 18 issue of *The Automobile* detailed the elaborate preparations. Thirty thousand dollars were set aside for decorations, and already "carpenters, sign-makers, wood-workers and painters are working zealously on the skeleton for the decorative creations." The large plaster statues "and other staff work" that had characterized earlier shows had been eliminated. The 1910 event would welcome visitors to the Madison Avenue side with a substantial Roman seat and fountain that permitted a view of the ranks of automobiles, motorcycles and accessories on the show floor. The low, grey stone abutment would curve, gracefully framing the exhibits, while, at the center and each end, water would "spray from the mouths of griffins and gargoyles upon the pool beneath." The waters would be colored with "cunningly hidden lights." Goldfish and water lilies would decorate the pool as well. The setting complemented the popularity of the automobile show, "becoming every year more important as a social event, at which the latest fashions in both cars and costumes are displayed."

A few weeks later, on November 30, the AMCMA met in New York to plan their competing January auto show at the Grand Central Palace. H.O. Smith of Premier chaired the meeting. The same day the members of the ALAM met in its 42nd Street headquarters chaired by Charles Clifton. Discussion apparently centered on the admission of former members of the AMCMA to the Association. The next day the ALAM executive committee met with Clifton again chairing. The committee was understood to have decided that "members of the AMCMA had been given an opportunity to obtain licenses upon reasonable terms." That afternoon, the executive committee of the NAAM met to discuss the 1910 Chicago auto show.

"Because of these meetings," wrote *Motor Age* in its December 2 coverage of the week, "and the annual session if the American Automobile Association, the city is filled with prominent motoring lights, both in the trade and in the sport, and in consequence there is great activity in local circles." This significant year had opened and closed with intense automobile industry activity in New York City, still the commercial center of the automobile business, despite the growing importance of Detroit.

In his diary that month, David Fergusson recorded another $1,250 bonus from the company—a Yuletide remembrance, perhaps.

As the year 1910 began, the final impact of Judge Hough's decision to uphold the validity of the Selden patent was still not entirely certain. There were still two 1910 New York automobile shows. The membership of the Licensed Association had grown as less determined holdouts gave in and joined. Meanwhile, the Ford Motor Co. and its allies pressed ahead with their appeal of the Hough decision in a higher federal court. Their determination seemed quite unshakable, and the winning ALAM had members still harboring less than total conviction that the patent was really valid.

As the ALAM show opened, another spectacular show car appeared on the Pierce-Arrow stand beside its other 1910 models. This time it was a large, completely equipped 66 HP convertible car designed to the order of company president George K. Birge for long distance touring. The January 20, 1910, issue of *The Automobile* reported that the car had "[s]pace for luggage, the utensils of a protracted tour, and the 'home comforts' which even a hotel limits." This weighty but powerful car seemed perfect for maintaining the desirable average of twenty miles an hour for long distance touring over available roads advocated by experienced tourists such as Harry B. Haines, who wrote for *Scientific American*.

The design of this Touring Landau model was assisted by Herbert M. Dawley, who now headed Pierce-Arrow's Art Department from "an office in a large room in the factory where a car could be brought in and photographed" by his own photographic assistant. Such photographs were compiled into albums that assisted customers ordering up special features and equipment. In his recollections for the Pierce-Arrow Society in 1968, Dawley remembered Birge wanted this show car to "embody every comfort which would enable him and Mrs. Birge to take extended tours in this country and abroad." Those "comforts" included a hinged basin with running water, cabinets for linen, thermos bottles and cutlery. A toilet was concealed behind a seat, and a bunk for sleeping could be provided by arranging seat cushions. Two-way conversation with the chauffeur was provided by a telephone. "How much the luxury appointments were used, (particularly the toilet), I never knew," Dawley wrote.

This lavish car, the second of three variations on the "touring" theme the company built for Mr. Birge between 1909 and 1911, was offered as a catalogue model. The firm even distributed a separate brochure, with photographs of the Touring Landau and its various details against a vast, rough-cut stone apartment building. At a price of $8,250, its purchase equaled

The 1910 Model 66QQ Touring Landau for the world traveler, offered at $8,250 (courtesy Pierce-Arrow Society).

the cost of a substantial home at the time. It is not known how many of these Touring Landaus were sold to customers, and none seem to have survived.

The Birge Touring Landau was used by the family for many years. It was their custom to spend part of the year in France, where they had a residence in Paris. A niece of Mrs. Birge told James Sandoro of the Buffalo Pierce-Arrow Museum that it was shipped to France every summer, apparently even after the death of George K. Birge, for Mrs. Birge to use for touring. The niece accompanied her on these trips for several years. According to her account as soon as the Touring Landau reached Paris it was put away and the Hispano-Suiza Mrs. Birge preferred was put into service. This practice was deliberately not disclosed to the press for fear of embarrassing Mrs. Birge back in Buffalo.

The refined Pierce-Arrow models for 1910 had gone into production in July of 1909, Pierce's usual season for new model introductions. Offerings consisted of three lavish but distinct six-cylinder "pleasure car" lines. These three versions were produced, with periodic improvements for nearly the next decade, and they were enormously successful. The most compact Pierce-Arrow in 1910 was the 36 HP, its 3,380 lb. touring car on a 125-inch wheelbase, powered by a 4 × 4¾ inch motor. The price was $4,000. Mid-range in Pierce line was the 48 HP 4½ × 4¾ inch six on a 134½ inch wheelbase. Its touring car model weighed 4,120 lbs. with a price of $5,000. The largest model, on a 140-inch wheelbase was the gargantuan 66 HP model, priced at $6,000 for the touring car. These weighed 5,400 lbs. and were powered by a mighty motor of 5¼ × 5½ inch bore and stroke dimensions. Its thirst for gasoline was phenomenal, as was it power. All Pierce-Arrows had T-head motors, with cylinders cast in pairs, dual ignition systems, seven main bearings and a "special automatic" Pierce-patented carburetor.

Their selective four-forward speed transmissions were mounted amidships behind a leather-faced cone clutch, driving the rear axle through bevel gears. The frame was channel-section, of chrome-nickel, heat-treated steel on the two larger chassis, carbon-manganese cold rolled steel on the 36 HP. Refinement was sedulously pursued by the company. Semi-elliptic springs supported the front of the car, three-quarter elliptic springs the rear. The Pierce-Arrow body factory continually developed a greater strength and variety of bodies for the three models, all assembled of complicated aluminum castings. Seats were carefully thought out, cushioned by deep, coiled springs topped by a thick layer of curled hair. The goal was to provide generous support to riders even for long distances over rough roads, the usual conditions obtaining at the time. Upholstery material—leather for touring cars, heavy fabric for sedans—was selected after tests in the factory laboratory guaranteed the required durability.

Pierce-Arrow made it a point to offer a selection of closed body styles suitable for varied formal use by its moneyed clients. Shorter chassis had 5-pass. Brougham and Landaulet offerings, while the longer wheelbase models included 7-pass. Suburban and Landau formal styles. Each range of models also included 2-pass. Runabout, 4-pass. Miniature Tonneau and larger 5-pass. Touring cars. The two larger models also offered 7-pass. Touring versions. The closed bodies entailed a premium of $1,000 or so above the corresponding touring car models. With a standard factory wage of around 35¢ an hour, these were very high prices. Nonetheless, the Pierce company told F.S. Edge, the famous Napier executive who visited the factory that year, that they had sold the entire production scheduled for the 1910 model year by December 1909. This was an output of 1,528 cars, according to a company recension table from 1920.

The situation suggested that factory capacity should be expanded. In addition, Pierce-Arrow was continuing its efforts to develop a practical heavy truck and enter a new market. The Turner Construction Co. of New York had added a 350 ft. four-story extension to the body buildings in 1909. A major reason for this increased production space was the extended time it took to dry coat after coat of the varnish finishes, which were the only automobile paints available at the time that could be mixed into various colors. Days of drying time were needed to get a good "carriage finish." As a result, much factory space was needed at all auto-

The 48SS chassis ready for body mounting (courtesy Pierce-Arrow Society).

mobile plants to accommodate freshly varnished bodies. Pierce-Arrow also laid out plans in 1909 for further plant expansion to be completed by the summer of 1910.

The Aberthaw Construction Co. of Boston would build additions that doubled the size of the power house and added a new storage garage for completed cars next to the Motor Test building on the far east-side of the plant. Most significant were two new four-story buildings erected east of the Manufacturing Building, one to contain rough and finished stock with room for some assembly, the other for nickel plating and additional assembly. To their northeast, and within the junction of these two buildings, a single-story truck assembly building was erected to produce a commercial line for the company later in 1910. As the years passed, this complex, further enlarged and known as "Building C," became the most important subassembly building in the plant. As these additions were completed the factory expected to employ 3,600 men and women. The machine shops were already working nights to keep up with production demands. By late summer, production space totaled 23½ acres, according to a story in the August *Horseless Age*.

The members of the AMCMA held an eventful annual meeting the third week of January 1910. *Automobile Topics* reported in the January 22 issue that the "articles of agreement which bind together the members" was for five years only, and "expires February 9." Considering the turmoil Judge Hough's decision had caused in the ranks of the independent organization, it was not clear that renewing the agreement was important, and eventually it lapsed.

One important effect of this confusion was the resignation at the meeting of Alfred Reeves as AMCMA general manager. He would shortly assume that same post at the ALAM,

Pierce-Arrow factory in 1910, now greatly enlarged from the original in 1906 by south extension of Office Building (*foreground*), additional story on Body Building (*to right*), and new four-story Body Building (*right rear*) (courtesy Pierce-Arrow Society).

where he and Charles Clifton began a long and fruitful partnership in automobile industry organizations. Clifton acted as the overseer and political strategist, while Reeves ran the front office and took care of day-to-day operations. Securing Reeves' services was seen as a sign of the ALAM's power over the industry at the expense of the faltering AMCMA.

On Thursday, February 16, Charles Clifton was in Washington, D.C., where he read a paper entitled "Inter-State Intercourse by Motor Vehicle" to a hearing at the Willard Hotel of the Senate Committee on Interstate and Foreign Commerce, chaired by New York Senator Chauncey M. Depew. The committee was considering a bill that would simplify crossing state lines in automobiles. Such traffic was still somewhat rare, and some states were very protective of their borders. It was certainly in the interest of the automobile industry to make such crossings as simple as possible.

The February 26 issue of *Automobile Topics* reported, in an article entitled "Col. Clifton Goes Abroad," that he and Mrs. Clifton were leaving that day "on a month's cruise on the steamship *Molke* to the West Indies and the Spanish Main."

"Since the decision in the Selden patent case," they wrote, "Mr. Clifton has devoted a great deal of time to association matters. He expects to secure a well-earned rest on his trip to the Caribbean Seas." Apparently, the Clifton children, 16-year-old Gorham and 6-year-old Alice, remained in Buffalo.

Two days later, *Motor Age* stated in an article titled "Reeves Visits Detroit" that Alfred Reeves had set out the week before to convince the Ford Motor Co. to join the ALAM. Since he had been, apparently, on good terms with Henry Ford when general manager of the AMCMA, Reeves may have felt he could make a persuasive argument without giving offense. Henry Ford, however, declined with what was described as "a stinging reply," and Reeves left Detroit that Saturday the 26th. "The A.L.A.M. wants it understood," he was quoted as saying, "that the keynote of its policy is the protection of the motor industry." This appears consistent with earlier "broad view" statements by members of the organization. Reeves then added: "It has reached the stage where precautionary measures are necessary." The "precautionary measures" were not stipulated, and no legal actions were announced, but the remark suggested that the ALAM was considering stronger actions against those companies like Ford that refused to join up.

While the Cliftons were relaxing on the Spanish Main, the industry was witness to a duel over the ALAM and the Selden patent by the two main antagonists in the dispute. Opening salvo was a declaration of Selden Patent policy in what was described as an "interview" with Charles Clifton that apparently occurred on February 22 in Buffalo and was then printed in the March 2 issue of *The Horseless Age*.

Clifton's argument, which doubtless presented the official position of the ALAM board, maintained the Licensed Association was intent only upon protecting an innocent public against dangers lurking in the booming automobile business. The first of those was said to be that of feckless investors being enticed into backing weak automobile projects in hopes of "overnight" riches. Clifton pointed out what in fact turned out to be an ever-increasing difficulty: that of entering the automobile business successfully. "Those who start companies at this time," he wrote, "forget that the makers now getting profits from the business are old timers, who, after years of work, have built up a line of products and organization for handling them which cannot be duplicated without a great amount of work at this keen competitive period of the industry."

The second danger Clifton described was that facing the hapless "innocent buyers" of cars that "infringed the [Selden] patent." This left those buyers open to "chances of litigation" and the "difficulty of trading that car in exchange for a licensed car when a new purchase is contemplated."

There had been no general policy by the ALAM to sue private owners of unlicensed cars, but that threat was certainly implicit in these remarks. While the official licensee of the Selden Patent was the Columbia Motor Car Co., inheritor of the now defunct Electric Vehicle Company's remains, Clifton was careful to point out that "the Association of Licensed Automobile Manufacturers has the right through its executive committee to say who shall and who shall not be granted the protection of the patent."

He went on to explain that "seventy-six standard American cars and two imported cars are now licensed." These companies, he maintained, covered the range of automobile offerings "from $485, the lowest priced car in America to the most luxurious machine of the automobile and coachbuilder's art, with makers in strict competition with each other." These makers made "almost 95,000 cars, or about 85 per cent of the estimated total production, and this year are expected to market not less than 160,000 machines." The thrust of these remarks was that nobody needed to patronize unlicensed manufacturers because the ALAM membership covered the entire market, offering cars all made by "excellent businessmen"; a fact apparently certified by their membership in the Licensed Association.

"With a view of protecting the public," Clifton continued, "and thereby increasing the popularity of the automobile, it has not been the policy of those who control the patent to extend its protection to new and untried or doubtful products." By these measures, the ALAM claimed to be a public benefactor. "It is the intention of the owners of the patent," he concluded, "to protect the exclusive rights secured by it to those who have become licensees by commencing suits against infringers of it." These remarks suggested that the ALAM was now embarking on an aggressive campaign against the unlicensed producers, their agents and customers.

The day after this broadside appeared, March 3, 1910, to be exact, *Motor Age* printed Henry Ford's withering reply to Charles Clifton and the ALAM. Ford declared that if motives of the ALAM were truly what Col. Clifton claimed, "it would be a most philanthropic undertaking."

"It should be," Ford continued, "and no doubt is, so evident to the public that the real motive of this war of the A.L.A.M. against the [unlicensed] motor car is a selfish one, and is neither to protect innocent investors from putting their money into new enterprises nor to protect buyers from buying cars for which they will not be able to secure parts, but is for the purpose of maintaining their present extravagant prices."

Ford suggested that the efforts of the ALAM would be better spent trying to get a court to enjoin unlicensed car companies from producing cars, rather than attempting to educate the public against buying them. He agreed with Clifton that the profits of older automobile producers encouraged formation of new companies to compete for the profits, but he suggested that many of the ALAM's "seventy-two varieties" were as likely to fail as newcomers. Open competition would see to that, and he suggested competition should be the policy of the industry instead of letting the ALAM select participating companies to license.

"The public," Ford insisted, "knows that all this campaign of education and all this expenditure of money for advertising is for the benefit of the seventy-two varieties, not for the benefit of the public, just as the same public knows that I am not building cars for the benefit of the public and that we are not conducting our campaign of publicity for the benefit of the public, but for the benefit of the Ford Motor Co. In so doing, however, we are proceeding along honest lines, a fact with which the public does agree."

Meanwhile, Ford made it clear that he was not caving in to ALAM pressures. "I can assure you," he wrote, "that while I am at the head of the Ford Motor Company, there will be no price that will induce me to permit my name to be added to those of the seventy-two varieties. I am going to continue our fight along honest lines as always and to trust to our courts, in which I have the greatest confidence, to see that justice is done."

Clearly, the Selden issue was not settled, "broad view" or no, but the automobile industry went on, regardless. In March the Pierce-Arrow Motor Car Co., perhaps as a way to promote the Touring Landau model, announced that they would have 66 HP models available by mid–July for "touring abroad." Then, on March 31, *The Automobile* reported that Charles and Grace Clifton had returned after "an interesting voyage," and "the pressure which Col. Clifton is accustomed to applying to affairs automobile will be felt again."

The resistance of Henry Ford notwithstanding, the industry powers at the upper levels of the ALAM exuded nothing but confidence that spring. Clifton's return presently blossomed into a notable public event that enjoyed widespread comment.

At the time, the City of New York was the location of the primary financial backers of the automobile industry, along with many others associated with its sales and service. Concurrently, several auto industry organizations, such as the AAA, the NAAM and the ALAM had their headquarters in the city. The Transit Building at 7 East 42nd Street was the site where several of these organizations had their headquarters. Business meetings were often held there. The prominent Hotel Astor, near Times Square, was used by the various associations for industry luncheons and banquets. It was also the starting point for other events like the New York to Paris race in 1908.

The industry banquets held there in the century's first decade were social events of the first order in the automobile industry. These were lavish Edwardian celebrations during which the leading men of the industry, dressed in black tie formality, ate well, drank well, joined together in song, made toasts, and enjoyed speeches by important men of the time. Charles Clifton fit into these events with the ease that came from watching his grandfather in Buffalo wine and dine political lions of the pre–Civil War era, and Brig. Gen. Peter C. Doyle of the 4th Brigade officiate at such events of high military decorum with the New York State National Guard.

So it was that on the evening of Thursday, April 7, 1910, some 175 members of the Association of Licensed Automobile Manufacturers and the press crowded the tables in the ballroom of the Astor for a rich meal and entertainment to celebrate the new strength of the association in the wake of the Hough decision vindicating the power of the Selden Patent and the collapse of the competing AMCMA. There may have been a business meeting that afternoon, before the evening festivities, but if so, it was not covered by the press. The banquet was covered extensively by both *The Horseless Age* and *The Automobile* in their April 13 and 14 issues, respectively. The honored guest of the event was Governor Fred Warner of Michigan, who gave the keynote speech. Lighter activities were arranged by General Manager Reeves and Secretary Downs of the Show Committee. Toastmaster was Joe Hedges, one of the organizers of the now-defunct AMCMA, who playfully professed himself as preaching his own funeral sermon, while also acting the part of corpse and choir.

Governor Warner gave a detailed speech to demonstrate the enormous impact that the auto industry was having in the Michigan economy, and expressed confidence that improved roads were on their way. From time to time the guests sang popular songs from sheets containing new topical lyrics devised by R.H. Johnston of the White Co. Arthur Brisbane of the New York *Evening Journal* gave a witty speech, urging that the feminine market be built up to loosen up "tight wad husbands."

The event was, according to *The Horseless Age*, "a tribute to the several men who have done especially marked work for the Licensed Association and nursed it to its present size and position." Chief among these was Col. Clifton, who received an engraved loving cup from the Association for his work "upbuilding the organization" as its president. The presentation was made by Col. George Pope. Clifton's speech of thanks began with the insistence that the basis of the presentation would have to be altered before he would be easy in his mind about receiving it. He maintained that it was the "efficient support by the other officers and members of the association" that brought about any success he had achieved.

He then made a plea for continued cooperation and for regarding the cup as a rallying point for the forces of the association. "The inertia of thoughtlessness and prejudice has had its say," he continued, according to *The Automobile*; "it has done its best to bar the onward march of the automobile, and the time has arrived when nothing remains but to continue along co-operated lines, looking at things broadly, and remembering that inherent worth must govern the combined efforts of the co-operators, and this will only be possible if worthy effort obtains at the behest of the individuals in their several walks."

As the Colonel turned to resume his seat amid applause, the toastmaster, Mr. Hedges, interrupted, and, when quiet was restored, told Clifton that every member of the association knew how much valuable time he had given over to association work. That was in the past and could not be recalled. But during all that time, Hedges went on, in which Colonel Clifton labored to build up the motor industry "he almost forgot he had a home. He could not forget that he had a help meet and the partner of his joys and sorrows, but if it had not been for the free service he gave the association, he undoubtedly would have spent more time in her company." Therefore, while the success of the association was sufficient reward in itself for Colonel Clifton, Hedges added, the association had decided to make some sort of amends to Mrs. Clifton for the loss of his company. To accomplish that purpose they were presenting Clifton with a Steinway baby grand piano that he was to give to her on their behalf. These presentations were the high point of the banquet. The ALAM had never been so strong before, and Clifton was clearly seen to be one source of that strength.

That same issue of *The Horseless Age* contained a story "reported on good authority" that the ALAM intended to file federal suits "in a few days" against seven motor car companies from various states that manufactured cars "which do not carry the Selden license tag." Such a story tended to confirm the intent that previous remarks by Charles Clifton and others in the ALAM suggested. Indeed, suits were filed against 12 manufacturers by the middle of May. By contrast, the Velie Motor Company of Moline, Illinois, filed a countersuit for a half-million dollars alleging the misrepresentations of the Selden group had resulted in damages to their business from its high initiation fee and reductions in production totals the association had imposed. Fifty-four members of the ALAM were named as defendants. Another suit against the ALAM by Carhartt Automobile Co. of Detroit was also filed, charging the association denied them a license in spite of promises to the contrary causing great expense to fulfill requirements. Norville Hawkins of Ford Motor Co. found, as he canvassed the Midwest looking to expand Ford's dealer network, that the ALAM had openly discouraged potential dealers by writing them letters pointing out the legal risks they ran as agents for an "infringing" make. Judge Hough's decision seemed to have increased the Licensed Association's aggressive attitude.

The Pierce-Arrow Motor Car Co. had some more positive news that spring. The April 13 issue of *Horseless Age* revealed the completion of factory expansion at the Buffalo plant, accompanied by a statement announcing that the firm intended to begin the manufacture of motor trucks. "It has been known," the magazine asserted, "in the inner trade circles for more than a year that the company had a truck on the road for experimental work. It is the belief of the company that through this two years of constant experimentation there has been evolved a commercial vehicle that goes far toward convincing even the most skeptical of those who have uses for motor trucks that they have reached the strictly practical stage in their development."

This account of truck development at Pierce-Arrow was later enlarged by the company's own history published some years later in *The Pierce-Arrow Salesman* for January 1919 and apparently derived from a letter David Fergusson wrote to vice-president May on September 16, 1912. Actually, Pierce began developing commercial vehicles in 1905, and by late 1906 a cab-over-engine design based on the 4-cylinder, 45 HP Pierce Great Arrow running gear with chain drive was nearly ready for construction and testing. It had a projected five-ton capacity, the size the Pierce board believed would be the most profitable.

Completion of this design was interrupted by the movement of motor car production to Elmwood Avenue in November 1906, and it was not until the spring of 1907 that tests began. After a two-year period of development, the board decided in early 1909 to construct 100 of these trucks, only to have the development stopped by a new assistant general manager, one H. Kerr Thomas, who left Napier in England for Pierce in September 1909. Thomas had considerable experience with trucks at Napier and previously with the English Hallford Co. Henry May was startled by a December 10, 1909, report Thomas submitted after looking over the Pierce truck plans, in which he called for a complete truck redesign. The production planned for early 1910 was halted in order make those substantial alterations. Kerr Thomas' suggestions became the new basis of the Pierce-Arrow truck. Its front axle was moved forward, the radiator and engine just behind. The load was positioned over the large rear driving wheels, the frame redesigned to flex with road irregularities and a transmission brake was incorporated.

This new design was the basis for a scheduled output of 200 trucks in early 1910, but for a second time the effort was halted. This followed comments by a Canadian truck user, who had experience with both chain-drive and Berna gear-driven trucks. After a visit to Toronto in late spring, David Fergusson told May that he was dead set against chain drive because of its high maintenance costs and short operating life. His conclusion was strengthened by his engineer brother's experiences at the English Leyland Company and the observations made by Pierce-Arrow's test drivers. Again, Henry May delayed production, and a careful evaluation of geared drives was carried out. Pierce had been a leader in the adoption of geared drives in its very first Motorettes, and their bias toward that drive system was already evident. After study of three types of geared drives, they chose to use a worm-drive, and May approved the use of Leyland hobs to cut the gears for those rear axles. Two pairs of worm gears had already been ordered from "Wrigleys" who, Fergusson reported, made the Leyland gears. Most of the rest of 1910 was spent working out this final design and testing it.

One interesting contributor to this development was the test driver employed. Francis W. Davis, a recent graduate engineer from Harvard University, was first hired at Pierce-Arrow in 1910 as a $12.15 a week inspector in the machine shop. This job was followed by work grinding transmission valves, and, still later, working on the carburetor line. It was preliminary training for Davis in the automobile industry on top of his college degree. He ended up some years later perfecting the basic design for power steering, now used universally.

His rotation through jobs at Pierce ended when he became test driver for the new prototype 5-ton worm drive truck, which he had also helped to assemble. According to historian Maurice D. Hendry, test drives consumed 10 hours a day driving not from a seat in a cab with a roof but on a seat box naked to the elements. At noon, Davis remembered bolting his meal and thawing out in the boiler room of the factory. Davis continued to work at Pierce-Arrow for several years in the truck department, where he was sure the opportunities would be great.

Production of the Pierce-Arrow cars for the 1911 model year went ahead into production in July 1910. Perhaps reflecting the company's focus on truck development, they were near copies of models of the year before. The biggest mechanical change was the lengthening of the stroke of the 36 HP to 5⅛ in. and the stroke of the 48 HP to 5½ in. The biggest body change was the application of front doors to some models.

The October issue of *Automobile Topics* commented on the attitude that the Pierce-Arrow company brought to its employment practices, convinced that "giving its employees sanitary and social advantages would secure for it a better class of workers." They described the new dining hall included in the south extension of the Office Building then being constructed on Elmwood Avenue that would enable 1,700 workers to sit down to a meal instead of the earlier 900. Amusements such as concerts and dances would also be organized for the space by the Pierce-Arrow Amusement Association. The new building would contain 3,042 full-length lockers for the workforce, located in the greatly-expanded basement along with "766 porcelain individual washbowls, each one of which is provided with hot and cold water faucets, soap and individual towels." Tunnels for use during Buffalo's inclement weather connected this basement with the factory production spaces on the other side of what the employees called "Main Street" between the buildings.

At this time, the automobile industry was absorbing a great influx of new ideas, new materials and new high-speed machine tools that permitted both more precision in manufacture and greater durability in service. They also allowed costs and, consequently, in some cases, prices to fall. The December issue of *Cycle and Automobile Trade Journal* printed an explanation entitled "No Logical Reason for Reduction in Price of High Grade Cars" written by Charles Clifton in his role as the Pierce-Arrow Motor Car Co. treasurer and sales manager. He emphatically rejected the idea that such cars as those Pierce-Arrow made were likely to reduce prices. "We can see nothing," he wrote, "that would cause a reduction in price." High-grade materials, labor costs and rubber remained high, and, since such cars were not made in quantity, and the factory facilities were extensive, makers were "very conservative as to quantity." The only price reductions in this sector of the market that the Colonel foresaw would be those of cars thrown on sale at reductions because of fear of bankruptcy or bank-

4. Showdown Over Selden (1907–1911)

ruptcy itself. "But this," he concluded, "must be a comparatively small group and can, at the worst, be only temporary."

Clearly Pierce-Arrow prices were not due to fall. Nor did they.

On another front, at what *The Horseless Age* called "the largest gathering ever held" by the ALAM, Charles Clifton was elected to his seventh term as president, by a unanimous vote of the organization's board of managers on Thursday, November 3. In fact, the entire slate of officers was re-elected, with a "vote of appreciation and endorsement of their work."

During this meeting, trade conditions were also discussed, "which from reports appear be even more healthy than at this time last year." The increase in the automobile business over the previous 12 months was said to have been almost 100 percent, "a record without parallel in other lines of trade." The report counted some 6,500 automobile dealers handling licensed cars at the time. And the board endorsed a "conservative policy with an increased care in the manufacturing and marketing of cars."

Later in the day, the Association Patents Committee met, and the following officers and directors were unanimously elected: Charles Clifton, president, Thos. Henderson, vice-president, Alfred Reeves, secretary and treasurer. George Pope, L.H. Page, L.H. Kittredge, Hugh Chalmers and R.E. Olds were named directors, along with Herman F. Cuntz, the expert on patent matters. This committee would oversee patents actually owned by the Licensed Association.

The Show Committee, chaired by Col. George Pope, also presented a report about the 1911 New York ALAM automobile show to be held (at the Madison Square Garden, naturally) for two weeks beginning on January 7. Special plans were made "to care for every one of the licensees, as well as accessory people." The Licensed Dealers' Association of New York was urged, in a resolution passed at the meeting, to co-operate and affiliate with the manufacturers in the automobile show. The impetus to gather all the forces of the industry into the ALAM was still evident as the year 1910 ended.

Shortly after, on November 22, 1910, the appeal of Judge Hough's decision in the Selden Patent case reached the U.S. Circuit Court of Appeals. Hearings in the case were held at the Old Post Office in Manhattan before three judges: Emile Henry Lacombe, Walter Chadwick Noyes, and Henry Galbraith Ward. Judge Lacombe presided. Of them, it was Judge Noyes of the Second Circuit who was a recognized expert in the patent field. Some 40 attorneys made very similar arguments to those they had made before Judge Hough. The last of these was received on November 25, and the judges retired to consider the volumes of testimony, exhibits, and briefs connected with the case. Their consideration could take as long as they needed.

The first 5-ton Pierce-Arrow prototype truck was finally completed in late December of 1910, in time to be taken to the New York show. The company had high hopes for its new offering. The event proved even more momentous than anyone imagined it would at the time, but for unrelated reasons. On the last day of the year, a Pierce-Arrow with an ambulance body was delivered to the Buffalo General Hospital.

The ALAM show opened in New York on Saturday, January 7. Pierce-Arrow cars sported front doors, and a racy new four-door touring style called the "Protected Touring" was introduced. The spectacular 66 HP model Pierce displayed at the show was again a touring landau sort of car. This time it was a five-passenger version with folding tops and very traditional lines called the George Washington Coach. It was named to evoke the memory of a traveling coach, powered by six horses, used by President Washington himself. The car was a very stylish affair as well. Once again, the new model had much storage space for tour books, tools, and parts. Fittings included a wash basin, toilet, and spaces to carry six steamer trunks. Road tours were a serious business in those days. Exterior door panels incorporated scenic paintings by artist Ernest Fosbery of Buffalo. The list price of this "George Washington Coach," at first, was $8,500, as compared to $7,200 for the more conventional Suburban model. The price soon climbed to an even $9,000, but even this dark green show car with the russet stripe did not get as much attention as Pierce-Arrow's new 5-ton Model R truck.

Every showgoer with any interest in the idea of motor trucks carefully observed the Pierce truck stand. Here was an unconventional and revolutionary approach to such vehicles in America. The motor was way up front, like a car, with the driver behind that, over the transmission. The rear axle was near the center of the load-bearing area at the rear, permitting a shorter turning radius while improving traction. The worm-drive, built by David Brown & Sons, Huddersfield, England, presented a dramatic change from the usual chains or complicated compound wheel gears. Notable for its quiet operation, it also had a power delivery efficiency of 95 percent, compared to the 80 percent to 85 percent for chain drive. The increased price of the axle was discounted by the reduced maintenance required and was said to reduce the vibration in associated components as well. Orders were already being taken for spring delivery when production was scheduled to get under way in Buffalo. But this dramatic show success was anticlimactic, compared to the news that broke the next week.

On Monday, January 9, the melodrama around the Selden Patent was brought to an

First R-1 truck at plant office entrance (1911) (courtesy Pierce-Arrow Society).

4. Showdown Over Selden (1907–1911)

abrupt end by the unanimous decision of the U.S. Circuit Court of Appeals, delivered (and largely devised) by Judge Noyes. While the Hough decision asserting the validity of the Selden claims was upheld, the Court of Appeals made an important limitation. It held that Selden made a decisive choice in the motive power for his gasoline wagon. That choice, the Brayton engine, had a very different operation than the competing Otto engine, and it had never been successful in powering a car, while the high-speed Otto had worked well continuously for 20 years. The court ruled that George Selden's patent covered only vehicles using the Brayton-type engine. "Every element in the claim was old," they wrote, "and the combination itself was not new.... [H]ad he [Selden] appreciated the superiority of the Otto engine, and adopted that type for his combination, his patent would cover the modern automobile." As it was, Ford and the other defendants "neither legally or [sic] morally owe him anything."

The triumph of the Association of Licensed Automobile Manufacturers had been overturned right in the middle of their prestigious New York show.

The Automobile reported that "the whole atmosphere seemed to take on an electric quality" as news of the decision passed among the show's participants. Everyone realized that the ALAM was now stripped of its major legal compulsion. Alfred Reeves' first impulse was to announce that the Licensed Association would appeal this decision to the Supreme Court of the United States. Shortly after, however, the "broad view" was again embraced by the ALAM. It had been the principle always favored by Charles Clifton because it avoided unnecessary conflict within the industry and strengthened its influence. Here, he could see a fine opportunity to unify the automobile manufacturers for their own good and for the good of the public. In any case, the Selden patent would have stood for less than two more years. An appeal would take up at least a substantial part of that time, costing additional money. It was better to make a public peace between the combatants.

This was done in as spectacular a manner as possible, covered by the January 21 *Automobile Topics* under the headline: "A.L.A.M. Banquet Is a Love Feast." Held at the Astor on Friday, the dinner was a suddenly genial celebration amid lavish food and drink that started with appetizers and champagne, passing through *Filet de Boeuf, Richelieu* and Duck *Glace' d'Aselles* and salad to fruit, cheese and *Petits Fours*, accompanied by more champagne (G.H. Mumm & Co.'s *Extra Dry* or *Selected Brut*) or 1905 *Haut Sauterne*. Liqueurs followed or Perfection Scotch Whisky and even *Appollinaris* water to accompany cigars or Philip Morris cigarettes.

Amid the dinner jacketed participants was none other than Henry Ford as the guest of honor, clad in a business suit. "President Charles Clifton voiced the general opinion," the magazine wrote, "when he referred to the decision of the Circuit Court of Appeals as one that made it possible to celebrate the unification of the industry. He went on to say that in defeat the A.L.A.M. found its victory, and that the old order was ended and it gave him pleasure to welcome in the new."

At this point, Clifton produced a churchwarden pipe of tobacco, which he first lighted, then drew a puff or two of smoke and turned to Ford, presenting the pipe, on which Ford drew a puff and raised to the crowd. At that point, "the applause became an uproar." Few trade association dinners before or after could match the drama of this one.

It was apparent, however, that the usefulness of the ALAM was over, and by the opening of the Chicago automobile show in February plans were put in place to establish a useful successor. The committee of organization was made up of C.C. Hanch of the Nordyke & Marmon

Co., Hugh Chalmers of the Chalmers Motor Co., Henry B. Joy of Packard Motor Car Co, Charles Clifton of the Pierce-Arrow Motor Car Co., Benjamin Briscoe of the United States Motor Company and Thomas Henderson of the Winton Motor Carriage Co. This committee determined the name, plan of incorporation, and other details that would enable the association to organize shows, handle patent litigation, encourage progress in mechanical and metallurgical subjects, and do "other things as may protect and advocate the interest of those companies comprising the corporation," according to the February 8 *Horseless Age*. By contrast, *The Automobile* in its March 2 issue warned that the organizers were a combination "that has for its object the acquisition of all the live patent rights that have a bearing upon the manufacture of automobiles."

Despite the controversy, by May 4, according to the May 31 issue of *Automobile Topics*, the organization had been incorporated and named the Automobile Board of Trade and its constitution and by-laws approved. The directors chosen to lead it were the same as the members of the organizing committee, except that Joy's place was taken by S.D. Waldon of Packard and Samuel T. Davis, Jr., of Locomobile was added. Charles Clifton had presided at a meeting earlier that day of the languishing ALAM, which took care of mere routine business. Clifton was chosen to head the new organization. Perhaps in recognition of that new position, he was also chosen to be an honorary judge at the Elgin Cup Race in Illinois that August 25–26.

In the meantime, *Automobile Topics* reported in its February 11 issue that Col. Clifton, acting as the ALAM president, had gone on record as opposing the plan by Governor Dix of New York to turn highway construction over to the state engineer. "The present idea of a commission of three men alternatively appointed for six year terms every two years has worked admirably in the brief two years of its existence," he stated. "Under the commission, for the first time we are getting State roads built to last. For the first time a regular system of patrol and repair work has been established that has saved the State millions of dollars. In short, the commission idea has resulted in a businesslike administration of our highways. This idea needs to be tried out thoroughly."

Pierce-Arrow President George K. Birge also strongly opposed the changes under consideration, saying "Under the State Engineer the roads were poorly built and not maintained. The abolition of the commission will restore this condition." Highway construction was becoming an ever-greater issue with motorists.

Concurrently, Pierce-Arrow's new 5-ton capacity Model R truck was going into production that spring. Orders were already in hand, but a notable achievement like the Pierce Great Arrow's victory in the Glidden Tour was desired. On Friday, June 16, 1911, at 2:05 a.m., a Pierce-Arrow truck left New York on a 24-mile jaunt to Boston with a capacity load of 20 barrels of oil that the consignee, the Standard Oil Co., had diverted to the truck when it discovered that the cargo could not reach Boston from New York on time Saturday either by rail or boat. The truck was fresh from a series of week-long demonstration events in Chicago, Philadelphia, New York City, and Newark. At trip's end, the truck arrived in Boston at 3:00 o'clock Saturday afternoon, having stopped to make short demonstrations at New Haven, Hartford and Worcester on the way, according to the June 24 issue of the *Morning News* of Wilmington Delaware. The truck consumed 51.5 gallons of fuel on the trip, keeping an average speed of 12.1 miles an hour, not far from the 13 miles per hour operating speed the vehicle was designed to hold through almost all conditions. The Standard Oil Co. had already ordered such trucks for its fleet, so this was a confirmation of its good judgment and Pierce-Arrow's

4. Showdown Over Selden (1907–1911)

claims for its performance under typical road conditions. This first year of its production, 100 of these trucks were built and sold.

There can be little question that the Pierce-Arrow Motor Car Co. took special pains to make working there as satisfying as it could. Many employees worked at the plant for decades. Vice-President Henry May supervised the factory, and he was known for a particular fairness dealing with conflicts, despite his somewhat prickly demeanor at times. All the same, this spring one Buffalo paper carried a story that reported a strike involving 600 "trimmers, painters and final-assemblers" at the plant that had lasted for a week. The employees, like many at the plant, were members of the International Association of Carriage and Automobile Workers. The problem had started with the company attempting to put these employees on "piece work." They preferred the "old system," and the union objected to the change. Buffalo Police Chief Regan had sent details from the Austin Street and Cold Spring police stations "to check any trouble." Company representatives were reported as hoping "the whole trouble will be satisfactorily adjusted in two or three days." However this particular difficulty was settled, the fact was that employees in the Pierce-Arrow plant worked under a piecework system in the future for many, many years.

The Automobile Board of Trade held its first quarterly meeting on July 6, which was covered in the July 15 issue of *Automobile Topics*. They met at the new organization's headquarters, the old offices of the ALAM at 7 East 42nd Street, New York City, with Charles Clifton presiding. Clifton noted that the Board of Trade had gone into operation on the first of that month. An important item of business was the naming of W.C. Leland of Cadillac to fill the vacancy on the board created by the decision by Thomas Henderson to retire from business. The board also apparently discussed patents and 1912 New York Automobile Show plans. The magazine also reported that Henderson "received a most joyous send off Thursday last, the 6th inst. at the Engineers Club, New York City." Among the many guests offering Henderson "glowing tributes" was Charles Clifton. The new retiree received an engraved silver loving cup "as an appreciation of the work done by Mr. Henderson for the industry."

The Charles Clifton family relocated during 1911 into a large property at 789 West Ferry Street, across from the extensive John Albright estate. Albright had established the first steel mill in the Buffalo area shortly after the turn of the century and was a leading figure in its business world. The Clifton home had been built in 1897–98 for Cassius M. Carrier. Chauncey J. Hamlin in turn occupied the house beginning in 1906. Charles Clifton evidently bought it from Hamlin. It was designed by the prolific Buffalo architectural firm of Green & Wicks in the style common in Buffalo at the time. A three-story house, its ground floor was of cut stone, while brown shingles clad the upper stories. There were two prominent half-timbered dormers on the front façade of its steeply-slanted roof. The dormers extended two stories down to the ceiling of the stone story. The house had several porches, and there was a *porte cochere* on the west side, which led to a carriage house at the rear.

Mark Clifton, the Colonel's grandson, remembered a visit he made to the house when he was five or six years old sometime in the late 1920s and recalled a garden in the back and an ornamental fish pond. Inside, the most memorable aspect for Mark was the dumbwaiter that took meals from the kitchen on the ground floor to the dining room upstairs ("My brother rode it once.") Such details as wood paneled walls and stained-glass windows also came back to Mark's mind along with floors "layered with oriental carpets" and a solarium "where they raised their plants" in the back. What Mark Clifton called a "garret for the servants" was

Clifton family residence (1911–1929) at 789 West Ferry St., Buffalo (courtesy Buffalo and Erie County Historical Society).

located on the third story, where "a cook, a chauffeur and a couple of maids" resided. Charles Clifton's mother, who had been living at 102 Richmond Avenue, then moved into the Cliftons' previous home at 61 Irving Place.

This year Clifton became the secretary of the Buffalo Club, as he had been before in 1897. He would keep the position for three years. The Colonel was also a member of the club's board from time to time through this period.

About the middle of July, the addition to the Pierce-Arrow factory was completed. A report on it appeared in the *N.Y. Evening Mail* on December 20, 1911, which called the plant "one of the show plants of the American Industry." The 3,500 workers were turning out the 1912 models, expected to total 2,000 cars by the next June. Eight cars a day were scheduled for assembly.

The new 36 HP, 48 HP and 66 HP models were largely unchanged mechanically, except for more powerful brakes and a longer stroke on the 66, making it a 5 × 7 inch six (824 cubic inches displacement). Some electric lights had been added, but headlights remained carbide gas models because Pierce-Arrow felt the electrical variety were not yet reliable enough to adopt, although they were confident of their eventual adaptability.

The body styling, however, was completely changed and revolutionary. The company was determined to have the coachwork reflect the character of the self-propelled vehicle. Both body designer James R. Way and Art Department head Herbert Dawley seem to have been uncomfortable collaborators in the new designs. Dawley later described Way as "a disciple of the Sphinx, because as a conversationalist he left much to be desired." Dawley had started his career at Pierce determined to unify the appearance of the various hardware on the cars. ("It had about as much uniformity as a patchwork quilt.") Later, as his work was more accepted by management, he had "sold Col. Clifton on the idea that the motor car design should depart from the conventional carriage design by reducing the seating space, presenting a smooth line and surface from front to back, thereby suggesting speed and eliminating a resemblance to a pregnant cow."

The 1912 Pierce-Arrows seem to have been the first attempt to fulfill Dawley's vision. They were still made of complicated cast aluminum panels, but the skill of Pierce's vendor, the Aluminum Castings Co. in Buffalo, had advanced to the place that much larger, more sculpted castings were possible.

Pierce-Arrow described the result in one piece of sales literature: "The greatest consideration has been given to the designing of the Pierce-Arrow bodies, both open and closed, for 1912 cars. In past years, the style of automobile bodies has progressed along the lines of the horse-drawn vehicle; the automobile body has been an adapted coach body. In producing bodies for the present series of cars, it has been the object of the company designers to construct a body essentially for an engine-propelled car, the contour of whose lines and curves and form is at once typical of great self-created and self-transmitted power." The exterior was cleared of as much extraneous machinery and fittings as possible. Operating controls were all brought inside the body itself. The eight body designs enclosed larger spaces and were carefully laid out for easy operation of the controls. Their lines were much smoother than the usual design, more shapely. The windows of closed cars had no wooden sashes. The glass moved up and down with mechanical lifts in the interior, rather than the conventional straps. These features made the cars stand out.

1911 48SS Landau, 135-in. wheelbase, with restyled cast aluminum body and sashless glazing at $6,200 f.o.b. (courtesy Pierce-Arrow Society).

As a part of the marketing plan, the company released a lavish catalogue illustrated with color plates and pen and ink sketches by Adolph Treidler to accompany careful descriptions of the features contained in the cars, along with photographs of the various models. The *San Francisco Newsletter* called it as "classy as the car itself." It was the second year in which such catalogues were used to promote the line, and both times such booklets were widely praised.

The Sunday, October 15, 1911, issue of the *San Francisco Examiner* contained in its "Automobiles" section a lengthy report of 21 trucks involved in what was called "The Big Truck Test." This had involved two trips by fully-loaded trucks: a morning run through the harbor area and an after-lunch climb of the famous Twin Peaks. The Pierce-Arrow carried 10,000 lbs. of flour up the hill, faster than the only other two trucks, both Whites, carrying such a heavy load. It was considered a very good showing, made better by the relative silence of their progress due to the worm rear axle gearing.

The company was very pleased with the interest in this new product and its satisfactory performance. Sales were so strong that when the year's run of truck production had ended fewer than 10 remained unsold. Accordingly, plans were underway to increase production greatly, should demand require it. The *New York News* reported in its October 21 issue, "the company has bought a plot of land of about 35 acres, there [Buffalo], adjoining the New York Central tracks at a cost of about $165,000." The plans included a large plant to be erected on this site that would produce "various kinds of commercial vehicles propelled by gasoline."

Automobile Topics for October 14 had covered the quarterly meeting of the Automobile Board of Trade in New York, chaired by Charles Clifton, the week before. Members of nine committees were chosen, covering such responsibilities as Trade, Show, Legislation and Law, Good Roads, Mechanical Cooperation, and Patents. Clifton seems to have been a member of any committee he wanted to take part in *ex officio*. He, in fact, attended a meeting of the Show Committee, chaired by Col. George Pope, in August at the 42nd Street offices, where they discussed decorations for the forthcoming Madison Square Garden show in January 1912.

The October 25 *San Francisco Chronicle* reported the visit of "Colonel Charles Clifton, treasurer of the Pierce-Arrow Motor Car Company of Buffalo, N.Y. and one of the leading automobile manufacturers of the United States." He and Grace were registered at the Palace Hotel on Market Street during a visit to California and had traveled from Los Angeles. "While here," the paper reported, "he spent considerable time with William F. Culberson, president of the Pierce-Arrow Sales company of this city, who is also the general coast representative of the Pierce-Arrow Motor Car Company." Clifton was, apparently, quite pleased with the automobile outlook in California and made it clear that he expected many from the East to send their cars there for vacationing in preference to Europe, especially in view of the year-round season in the Golden State. He called the state the ideal spot for automobile touring. The couple expected to return east by way of the Pacific Northwest and northern states.

The various Buffalo city papers all had extensive stories on Thursday, November 23, 1911, about the "automobile parade" that took place the evening before and was part of "Industrial Week," a celebration of Buffalo industry. While the *Express* described the evening's weather as "chilly and disagreeable," crowds lined the streets to watch a mile-long parade of Buffalo-made automobiles and trucks, gasoline and electric powered. The parade started at 8:30 from the corner of Main and Exchange, the corner where Charles Clifton's Grandfather

Dorsheimer's hotel stood, and where he remembered parades in the city starting or ending all through his childhood. The parade traveled up Main Street to Summer and curled though the eastern sections of the city to as far east as Jefferson. The parade was led by an Atterbury truck, with a white statue of a bison named White Ted "lit with electric lights," followed by a band on another Atterbury. After that, the following makes paraded current and early models, apparently supplied by local owners: Thomas-Flyer, Atterbury, Babcock electrics, Victor motor trucks and fire apparatus, Thomas Motor Cab, Denniston commercial electrics, Automatic Transportation indoor electrics, Van Waggoner, Kopp trucks and, last, Pierce-Arrow.

Pierce ran more than 20 vehicles in the parade, counting the Pierce patrol wagon, the ambulances for Buffalo General and the Emergency hospitals, and Palmer the Florist's delivery wagon. Models from the ten-year span, 1902 to 1912, appeared, courtesy of their owners. Their performance was faultless. The earliest closed car was a 1906 Great Arrow, the earliest six-cylinder from 1907. Pierce-Arrow stressed that all the cars in the parade had been in service since constructed. Perhaps the most interesting of them was a car described as a "garage truck" that had traveled 163,000 recorded miles. This car sounds very much like the early four-cylinder car used for miscellaneous transport around the Pierce-Arrow factory by shipping superintendent Charlie Brenner and known as the "Skidoo Wagon." Over 600,000 miles had been recorded on this little vehicle when it was broken up for scrap in 1919.

Six Model R trucks were in the parade, loaded to capacity by their Buffalo area owners: Spaulding & Spaulding, Empire Limestone Company, Standard Oil Company, J.F. Kulp & Sons Company, Phoenix Brewing Company, and Magnus Breck Brewing Company. Five new 1912 Pierce-Arrow cars were in the parade, representing both closed and open styles and all three model lines.

So proud was Pierce-Arrow of this demonstration of its 10 years of progress that it had a bronze medal designed and cast as a souvenir for those who "have made possible the phenomenal growth of this company," according to a story from the Omaha *News* of December 10, 1911. These medals were titled "Ten Years of Industrial Activity." One side depicted a miniature of the first Motorette in the hands of a young workman. On the obverse was a mature figure holding a miniature of the 1912 Vestibule Suburban closed car, inscribed "Pierce-Arrow Motor Car Co. 1911."

Near the close of 1911, and anticipating the spring season, Pierce-Arrow released a booklet entitled *Over El Camino Real in a*

Obverse side of medallion cast to commemorate 10 years of automobile building at Pierce (courtesy Pierce-Arrow Society).

Pierce-Arrow Car. It was the account of a 20-day trip made in May of 1911 by Pierce-Arrow President George K. Birge with his wife, his daughter, and son-in-law to places in California between San Francisco and San Diego. According to a review of the booklet in the *San Francisco Examiner* of December 15, 1911, the book contained "forty-seven half-tone illustrations of scenes along the route, while the cover shows, in color, a cowboy of the romantic type watching the approach of a motor car along a road through the mountains." This illustration by artist Edward Borein of California was also used in Pierce-Arrow's national advertising at the time. The text gave a romantic image of the trip. "In Southern California," it glowed, "everything in nature and in and about the homes looked clean, fresh and prosperous. The wild flowers and roses were more abundant and beautiful than we have ever seen, even in beautiful Florence [Italy]." It may well be that research for this booklet was made using the same Touring Landau car Birge had ordered up from Herbert Dawley for a show car.

During 1911, the Pierce-Arrow Motor Car Co. had introduced a whole new line of heavy-duty commercial vehicles, expanded its production facilities, cleared the way for even greater expansion and produced a ground-breaking style in its three highly successful pleasure car lines. It had become a great Buffalo institution as well. The *Express* remarked in a December 31 story, "Made in the city, in the largest industrial plant within the limits of Buffalo, and with a greater number of employees than any other concern, the Pierce-Arrow company has always taken a certain amount of pride in having its exhibit of cars represent in its way its standing in the community." There was a great contrast between its standing 10 years before as a bicycle producer with an experimental line of motor cars and that of the successful and prestigious automobile giant whose products now graced even the White House.

The year had also seen resolution of the greatest patent controversy affecting the automobile industry. In all these accomplishments the impact of Charles Clifton could be seen. There would be more.

~ 5 ~

Conflict and Character (1912–1913)

> Col. Clifton was one of Buffalo's most highly esteemed and useful citizens and a leading figure in its business life. His kindly and sympathetic nature was nobly expressed in his many and bounteous charities, which as far as possible he kept from public notice. To a career of notable achievement in the realm of business, he united a record of fruitful, unselfish service to his fellow man.
>
> —*The National Cyclopaedia of American Biography*

The debris from the collapse of the ALAM in 1911 was still scattered around the automobile industry at the start of 1912, although the Automobile Board of Trade had taken charge of several of its components. Of course, there was also another trade association in the industry, the old NAAM. The unanswered question was, "Are these two organizations both necessary?" Various complications prolonged the search for an answer to this question.

So, the two New York automobile shows went right ahead as planned, but now projecting a cooperative intent. *Automobile Topics* headlined in their January 6 issue, "Twelfth and Final Motor Vehicle Exhibition in the Historic Madison Square Structure in New York Opens with Peace and Prosperity in the Industry." This described opening night for the New York Automobile Show sponsored by the Automobile Board of Trade, which corresponded to the Licensed Association's show in 1911 but lacked the former's contentiousness. Then, four days later, the NAAM show opened uptown at the Grand Central Palace. Any make could have theoretically been in either show, or, perhaps both. The division over the Selden patent was gone, but two shows were held anyway. The NAAM, having assumed sponsorship of the previous "Independent Show," graciously made a special attempt to smooth any resentments by inviting "every exhibitor at the Garden to attend the Palace opening, and to transport the entire army of trade men to the site in automobiles," according to a January 6 story in *Automobile Topics*. The automobiles, furnished by the NAAM exhibitors, were scheduled at half-past seven that evening to pick up their guests at the Garden and deliver them to the Palace by eight o'clock. The first car would contain "Col. Charles Clifton, president of the Automobile Board of Trade and William E. Metzger, president, and a large delegation of the executive committee of the N.A.A.M." The Palace was expected to be the location of the now-unified New York Automobile Show for the next five years, and this would give the visitors a chance to see the facility. This aspect of doubled sponsors would end, anyway.

Earlier that same week, both the remnants of the ALAM and the succeeding Automobile Board of Trade had met to conduct yearly business, each meeting being chaired by Charles Clifton. In the case of the Licensed Association the only business was to hear Clifton's final report and tender thanks to the officers and the executive committee for their services, according to *MoTor* for January 11. *The Automobile* of that date reported the Automobile Board of Trade on January 9 had held their annual meeting, at which President Clifton and the other officers were reelected unanimously. Reports from committees were heard, after which the committee members were all reappointed for 1912. Committees included "patents, general trade, statistics, shows, legislation & law, intercourse & arbitration, good roads and mechanical improvement." Charles Clifton had previously been named a member of the NAAM's auditing and legislative committees.

Activity next shifted to Chicago, where the local automobile show opened at the beginning of February. As reported in the February 8 issue of *Motor Age*, a special banquet took place for automobile dealers sponsored by the Chicago Automobile Trade Association on the evening of the First. Speakers included Charles Clifton, W.E. Metzger, Hugh Chalmers, Henry Ford, E.P. Chalfant, and R.D. Garden, the New York City Pierce agent. Beyond the speeches, however, dealers' representatives had the day before set up a National Automobile Dealers Association (NADA) that would become a vital contributor to automobile merchandising.

The executive committee of the NAAM met on Wednesday, March 6, in New York for the ambitious purpose to "Absorb the Board of Trade," according to a headline in the March 9 *Automobile Topics*. The NAAM was the earliest association of American automobile producers, having been organized at the very dawn of the industry in November 1900. The NAAM was also the largest auto manufacturers' association. It had originally even allowed accessory manufacturers to join until they formed the separate Motor and Accessory Manufacturers Association. It was a big tent. That another manufacturers' group was ever set up was due entirely to the dispute over the Selden Patent. After the showdown between the "licensed manufacturers" candidates for the NAAM board and those representing "independent manufacturers" resulted in the slate of the licensed manufacturers' winning control in January 1905, the NAAM tried to steer clear of the conflict as much as possible. They sponsored the Chicago automobile show but had not taken an active part in either of the New York shows. The organization actively supported the American Automobile Association (AAA) and their competition and good roads efforts with donations. They also helped fund Andrew F. Johnson's National Carriage Builder's Technical School in New York City, which was the major training program for automobile body design and construction across the industry.

The Automobile Board of Trade, by contrast, was pretty much just the remnants of the Licensed Association of Selden patent supporters. It had been founded in 1911 after the U.S. appellate court limited the scope of the patent. The Board's single important asset was the Association Patents Company, organized in 1905 to hold the patents owned by the licensed association, the Selden patent itself being only managed not owned by them. This asset was then transferred to the Board of Trade. The old ALAM was now left with only some remaining routine litigation that was expected to be disposed of shortly, and the organization would then be dissolved.

The *Automobile Topics* article described several difficulties to achieving the proposed absorption of the Board by the older NAAM. Some of the difficulties were legal. For example, the NAAM was chartered in Connecticut, and state regulations had the potential to interfere with the division of any part of its surplus among members. This raised the question whether it would be necessary to take out a charter in a less obstructive state in the future. Another roadblock was the patents company. This was organized largely as a defense against members having to pay license fees to outsiders, what the association described as "tribute." Another goal was to prevent "unnecessary friction and litigation between its members" over patents. This remained a continuing problem. The Automobile Board of Trade also staged the profitable Madison Square Garden New York automobile shows the Licensed Association had commandeered years before. These were some of the conflicting ambitions to placate if the merger was to be consummated.

The NAAM executive committee considering these problems was made up of W.E. Metzger, Charles Clifton, S.T. Davis, Jr., S.D. Waldon, H.O. Smith, H.H. Rice, A.L. Pope, L.H. Kittredge, R.D. Chapin, Alfred Reeves, W.C. Leland, G.W. Bennett and S.A. Miles, the NAAM general manager. At the March 6 meeting C.C. Hanch and Col. George Pope also attended. Apparently even naming the proposed combination was controversial, though the current "National Association of Automobile Manufacturers" seemed to enjoy a majority support among this particular group, perhaps understandably.

It was C.C. Hanch of the Nordyke & Marmon Co. who evidently brought up the greatest number of concerns about the combination. These were answered by George W. Bennett of the Thomas B. Jeffery Co., "The latter taking a very active part in championing the merger," according to the reporter. The Jeffery Company and its founder had a long history of successful opposition to patent claims, having opposed Col. Pope's extensive bicycle patents years before. Jeffery also ignored Selden patent claims successfully, although others, especially Henry Ford, fought them directly in court. Putting the collected automotive patents in the hands of the largest automobile trade association may have held particular appeal to this company.

A committee was eventually selected to work with the Board of Trade directors to accomplish the projected merger of the two organizations. Albert Pope would chair, and the other members were George W. Bennett, Roy D. Chapin, William E. Metzger and Samuel A. Miles. *Automobile Topics* concluded that "the difficulties to be encountered by the committee, while important, are chiefly matters relating to detail." The steps toward union appeared to be proceeding methodically, albeit slowly.

That same day the NAAM received a report from a two-day session of its truck committee. During that meeting Col. Clifton had delivered a talk on trade conditions. The 40 representatives of commercial car makers made recommendations regarding load ratings, overloading, body weight, and allowable speeds. "All of these were ratified by the National Association," *Motor Age* reported, "with the exception of the 90-day manufacturing warranty clause which has been held over a month pending some legal aspects of the case." Some SAE standards regarding truck wheels and tires were also approved. The growth of the motor truck market was evident.

Both *The Automobile* and *MoTor* noted that automobile makers, especially those in the higher-priced brackets, opposed the lowering of duties on imported cars from the prevailing 45 percent to 40 percent proposed in the Underwood Tariff Bill then being considered by Congress. Charles Clifton, Henry B. Joy of Packard Motor Car Co., and Wilfred C. Leland of Cadillac Motor Car Co. were scheduled to testify in opposition at an April hearing before the U.S. Senate committee considering this change. It was the manufacturers' contention that higher-priced cars would suffer more as a result of the reduction because labor costs were a greater proportion of their cost of manufacture. In mid-range cars of "very moderate price" the average was $90 per car as compared with "certain high-grade cars" with costs of $1,322. Other makes presented their testimony including Locomobile, Peerless, Premier, U.S. Motor Co., Nordyke & Marmon, Pope, Hudson, Waverly Electric and Overland.

At the quarterly meeting of the Automobile Board of Trade in New York on April 5 the spring selling season was reported by *Motor Age* in its issue of April 11 as "now in full swing, with demand for cars at a point that is pressing the production departments of all the makers." Although the weather in northeastern states was cold and stormy, reports from the South and various other sections of the country "indicate sales far in excess of previous years." The NAAM also held its quarterly meeting, the magazine reported, admitting the Velie Motor Vehicle Co., and anticipating Warren, King, and Federal truck would soon join. "The tenor was that business is excellent at the present time," the magazine reported, using Charles Clifton's exact description. "Nearly every factory is working overtime and the only complaint seems to be the scarcity of freight cars." It appeared 1912 would be a very big sales year.

Late in the spring season, *The Automobile* detailed the shortage of railroad cars. In its April 25 issue W.K. Vanderbilt, Jr., who managed several important railroads including the giant New York Central, which served many of the automobile factories, was quoted as saying the congestion was caused by those receiving the cars of automobiles for consignment not emptying them out quickly, surmising that they did not have the money to cover the costs of the vehicles due upon receipt. Some 50,000 automobile cars were presently in use for such shipments, according to Vanderbilt, and their movement since the first of the month had returned to almost normal. He pointed out that freight car speeds had risen from an average of eight miles a day in 1907 to about thirty. The magazine reported that, of the 40,365 automobile shipping cars owned by U.S. railroads, the New York Central owned 12,000 and 2,500 more were under construction. "The strenuous conditions imposed upon the trade during the continuance of the recent blockade," they wrote, "have resulted in a concerted protest by manufacturers against the possibility of recurrence in the future."

In response to Vanderbilt's statements, Col. Clifton released a statement on behalf of the manufacturers that said, "With such a winter as we have had and with so much congestion as there has been among the railroads, it would not be very unusual if, when the clean-up came, there should be a very large number of automobiles consigned to New York delivered within a short space of time. When the backward spring is taken into account, such a condition is not to be wondered at. I believe these factors are much nearer the truth than anything involving overproduction."

Meanwhile, the Pierce-Arrow Motor Car Co. was deeply involved with an expanding truck business. The second run of 100 5-ton trucks went into production in January, classed as R-2 models. Demand was strong. The company had, however, found that the merchandising of trucks differed from that used for pleasure cars. A story based on their press release published in the *Philadelphia Ledger* of May 13 pointed out that truck salesmen also had to be experts on traffic that trucks could carry. They needed to help customers appreciate the "wide scope of heavy traffic duty done by our trucks." The range included hauling oil field machinery in California, wool and milk in Boston, municipal dump work in Seattle, ice haulage in Jacksonville, farm products in Geneva (NY), mining products in Victor (CO), delicate machinery in Brooklyn and Dayton, beer, sand, coal, and safes in Buffalo, and so on and on. This range meant that mechanical men in the cities were called to the factory "at regular intervals" to train them on ways to help owners get the best service from their trucks by helping them organize their programs to facilitate repairs and replacements, operate trucks economically, and reduce strains on them. The company had a force "of practical truck engineers, who are constantly on the road in the interest of the owner. Not only are these men truck engineers," the article continued, "but they could also qualify as traffic engineers, their experience in handling of haulage problems in many cities under a wide range of work fitting them to advise on the scope of usefulness of the motor truck under conditions [sic]." Pierce-Arrow vowed to "stand unqualifiedly behind this truck."

Along related lines, the company publicized its "general invitation to visit the Pierce-Arrow factory" that extended to anyone interested. This effort was described in the *Boston American* of May 15. The company said that hundreds of visitors took such trips through the plant every year, "and the company has done what it can to make the visit an interesting one by providing guides and mapping out a route for them to follow." Those guides were admonished that "any one coming here with a desire to see the plant is the guest of the Pierce-Arrow Motor Car Company and is to be treated as such in every respect."

In May, according to an article in the May 23 issue of *Motor Age*, the Automobile Board of Trade had taken over the management of the January 1913 New York Automobile Shows at both the Madison Square Garden and the Grand Central Palace. Accordingly, a supervising committee for the shows was named. Chaired by Col. George Pope, it was made up of Charles Clifton, Alfred Reeves, and Merle L. Downs.

By that time the Pierce-Arrow Motor Car Company was readying its 1913 models to go into production in July. They would mark a great advance over former models, even though the body styles were virtually unchanged. There were, again, three models, now labeled 66-A for the 66 HP, 48-B for the 48 HP, and 38-C for the new 38 HP. That last model was now larger, with a bore of 4 inches. All models boasted a full-pressure lubrication system, which was an important advance. Their wheels sported Pierce-Arrow "Johnson Patent" demountable rims. A Westinghouse generator system furnished electric power for all lamps. The carbide headlamp was clearly passé.

Most impressive to buyers, however, was the fact that the car could be started from the driver's seat, with no hand cranking required (hopefully). This was the year that Cadillac had adopted the first electric starting system for production cars,

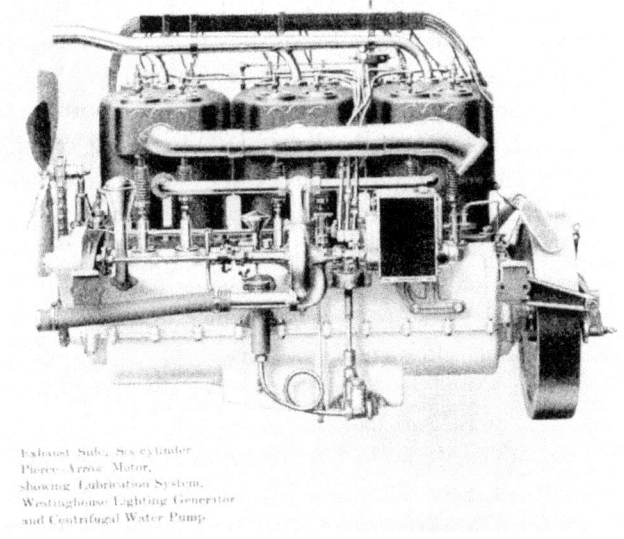

Exhaust side of Series 1 Pierce-Arrow motor (1912), now with pressure lubrication (courtesy Pierce-Arrow Society).

developed from Coleman patents by Charles Kettering and Edward Deeds of the Dayton Engineering Laboratories (DELCO). This bold improvement resulted in the second Dewar Trophy awarded to Cadillac. (The first had resulted from its demonstration of interchangeable parts in 1908.) Suddenly there was an industry-wide effort to perfect mechanical starting systems for the gasoline car. More than a dozen electric starter systems alone were developed. There were other types as well, including carbide gas starters and compressed air starting systems. It was this last that Pierce-Arrow decided on for its lines of "Series" models. The power to start the heavy six-cylinder engines was furnished from a tank filled with compressed air by a four-cylinder pump connected to the transmission counter shaft. The system worked if the tank had sufficient air. Unfortunately, over time, leaks developed and efficiency fell off. Pierce engineers felt it was more reliable than electricity and could be manufactured by Pierce itself. It proved to be only a temporary solution. All the same, it was an exciting development for anyone who dreaded hand cranking the motor.

Another 48 HP model, known as the 48-D, was marketed that year beginning in May. It apparently used a different electrical system and a carbide gas starter system. Fewer than 100 of those cars were made.

Promotion of Pierce-Arrow's 1913 cars featured full color advertisements in the carriage trade magazines such as *Country Life, Vogue,* and the early *Life*. A lavish catalogue was again issued, illustrated with photographic images of the many body styles, mechanical features, and pages of full color plates by Adolph Treidler illustrating the cars in spectacular settings. Pierce-Arrow had fewer than 100 outlets worldwide, yet demand was enough to encourage them to produce some 1,800 copies of this impressive advertising piece for its "Series One" line of cars. Prices ranged from $4,300 to $7,300 for catalogue models. The company welcomed special orders as well, and those prices could reach very high levels. Such customers were turned over to Herbert Dawley and the Art Department. In fact, it was for just such orders that Clifton apparently had hired Dawley, who recalled for historian Maurice D. Hendry in 1970 the special order for Seymour H. Knox of Buffalo that he carried out at about this time. Knox was the founder of the Knox 5 & 10¢ stores, which he sold to F.W. Woolworth for a substantial sum. Knox came to Pierce one spring with an order for a custom-designed car to be completed by his wife's autumn birthday. The car had carved Circassian walnut interior trim and custom woven upholstery with the lady's monogram displayed in the center of each tonneau seatback section. A matching chauffeur's uniform was tailored for the car as well. Hendry recorded a price of £18,000, which would have been $90,000 in those days—some million dollars today. Since Dawley had carte blanche this was possible, although even if the price actually was $18,000 it would have been stupendous with its chassis price being less than half this sum. Knox was quite willing to spend for his wife, however. The majestic Cass Gilbert designed mansion he built for her in 1915–1918 on Buffalo's Delaware Avenue still stands, although Knox himself did not live to see construction even start. It was the sort of house the Pierce-Arrow car was built to serve.

The NAAM Executive Committee held its usual mid-summer meeting on July 30 at a most unusual place—"240 feet above tidewater" at "Clifton," the summer home of its general manager, Sam Miles, at Christmas Cove, Maine. *Automobile Topics* described the event as "three days of rollicking good time." Charles Clifton was among the guests along with W.E. Metzger, Thos. Henderson, W.T. White, Albert Pope H.H. Rice, R.D. Chapin, and Alfred Reeves. These worthies constituted "about one half of the house party," according to the

5. Conflict and Character (1912–1913)

report, and until the evening of the third day discussion of business resulted in a fine being assessed payable to Col. Pope. The collection was not large. What was the actual business? "Real old shore dinners of steamed clams and lobsters, sweet potatoes and corn, with all that goes with them, had been daily features with all-night card parties and pool and fishing and luxurious bathing—bathing that is in a cement pool of steam-heated sea water pumped up from the bay below." The agenda for the business meeting was not extensive and included 1913 show plans, publicizing trucks at the show and the content of "standard caution plates for trucks." This was an appropriate list for the circumstances because Miles was the manager of the Chicago Show. The dinner that followed the business meeting was the end of the party for most, but not all, guests. These summer gatherings around industry business became a tradition for several years.

The *Boston Herald* noted in its July 16 issue that "Col. Charles T. Clifton, treasurer of the George N. Pierce Company [sic], builders of the popular Pierce Arrow motor cars," had been a guest at the J.W. Maguire agency. Clifton was quoted as being "greatly pleased" with the success of the Boston outlet, and told many stories of the increase in Pierce business during the year. (The lack of a middle name for the Colonel was a continual difficulty for reporters. Several were willing to supply a missing initial in their coverage over the years.)

That same month there was further evidence of the growing sales of Pierce-Arrow cars. Sam Breadon announced he planned to erect a new home for his Western Automobile Company at Washington and Euclid avenues in St Louis. Meanwhile, the Foss-Hughes Company, the leading mid–Atlantic Pierce-Arrow agents, announced a new headquarters would be erected for the Washington, D.C., agency at 1220 Connecticut Avenue and another at Elmwood Avenue and Plenty Street in Providence, R.I., where it would be convenient to Narragansett Pier, Newport (where the company operated a service garage at the Casino), Watch Hill, New London and the road to New York City, according to a story in the August 11 *Philadelphia Inquirer*.

An August 27 story in the same paper carried news of a contract between the Pierce-Arrow Motor Car Company and the Aberthaw Construction Company of Boston to construct more additions to the Buffalo plant. These included three stories to the "truck assembly building" as well as other structures. Plans were already being completed. Construction was to begin within the next few days and be finished, ready for occupancy, by the first of the year. It would add "several acres of good floor space." This was additional space in Building C, the Sub-Assembly Building.

An organization chart for the Pierce-Arrow engineering department dated August 19 shows Henry May as general manager and H. Kerr Thomas as the assistant general manager. David Fergusson was "Mechanical Engineer" for pleasure cars with Charles Pleuthner in charge of the "Drafting Room," Charles Sheppy as "Experimental Engineer" and a Mr. Cox heading the "Metallurgical Dept." Car testing was headed by Edward Retling. John Younger was the mechanical engineer for trucks. A Mr. Smith was in charge of the truck drafting room, Dr. Schwarz was experimental engineer for trucks and truck tests were supervised by Mr. Ulrich. The factory was hiring. "There's a Job for You at Pierce's" read the bills inside the International's streetcars traveling around the city.

Automobile Topics covered the NAAM September convention in its September 7 issue. "Hold Conference on Consolidation" read the headline, the text reading: "Consolidation of the Automobile Board of Trade with the National Association of Automobile Manufacturers was brought closer to consummation this week by a conference on Tuesday night, 3rd inst., at which representatives of both organizations met in committee session." The report disclosed no major obstacles but mentioned there were many details to be settled. The executive committees of both organizations met the next day to iron out some of those details. Charles Clifton was, of course, a member of both organizations.

More construction at the Pierce-Arrow plant was disclosed in the November issue of *Motor Truck*, which reported that along with the three stories being added to the truck building an additional story would be added to the three-story body building. Reportedly, the factory contained 23⅓ acres of floor space that also sported 18 acres of glass in the sides and roofs of the buildings. Employees numbered 3,850.

Business held over from the Detroit meeting of the NAAM was taken up at the December meeting. According to *Horseless Age* committees were set up to deal with used cars and yearly models. "In response to the invitation of the Carriage Builders' National Association, Charles Clifton and H.H. Rice were appointed members of the advisory board of the C.B.N.A. Technical School, "to which the N.A.A.M. has been a contributor each year." Charles Clifton now had an inside view of how automobile stylists and constructors were trained. The Colonel was, evidently, not at the meeting itself. The *Boston Post* reported on December 11 that J.W. Maguire had left for Buffalo the previous evening to spend a few days at the Pierce-Arrow plant and "to visit Colonel Clifton, who has been on the sick list for the past few weeks." Mr. Maguire was planning to supervise the shipping of two Pierce-Arrows he had sold, one to Paris and the other to Cape Town, South Africa.

The two automobile industry associations (i.e., the NAAM and the Automobile Board of Trade) were still active at the start of 1913. *The Horseless Age* and *Automobile Topics* both covered their separate meetings during the New York show in early January. The focus of the NAAM executive committee meeting on January 8 was on several issues that included adding

Aerial view of the Pierce-Arrow factory at 1695 Elmwood Avenue in 1911, showing (*from left to right*) shipping garage, metal treatment shops, receiving room and power plant (along Belt Line railway); machine shop, truck assembly and nickel plating building (4 stories); office building and extension along Elmwood Avenue; assembly hall (*center*), and body buildings along Great Arrow at the south (courtesy Pierce-Arrow Society).

an Indianapolis automobile show in March. The show committee also revealed a plan made with the organizers of the 1915 Panama-Pacific Exposition to erect a "special automobile palace" on the Golden Gate Park exposition grounds in San Francisco. It was projected to be 350 × 600 ft. in size, housing "all the exhibits of automobiles, motorcycles and accessories." The committee decided to submit the plan to the membership for approval. The report of the contest committee reported a tentative agreement it had reached with the AAA contest board that would give the NAAM the authority formerly held by the Manufacturers' Contest Association. There was also a discussion of the Motor and Accessories Manufacturers recommendation that the warranties of cars be invalidated if their pneumatic tires were filled with substitute filler preparations "that have been placed upon the market within the last year or so." President W.E. Metzger presided, A.L. Pope, R.D. Chapin, L.H. Kittredge, S.T. Davis, Jr., W.T. White, H.H. Rice, W.C. Leland, H.O. Smith, G.W. Bennett, and H.B. Joy attended, as did Charles Clifton, Alfred Reeves, and General Manager S.A. Miles.

When the Automobile Board of Trade had its annual meeting on the 14th, some 65 members attended. Charles Clifton presided. The membership unanimously approved the plan worked out for consolidation of the two organizations by the committee charged with the task. "As a result," *The Horseless Age* reported in its January 15 issue, "a new organization to be known as the Automobile Chamber of Commerce will be created, whose membership will consist of the members of the two associations." The NAAM executive committee had already agreed to the plan "for themselves and for their companies." The Board of Trade reelected its officers and then heard committee reports that included one by George Pope of the Show Committee, which extolled the success of the current show at the Grand Central Palace and the Madison Square Garden, which witnessed record attendance on Saturday and Monday "with every indication of even greater increasing attendance during the week."

On February 1, 1913, Herbert M. Dawley filed an application for a patent with the United States Patent Office. Along with his signature were those of a Pierce-Arrow company attorney and two witnesses. The patent would be granted on May 12, 1914, with the number 1,096,802. It became one of Pierce-Arrow's most prized possessions. Its title was "Headlight Construction for Vehicles."

It is likely that Pierce realized long before the final first series cars had been assembled in the late spring of 1913 that their compressed air starter system had not proved entirely satisfactory and began development of an integrated starter and electrical system. A January 1913 newspaper article boasted of Pierce-Arrow's "single wire, positive ground" electrical system in which the car's chassis was the return circuit. That was a part of it. Placement of the electric headlamps appears to have been the focus of considerable energy as well. The first series cars had their lamps mounted at about knee height on stanchions attached to the front frame, the same way as the previous carbide lamps were placed. The speed at which an automobile ran put a premium on the reach of the light from the headlamps, and a need to improve the illumination was obvious. To assist, the company set up a location in the plant where photographs could be taken to compare the coverage of various available headlamps. Herbert Dawley concentrated on finding a headlamp location that would illuminate the roadway as effectively as possible. Descendants of factory manager Henry May mention a discussion within the family at this time concerning lamp placement, including the suggestion by Henry's wife Emma that they be placed on the front fenders. As we will see, Charles Clifton played a documented part in the outcome of this effort as well.

1913 48-B touring car sporting electric lights and living up to its name in the West (courtesy Pierce-Arrow Society).

At some point, evidently in 1912, Dawley decided to design a mount for electric headlamps that attached to the crest of the front fenders, which improved illumination, especially on turns. These new housings were built up of sheet metal, open at the end like a horn. The wiring and bulbs were placed inside; a glass lens sealed the opening. Unfortunately, his enthusiasm for the placement was not shared when he showed it to the engineering department. "And who the hell would want a pair of frog's eyes sticking up in front of him?" was one response that he remembered. "My dander was up," Dawley reported later. This was not the first opposition he had encountered, and he knew the drill. He carefully developed working drawings, photographs, and analyses. His closing argument was that the lights he designed would also serve the purpose of gun sights, helping the driver aim the car down the road. He then packed up his proposal and appeared at Colonel Clifton's office.

"I sought an interview," Dawley recalled in his inimitable style, "and went armed to the teeth. Up to then he knew nothing of the idea. When I entered his office, he was reading *The Wall Street Journal*. (He was forever reading it.) He peered at me over the top and said, 'Yes, son?' he then disappeared again. I stood still and said nothing. After quite a pause, he reappeared and said, 'Have you something to say to me, son?' I said, 'Yes, sir, but I wish to talk to *you*, not the *Wall Street Journal*.' He looked at me coldly for a moment, but I detected crinkles at the corners of his eyes. He meticulously folded the paper and placed it to one side, removed his glasses and put them on top of it, folded his hands, leaned forward on his elbows and said, 'Now will you consent to tell me your story?'"

Dawley described Clifton's response to the proposal as "enthusiastic," suggesting a conference "with Mr. Birge and my superior Mr. Carl Blakner." The conference produced two more officials "emphatically" in favor of the idea. Their response to "the factory's opposition" is revealing. Instead of provoking a confrontation, Clifton and Birge hired an outside builder at their own expense to fabricate prototype lamps to mount on one of Birge's Pierce-Arrows. Dawley followed the project through for them. "When that car appeared at the factory, equipped with the fender lights, there was much wagging of heads and ill-concealed smiles!" he remembered.

There is no documentary evidence placing the patent application in relation to these events. What we do have is Dawley's conclusion that the new headlights were adopted, "but optional." Demand quickly made them standard. They seem to have first been attached to production cars in the late spring of 1913.

"Col. Clifton suggested several times that I try to devise something that would be a distinctive feature of the Pierce-Arrow," Dawley wrote. "The fender headlamps did it but that they fulfilled this suggestion was an accident."

Meanwhile, out on Long Island City, New York, Harrold's Motor Car Co. was erecting a stunning new service garage as covered by *The Automobile* at about that time. It was designed to employ "at least 200 men" in service activities for its customers in New York City and surrounding areas. At this writing, the four-story building still stands at 34–01 38th Avenue, convenient to the Queensboro Bridge. Attending to Pierce-Arrow cars and trucks in the metropolitan area obviously required substantial infrastructure.

In San Francisco, the *Call* reported in its February 23 issue that "the Pierce-Arrow Sales company has been forced out of its Van Ness Avenue location to make way for the civic center buildings." In fact, temporary quarters had already been erected to the south at the corner of Geary and Polk streets "pending the completion of its new home on the opposite corner." This was to be another four-story construction "and will be in keeping with the high quality of the Pierce-Arrow car." W.F. Culberson, the company head, was said to have spared no expense fitting out the temporary quarters to care for its patrons in the meantime.

In Buffalo, a local paper reported that Julian D. Eltinge appeared "last week in the Fascinating Widow." While in town, Mr. Eltinge decided he would look over the Pierce-Arrow plant, and a 48 HP seven-passenger touring car was sent out to bring him there. After his tour, the actor was so satisfied with what he had experienced that he bought the very car, writing his check on the spot, and rode the car back into town. "I want a car I can depend on," he was quoted as saying.

Sometime during 1913, Col. Clifton undertook another of the sort of projects that more and more typified his life. This was occasioned by his dissatisfaction with a particular piece of stained glass over the altar of the as yet unfinished Christ Chapel at Trinity Church. Clifton had been a neighbor of Trinity's rector, the Reverend Cameron Davis, when living on Irving Place, and they had become close friends. In passing, the Colonel mentioned to the rector that he would happily replace the window with something more finished, but his offer was refused because, as Davis pointed out, the window was a memorial. Clifton suggested the project be further researched, and, when Bertram Goodhue, the famous architect, visited Buffalo, Davis asked him for his professional opinion. It turned out that Goodhue expressed interest in the project only if it involved finishing up the whole chapel. Clifton quickly offered to underwrite the effort personally, hiring Ralph Adams Cram along with Goodhue to oversee the design and construction. The chapel was completed in 1913. Charles Clifton ordered carved in the marble floor near the altar this memorial to his little daughter: "To the Glory of God and in loving memory of Katherine Gould Clifton, 1892–1902."

On a more commercial note, the February issue of *Motor Field* noted that Pierce-Arrow trucks "are everywhere admitted to possess the certain required qualities that make for a successful heavy truck." They especially praised its ease of maintenance and repair. "The worm drive in its operation is smooth and silent," they reported, "and it is not necessary to have a noisy vehicle." The magazine also spent several paragraphs describing the hydraulic hoist developed by the company "resulting from a growing demand by those whose business requires an end dump body giving a sufficient angle tilt that will cleanly and quickly discharge coal, sand, gravel, asphalt, and like commodities."

Among the issues that entangled the NAAM that spring were aspects of automobile shows, specifically the shows that the organization itself, assisted by the Board of Trade, sponsored in New York and Chicago. The regular monthly meeting of the NAAM executive committee, of which Charles Clifton was a member, held in Chicago on February 5 had spent a good deal of time attempting to decide if their sponsorship of these shows was still necessary. Their original purpose had been to publicize these revolutionary new vehicles and demonstrate their usefulness to unlearned amateurs. There was a groundswell of opinion that local dealers might be better fitted for the job now that the automobile was an accepted part of daily life. In addition, there was disagreement about the proper time to stage them because almost all manufacturers introduced their offerings for the next calendar year the summer before, and the shows were months later. When the executive committee next met on March 5, the truck show was the subject of discussion. The board recommended it no longer be sponsored by the organization because of "low interest." At least that was the report in the March 8 *Automobile Topics*.

Low interest also had derailed the plan to construct an "Automobile Palace" at the projected Panama Pacific Exposition scheduled for the summer of 1915 in San Francisco to celebrate the completion of the Panama Canal. So little interest had been shown "that it appears that no special building for automobile exhibits will be erected," observed the *Automobile Topics* reporter. "The original proposition of the Exposition management to give 60,000 square feet of space in one of the regular exposition buildings will probably be accepted," he wrote, "as it is not likely that more than this amount of space will be required."

A report from the NAAM special fuel committee was presented by Alfred Reeves. The committee had been set up to investigate the rise in fuel costs and the "possibility of adopting a lower grade of fuels." The investigation was still in the early stages, but "a number of conferences" had been held with representatives of the fuel suppliers, and the SAE was going to be "requested to appoint three members to cooperate with the engineers of the oil producers in an investigation of fuels and carburetor requirements."

The consolidation of the NAAM with the Automobile Board of Trade into the Automobile Chamber of Commerce was now on the verge of completion. The Chamber's first meeting was scheduled for March 19 and until that time the incorporators would act as the officers until their formal election.

Support for the planned Ocean to Ocean Highway was also discussed, as was the content of Massachusetts and New York state automobile registration laws.

Automobile Topics reported a little levity, too, or at least that was the tone of the coverage. Members of the NAAM attending the meeting were "amused and gratified to learn through [general manager] Sam Miles that they are all members of the famous 'Money Trust.'" The residents at Christmas Cove, Maine, site of Miles' summer home, were engaged in a "hot political fight" that pitted Miles and some of his neighbors against "the old residents in matters of taxation, school house locations and road improvements." Evidently, the local newspaper had launched an attack on Miles, asserting that he and the friends he entertained there during the summer, including many automobile executives, were all members of this "Money Trust." Board members found themselves lumped in with the usual economic villains such as those controlling railroads, packing companies, coal mines, and steel mills. That such comparisons were even possible demonstrated how large and important the automobile industry had become during the previous decade.

Automobile Trade Journal in its April issue finally announced, "The long pending merger of the Automobile Board of Trade and the National Association of Automobile Manufacturers into the Automobile Chamber of Commerce has been assured." On March 17, a 25-year certificate organizing the new body had been filed "under the corporation law of New York state, and approved by the state Supreme Court." Charles Clifton was elected NACC president, Wilfred C. Leland vice-president, Roy D. Chapin secretary, and George Pope treasurer. They and 11 additional board members would serve until June 4, 1914, when the annual meeting would be held (i.e., the first Thursday after the first Wednesday in June).

The objects for which the Chamber was organized were listed:

"To foster the interest of those engaged in the trade or business of manufacturing automobiles and all of the self-propelling vehicles;

"To reform abuses relative thereto;

"To secure freedom of its members from unjust or unlawful exactions;

"To diffuse accurate and reliable information as to the standing of merchants and others dealing with members, as to all inventions, patents, processes or devices designed or intended for use in, upon or in connection with such vehicles, and manufacture thereof, as to the state of the art relative thereto, and as to the condition and development of the trade in which the members are engaged in the United States and foreign countries;

"To procure uniformity and certainty in the customs and usages of such trade;

"To promote the construction of better highways;

"To advocate the enactment of just and equitable laws affecting members;

"To settle differences between members;

"To promote a more enlarged and friendly intercourse among businessmen engaged in such trade or dealing with persons engaged therein;

"To acquire by grant, gift, purchase, devise or bequest to hold and dispose of such property as the purposes of the corporation shall require, subject to such limitations as may be prescribed by law, including inventions, letters patent and processes, or right thereunto, for the benefit of its members and not for pecuniary profit."

In the May 17 issue, *Automobile Topics* reported "Sign painters this week erased the names of the National Association of Automobile Manufacturers and the Automobile Board of Trade from the doors of their adjoining headquarters on the tenth floor of the Transit Building, 7 East 42nd Street, New York City, and, instead, painted the name Automobile Chamber of Commerce." Samuel A. Miles was quoted as saying, "So far as active work is concerned, the National Association of Automobile Manufacturers, organized thirteen years ago, and the Automobile Board of Trade, organized two years ago, ceased to exist on Wednesday and Thursday of last week when, by a number of meetings of the directors, executive committees and members it was arranged to transfer all of the affairs of both associations to the Automobile Chamber of Commerce." This at last brought an end to the effects of the Selden patent suit in the automobile industry.

An upstate New York newspaper apparently about this time carried a story about the

1914 Model 38-C-2 five passenger touring car, exhibiting Herbert R. Dawley's freshly adopted fender headlamps (courtesy Buffalo and Erie County Historical Society).

1913 Pierce-Arrow line together with an interview with the Pierce-Arrow dealer in Syracuse and Utica, A.A. Ledermann. Mr. Ledermann, known to his friends as "Tony," began his automobile career in Brooklyn, New York, helping to assemble imported DeDion automobiles in 1899. By 1901 he had moved to Utica, where he became a road tester for the Remington Auto Company. Shortly after, he was hired by the Miller-Mundy Company there, who ran a large garage. This work with Pierce cars gave him an entry to the Geo. N. Pierce Co. itself, where he became chief of the experimental department. Within six months he had worked in every mechanical department of the plant. A skillful driver, Ledermann was sent to the New York dealer to demonstrate cars there. By 1905 he was made "trouble man" for Pierce and "traveled every state from coast to coast" as a specialist mechanic for Pierce cars. When in Buffalo he was also head of instruction at the plant's school, an important part of the Pierce program in the early days. He drove the first six-cylinder car in test runs and the Glidden Tour of 1906, perhaps as a relief driver. According to Ledermann, this car was known on the tour as the "Express Car." He opened a dealership in Utica in 1901 and two years later opened the Syracuse outlet. He concluded from this wide experience with motor cars from pioneer days that the improvement in power to weight ratios over the years was what had made the cars practical. "This solution of the weight problem," he was quoted as saying, "the change in body designs, the advent of the six-cylinder, the self-starter and electric lighting systems are, to me, the greatest improvements in motor car building." Ledermann's admiration of the Pierce-Arrow and its producers extended even to naming one of his sons after Charles Clifton.

In May 1913, production of the revised Series Two Pierce-Arrow cars began. The new models were decidedly different looking because of the headlamps mounted on the front fenders, and parking lamps sunk into the face of the firewall. In addition, the windshield was supported with additional internal bracing eliminating the need for leather straps attached to the front frame. There also was an electric license plate lamp and a "combination oil and electric signal lamp" at the rear. The electrical system was more complex, driving the Westinghouse starter. Many new courtesy lamps had been added and an electric horn augmented the bulb horn. Brightwork was now nickel-plated unless otherwise ordered. Much publicity centered on the unconventional new headlamp placement. No one knew if the engineers' distaste for their appearance would prove widespread. Fortunately, while just under 2,000 of the previous model had been assembled in 1912–1913, the output for the Series 2 with the fender lamps would increase to nearly 2,500 along with about 1,500 trucks.

Automobile Topics for April carried a story about problems in the motor truck industry. Col. Clifton was quoted extensively about the challenges and noted failings in "engineering, salesmanship, executive departments and finance." He felt that too many trucks were designed without an understanding of American road conditions, that too high buyer expectations were encouraged by sales staffs, and some high sales expectations were disappointed due to "overbuilding of commercial cars that were not acceptable to the purchasers." He was, nonetheless, still optimistic about the long-term market potential for trucks. "I believe," he concluded, "there is a great future in the American field for the commercial vehicle motor driven, but I believe it will only come in its fulfillment when the product fulfills the reasonable expectation of the purchaser. It is an instrument of efficiency and should be as carefully considered as a locomotive or a dynamo; in its handling it should receive the same scientific use

A mere (!) runabout mounted on the gargantuan 66 HP Series 2 chassis of 140 inches, driven by an 824.7 cu. in. six (courtesy Pierce-Arrow Society).

and care. It should be marketed honestly and truthfully. Those who are entitled to credit should have credit, and if the product is right I do not believe that any banker would hesitate to lend upon the security." Although the Colonel was optimistic, even he did not foresee the impact the truck market would soon have on the industry and, especially, Pierce-Arrow.

Pierce-Arrow was strongly marketing their trucks. A story in the June 15 issue of the *Buffalo Sunday Times* reported a program to publicize trucks and their uses. "On Friday evening of this week," they wrote, "the Pierce-Arrow Motor Car Co. will exhibit at its show rooms, No. 754 Main Street, moving pictures of Pierce-Arrow trucks as used in this city in the various lines of business. The loading and unloading devices in conjunction with the trucks," they added, "will be very interesting to all." Herbert Dawley in a letter to Francis Davis written in 1969 recalled his experience with moving pictures and Pierce-Arrow trucks. In the early days of the truck, it seems that Thomas Edison was called in to help take moving pictures of trucks. "Perhaps you remember," Dawley wrote, "that we took motion pictures of many types of trucks in operation. Edison had perfected a method whereby three thousand feet of pictures could be included in one reel of five hundred feet. He had perfected a projector for showing them which was portable and relatively inexpensive. By this method, the agents could show a prospect the type of truck he was interested in, thus obviating the necessity of carrying a large inventory." It may be that the news story describes a tryout of that system.

The first annual meeting of the new Automobile Chamber of Commerce (NACC) had been held at its headquarters in New York on June 4, according to an article in the June 10 issue of *The Horseless Age*. It was "the largest gathering of automobile officials that has ever been held since motor car building became and industry." There were representatives from 74 companies at the meeting and the annual luncheon, held at the Biltmore Hotel, part of the new Grand Central Terminal complex, which was displacing the old Astor in the industry's affections. The election of officers merely approved those elected before with the addition of second vice-president, Windsor T. White, from the commercial division and another second vice-president, H.H. Rice, from Waverly Electric representing the electric division. Reports were heard from the committees on freight traffic, legislation, good roads, electric vehicles, commercial vehicles, patents and shows. The last committee had charge of the 1914 shows in New York and Chicago, which would be for pleasure cars only and would last a single week instead of two, as before.

The report noted that "More than ordinary interest in the patent situation recently developed in the automobile industry, together with the various other co-operative matters handled by the chamber, accounted for the record attendance." The Chamber had taken over the patents held by the ALAM Board of Trade, and the trade took seriously its promise to protect members from "unjust or unlawful exactions."

At the director's meeting afterward, the board decided to hold its regular July meeting again at general manager Sam Miles' summer home in Christmas Cove, Maine, as the predecessor organizations had done for the past two summers. It is not recorded how Miles' neighbors felt about this decision.

September marked another expansion of Pierce-Arrow's commercial lineup with the introduction of the Model X truck. This smaller model had a capacity less than half that of the R model, 2 tons as compared to 5 tons. It retained the worm-drive rear axle design in a chassis length of 150 inches or 180 inches, at least a foot and a half shorter than the heavier model. Likewise, the 4-cylinder T-head engine was smaller: 4-inch bore by 5½-inch stroke.

Wheels were universally 36 × 4-inch solid-tired, but the Model X had dual rear wheels, another trait it shared with its older stablemate. It had a somewhat higher road speed and retailed for a chassis price of $3,000 f.o.b., $1,500 less than Model R. A run of 500 such trucks was scheduled, which took more than a year to complete.

At the November meeting the Chamber's board supported various state commissioners working on ways to encourage "uniform automobile laws," according to a story in the November 8 *Automobile Topics*. The NACC offered their cooperation and their board room in New York as a meeting place for the several commissioners. Col. Clifton was absent from this meeting, "being on a trip to the Pacific Coast."

At this point the automobile industry and the wider economy were adjusting to a downturn in business. The industry had not had to deal with such issues for a decade, during which it relentlessly expanded. *Automobile Topics* interviewed Clifton for its December 18 issue, pointing out that "His views have the double value of being those of an official of one of the foremost automobile manufacturing companies and those, also, of the president of the national organization of motor car makers, his dual position giving him unusual opportunities of observation and information."

Clifton's view was that the conditions, found not just in the United States "but throughout the world," were a reaction to "a number of years of rapid expansion and development." This was especially true of the automobile industry which had in 10 years "wholly transformed one phase of urban transportation." He urged calm and thoughtful responses, warning against "exaggerating the present activity and future production of the big automobile manufacturing centers." Above all, confidence was needed, "and lies and exaggerations, either pessimistic or optimistic, serve to destroy that confidence. The industry is strong and prosperous enough," he stressed, "to require no boasting! There can be no wild and unconsidered development based on mere hope and optimism. Its progress now must be based on sound business judgment, which means expansion and increase only where a sure market has been found."

Pierce-Arrow was in a strong position, as Clifton well knew as treasurer. Although its profits had declined a bit, they still topped a million dollars a year. There seemed every reason for confidence. The company had assembled just under 2,000 vehicles the year before, mostly pleasure cars. Trucks were, as yet, only a successful sideline.

~ 6 ~

Excellence in Every Desirable Particular (1914)

> One of the great foundation stones of the automobile industry has been the unparalleled leadership which it has enjoyed in Colonel Clifton. His clear vision, his ability to see essentials, his optimism, his understanding of economics have always made him a sane guide for others to follow. All his associates deeply regret his retirement and recognize that he has set an example and established principles which will be an abiding and permanent guide for this business.
>
> —Alfred P. Sloan, Jr., on Clifton's retirement from the NACC presidency

When 1914 began, nothing foreshadowed the catastrophic events that would ultimately transform the whole world. Charles Clifton himself would find widespread industry controversies to cope with as well, but the calendar year opened quite routinely with New York and Chicago automobile shows. This year, Pierce-Arrow displayed no spectacular show cars. Perhaps the new headlamp placement was considered attraction enough, and the new, smaller Model X-2 truck expanded commercial vehicle interest. Both shows seemed to generate little controversy, and their NACC sponsorship was successful.

The directors of the Chamber were in Chicago on Wednesday, February 4, for a regular meeting, chaired by Col. Clifton. Those present included W.C. Leland, R.D. Chapin, W.E. Metzger, Hugh Chalmers, L.H. Kittredge, Alvan Macauley, H.O. Smith, W.T. White, H.H. Rice, J.N. Willys and general manager Sam A. Miles. Along with other routine business, they approved January dates for the next year's "National shows" in New York, according to *Automobile Topics'* coverage of the meeting in the February 7 issue. Their next meeting at the end of the Chicago show enabled the directors to note a very satisfactory show attendance, encouraging them to quickly approve all 1915 show dates without the controversy that had surfaced the year before.

The directors' meeting was covered in the *Automobile Topics* March 7 issue and revealed that Miles had given up his NACC general manager position to Alfred Reeves. "Nevertheless," the magazine observed, "Miles will continue to have a big hand in the management of the New York and Chicago automobile shows." He was still an important figure, having been active in the NAAM from its beginning. His retiring had, apparently, been brewing since the Chicago directors' meeting. Alfred Reeves had recently left his position as vice-president of the Hartford Suspension Co., disposing of the accompanying stock he owned in anticipation of the change. "No other selection," *Automobile Topics* wrote, "could possibly be so enthusiastically and pleasurably received in the trade as that of Reeves for the post. He is peculiarly qualified for the duties, by temperament, ability, and experience."

In his report as chair of the NACC's show committee, Sam Miles noted that "the exhibitions at New York and Chicago this year were the most successful in the history of the industry, there being substantial increase in the box office receipts at both places, while the makers reported business far in excess of what shows have supplied in the past." It was Miles' plan to henceforth devote his "entire time" to the management of the two shows, along with some additional "personal interests."

Considerable time in the meeting was also devoted to a discussion of various state proposals related to the licensing and use of automobiles as their popularity grew. The board adopted a declaration of policy to "discourage by all proper means" actions by states or other legal jurisdictions attempting to impose several kinds of measures, namely: local license fees and operating rules beyond state requirements; burdens on cars not imposed on horse-drawn vehicles; double taxation of automobiles by using personal property tax beside the license fees; special local laws to restrict or regulate the industry or trade; and local laws requiring "the use of specific or proprietary devices or attachments" in addition to standard equipment supplied by their manufacturers.

A report was also given by Roy D. Chapin, who chaired the committee on good roads. Highlight of his presentation was an account of progress made on construction of the Lincoln Highway from New York to San Francisco. He noted that many cities through which the highway was scheduled to pass had already changed the names of streets over which the highway was to run to "Lincoln Highway."

It turned out that this meeting would mark the temporary end of such sanguine gatherings. Conflict suddenly arose when *The Horseless Age* printed in its March 11 issue a statement under the signature of Alvan Macauley, the president of something called the Kardo Co. Macauley was well known to the NACC. In fact, he was a member of both its patent committee and its board. Packard had hired him away from Burroughs Adding Machine Co. in 1910 to be their general manager. He would go on to great respectability and success during the next thirty years.

The surprising Kardo Co. statement revealed it was the owner of nine patents covering various components used in automobile rear axles. The individual patents had formerly belonged variously to Packard Motor Car Co., Peerless Motor Car Co., and the American Ball Bearing Co., all of which had Ohio connections. After encountering some conflict among themselves over these patents, the three firms had pooled them that February in the Kardo Co., chartered in Ohio and capitalized at a million dollars. Each of the three patent contributors appointed both an executive and a board member for Kardo. The patents covered such things as anti-friction bearings, pinion gear mounting and adjustment, bevel gear drive, removable covers allowing access to components for inspection and repair, dust-tight gear casings, locking mechanisms for selected gear shifts, compensating mechanisms to adjust for the rise and fall of rear axles in operation, and removable axle shafts.

"The patents are now owned by the Kardo Co.," Macauley announced. "Some licenses under them have been granted and the company is negotiating others at the present time. Of course, the usual royalty will be made, and manufacturers will receive licenses that will insure them the right to make and sell to their customers axles that are free from charges of infringement. It is sincerely hoped and confidently expected that no litigation whatever will be necessary to the accomplishment of this constructive work." Events would soon prove such confidence was misplaced.

In fact, opposition to these plans arose almost instantly. *The Automobile* a week later carried an editorial below the masthead titled "Removing the Lid," in which it asserted that the Kardo plans would undermine NACC attempts to "prevent widespread litigation among companies." Such a plan would, as a result, disturb "public sentiment in general." The magazine foresaw this "embroiling the whole industry in a maelstrom of patent litigation" as heretofore hidden patents would be brought out by automobile companies and used to collect royalties from other makers.

The issue raised by this conflict centered on the way patents should be used in the young automobile industry. The technology used in auto making was sophisticated and constantly changing. New ideas were continually tried out, thereby improving the product. Companies patented ideas that looked promising largely as a protection against a similar idea someone else might develop independently. What is today called "industrial espionage" was quite rare in the industry, probably because the effort just to keep producing cheaper and more reliable cars was about all anyone had time for. The idea of producing an income stream from patents was not at all what the business was about. A great exception to that, of course, had been the Selden patent conflict, settled only three years before after a long battle that everyone well remembered. To many of the principals in that previous struggle the attitude of the Kardo Co. was uncomfortably similar to that of the old Electric Vehicle Co. Those earlier claims had been commandeered by the industry itself in 1903 for the benefit of the early producers

THE MEN BEHIND THE KARDO COMPANY

The Kardo company executives in 1914 (*left to right*): Walter C. Baker, F.S. Terry, Alvan Macauley, Edward Rector, Edward R. Alexander, Milton Tibbetts, Fred C. Dorn, and Theodore W. Fretch (author's collection).

at the cost of a long conflict between factions inside the gasoline car industry. There now arose a groundswell of resentment against Kardo's plans inside the NACC.

Charles Clifton, as NACC president, now faced the third patent conflict of his business life. The first had involved his brother-in-law and ended with Clifton's dismissal from the starch company. The second was the Selden patent struggle itself, which had taken years to work through, although it ended with almost a feeling of triumph inside the industry. During those years Clifton made it clear that he felt the best outcome would be the unification of auto associations into a single organization, and that the punishment of "outsiders" by the Licensed Association should be avoided. When the succeeding NACC was developed, patents it held were open for sharing by all members, and conflict over patents was discouraged. As Alfred Reeves, Clifton's right-hand man in the NACC, described the situation to a congressional hearing in 1938, "[T]he manufacturers were having great difficulty getting out production; they didn't want to be bothered with patents; they didn't want to sue one another."

That was not, however, a universal opinion in the industry. In a letter to the editor of *The Automobile* dated March 30, 1914, Milton Tibbets of Packard Motor Car Co., in rebuttal to that magazine's "Removing the Lid" editorial, wrote, [T]here is probably not another industry in which there has been so much wholesale appropriation of patented features." Tibbets was a member of the Packard legal department. He also represented Packard on the Kardo board, so he was not speaking as a disinterested bystander. In his letter, titled "The Kardo Situation, an Analogy," he compared this "appropriation" to the occupying of land without paying the owner rent. In such a situation the owner has recourse to the court to compel payment for the use. Likewise, Kardo merely expected rent, in this case royalties, for the use of the patents' features by other automakers. "If an unreasonable attitude is assumed by them [automakers]," he wrote, "they can hold themselves and not the Kardo Company responsible for 'embroiling the entire industry in a maelstrom of patent litigation.'"

The battle was now joined and the obvious next step was litigation. Kardo had only to sue an automobile company for infringement to start the process. During upcoming meetings of the NACC, members of its board had this possibility, if unspoken, always in their thoughts.

Yet another issue arose for the April 2 meeting of the board in New York City, but the industry united in its response. The railroads that supplied most transport into and out of automobile factories proposed to raise charges for switching and placing the railroad cars for loading and unloading. They also wanted to stop the shipment of both trucks and pleasure cars in the same freight cars. The reason for these changes was said to be the necessity for using 40 ft. boxcars for the service, although the automobile companies pointed out such cars were used "for many commodities." They felt the new rules would be used to discriminate against automobile companies and decided to send members of the Chamber to argue against the proposals at the Interstate Commerce Committee hearing on April 16.

Another bit of NACC business indirectly involved the Kardo patent controversy: Windsor T. White and Wilfred C. Leland were appointed to the NACC patent committee, replacing newly resigned members Alvan Macauley of Packard and L.H. Kittredge of Peerless Motor Car Co. The two resignations seemed to show disagreement with the policy of the committee related to patents and endorsement of Kardo, with which they were both associated. Another topic the board discussed were ways they could assist the Touring Board of the American Automobile Association (AAA) to promote an early summer "National Touring Week."

The next NACC board meeting took place on May 6 in New York. The evening before, Charles Clifton gave a dinner for the NACC officers and directors at the Biltmore "as a personal recognition of the co-operation of his associates in the organization and launching of the National Automobile Chamber of Commerce," according to *The Automobile*. Clifton noted that the inspiration for the meeting had come from a passage in a Berton Braley poem warning against a spirit of competition that allowed "forgetting the real man and the true friend." His guests were described by *Automobile Topics* as celebrating Clifton's "leadership in organization work, his well-known spirit of co-operation and his admiration of men who accomplish things." The evening was apparently a great success, doubtless the Colonel's intent. In June, the NACC annual meeting would elect officers. Wining and dining important constituents was a natural step for anyone trained in politics, which Clifton had been, born as he was into a political family.

"Aside from the optimistic spirit which prevailed as a result of trade reports received throughout the country," *The Automobile* reported of the Colonel's dinner in its May 7 issue, "there were some delightful reminiscences of the early days of motor car manufacture, practically every one of those in attendance having been in at the birth of the motor car in America. The graphic descriptions of tours and races won and the obstacles overcome and the tales of the beginnings of many of the big motor car companies, made the affair so interesting that it is certain to become an annual fixture."

"The officers and directors of the Association who were Colonel Clifton's guests," the article continued, "included Colonel George Pope, Wilfred C. Leland, S.T. Davis, Jr., H.H. Rice, Windsor T. White, R.D. Chapin, C.C. Hanch, Alvan Macauley, Wm. E. Metzger, Albert L. Pope, L.H. Kittredge, S.D. Waldon and Alfred Reeves."

At the board meeting the next day the patents committee submitted "an important report," but what it contained was not publicly disclosed. That it touched on the issues raised by Kardo is likely. It can also be safely assumed that the Kardo plans remained on almost everybody's mind as the summer's weeks passed.

The annual meeting of the National Automobile Chamber of Commerce took place Thursday, June 4, 1914, in its Transit Building headquarters. According to the June 10 *Horseless Age*, it was "the largest gathering of automobile officials that has ever been held since motor car building became an industry." Representatives from 74 automobile manufacturers were present at the business meeting and the annual luncheon held at the Biltmore. The magazine remarked that "More than ordinary interest in the patent situation recently developed in the automobile industry, together with the various other co-operative matters handled by the chamber, accounted for the record attendance." Reports from the committees on traffic, legislation, good roads, electric vehicles, commercial vehicles, and shows were heard, as well as from the patents committee.

The main business of the meeting, however, was the election of directors and officers for the NACC, that were listed as follows: President, Charles Clifton (Pierce-Arrow); Vice-President, Wilfred C. Leland (Cadillac); Second Vice-President, Commercial Division, Windsor T. White (White); Second-Vice President, Electric Vehicle Division, H.H. Rice (Waverly); Secretary, R.D. Chapin (Hudson); Treasurer, George Pope (Pope-Hartford), General Manager, Alfred Reeves. These men were the core of the group who would deal with the Kardo controversy. The directors were, besides the former, S.T. Davis, Jr. (Locomobile), C.C. Hanch (Marmon), Alvan Macauley (Packard), W.E. Metzger (Argo), H.O. Smith (Premier), Albert

L. Pope (Pope-Hartford), L.H. Kittredge (Peerless), John N. Willys (Overland), and E.R. Bensen (Studebaker).

Press coverage of the event, however, focused on the Kardo controversy. Except for the story in *Horseless Age*, which hardly mentioned the subject, headlines in the other industry publications verged on the alarmist: "Kardo Explodes Patent Bomb," led into the *Automobile Topics* coverage of June 6 that was summarized in this outburst: "The explosion took place when it developed that the owners of the Kardo group of patents want the automobile manufacturers to pay something like two and a half million dollars a year in royalties on rear axles with bevel drive." They described the result as a "flood of protest such as the rooms in Forty-second street had never heard before."

The Automobile focused its outrage on the Kardo attempt to frustrate the NACC patent policy. "When the report of the [patent] committee was presented at the general meeting it was the consensus of opinion that it was not ethics [sic] on the part of these companies to organize a separate patent-holding organization when the National Automobile Chamber of Commerce has a special patent department and had a patent committee on which both the Packard and Peerless companies were represented, but which representatives resigned some time ago." The patent committee, meanwhile, was itself conducting "an exhaustive examination" into the patents held by Kardo. It was not clear if any company had yet taken out a license to use Kardo's patents. Opposition, in fact, seemed to be quite widespread. However, no litigation had been started, either.

Pierce-Arrow began assembling the first of their 1915 models that June, and they had

The elegantly restyled Series 3 body for 1915 crowns the 38 HP touring car, seating five and listing for $4,300 at Buffalo (courtesy Pierce-Arrow Society).

certainly not taken out a Kardo license. However, this can be seen as a more significant introduction than it first appeared to be. These vehicles would amount to templates of Pierce offerings for some years to come. The new cars showed extensive revisions to both chassis and bodies. The firm declared: "The result of several years experimental work, the 'Series Three' Pierce-Arrow models incorporate numerous refinements of chassis and body design which make them the most satisfactory vehicles yet produced." One major chassis refinement was the lowering of the frame 2½ to 3 inches. This allowed lowered roofs on the bodies, but also required that the fuel tank be moved to the rear, where a pressure system now supplied gasoline to the carburetor, which, in turn, was raised up to the engine from its old position below the chassis sides. Several minor changes were also made in the operating controls, now placed in a cluster on the dash for convenience. Locks with universal key secured engine hood sides, dash cabinets, tool compartment and spare tire carrier. A complete double ignition system, one by battery and the second by Bosch magneto, was provided against breakdowns while touring, and Goodrich "Silvertown" tires were adopted on all models. The three lines, 38-C-3, 48-B-3 and 66-A-3, were unchanged in price from the three models of 1914.

Body lines were not merely lower, but noticeably more integrated and sensuously curved as well. The fender headlamps were reshaped from a convex to a concave curve atop the new, larger front fenders. It was clear that this was now considered the standard headlamp placement, although separate lamps on crossbars were still available. Parking lights were delicately molded into the dash. The body silhouette had been noticeably revised from that of the 1912 designs. There were now two lines of closed cars: "Dome Roofed" and "Flat Roofed." The former, considered the standard, had higher ceilings (to clear the towering headgear then fashionable); the latter had more glass area. Broughams (5-passenger closed bodies), Landaulettes (5-passenger, folding rear roof), Suburbans (7-passenger closed bodies) and Landaus (7-passenger, folding rear roof) were available as either domed roofed or flat roofed cars. Vestibule models of these chauffeur-driven limousines closed the front compartment sides with doors and windows. Just about every use for a formal vehicle could be accommodated with this range of bodies. Indeed, examples of them were used at the Executive Mansion in Washington under the lease program by the company. President Wilson, despite his previous opposition to all motor cars, enjoyed the Pierce-Arrows hugely. So had his predecessor, William Howard Taft, who purchased one of his White House Pierce-Arrows as a used car from the company at the end of his term in 1913, after using it campaigning in New England during his unsuccessful re-election bid the year before. Charles Clifton himself handled that sale.

It was common at the time for customers to purchase an additional open touring car body to substitute for the heavy closed bodies during the summer. The White House likewise adopted this approach. In such instances, the out of season body was removed at the agent's service garage for storage while the alternative body was used. This service for many clients is one explanation for the vast storage spaces in metropolitan Pierce-Arrow service garages of the time. Drying the expected refinishing of the varnish paint each year took up additional space. Pierce-Arrow's range of open cars included a Runabout with folding top and disappearing seat at the rear and a Runabout with metal coupe top. These sporty types had a more raked steering column. Touring cars came in four, five, and seven passenger versions. The Art Department offered services to patrons that ranged from selecting individual colors and materials, equipping the car with individual accessories, all the way to the development of a completely individual custom body to order. The factory had grown to more than twice its original size, with site space remaining for yet further expansion. Pierce-Arrow was Buffalo's largest employer. The International street railway had an expansive arrival and departure area right behind the Fire House to the south of the Pierce plant for its commuting employees.

One turn in the luxury car market that summer pleased the firm greatly. Its great Cleveland rival, the Peerless Motor Car Co. had decided to withdraw the 60 HP model, its entry in the ultra-high-priced market. With this Peerless had competed against the 66 HP since 1912. Pierce-Arrow was now able to boast to its dealers, "There is no car on either the European or American markets that can be compared with the Pierce-Arrow 66. In other words, we have no competition to contend with in connection with this truly wonderful model." The gigantic 66 was sold by the company to as many as 300 customers a year at a $6,000 price for the seven-passenger touring car and some $1,250 more for closed models. It was the rarified ultimate in the market.

The Pierce-Arrow car enjoyed a worldwide reputation for excellence, and the Pierce-Arrow Motor Car Company was an institution devoted to production at as high a standard of quality as could be set for its entire line. This determination radiated from the wood-paneled halls and stained-glass-embellished front office itself. Charles Clifton was heard to say on numerous occasions that his goal was to match the high character of the product with that of those who produced it. "I want to say to you gentlemen," he remarked at a company meeting in 1917, "that I am proud of this organization because I believe that the human character here is the counterpart of our product." It was often repeated in company literature that its policy was simply to produce the finest cars possible, setting the selling price at a level to pay for such construction plus a reasonable profit. Demand remained strong.

The Pierce-Arrow factory was supervised by general manager Henry May in a thorough and uncompromising manner that assured the product would be as perfect as design and construction could achieve. Secretary Laurence H. Gardner described him as "the brains of the Pierce-Arrow factory." May's hard work at the old George N. Pierce Co. from its inception in 1878 developed his skills over many years in many capacities, for which he was awarded a partnership by its founder. He was especially respected for his fair handling of disputes among employees. H. Kerr Thomas, a highly-trained and exacting English engineer, was May's assistant superintendent. John Guider supervised manufacturing departments, Robert Gerlatch assembly departments and George Cooke the body departments. It was the management's decision at the time, that each step to machine the individual parts would be inspected so no effort was wasted on imperfect work. Under Walter Newsome, inspection was systematic. He presided over 135 inspectors through a general foreman and six sub-foremen. In the early years on Elmwood Avenue each piece was taken into the inspection department after every operation. Later, inspection was carried out at the individual machines. In either case, imperfect parts were discarded. The many parts purchased from outside suppliers were also carefully inspected upon receipt to assure quality. Eventually, a separate building on Elmwood Avenue was erected to house the scientific laboratory that tested materials used in the product. Problems with particular parts were referred to James F. Bach, foreman of the manufacturing research department that carefully investigated difficulties and contrived their solutions. The vital metallurgical department at Pierce-Arrow was headed by M.H. Medwedeff, according to the Pierce-Arrow house organ *The Arrow* of April 15, 1919. Medwedeff also supervised the heat-treating processes carried out by "Mr. Pendegrast, assisted by Mr. Maeder and Mr. Hunt" on the north edge of the plant grounds. These operations were crucial to the durability of the mechanical components.

Herbert M. Dawley's 1968 reminiscences disclose the strong characters of those who oversaw the production of Pierce-Arrow cars. As an example, Dawley recalled Hans Buerk, head of the tool and experimental parts department: slight of stature, wearing "thick-lensed glasses," who conversed "squarely in front of you at a distance of only a few inches." His whole department was filled with craftsmen. "It was inspiring," Dawley wrote, "to watch these master artisans working at precision lathes, universal milling machines and other complicated machines as they made gauges, jigs, templates and other devices used in the factory for maintaining highly accurate production."

Constructing engines was especially exacting. Each completed motor was tested in a building at the back of the plant. "Here," Dawley wrote, "the heart and pulse of the Pierce-Arrow was being analysed [*sic*] and recorded by men who went about their work with the quiet, cool deliberation of surgeons. Should they detect a flaw, the motor was disassembled and the trouble corrected. Then back to the block it went for more testing." To make the tests and run-in the mating surfaces, the motors turned large fans, each specifically designed to

Inside the machine shop (later Building "A") of the Pierce-Arrow plant in 1915 (courtesy Pierce-Arrow Society).

provide the appropriate load for the particular motor being tested. "The sound filling the laboratory," Dawley wrote, "was overpowering and rivaled the grandeur of a Wagnerian opera."

The procedure was of paramount importance. This was made abundantly clear by Frank Merrell writing for the Pierce-Arrow Society in 1983 [*The Arrow*, Fourth Quarter, 1984]. Merrell described the way that the individual parts of the motor of his Series 4 were each marked so that they could be accurately reassembled in the field to the exact factory specifications by mechanics trained to do so in the factory classes. "To remain in this same perfect condition," Merrell wrote, "required, therefore, that in factory reassembly, after running-in, or in any subsequent field reassembly, every part, nut and bolt must be replaced in exact original order and be torqued to the exact original figure as when originally run in." Pierce-Arrow earned its reputation for reliability and service the hard way.

The original concept of the Pierce automobile was laid down by David Fergusson, the chief engineer, who also guided its evolution. He was rightly regarded as a pioneer in automobile development, having designed and built gasoline-powered vehicles in England from 1898, moving to the United States two years later. He had been an ardent bicyclist and was

The motor testing room on the far east side of the plant in the early years. Note the cages that surround the fans which absorbed the power of engines under test (courtesy Pierce-Arrow Society).

a determined test driver in the early years. Pierce hired him to head their automobile department in 1901, and he continued at that post, usually in renewed yearly contracts awarding him steadily increased salary and bonuses. He was active in industry engineering associations, including the SAE for many years, and was well acquainted with the trends in the art both in America and abroad, especially England where his brother worked for Leyland. Fergusson put a high value on reliability and strength, sticking with proven approaches, carefully providing proper lubrication and protection of moving parts from road dirt. Matching his dedication was that of Charles Sheppy, the Pierce experimental engineer. The struggle between these "two rare personalities" was described by Herbert Dawley as "a donny-brook."

"Ferggie was a Yorkshireman," noted Dawley, "whose manner of speaking gave the impression he was a Scot. He had other characteristics which confirmed that suspicion! His appearance belied his reputation as the brilliant Pierce-Arrow engineer. When he shaved was a mystery, because he always needed one. Same for his hair. His clothes were ill-fitting…. However, all these idiosyncrasies disappeared when you came to know David Fergusson the engineer. He had unusual powers of concentration and was an attentive listener. Because of these virtues and his brilliant mathematical mind, he created motors that knew no rival."

His erstwhile adversary was the experimental engineer, known around the plant as "Father" Sheppy, who presided over the company testing program as improvements were developed. Sheppy had worked at Pierce on its early automobile experiments in 1900 before Fergusson had even arrived. Their later encounters, in Dawley's words, were "like watching Dempsey and Firpo tangle." Briefly, Fergusson's carefully developed experimental car would be placed in the hands of Sheppy and an assistant, who disappeared "with the fiendish intent of driving it through or over every obstacle, seeking the worst roads and extremes of altitudes and temperatures to be found in this cotton-pickin' land, until it hollered 'Uncle' or fell apart." Weeks afterward they might return by train, having shipped the car. If that occurred it was Sheppy's round. On the other hand, they were known to return in the car, with the motor purring but the body looking like the "Wreck of the Hesperus" and the passengers "resembling men in the business of haunting houses. This would be Ferggie's round." Sheppy was especially proud of his driving prowess and was fascinated by the intricate challenges of carburetors. Over time he perfected the Pierce-Arrow reed-valve carburetor, for which he applied for a patent on August 6, 1912. It was granted patent 1,213,914 on January 30, 1917.

The Pierce-Arrow car was a commanding presence on the road, due to both its size and its demeanor. Passengers were surrounded by the unconventional, cast-aluminum body in various styles, designed and manufactured in the body factory along the south side of the Pierce-Arrow plant beside what became Great Arrow Avenue. This was considered a matchless selling point by the company. Even S.F. Edge had remarked during his visit to Pierce-Arrow in 1909 that the strength shown by their cast aluminum bodies of the time "seemed so enormous to that which one reasonably might require in a motor car body." The company took pride in the fact that their cast aluminum bodies had survived with only minor damage from even violent encounters with moving trains.

There was also the style factor. Herbert Dawley, head of the art department, spoke on the subject to a Pierce-Arrow dealers' meeting at the factory on September 15, 1914. He explained that the Pierce-Arrow objective was to produce a vehicle unlike anything that had ever come before. The current Pierce-Arrow was, Dawley contended, "a distinct type of vehicle. It has the sturdiness of a Roman Chariot, the refinement and privacy of a Sedan Chair;

the comfort and convenience of a horse-drawn brougham, plus a slave under the hood whose magic eliminates the old values of space and time."

The body castings were made for Pierce-Arrow by the Aluminum Castings Co. of Buffalo at their Elmwood plant using a complicated method similar to that used to make art castings. The material was Lynite No. 103, a trademark aluminum and copper alloy furnished by the Aluminum Company of America. After inspection upon delivery to Pierce-Arrow, the individual panels were cleaned and assembled into complete bodies in the body assembly area of the North Body Building. The panels were fastened together using cold hammered steel rivets. Ash wood members were added to furnish floors and tacking strips for upholstery. They also added some structural strength. Then the completed bodies were sent to the paint shop for finishing under the watchful eye of "Mr. Mac" McLaughlin. Final finish and trim took 22 days to complete. This followed the 30 days it took to accomplish body assembly. Total assembly time to complete a Pierce-Arrow car, then, totaled nearly two months from receipt of the order to the showroom.

Upholstery and trim were applied in the South Body Building under the supervision of Frank Holland. Tobacco chewing seems to have been almost endemic to the employees of the body buildings. Even fastidious James R. Way chewed it. Holland's own brand was Piper Heidsic plug, soaked, so he claimed, in rum and honey. Dawley seemed to retain an especially sharp recollection of the trim department. "Even the workers seemed to be of another genus from the standard homo sapiens. A cheerful atmosphere pervaded the place." The artisans

Assembling the cast aluminum panels into finished bodies upstairs in the body building. Completion took a month (courtesy Pierce-Arrow Society).

impressed him with delicate care at their work and also their coarse language. Most impressive of all seemed to be their unerring skill aiming their spitting tobacco into an unseen box of sawdust amid all the luxurious fabrics with which they worked.

The lines of Pierce-Arrow's bodies by now had attained a distinctive style and would show little alteration for the next five years. James R. Way, the body engineer and designer, had developed their technology over the previous decade. Dawley, who, as head of the Art Department, had continual interaction with Way, noted that his office and shop "were Sanctum-Sanctorum, forbidden except to a chosen few." Way himself was taciturn in the extreme. Dawley remembered: "save for a housekeeper and a cat, he lived the life of a recluse." Dawley's attempts to change body lines "presenting a smooth line and surface from front to back" met with resistance from James Way. Nonetheless, the two men seemed to have worked out an effective collaboration. Dawley had even convinced Way to adopt the sculptor's method of modeling proposals in clay over an armature. Compared with the competition, Pierce-Arrows showed a rather advanced line, except for their stubborn refusal to adopt the conventional left-hand driver's seat with center control.

Thus, the driver of a Pierce-Arrow rode tall at the right front of the car, in most cases next to the cache of two large spare tires on the right-hand running board, and behind the hefty steering wheel, a formidable control for the direct and sensitive steering Father Sheppy demanded. A massive shift gate for the four-speed and reverse transmission was positioned comfortably to the right, substantial clutch, accelerator, and foot brake controls before. Around the driver arose a truly monumental enclosure for passengers. These were the Pierce-Arrows that carried the company reputation to unmatched heights of service and prestige.

James R. Way, long-time body engineer and designer at Pierce with a Series 4, 38 HP French Brougham: "...save for a housekeeper and a cat, he lived the life of a recluse" (courtesy University of Michigan Special Collections).

As summer of 1914 progressed, the controversy over the Kardo claims continued to ferment. At the same time events in Europe moved relentlessly to World War. While little was heard from the Kardo Company itself, there is no doubt that they encouraged the thought that manufacturers should sign up with them for licenses to pay royalty and use their patents. In fact, the July issue of *The Automobile Trade Journal* supported that idea in an article titled "Formation of Kardo Company Prevents Litigation." Its contention was that Kardo had eliminated dispute amongst the three organizing companies by exchanging licenses. "Other concerns wishing to avail themselves of licenses under the Kardo patents," they wrote, "now have the opportunity to do so." The company had devised a plate, carrying the statement "Licensed under Kardo patents," suitable for mounting on cars that were properly licensed. One was shown as an illustration to the article. In its August issue, *MoTor* noted that both Packard and Peerless had included the statement in their advertising.

The automobile magazines of late July covered the NACC board meeting earlier that month, which was again held on Sam Miles' summer estate at Christmas Cove, Maine. The event started on Saturday evening, July 18, when Miles' guests arrived by boat from Bath, having traveled from the Boston & Maine railroad station in Portland to Bath by motor car. That evening the festivities began, during which the 24 guests were broken into two teams (the Blues and the Grays) to compete for points playing baseball, pool and billiards, water sports, clay pigeon shooting, fish catching, and high jump. Shop talk was again fined. Breaks were provided by a clambake on Sunday afternoon and a fish fry after the fishing contest on Monday. In the end, the two teams were tied exactly in points, permitting a rematch at the 1915 meeting. Clifton was part of the Blue team, playing "assistant first base" during the baseball game. Photos of the gathering published in the July 30 issue of *The Automobile* depict the tall figure of Clifton in a dark business suit and open wing-collared shirt, his bald head covered with a reflective white cap against the fierce Maine sun. The guests were the customary board members, along with counsel Charles Thaddeus Terry and Winton Motor Car Co.'s Thomas Henderson.

At the actual board meeting, chaired by Clifton, on Tuesday the 21st, the brand-new Dodge Brothers company of Detroit was admitted to NACC membership. Their factory had just started production. Reports were received from the committees on patents, traffic, good roads, legislation, and shows. The board also endorsed the plan to organize a commercial vehicle committee to oversee a commercial vehicle convention, to be scheduled at the September board meeting on the first Wednesday of the month. The August meeting was vacated. In its coverage of the session, *Automobile Topics* reported that "the patent situation has loomed somewhat large of late, and while nothing definite has been disclosed as to the probable disposition of one or two

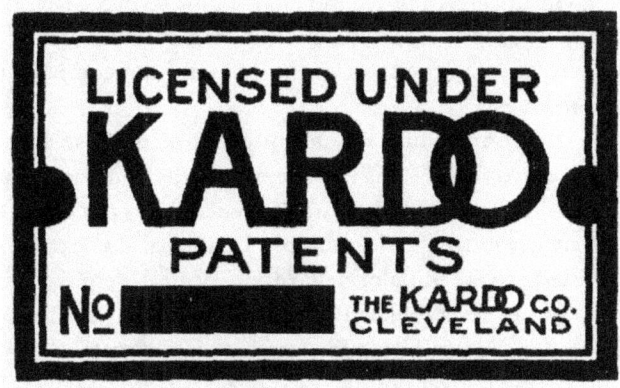

Kardo Patent License Plate.

The patent plate made up for prospective licensees of the Kardo patents to sport (author's collection).

important questions that are likely to come up in the fall, it is known that the Chamber will preserve an attitude of preparedness that is somewhat suggestive of the armament of nations." The budget, they noted, carried a generous item appropriated to support "careful scrutiny" of even foreign patents that might become threatening.

Two days later the Empire of Austria-Hungary delivered its ultimatum to the Serbian government demanding redress for the assassination back in June of Archduke Franz Ferdinand, the empire's heir. By August 1 the great European war had commenced, pitting Germany and its allies against France and associated powers. Shortly, many American plans to enlarge sales of cars in Europe had to be abandoned. American travelers found themselves blockaded on the Continent as masses of troops commandeered the means of escape. Financial markets suspended trading. Within weeks, German forces had invaded Belgium and northern France, destroyed an entire Russian army in East Prussia, and encountered the declaration of war by Great Britain and its commonwealth.

The August 26 issue of *The Horseless Age* reported Col. Clifton's appointment of members to all the committees that carried out the business of the NACC. Along with the committees reporting at the July board meeting were two more: Electric Vehicle and Commercial Vehicle. The appointees would serve for a year. Clifton always made the expectation clear to those accepting positions that an energetic personal involvement would be required. Over the years few officers ignored this mandate.

During the first week of September, the battle of the Marne brought an end to the Imperial German Army's advance on Paris, and to their plan to win a quick war. Widespread confusion about that battle and the events preceding continued for days. It was certainly on the minds of the Pierce-Arrow agents who gathered in Buffalo on Monday, September 14, for a three day "Pleasure Car Salesman's Convention." Sometime during the course of their meeting, Col. Clifton remarked that the enormity of the European conflict meant the world would not be the "same old world" as it had been before. His comment illustrated the shock universally felt, and his prediction was borne out by events.

As well as treasurer of the Pierce-Arrow Motor Car Company, Charles Clifton was also chairman of its Executive Committee, which included George K. Birge and Henry May. George K. Birge himself, it might be observed, owned nearly half the shares in the company. The organization had not appreciably changed since its recapitalization in 1909. "The owners, the board of directors, and the executive officers of the Pierce-Arrow Motor Car Company are one and the same group of men," the company proudly declared in a publicity booklet that year.

Perhaps most significantly, Clifton was also described as "Executive Head of Commercial Departments." This was the part of the company that distributed and sold its vehicles. Since the September salesman's convention was put on by the commercial departments it could be rightly judged Clifton's show. Dealers and salesmen from 40 cities were present. Well represented were Buffalo, New York City, Philadelphia, Chicago, Washington, D.C., and Baltimore, as were several New England cities such as Boston, Providence, New Haven, and Pittsfield. Some Midwestern cities, such as Cincinnati, Dayton, Milwaukee, and Grand Rapids, had representatives present. So did Jacksonville and New Orleans in the Deep South. The extreme reach was Denver, way out West. No representatives from outlets west of the Rockies appeared at all, despite strong dealers in San Francisco and Los Angeles, Seattle, and Portland. Canada, however, had representatives from Montreal and Toronto. Sometime during the convention chairs were brought outside to the entrance at the north end of the Office Building and a panoramic photograph was made of the attendees, ivy-covered office windows behind them. In the center front row sat Henry May, general manager of the Manufacturing Departments in a light suit beside Charles Clifton, who looked at his ease in customary dark suit and tie, his hands partially covering the hat on his lap.

The first two days of the three-day conference were heavy with company presentations. Sessions involved demonstrations along with explanations of features in the car construction, style, and equipment. Most apparent was an emphasis on the importance of the sales program for them. Chairing the meetings was J.H. "Jack" Fassitt, who was a leading figure at the Foss-Hughes Co. of Philadelphia perhaps the most extensive Pierce-Arrow distributor in the country, with outlets at Baltimore; Wilmington, Delaware; Providence and Newport, Rhode Island; and Washington, D.C. Special trolley cars carried those attending the convention each morning, at 9 o'clock "(Sharp)" according to the program, from the Lafayette Hotel up to the factory. The program for Monday, September 14, included talks by W.B. Newlin on "Selling efficiency," H.K. Thomas on "Factory practice," plus a factory tour. A dinner was held at the Lafayette that evening at 6:30, followed by "Theatre."

Charles Clifton presented a talk entitled "An Explanation Not an Apology" at the morning session on Tuesday that opened with his reason for not being present to welcome attendees the morning before. "I have been away with my car for three days," he explained. "Of course," he continued, "when you get out next to God's green earth and in the sunshine, you get a lot of the cobwebs swept away; and I am here this morning without any cobwebs." But Clifton's presentation was really a sales talk extolling the newly redesigned Series Three. He insisted that he had not fully appreciated its virtues until he had a lengthy drive in it. "I am frank to say that the President of this Company did not know what a good thing has been produced." Having taken his superior on a 32-mile drive the previous Sunday afternoon, he quoted George K. Birge saying upon leaving the car, "I have never ridden in a car that gave me the extreme sense of luxury that that car does, in point of power, in quietness and ease of riding." Clifton further noted, "And he has been a good deal of a crank about that." Clifton's touring went on the next day. "Yesterday afternoon we had reached thirty-five miles an hour from Geneva to Buffalo," he continued, "the roads being fair to average, some of them very fine state roads. We had all the conditions of traffic also. My wife was with me, as well as the driver; and we both came back absolutely untired. I do not believe that there is a car made that you can do the same thing with and have so little physical tiredness."

Clifton then pivoted to his actual point: That the Pierce-Arrow was best appreciated only when driven and ridden in. "I think that car is a car that should be out," he emphasized, "that people should be persuaded into buying that car by the car's actual accomplishments; and I feel that the man who sets it up on his floor and puts a railing around it, is only to be compared to the old parable of the talents, which you all learned, of course, in Sunday School." He urged the sales staff to build enthusiasm for the car from use and suggested that "it might be a good idea for us to do a good deal more bugle blowing than we have," feeling that there was a larger market waiting to be cultivated. He mentioned a *Saturday Evening Post* magazine ad campaign of the past spring that had cost $18,000–$20,000. "We are not afraid to spend the money to get results to help you," he concluded, "but primarily, in my judgment, you have got to help your selves." Applause greeted this concluding observation. An admonition from the chair at the end of Tuesday afternoon's talk on body design and construction by Herbert Dawley gives a sense of the social side of the convention. "I want," said Fassitt, "the late-rising poker players and the early-rising golf players to be here tomorrow morning at ten sharp." Likely among the golfers was Charles Clifton himself.

Time was set aside at 2:00 p.m. Wednesday, the final session, for the dealers to discuss among themselves some of their concerns about the actual selling arguments needed for success with the new models. While Mr. Fassitt chaired the meeting, it would be led by direction of Henry Paulman from the Chicago agency along with chief engineer David Fergusson and W.B. Newlin, who was sales manager for passenger cars. The purpose was to increase understanding of the mechanical features of Pierce-Arrows and the competition's arguments. "I contend that a properly fortified salesman," Paulman began at the start of the session, "should know his competitors' weaknesses as well as he knows his own strength." The ensuing discussion was lengthy, Jack Fassitt noting at the close, "We are getting a little short in our time. The special car [doubtless a streetcar to the downtown hotels] is usually outside just at five o'clock."

The transcript from the session, published later in *The Pierce-Arrow Salesman* which Mr. Newlin himself edited, showed that the interest of the salesmen was most sharply focused on sales arguments, especially countering those of competitors against Pierce-Arrow features. The most extensively discussed issues were comparative car weights and prices, clutches, engine mounts, rear axles, and right-hand drive vs. left drive. Some comments from the discussion are of interest, including this one by Mr. Newlin: "I believe it is a fact that we can accentuate very strongly that the present cars of the three series are the lightest 6-cylinder cars of their class manufactured today." This remark was part of an extensive discussion of car weights and prices that compared Pierce-Arrows with Locomobiles and Packards, the two competitors the salesmen seemed most concerned about. Another discussion involved Mr. Fergusson explaining how the forged-steel arms supporting the Pierce-Arrow engine on the frame were both lighter and stronger than the manganese bronze used by Locomobile for crankcase and supporting arms. There were in the meeting room, evidently, both a Pierce-Arrow chassis and a blackboard, which Fergusson used to make his points during this discussion and a related one about "three-point engine suspension." The advantages of right-drive over left (which Newlin called "learning to be left-handed") were argued in a lengthy discussion. The most forceful point seemed to be that the driver could see the right edge of the road better with right-drive, thus avoiding driving into a ditch. This was generally seen as a greater hazard than avoiding oncoming traffic, indicating the relatively uncrowded roads of the time. The newly adopted split front seats made exit on the right side of the car at the curb much more convenient, negating at least that criticism of the right-drive position. The Packard rear axle and transmission were also discussed, Fergusson pointing out the problems with ride quality given its greater unsprung weight: "The weight should come inside the axles if possible," Fergusson insisted. This was also an argument in support of Pierce-Arrow's placement of the spare tires on the right running board, rather than at the rear. The cone clutch of the Pierce-Arrow was derided by both Locomobile and Packard, both using disc clutches. Mr. Newlin was most defensive about the cone clutch, which he maintained was smoother and easier of action. His most interesting argument was that the cone clutch allowed the driver to "use the store-up energy in a racing fly wheel to jump the car out of a hole as in a railroad crossing, otherwise the engine would be stalled." After a particularly long technical discussion about radius rods, Newlin concluded, "The majority of people who ask you your reason for doing this or that could not understand the real reasons at all when they were given." This discussion reflects the life of a Pierce-Arrow agent in 1914.

The sales materials used by the salesmen in their efforts were provided by the advertising manager, E.H. Rounds, who was also assistant treasurer to Charles Clifton. The chief copywriter was quite probably William "Bill" Baldwin, who had a long tenure at Pierce-Arrow extending, in fact, right up to the end. Baldwin had a winning personality and a particular talent for short and evocative lines, which provided the relatively tiny block of copy Pierce used in its advertising. Copy for catalogues was much more extensive, but also had a very literate quality. For the current Series Three models, the company had put out a single catalogue, printed by Bartlett-Orr, with details of all three models in the series, rather than the three separate model volumes of the year before. Illustrations were careful engravings of the cars, with details of their mechanical and coachwork features taken from photographs. More impressionistic illustrations made from etchings signed by the artist A. McKinnon in the form of scenes of Pierce-Arrows touring in Scotland appeared as well. It continued the firm's tradition for artistic promotion.

A distinctly new format was used in advertising this year's cars. James Alfred Clarke, the art director at Calkins & Holden, Pierce-Arrow's New York advertising agency, developed the many lavish advertisements that appeared in such high fashion publications as *Life, Vogue,* and *Country Life,* among others. These consisted of very finely executed line drawings, usually colored in with strong colors, but with plenty of white space as well. A central panel showed a scene involving a Pierce-Arrow car in the service of social prominence: a shopping trip, on the way to the Harvard-Yale game, loading passengers for an evening's dining, etc. These were enhanced with a deft description in the copy extolling the attributes of the Pierce-Arrow that made it so appropriate for such occasions. Flanking the main panel were two narrow depictions of the passengers in other settings during the event. Always, hidden away somewhere, were the initials RC—those of "Rene" Clarke, James Alfred's professional identity.

Some years Pierce-Arrow hired a single artist to produce, through Calkins & Holden, all the advertising art for the current model. The artists they employed have today a high reputation among connoisseurs. As the late Beverly Rae Kimes wrote in *Automobile Quarterly* (Vol. 14; No. 3, 1976), "[T]here was nothing to compare with the formidable series produced by Calkins & Holden for the mighty Pierce-Arrow."

The way Pierce-Arrow treated the artists it employed was as exceptional as the advertising itself. Adolph Treidler, who produced advertising art for Pierce from time to time for more than a decade, explained to Bernard J. Weis of the Pierce-Arrow Society in 1980 how its approach to the work contrasted with that of the usual client. Unlike the normal proceedings, Pierce told Calkins & Holden their plans and provided an artist like Treidler a car to use to model his illustrations. Treidler remembered that Herbert Dawley would bring a car to some picturesque locale, say New England in the fall, and Treidler would use his "fifteen dollar Kodak" and make photographs. Pierce-Arrow agents would also allow Treidler to photograph cars on display. He would then use the appropriate photos to lay out a proposed illustration in tempera and take it to the agency. Pierce-Arrow would buy the art and related copy (if they did not provide it themselves) along with the finished layout. They never edited Treidler's work, or, apparently, even suggested changes. This was a stark contrast with the client deciding what to include in advertising, usually by committee, and the artist getting specific instructions for any illustrations, every step being approved with initials on the layout.

Triedler confessed that his experience with Pierce-Arrow made him impatient with this conventional approach, and he was fortunately able to find more tolerant clients on his own. He worked into his 90s.

When the new models came out, Pierce-Arrow had already made a careful record of all their features using its own photographic department. The commercial manager would send a car out with a company photographer, perhaps Charlie Estabrook, to a place with good light. During this period Pierce was partial to the golf course environs on South Meadow in Delaware Park. Many side views of cars show a particular ash tree, displaying winter bareness or verdant summer foliage, in the background. The large-format view camera made very sharp images and furnished the basis for catalogue engravings. The photographers also recorded operations at the factory and plant personnel. Every detail of the marketing was carefully thought out, and only the best would do.

It is interesting to observe that, while Col. Clifton was very much the "Executive Head," he made no attempt to be the center of activity in the "Commercial Departments" he headed. His approach, as Herbert Dawley's experience shows, was to give responsibility to individuals and allow them to grow into their positions. All the same, he was the most notable single personality at Pierce-Arrow. In his 1913 *Hoo's Hoo and Wat's Wat in Gasoline*, Henry Caldwell was only slightly tongue in cheek when he wrote, "There is neither a Pierce nor an Arrow in the whole establishment. It's all Clifton." His was a case of thoroughly competent leadership, largely by example. Consistent with the company culture, the Colonel's expectations were high. His anticipated response guided almost everyone in the organization. Henry May, too, had absolute respect in the manufacturing sector of the company. But neither man was in control of Pierce-Arrow itself. George K. Birge and his close friends William B. Hoyt and William H. Gardner owned by far the majority of shares in the Pierce-Arrow Motor Car Co. It appears altogether to have been a very tight operation, if occasionally contentious, run on a basis of mutual respect.

The European war insinuated itself unexpectedly at Pierce-Arrow during those fall months in the form of orders for 300 Model X 2-ton trucks. This order was put together for shipment in October and was accompanied to France by E.C. "Ted" Selman, a young Australian immigrant invited to work at the plant by H. Kerr Thomas the previous April. The whole deal was seen as a bit of a windfall for the truck division, with no expectation that it would be repeated. An order for 300 R6 5-ton trucks would follow shortly thereafter.

At the October 7 NACC board meeting, the Kardo attempt to promote the licensing of its rear axle patents by automobile manufacturers was publicly and officially opposed in the name of the Chamber itself. The board passed a resolution to oppose attempts to "exact tribute" from automakers through such payment of royalties on patents. The timing of this action suggests that it might have taken months of persuasion by Clifton and Alfred Reeves, but eventually a strong support was gathered for such a stand. It also amounted to a line in the sand with respect to the issue, almost daring Kardo to try to impose their wishes through court action. This new board policy was revealed in a circular letter from the NACC published on October 23, 1914.

The next NACC board meeting was held on November 5 in New York. Apparently, its earlier plan to set up a motor truck show for the fall at the September meeting had not succeeded. On the agenda this November Thursday were the final preparations for the Fifteenth National Automobile Shows at New York and Chicago in January of 1915. The board decided

6. Excellence in Every Desirable Particular (1914) 109

A French Army 5-ton truck at the factory. Many more were shipped to the war zone in wooden boxes to be assembled at pierside (courtesy University of Michigan Special Collections).

that, while members offering motor trucks for sale could not display them at the shows themselves, spaces for them to meet dealers and show goers would be available at both shows. The 31 members manufacturing trucks, according to the November 11 *Horseless Age*, "will have to content themselves with a display of illustrations and the distribution of catalogs." The board also appointed a committee to "make arrangements for the annual dinner to be held during the New York show."

Despite complaints of "hard times" and the "detrimental effect" of the European War, the NACC traffic committee reported that October carload shipments totaled 10,225, a substantial increase over the October 1913 total of 7,694. The effects of the war were now evident in a rather unexpected way. In fact, the falling export sales of American automobiles seemed to be at least partially offset by the increasing export of trucks to the combatants. This situation was now well appreciated by Pierce-Arrow itself. The NACC board accepted the Allen Motor Car Co. of Fostoria, Ohio, as a member firm during this meeting.

At the United States District Court in Chicago on November 11, 1914, the Kardo Company, Cleveland, Ohio, filed suit against the Studebaker Corporation, Detroit, Michigan, charging infringement of Kardo rear axle patents. Kardo had now crossed the NACC line in the sand. Reporting the event, *Motor Age* noted that "the Kardo company has made many overtures to car manufacturers with the apparent intention of having them take out licenses to build axles on a royalty basis. Up to this date none of the manufacturers has taken a license."

That same day the NACC released a prepared statement: "Officials of the National Automobile Chamber of Commerce believe that makers as a unit are opposed to any effort on the part of Kardo Co. to exact tribute from the motor car industry on the eight or nine patents which it has secured from inventors with a view solely to secure revenue and not with the thought of protecting its product." The chamber also announced that it had secured the services of "the ablest counsel" for the matter, namely, Fredrick P. Fish of Fish, Richardson, Herrick & Neave, to "defend NACC members who are attacked." The battle lines were now openly joined.

The Automobile for Thursday, November 26, 1914, reported, on page 999, Col. Clifton's call for a special meeting of the entire membership of the NACC for 11 a.m., December 3, 1914, at the New York offices, "at which time the attention of the entire chamber will be drawn to the present litigation of the Kardo company on floating axle construction and other patents. It is expected that the national chamber may consider the advisability of defending suits brought against its members by the Kardo company."

Out of the winter cold, representatives from 56 automobile manufacturers gathered in the NACC meeting rooms of the Transit Building that Thursday in December. Their first decision would be whether the Chamber should take up all defense against the Kardo claims. There seemed to be a preponderance of opinion favorable to that course. Against it stood the immovable opposition of Henry Joy, president of the Packard Motor Car Co. Henry Joy and Samuel T. Davis, Jr., of Locomobile were the only others present beside Charles Clifton who had also attended the great 1903 showdown over the Selden patent in William Collins Whitney's drawing room. Now another showdown loomed. Joy had already published his answer to the NACC's October circular letter. His reply was in the form of a letter to Studebaker vice-president E.R. Benson. It contained a strong defense of the value of patents to their inventors and those who purchased them from inventors. It was Joy's contention that patents were an inducement for innovation and improvement and any move to limit returns on them would discourage that beneficial effect. "The declaration by the Chamber, therefore," Joy wrote, "seems to be equivalent to a declaration that the Chamber is opposed to recognizing the patent rights of anyone and that its individual members may therefore infringe the patents of anyone with impunity, and hold themselves immune from any accounting, because of its membership in the Chamber. I am not in sympathy with any such attitude. I do not believe the public is, or will be, in sympathy with it, and I am sure the courts will not be." Henry Joy read the letter to the session. Alvan Macauley and M.J. Budlong of Packard had accompanied Joy to the meeting. The other two owners of Kardo, Peerless and American Ball Bearing, had sent no representatives.

Despite Joy's determined opposition, the NACC membership voted to take over defense against the suit Kardo had filed against Studebaker, and further decided that any similar suit would be similarly defended. Then the discussion shifted to a more long-term solution to the whole patent conflict question. The members regarded patents as necessary to the development of improved automobiles, but patent fights between automakers were regarded as a threat to the growth of the industry. While the automobile manufacturers each owned many patents, few of them were essential to the individual make, being held as a sort of defense against suits by others. In the December 10 issue of *The Automobile*, Alfred Reeves' remarks summarized the issue as being whether the patent interests of a single manufacturer "are more important than the entire balance of the industry." Reeves pointed out that there were at least six or seven important patents on each part used in an automobile, every one a potential source of conflict. Ownership by NACC members totaled 900 to 1,000 patents. The solution proposed was for all the manufacturers to agree to let their individual patents be used by other manufacturers who allowed them similar patent access. This idea was called cross-licensing. "Naturally," *The Automobile* reported, "when the cross-licensing idea was proposed, there was an animated discussion although this was all along the same lines."

After the discussion, nearly one-half the companies represented at the meeting agreed to open their patents to other members who reciprocated. Charles Clifton, on behalf of the Pierce-Arrow Motor Car Co., was the first to sign the agreement, which was to go into effect when 61 companies signed it and at least 300 patents were included. It would last for 10 years, after which it could be renewed. Revolutionary patents of great value to the manufacturer were specifically exempted from the cross-licensing agreement. By the end of that Thursday it seemed likely that most automakers would agree to the plan. It appeared that Charles Clifton's goal of eliminating patent disputes from the still-growing automobile industry might be achievable.

This and other effects from the events that roiled the automobile world in 1914 would continue for years. Changes were in the air.

~ 7 ~

Unexpected Bonanza (1915–1916)

> When you visit the great Pierce-Arrow Asylum in Buffalo, the man you hear about and probably see, if your business is large enough to reach him, is Col. Clifton. There is neither a Pierce nor an Arrow in the whole establishment. It's all Clifton. The Colonel speaks, writes and moves for the company. He is as absolute as the colonel commanding a fortification. Every department is fairly gummed up with the Colonel and what he wants or what he doesn't want. As you enter the building, suggestive of a government hospital, or an ideal old folks' home, you are impressed in the reception chamber with the importance of the Colonel. As you go down the hall to slip the purchasing agent a bit of graft the Colonel sticks his head in and catches you. As you pass along into another department, the Colonel has preceded you. As you pass along to inspect the wheel department, the Colonel has preceded you and his form is just passing along into another department. In the big machinery halls the Colonel flits constantly by, sticking his nose in this and his fingers in that. In the body department if you seen anybody it is the Colonel. Then you go into the workmen's dining room at the top of the factory and there is the Colonel feeling the pulse of the stew and subjecting the butter to a microscopic examination. He is the Pierce-Arrow and the Pierce-Arrow is the Colonel.
> —Henry Caldwell, *Hoo's Hoo and Wat's Wat in Gasoline*, 1913

On the second day of January 1915, the Fifteenth National Automobile Show began its eight-day run at the Grand Central Palace in New York City. The NACC was the sponsor; its general manager was Sam Miles. Over 300 exhibitors were present, including 95 "makers of complete cars," according to the January *Automobile Trade Journal*. Accessory manufacturers and motorcycle builders furnished the rest of the displays. With the European war in full swing, the United States was among the very few countries still manufacturing pleasure cars. A few Italian cars were still available, but the industry had retooled in northern Europe, and was now supplying war materials. This circumstance made the New York show even more important than before. Still, the *Journal* noted that "Anyone looking at the automobile values of today must appreciate that (keen and almost savage as competition may be among makers in the fight for public favor), the simple, reliable and handsome offerings would not be possible except that co-operation, not entirely altruistic, has existed ever since the industry was entitled to a name."

That was a sentiment shared by Charles Clifton when he acted as toastmaster at the NACC Banquet Tuesday evening the 5th of January at the Waldorf-Astoria Hotel down on 34th Street. *The Automobile* in its January 7 issue reported Clifton's observation that the automobile field is "different from any other in that everyone seems to know one another and hence the petty rivalries engendered by business competition vanish under the friendship which permeates the industry." The 480 attendees also heard Irwin S. Cobb describe his experiences in the far-off war zone. But Clifton's description seemed proved out when Henry Joy of Kardo and Packard was seen to waltz with Alfred Reeves of the NACC down the center aisle of the banquet hall, "in an improvised parody entitled 'It's a Long Way to Judication.'" Clearly, the NACC cross-licensing agreement of the month before had not ended the rear-axle patent controversy. Two weeks later the same show would reopen at the Chicago Coliseum and First Regiment Armory.

On January 28 Clifton rounded out the membership of the NACC's legislative committee with the appointment of J. Walter Drake, sales manager of Hupp Motor Car Co., to join H.H. Rice of Waverley, chair, and J.I. Farley of Auburn.

Charles Clifton's mother, Elizabeth Dorsheimer Clifton, died in Buffalo on March 31 at the age of 83. She had seen the Niagara Frontier transformed from barest civilization to a rapidly growing industrial city. Her children had been themselves strong contributors to its growth. Although the family had its divisions, especially between Charles and the Gilbert family, it was easy to feel some little pride in its accomplishments.

The direction the automobile trade was now taking revealed itself clearly by spring. Reports to the NACC directors meeting on April 7 in New York showed a record automobile and truck business over the first three months of 1915, according to the April 10 *Automobile Topics*. Those present, Clifton, Wilfred Leland, E.R. Benson, S.T. Davis, Jr., C.C. Hanch, Wm. E. Metzger, H.H. Rice, and Alfred Reeves, heard that March shipments rose 25 percent over March 1914. Perhaps as a bit of a celebration, the board voted to again accept Sam Miles' invitation to hold its July 10–14 meeting at his Christmas Cove, Maine, summer home.

Pierce-Arrow found demand for its trucks growing among the allied combatants as the spring advanced. Its London agent, Norris Perry, was assigned to negotiate contracts with a French purchasing system deeply influenced by powerful interests. Perry unfortunately lost his life returning from Buffalo to England in early May on the Cunard liner *Lusitania* when it sank as a result of a German U-boat's torpedo. By this time Ted Selman had set up an elaborate receiving port at Le Havre for arriving Pierce-Arrow trucks used by the French Army.

The NACC event held in Detroit on May 5 and 6 highlighted the truck industry's growing importance. It was a convention of 200 delegates attempting to chart a course to develop the market for these new vehicles. According to *The Automobile*, makes represented included Adams, Armleder, Atterbery, Autocar, Baker, Chase, Commerce, Couple-Gear, Denby, Federal, General Motors, General Vehicle, Indiana, Kalamazoo, Kelly, Kosmath, Macan, Mack and Saurer, Moon, Menominee, Packard, Pierce-Arrow, Reo, Republic, Selden, Signal, South Bend, Standard, Sternberg, Studebaker, Velie, United, Walter, Waverley, White, and Wilcox.

At the Detroit Statler Hotel that Wednesday morning, the NACC board met and a get-acquainted event for participants in the convention began at 12:30. Clifton gave a welcoming address at 1:30. Two Pierce-Arrow truck executives also spoke about general issues. Robert O. Patten, sales manager, explained how dealers could "make money selling trucks." And H.

Kerr Thomas, the assistant factory manager at Pierce-Arrow, gave a presentation titled "Can a Standard Load Rating Be Devised and Approved?" The meeting appeared to be a success, and it should have been. It was timed perfectly. Pierce-Arrow, among others, had witnessed a sudden rise in truck sales. It had taken seven months in 1914 to sell 200 R-5 trucks and fifteen months to sell 500 X2–2-ton models. At the end of 1914 the rush began: three months sufficed to sell 200 R-6 models and the next 500 X models would be cleared out in half the previous time. To a greater extent than ever before in military history, the Great War was becoming mechanized. Horsepower from gasoline engines was the future.

That year, Charles Clifton became president of the Board of Trustees of the Buffalo General Hospital. This was the same institution that had treated him years before and had pressed him for payment when his finances were thin. His actions at Buffalo General would illustrate what his friend Rector Cameron Davis called "getting even."

At almost the same time, Clifton was faced with some new challenges. One of those resulted from the death of an owner-director of the Pierce-Arrow Motor Car Co., William Ballard Hoyt, who passed away quite unexpectedly on June 11, 1915. His place as director and legal authority for the board was taken by Thomas B. Lockwood, another attorney, who, incidentally, was married to George K. Birge's daughter Marion. No great difficulty came to Pierce-Arrow or Clifton from these changes, but the long continuity of the company was altered.

Most troubling to Charles Clifton must have been his son Gorham, who had reached his majority in November of 1914. Gorham did not seem to have either ambition to achieve or the self-control to succeed. Maurice Hendry quotes Herbert Dawley as saying flatly that Gorham, 13 years Dawley's junior, "was a disappointment." It resulted in a curious transfer—the Colonel always addressed Dawley as "Son." "He fastened on me," Dawley remembered. Gorham's own son, Mark Clifton (originally named Gorham Clifton, Jr.), described his father as "an incurable alcoholic." Back in 1915, 21-year-old Gorham was mostly focused on playing golf. His one accomplishment seems to have been that of a golf champion in Pennsylvania about this time. Any academic record Gorham had is not known, and his vocational career was almost non-existent. In this pre–World War time Gorham had a reputation for being a "man about town." Being the son of a well-to-do and prestigious business executive gave Gorham easy entry into society. His lack of productive direction would remain a deep concern for the rest of Charles Clifton's life.

Grace Gorham Clifton during the World War in her Red Cross uniform (courtesy Michele Clifton).

Grace Gorham Clifton made no recorded public comments about her son or concerns about his behavior. She was known only as a housewife, mother and socialite in Buffalo. She was a member of the Garrett Club, the Twentieth Century

7. Unexpected Bonanza (1915–1916)

Club (the first club in the United States organized and run by women), and Trinity Episcopal Church. She was interested in the Children's Hospital of Buffalo, paralleling the interest her husband had in Buffalo General Hospital. Mary Budik Gorham recalled Grace as "the sweetest and most beautiful lady" and also a woman who was always straightforward and honest. "She never hid her feelings on a particular subject." Among Charles Clifton's associates she was known as "Lady Grace." At this time Alice, the couple's youngest child, was a 12-year old schoolgirl.

The Automobile for July 1 reported that the cross–licensing plan formulated by the National Automobile Chamber of Commerce had been "more than accomplished." While various makers were still waiting for approval to join from their boards, the required 61 companies controlling 300 patents had already signed, and the agreement was considered nearly complete. The magazine generalized that "the greatest trouble has arisen from patents of trivial character and minor importance, the evils of which are overcome by this agreement when it becomes operative."

The summer meeting of the NACC directors and others, totaling 35 guests, met at Christmas Cove on July 10 for "the usual program of fishing, swimming, baseball, and other sports," according to *The Automobile* of July 15. "Mr. Miles has every facility for entertainment at this big estate here," they noted, "with its miles of lake front, its salt water swimming tank and all the other essentials." The "holidaying" took the first two days, and the business meeting began on Tuesday the 13th, chaired by Clifton. Other participants included C.C. Hanch, Thos. Henderson, Chas. Thaddeus Terry, Carl P. Pelton, J. Walter Drake, Wm. E. Metzger, H.H. Rice, Alfred Reeves, C.M. Hall, Chas. E. Thompson, James H. Foster, H.M. Swetland, F.A. Nickerson, R.D. Garden, Albert L. Pope, Wm. M. Sweet, Thos. J. Wetzel, T.C. Billings, and D.J. Post. Messers Nickerson and Garden were the Pierce agents in Portland, Maine, and New York City respectively.

In fact, Nickerson had helped start the Pierce Company on the road to automobile development by helping to build the very first experimental car Pierce assembled in 1900.

The report of the transportation committee doubtless evoked a greater response than any other topic on the meeting's agenda. June 1915 carload automobile shipments more than doubled over the year before—15,308 as compared to 7,492 for 1914. The economic downturn was clearly over. Some intense discussion involved "the desire of almost all the makers to have a uniform time for announcing annual models." This decision was nonetheless postponed until a later meeting. There was a report on progress standardizing automobile tire treads, and one "on the tendency of legislative bodies to give the jitney bus a fair hearing before passing laws affecting its operation." This would be another continuing issue. Not a lot of progress seems to have been made at the meeting, but the guests certainly seemed to have enjoyed themselves.

That same month *The Automobile* noted that L.P. Kalb had left the Pierce-Arrow engineering department and was now an engineer at the Kelly-Springfield Motor Truck Co.

An unusual Pierce-Arrow advertisement appeared in several magazines that July, the usual moment for the company's new model announcements. This publicity piece was all text, headlined "Pierce-Arrow Announcement of Policy." The announcement promised that "no radical change in its present six-cylinder power plant will be made during the next eighteen months." The "Series Three" models would also be continued unchanged for the rest of 1915. The company seemed confident that only minor refinements would need to be added for

1916. In fact, they declared, "complete satisfaction to the owner" was furnished by its present line of Pierce-Arrow cars. This policy appeared to be a response to the revolutionary Packard Twin-Six introduced on May 1. Pierce-Arrow archly countered with the contention that "the policy of this company is averse to the introduction of novelties for the purpose of securing a more spectacular selling argument." A contrasting Pierce-Arrow advertisement appeared in other publications that same week. It depicted a yellow touring car in a luxuriant country house garden setting, the rendering probably by Myron Perley, and with elaborate thick borders resembling an antique tapestry. The copy was a single sentence: "Justifiable confidence rides beside the man who drives or is driven in a Pierce-Arrow Car."

Pierce-Arrow's sales were climbing in both car and truck lines. Allied armed forces were extending very profitable orders for Pierce-Arrow trucks. According to Brooks Brierley in *There Is No Mistaking a Pierce-Arrow,* purchases by the government of France in 1914 of Pierce-Arrow trucks were under terms that proved particularly profitable for Pierce-Arrow because they allowed the company to keep the discount allowed for a wholesaler. The French seemed very satisfied with the trucks purchased, but dealing with them revealed many complications, some of which were hashed out in court over the years. The first public complication for Pierce-Arrow with these contracts appeared in New York newspapers in the summer of 1915 when one daily printed a dispatch from Paris purporting to show that J.P. Morgan & Co., a strong supporter of the Allied cause in neutral U.S.A., had arranged to contract the entire truck output of Packard, Pierce-Arrow, and White to the French government for an indefinite period. Each of the makers was quick to deny any such contract had been made, or that it had any knowledge of any such negotiations. It was Charles Clifton as Pierce-Arrow treasurer who made that company's denial, coupled with emphatic stress on the importance "of the very desirable and permanent domestic trade," according to *The Automobile* of August 12. All the same, sales of Pierce-Arrow trucks to the Allied armies, directly or through the firm of Gaston, Williams & Wigmore of London, would total nearly 2,500 by the end of the year. During this time the same importer ordered 290 38-C-3 Touring Cars in two separate orders for delivery to Petrograd, Russia. It is not clear if these were part of a military order. The Russian armies also used Pierce-Arrow trucks.

The September 9 issue of *The Automobile* covered the previous day's NACC directors meeting in New York City. Attending this meeting were Clifton of Pierce-Arrow as chair; Alvan Macauley, Packard; Cal H. Pelton, Maxwell; R.E. Olds, Reo; H.H. Rice, Waverley; W.H. Van Dervoort, Moline-Knight; Wm. E. Metzger, Argo; Windsor T. White, White; J. Walter Drake, Hupmobile; Howard E. Coffin, Hudson; John N. Willys, Willys-Overland, and manager Alfred Reeves. Again, the big news was from the traffic department. August shipments were 15,141, nearly double the 8,352 of August the year before. This situation produced "a pronounced shortage of freight cars due to the tremendous demand," and forced the traffic department to take up the matter "with every railroad in the country," hoping to prevent automobile freight cars being used for other purposes. It was an early instance of what would become an intractable and, eventually, critical transportation problem.

Committee reports included patents, good roads, jitney busses, and a preliminary report by the *ad hoc* committee attempting to come up with a uniform time for the announcement of new models. Their final report was expected to be finalized by a meeting to be held later in the month.

Plans were laid out for the drawing of spaces for the 1916 New York and Chicago shows to be held at the offices of the Chamber on Thursday, October 7, members drawing in the morning and non-members in the afternoon.

Alfred Reeves reported that he had finished the organization of service managers in Indianapolis and was moving on to set up such organizations in Detroit, Chicago, and Cleveland. On a sadder note, "Resolutions of respect and sympathy were tendered to the family of the late S.T. Davis, Jr., the recently deceased president of the Locomobile Co. of America, 'who was one of the organizers of the national body.'" Mr. Davis was a board member in several automobile organizations. The Locomobile Company never fully recovered from his loss.

In its story covering this meeting, *Automobile Trade Journal* mentioned that "the annual hand book of the 97 companies holding membership in the N.A.C.C., to cover the 1916 models, will be issued at show time with even more complete information than in past issues." The details added included the material used in vehicle wheels, methods of engine lubrication, electrical voltage data, wiring system type, gasoline supply system, type of clutch, type of steering gear, rear axle and drive details.

The November issue of the *Trade Journal* reported that Pierce-Arrow had created a new position of "Commercial Manager" to work directly in association with Charles Clifton. Appointed to that position was W.J. Foss, who "has been associated with the Pierce-Arrow for the last ten years as treasurer of the Foss-Hughes Co., distributor of Pierce-Arrow products in Philadelphia, Baltimore, Washington, Wilmington, Providence, and Newport." Foss was to be in charge of "every commercial activity of the firm, including the selling of automobiles and trucks, advertising, publicity and service." Mr. Foss entered the Pierce-Arrow management at a time of rapid growth and had a noticeable impact on its operations.

The December 9 issue of *The Automobile* reported that Charles Clifton had been an honored guest and speaker at the Board of Commerce on November 30 in Detroit. About 250 prominent men in the automobile industry, "not only from this city, but from other States, listened to Mr. Clifton's talk on Co-operative Competition."

Clifton was back in Detroit on December 9 for what *The Automobile* called a "monster banquet" at the Ponchartrain Hotel sponsored by the Detroit Section of the SAE. On this occasion, Clifton's remarks covered the history of the automobile industry, during which he pointed out that experimental automobiles had first appeared only a generation before. The famous 1896 Thanksgiving Day "so-called race in Chicago" was noted as the start of automobile acceptance. Contestants had tried to qualify, attempting to cover a 33-mile course in 9 hours. An early snowfall prevented that accomplishment, but the prize was awarded anyway due to their valiant struggle against road conditions. He contrasted this with the capabilities of current automobiles and called their success an example of "the greatest co-operation the world has ever known." He affirmed that such get-togethers as this demonstrated united effort as the industry grew. Clifton also paid special tribute to the city of Detroit itself and its relationship to automobile production. "Whenever anyone sees an automobile," Clifton noted, "he thinks Detroit." He considered that a great asset to the city. Other banquet talks were given by Nicolas Kouznetzoff of the Imperial Russian Government, Isaac Marcosson, publisher of the *Detroit News*, who spoke on "War and Business," and Arthur Nealey, boy president of the Illinois Model Airplane Club, who demonstrated model airplanes in flight to support his predictions about the future of aviation. All in all, it was a very forward-looking gathering.

On December 18, William H. Gardner, one of the five Pierce-Arrow Motor Car Co. owners and a board member, died "after a long illness" at his 255 North Street home, just down the street from that of George K. Birge. Gardner had been an important figure in the management, although without specific duties. His investment in the company passed to his heirs, including his son Laurence H. Gardner, who doubtless took his place on the board. Laurence already held the position of company secretary.

This year had seen the passing of three people who were close to Charles Clifton, now 62 years old. The deaths of long-time associates and family would have an increasing impact on his life.

The New York Automobile Show opened the first week of January 1916, but at the NACC banquet at the Waldorf on the evening of Wednesday, January 5, Charles Clifton did not preside due to illness. Wilfred C. Leland of Cadillac Motor Car Co., the NACC vice president, took his place, and some 300 men attended. It meant that Col. Clifton missed the scene, described by *The Automobile* the next day, during which five "huge, burlesque medals were hung by red ribbons around necks of the recipients." These worthies were John N. Willys, designated as the "prince of production," Harry W. Ford of Saxon for his skills at financing, George Kissell as "the Knight of the All-Weather Body" and John F. and Horace E. Dodge, for their joint accomplishments, awarded a single medal split in two pieces, each brother taking half. Gorham Clifton was pictured at a company luncheon held the next day at the Biltmore. He was employed at the Foss Hughes dealership in Philadelphia.

At the show itself, the Pierce-Arrow "Series Four" made its first appearance, which was a most unusual winter introduction for the firm. Maintaining it had worked for over two years toward this "better car," the company insisted its success was "appreciable, though it takes more than a cursory inspection to notice what we have succeeded in accomplishing." Prices were unaltered from 1915. Owners of Series Three cars were assured they did not suddenly

1916 38-C-4 sedan body for the owner-driver: two doors, seating seven passengers (courtesy Pierce-Arrow Society).

own something obsolete. Outward changes were very subtle—open bodies now had a slight roll at the top. A newly fashionable body, the French Brougham, was introduced, being a close-coupled formal car with a closed tonneau and an open chauffeur's compartment. This style eventually came to be known as a Town Car, since it was clearly for urban use, displaying the chauffeur and footman in the open, while concealing the owner in the shadowy enclosure behind. An "extension top" and side curtains protected these retainers in inclement weather. By July an unusual closed car was introduced as the industry struggled to work out a final sedan configuration. This 38 HP flat-roofed car was called a Brougham Sedan. It seated five, but also had two jump seats with no arms. There was no partition between front and rear seats. Its rear door opened into the right side tonneau behind the driver's seat. A single front door opened to the left front seat. Seat occupants could also pass between the individual front seats to sit. A sportier Four Passenger Touring Car with lower body sides was also added to the line. Mechanically, Westinghouse ignition was adopted in place of commutator and coil. The water manifold was also redesigned. Placements of water pump and magneto were changed, and oil pressure boosted. Charles Sheppy improved his carburetor with a combined mounting of the three reed valves that opened in sequence to provide a smooth response when air requirements increased under acceleration. A mixture adjustment was available to the driver from the steering column. The small introductory brochure promised a complete catalogue would be shortly available on request. And, indeed, before the year was out a typically lavish color catalogue for the Series Four was printed, with illustrations again by A. McKinnon, this year unmistakably of the American West. "It is our desire," intoned the copy, "to build a car with the highest possible average of excellence in all desirable particulars." The declared intention, or, perhaps, hope, was to produce this series of cars with only running detail changes through 1916 and 1917.

In fact, the Pierce-Arrow Motor Car Company was facing a number of unprecedented challenges as 1916 began. Pressure to produce much more rapidly rose from the seemingly endless demand for trucks by the Allied powers fighting in Europe. Great Britain, France, Belgium, Russia, and even Portugal absorbed every truck that Pierce could export. About a thousand of both X3 and R7 (and improved R8) models would be exported in 1916. Before the war, truck production had totaled about 200 a year for each type. It was now a considerable exertion to fill the orders pouring in. Even pleasure car production was affected. An article explaining the problem appeared in the *Pierce-Arrow Salesman* for February 1916, titled "Factory Production and What It Means," penned by H. Kerr Thomas, assistant general manager and factory superintendent. It was written mostly to explain why agents could not obtain deliveries as fast as customers desired the vehicles.

"Owing to the foresight of the Directors of the Pierce-Arrow Motor Car Company when the plant was originally constructed," he wrote, "ample provision was made for taking care of what was then the regular output.... In fact, until about fifteen months ago, it could not be said that the full capacity had anything like been reached." Then, however, "it became suddenly necessary to double the output." This increase had to be accomplished with practically no new machinery. Thomas then explained mathematical calculations showing that during the previous 12 months "more than ninety percent of the actual, theoretically possible production was produced in the Pierce-Arrow factory." His essay shows how Pierce-Arrow went about production. For one thing, it took about five months from the time orders were put into the factory before vehicles were actually produced. "The reason being," he wrote, "that

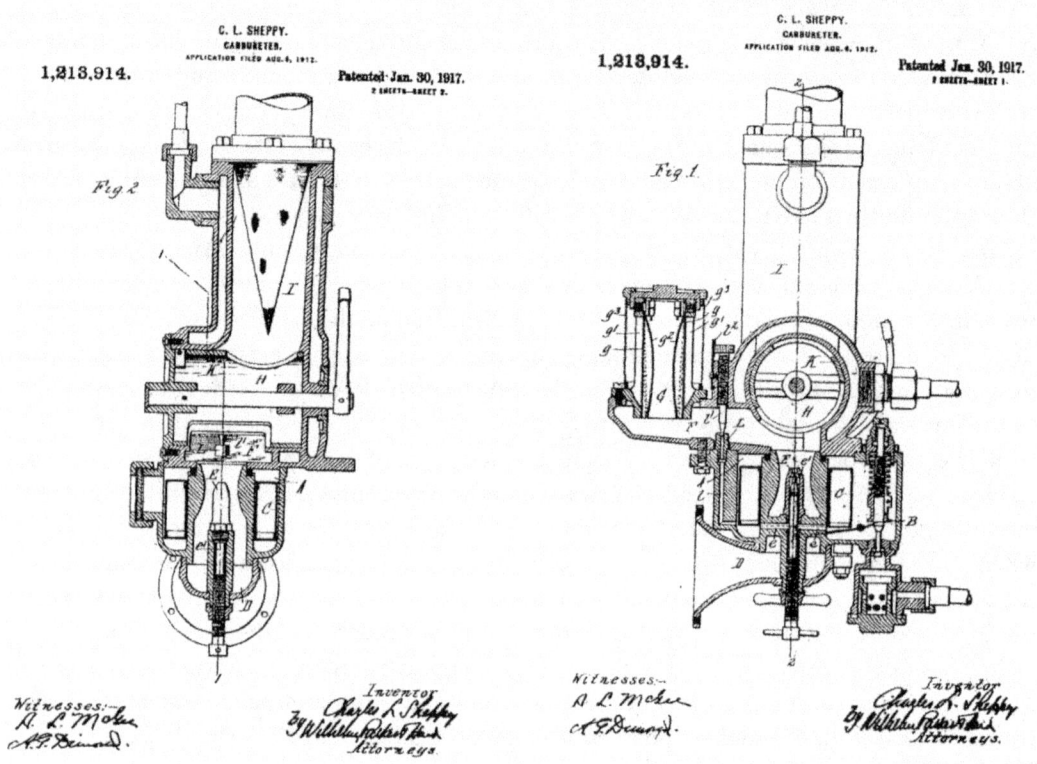

Patent drawings for Charles Sheppy's reed-valve Pierce-Arrow carburetor.

in factory production, a large number of similar parts must be made at one time and that when all the parts are made, the necessary time must elapse for assembling and painting and testing." Thomas remarked at how unhampered such production was unless the factory was asked to make "one special car or even one special detail about the car and the whole balance of production is disturbed." It took three days just to put instructions for a new order into the factory, and from three to four weeks to end a production run early. "This, no doubt, seems to imply a large amount of that substance which is generally known as 'red tape,'" he admitted. "It is, however, actually the necessary result of an organization big enough to undertake big things." It should be pointed out that at that time the automobile and truck industry in England, where Thomas was trained, could not produce such goods as Pierce-Arrow made in the quantity Pierce-Arrow achieved. So, Pierce was certainly big enough to "undertake big things."

On March 3, the Pierce-Arrow Motor Car Co. raised its wages 10 percent across the board. This was more than two years after Henry Ford had raised his company's wage to the lofty level of $5 a day, evoking approval by the public at large and the dismay and protest of the auto industry's leaders.

As the pressure from war orders grew, more production space was required. The three-story laboratory building for testing materials and parts went up north of the Administration Building in 1915. To supply spares to its growing international market, a 110,000-square foot service parts production and warehouse building was erected that same year beside the railroad siding at the northeast corner of the plant. The next year a 106,000-square foot extension of the South Body Building beside Great Arrow Avenue was completed. The North Body Building would be similarly extended in 1917. Considerable room remained on Pierce-Arrow's 2-acre site, and an additional plot purchased earlier was also available for expansion, if needed. Such a necessity now seemed likely. Pierce-Arrow's output and pre-tax profit had both more than doubled in 1915 over 1914.

Records of the routine Tuesday discussions within the Pierce-Arrow engineering department for 1916 show the scope of its efforts that year as they included intense study and discussion of design suggestions, test procedures and the effect of various materials on production. Sessions over time involved David Fergusson, Charles Sheppy, John Younger, H. Kerr Thomas, Charles F. Magoffin, E.H. Spencer, and Otto M. Burkhardt. The last would be appointed to the newly created position of Mathematical Research Engineer at the September 26 meeting. Henry May made his presence felt at some of these gatherings. Shortly after the year began, the design of an experimental "little six" was shelved even before it had been completed. All year long attention was focused on gear box issues. It was the noise of the current gears that was a matter of concern. One possible solution was the Entz electro-magnetic transmission, as installed in the Owen Magnetic cars marketed about that time. Such a transmission was installed experimentally in a 38 HP car that Henry May and his wife drove to Watkins Glen over the Decoration Day Holiday that May as a test. The Entz transmission was, however, found unsatisfactory by late June. At the February 8 meeting there was considerable discussion about the manufacturing costs of the Pierce-Arrow reed-valve carburetors that Mr. Sheppy had developed, citing "an enormous number of special tools." Their produc-

A plant 5-ton truck brings production machinery into the Pierce factory (courtesy University of Michigan Special Collections).

tion continued, however. Brakes were also a repeated item for discussion all year. Obtaining successful lining material seemed to be the main concern. Thermoid brake liners, for example, were tested in March on the test hill at Pekin, NY. An improved worm drive truck gear from David Brown & Sons was discussed on July 25. A long discussion of road testing took place on June 6 involving "Mr. May," who then ordered tests of all completed cars unless there were "very unusual circumstances." He also decided five senior executives should use newly completed cars each weekend to monitor production. Suggestions by Henry May seem to have been agreed to without discussion at these conferences.

Under development that early spring was an experimental 12-cylinder Pierce-Arrow automobile engine. At one point it was described as a 38 HP size, allowing it a bore of some $2\frac{7}{8}$ inches under the NACC formula. This engine had been under test at the end of 1915, and a running chassis powered with it was tested on the road into the summer of 1916. Tests revealed gasoline consumption of 9.28 mpg over a 305-mile mountain route in July. However, this design was then allowed to languish, perhaps because of increasing war work. More sustained effort began with the layout in early April of a $4\frac{1}{2} \times 6\frac{3}{4}$ inch 12-cylinder "Aero Motor." Fergusson made a sketch design for April 18, which was then approved for working drawings. This motor was, unexpectedly for Pierce, a valve-in-head design with cylinder liners. By the end of the year, and after various modifications, materials were purchased for assembling sample test engines. Only this aircraft motor proposal seems to have had enough momentum to produce an actual production design.

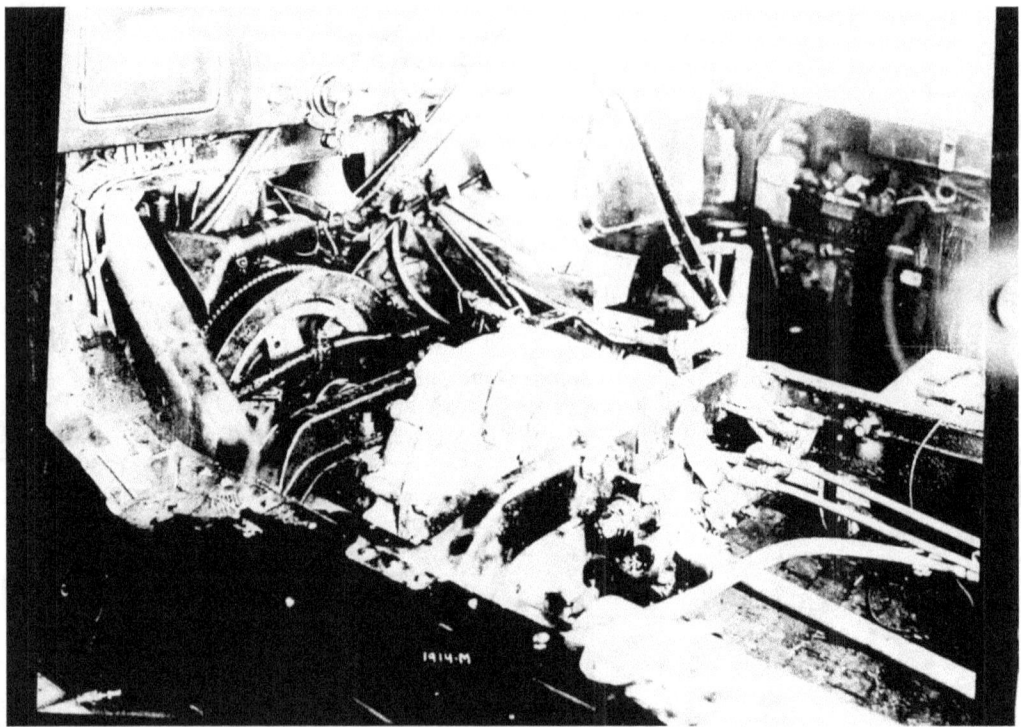

A test chassis with an electromagnetic transmission (probably an Entz) installed at the Experimental Department. Another version, the Elma, was later tested as well (courtesy University of Michigan Special Collections).

At the May 9 meeting it was decided to use one bank of the "Aero Engine" design as the basis for a new 66 HP automobile engine. A week later a tentative gear ratio for this experimental model was set at 3.261 to 1. This engine may have been "the new 6-cylinder motor" discussed at the meeting in August. David Fergusson submitted to the committee "new designs for the valve-in-head pleasure car motor" late in the year at the December 5 meeting. Production car designs, however, never went in this direction, and this proposed engine may never have been completed or placed in a chassis for testing.

This year, Charles Clifton began his efforts to improve Buffalo General Hospital, which he remembered well from earlier days when he had difficulty meeting his obligations to them during an illness. After some serious thought, Clifton prepared to present "a gift of astounding proportions," according to Evelyn Hawes in her history of the institution, titled *Proud Vision*. "It was to be an entire new hospital building," she continues. "After much reflection he had decided to give the completed structure, rather than an endowment." Pointing out that the daily expenses of a hospital, "like Tennyson's brook, [run] on forever," Clifton believed that covering those was a separate problem from providing facilities, and he urged that the number of subscribers to the hospital's Guarantor's Fund should be enlarged. The building itself, known as Memorial Hall when completed, was known as "the finest building of the hospital."

Automobile Trade Journal for July covered the annual meeting of the NACC in New York City on June 7 and 8. "Charles Clifton, of the Pierce-Arrow Motor Car Co., was again elected president of the organization," it reported, adding that it was a "record meeting" of automobile manufacturers. During this session, the manufacturers went on record as being "opposed to the Tavernner Bill now before Congress, which has for its purpose the prohibition of the use of time studies and premium or bonus payments in connection with work of the Government." This was seen as preventing "efficient methods in private manufacturing industries." Committees reporting at the meeting left the impression that "the automobile trade is enjoying its greatest period of prosperity with apparently no diminution in the demand for American made motor cars in this country and abroad." Clearly motor trucks were a part of this demand, and the commercial car makers held their own convention "at which many standards were adopted." They also decided that no truck show was necessary in 1917. Service policies for both cars and trucks were also agreed upon.

Other officers of the NACC elected at the annual meeting were "Vice-president, Wilfred C. Leland (Cadillac); second vice-president, Hugh Chalmers (Chalmers), Gasoline Division; second vice-president, Windsor T. White, (White), Commercial Vehicle Division; second vice-president, H.H. Rice (Waverley), Electric Vehicle Division; secretary, R.D. Chapin (Hudson); treasurer, George Pope; general manager Alfred Reeves."

The ongoing civil war in Mexico impacted the Pierce-Arrow Motor Car Co. in the summer of 1916. President Woodrow Wilson had sent a punitive expedition under the command of General John J. Pershing into the troubled country after a raid on Columbus, New Mexico, by the bandit Pancho Villa on March 9. The objective was to find and punish the bandits, but the attempt turned out to be lengthy. Then, on June 21, Mexican troops, encouraged by German diplomats bent on provoking a war between Mexico and the United States, attacked an American scouting party at Carrizal, killing 12 and capturing 23. The president immediately called out the National Guard to help guard the Mexican border against attack. Among those forces were members of the New York guard in Buffalo. Laurence Gardner, who was the Pierce-Arrow company secretary, for example, was a member of the local 74th Regiment.

Some of those called up had to leave their employment at Pierce-Arrow, and the board of directors on June 23 voted to pay those employees their hourly and weekly wages, less their pay from the government. Married men with dependents would receive full wages, the others half wages. In addition, the company guaranteed those employees re-employment by the company when their term of service ended. The company estimated that about 80 employees would be affected by this decision.

That summer, in its July 27 issue, *The Automobile*, in an article datelined Christmas Cove, Maine, noted the "Officers and directors of the National Automobile Chamber of Commerce, Inc., are enjoying their annual sojourn here as the guests of Samuel A. Miles." The actual meeting took place on Tuesday the 25th, its business "being mostly of a routine nature." The National Automobile shows and their decorations were discussed, as was "the patent situation." The usual pleasure before business program obtained, involving "fish fries, clam bakes, and general sports." The guests present were mostly the same as those attending in 1915. Mr. Pelton, Mr. Hall, Mr. Foster and Mr. Billings were absent, replaced by John N. Willys, Windsor White, A.G. Batchelder, and John C. Wetmore.

Spaces for the National Automobile Shows at New York and Chicago were allotted on October 5 when representatives from 98 automobile firms, including five that manufactured electric cars, met at the NACC headquarters in New York. There were 14 more makes accommodated for the 1917 shows than for the shows one year before. Ten other makes had left the market entirely, and White and Locomobile had decided to show only in the more exclusive Importers Salon at the Hotel Astor in January. Twenty new makes of cars would debut in New York, including such makes as Liberty, Roamer, Jordan, Doble, and, believe it or not, Ben Hur. For the third time in as many years, John N. Willys had the honor to select the first space for Overland because it was the largest-selling make in the NACC. Ford was by far a larger seller than Overland, but Henry Ford refused to join the organization. The makes drawing spaces following were Buick, then Studebaker, Dodge, and Maxwell, presumably in sales order. Eventually all 98 were placed on the four floors of the Grand Central Palace in New York and the Coliseum and First Regiment Armory in Chicago. NACC General Manager Sam Miles presided at the drawing. Prior to that event Charles Clifton presided at a routine meeting of the board that morning before the allotments began.

The Pierce-Arrow sales agents from around the country met in Buffalo at the factory on Thursday, October 26, to prepare for the New York and other automobile shows in early 1917. Col. Clifton gave a short welcoming speech noting, among other things, "I believe the future belongs to the young men." He expressed confidence that the "future is in your hands, and I believe it is more secure than any in my recollection, because I believe the young men of today are better equipped than the young men of any other day that I can recollect." This must have been a surprise coming from a man who saw young Buffalonians depart to fight in the Civil War. "One thought I want you to take home," he concluded. "There are certain firmer virtues that stand out predominately—that stand out everywhere today—with regard to character, and these firmer virtues are honesty and fidelity." This was yet another indication of the importance character had in Charles Clifton's approach to life and work.

On the last day of October, a notice on the company letterhead went out above the signature of Assistant General Manager and General Factory Superintendent H. Kerr Thomas that implied an organizational shuffle. The next morning, Saturday, "the organization of the Experimental Work in the factory will be changed as follows": Charles Sheppy would be

The Series 4 Pierce-Arrow motor (courtesy Pierce-Arrow Society).

"CONSULTING EXPERIMENTAL ENGINEER." The mere experimental engineer would be Mr. Magoffin, "having entire charge of the experimental work being carried on in or by the Experimental Department." Robert Gerlach would be in charge of the Motor Test Room. Mr. Fergusson would take charge of pleasure car testers, and Mr. Younger would be in charge of truck testers. These changes were made "to meet the growing requirements of the factory, and by relieving Mr. Sheppy from the routine work of the Experimental Department, he will have time to assist any of the factory departments with his advice, both in the development of new designs and in improving the quality of the product." The heads of factory departments were encouraged to employ Mr. Sheppy "in order to obtain the benefit of his experience." This notice suggests that Charles Sheppy would have a wide impact on Pierce-Arrow offerings in the future.

The members of the NACC board met on Thursday, October 30, and Clifton again was chairman. They discussed two important topics. The first was the report submitted by the traffic department showing that, once again, automobile shipments for October 1916 had greatly outpaced those of that month in 1915. The total reached 19,510 carloads as compared to 17,848. Notable was the shrinking margin in the October comparisons. Some months in 1916 had more than doubled the previous year's shipments.

The second topic centered on the wide variations state legislatures had when making laws affecting automobile use. Laws in some states also had the effect of slowing the growth of the commercial vehicle industry. Clifton as president of the NACC was chosen to "act as a national councillor representing the automobile manufacturers' organization in the Chamber of Commerce of the United States," according to the November 8 issue of *The Automobile*. Already, the NACC counsel had argued a case involving the constitutionality of one state registration law being considered by the U.S. Supreme Court. The main concern was that state automobile registrations might be used to charge further registration fees from vehicles already licensed in another state.

Tuesday, November 7, 1916, was Election Day. The voters would decide between the re-election of Woodrow Wilson, campaigning under the slogan "He Kept Us Out of War!" or rival Charles Evans Hughes. Charles Clifton, an enthusiastic admirer of Wilson's critic, Theodore Roosevelt, doubtless supported Hughes, but it is nearly certain that his attention that day was focused on things other than the election. That morning's papers carried a short

View of the Pierce-Arrow factory as enlarged by the fall of 1916. New construction includes the Parts Department behind the truck factory at the left, the Laboratory on Elmwood and an east extension of the south body building beside Great Arrow (courtesy Pierce-Arrow Society).

wire service article noting that a new company called the Pierce-Arrow Motor Car Corporation was in the process of being formed to take over the holdings of the Pierce-Arrow Motor Car Co. Wall Street powerhouse J. & W. Seligman & Co. was heading a syndicate that would underwrite issuing 100,000 shares of 8 percent convertible preferred stock and 250,000 shares of common stock to consummate the deal. As a part of it, the outstanding $1,250,000 in 6 percent bonds of the Pierce-Arrow Motor Car Co. would be retired February 1, 1917. The same page of the *New York Times* on which the story appeared also carried this advertisement: *C.C. Kerr & Co., 15 Wall Street, N.Y., Pierce-Arrow Motor Corporation bought, sold, quoted N.Y. Curb.* This was a momentous change. Pierce-Arrow stock had never before been publicly traded.

By Thursday morning, while President Wilson's re-election was still uncertain, details of the Pierce-Arrow transaction were more complete. *The Automobile* that day explained that the new capital would be used to increase factory facilities. The magazine added, "George K. Birge, now president of the company and prominent in the wallpaper business, will retire, and Col. Charles Clifton, now treasurer of the concern and for several years head of the N.A.C.C. will succeed him." It was also widely noted that the preferred stock would be "redeemable at 125 and accrued dividends," being convertible share for share with common stock. Funds to repurchase the preferred shares would be accumulated when dividends on the common stock exceeded $5, after which $1 per share would be set aside for redemption of the preferred. Such redeemed shares converted into common shares would then be available for corporate purposes. The next day's *Wall Street Journal* looked over the price paid to purchase control of Pierce-Arrow. Mr. Birge had insisted that his 7,000 shares of Pierce-Arrow Motor Car Co. stock were worth a thousand dollars each. To obtain all the issued shares would take $15 million. Adding a 10 percent transaction expense brought the purchase price to $16,500,000. The *Journal* concluded that the company "should have on January 1 about $15,000,000 in assets including real estate, buildings, equipment, inventories, cash, etc." They added that Pierce-Arrow was currently earning a half a million dollars a month, and that the earnings since 1912 had been:

1912	(July 1, 1911, to June 30, 1912)	$2,142,000
1913	(July 1, 1912, to June 30, 1913)	$1,464,000
1914	(July 1, 1913, to December 31, 1914)	$1,714,000
1915	(January 1, 1915, to December 31, 1915)	$4,301,000

There seemed to be good reason for changing a fast-growing company like this from a closely held corporation, as it was, into a public corporation. The syndicate behind the deal would receive for the $16,500,000 it raised $10 million of the preferred stock and 180,000 shares of common. "The bankers and their associates," the *Journal* concluded, "will find their profit in the remaining 70,000 shares of common stock." *The Wall Street Journal* calculated that "on a peace basis" the company could expect to earn between $3 million and $4 million a year. Before the week was out, President Wilson had won reelection.

None other than Clarence Barron himself turned up at the Pierce-Arrow factory in Buffalo sometime in early December. His weighty observations appeared in the Saturday, December 9, edition of the *Wall Street Journal*. He saw the reorganization of the Pierce-Arrow Motor Car Co. as confirming the "evolution of the motorist from the place of the lower priced to that of the higher priced cars." Every bit as important was that "demand for the Pierce-Arrow five-ton truck is so large in this country that all foreign or war orders have had to be declined." This convinced him that the larger future profits of the company would be achieved from truck sales. While future car sales by Pierce-Arrow might reach as high as 6,000 cars a year, he felt, the truck field offered almost limitless possibilities. "It is believed," Barron wrote, "that the motor truck department will be the first to outgrow the magnificent concrete buildings on the 25 acres within what was formerly the Buffalo Exposition ground, and demand the construction of new buildings on a 40-acre tract owned nearby." Already the gross business of Pierce-Arrow totaled about $20 million per year, employing nearly 7,500 people. "The business of the concern should be doubled every prosperous period of three or five years," Barron concluded. Pierce-Arrow was becoming a giant.

At about this time, influenced by Charles Clifton, Herbert R. Dawley left his position as manager of the Art Department at Pierce-Arrow. That fall the Laidlaw Company of New York, a supplier of upholstery materials for automobiles, inquired of Dawley if he would consider a position with them. "I told the Colonel about it," Dawley recalled for Maurice Hendry 50 years later, "and a short time later he called me into his office. He knew of impending changes, and said 'Things are going to happen around here, son…. You're a luxury in most places around here, son, and so my advice to you is—take that job!'" Upon his leave-taking, Clifton handed Dawley a sealed envelope, asking that it not be opened until he reached his new post. "I did as he asked," Dawley continued, "and found the contents to be a personal cheque from the Colonel for a substantial sum and a little note which said simply, 'Thank you—Charlie Clifton.' That's the kind of man he was. He was a marvelous man. He could think twice while the others were getting ready to think. Made 'em look like stodges."

The financial proceedings to reorganize the Pierce-Arrow company were completed by early December. A story datelined December 5 at Buffalo and appearing in *The Automobile* of December 7 noted the transfer of "the present company to the Pierce-Arrow Motor Car Corp. will be made tomorrow." The proposed directors were: Charles Clifton, president; Henry May, vice-president; W.J. Foss, Buffalo; J.F. Alvord, president of the Torrington Co.; W.S. Cox, of J. & W. Seligman & Co.; C.J. Schmidlapp, vice-president of the Chase National Bank; J.G. Dudley of Buffalo; Albert Strauss of J. &. W. Seligman & Co.; and C.H. McCullough vice-president and general manager of the Lackawanna Steel Co. of Buffalo. The recently chartered Pierce-Arrow Motor Car & Truck Co. had been incorporated by L.D. Adkins, R.J. Trimble and E.S. Hemphill on December 2, 1916, to merge with the earlier Pierce-Arrow Motor Car Co. The name of the combined companies was then changed back to the Pierce-Arrow Motor Car Co. on December 7, 1916.

On the evening of December 5, Charles Clifton "gave his annual complimentary dinner to the [NACC] directors at the Hotel Biltmore," according to the December 7 issue of *The Automobile*. The next day the board met and received news of automobile shipment totals that November of 17,250 carloads, 112 more than in November of 1915. There was considerable impatience in the industry with the continuing shortage of suitable freight cars and "cars being arbitrarily used in other services." The Interstate Commerce Commission was set to meet with the representatives of the Railway Association to try and alleviate the freight car shortage. The board anticipated the railroads would soon advance per diem charges for the use of freight cars from the current 45¢ to $1.00 or even $1.25 a day to speed up unloading. Exports of automobiles and trucks had reached new heights as well. Estimates for the total value of exports in 1916 already were estimated to exceed $160 million. The board decided to call a meeting of export managers in January to work through related problems.

For Charles Clifton it had been an eventful year. At age 63, he was now the actual, titular head of Pierce-Arrow Motor Car Co. To prepare his selling forces for the changes they would face he issued an explanation. "The reorganization of the Pierce-Arrow Motor Car Company," he wrote for *The Pierce-Arrow Salesman* in December, "was effected because of the desire of President George K. Birge to retire from active business. The remaining members of the old Company felt that the maintenance of past successful policies could be best guaranteed by changing the form of organization into a public corporation rather than continuing the old closed partnership.

"The change means absolutely nothing so far as the established policy of the Company is concerned. It will manufacture and sell along precisely the same lines which have marked it in the past, and the conduct of its business will remain in the same hands." In fact, the only change in executive management was that Clifton's previous position as company treasurer was now held by Walter C. Wrye. Challenges related to the war had already appeared—inflationary movements were occurring in both materials and labor costs. As a result, Pierce-Arrow prices were being raised to cover them.

~ 8 ~

War Work
(1917–1918)

> He has never tried to dominate, always seeking rather to guide and advise. He has been a chief of the "silent" type, believing that diplomacy and common sense will accomplish more than any attempt at steam roller methods.
> —*Automotive Industries*, March 5, 1927, at the Colonel's retirement

The New York Automobile Show for 1917 was held the week of January 7 at the Grand Central Place. This year, among its four cars on display, Pierce-Arrow presented a spectacular show car—a 48-B-4 Suburban fitted out to evoke the "simplicity and grace of the designs used throughout the Adam period," according to the description in that month's *Pierce-Arrow Salesman*. The exterior of this impressive formal model was finished in glistening black, sporting a quarter inch blue stripe split with a hairline of white. The chauffeur's seat was plain black leather; bright work was "dull nickel" and the pillar lamps "are of special design and will carry an extra charge when applied to other models."

The description of this show car suggests it was a late, perhaps even final, product from Herbert M. Dawley before his departure from Pierce-Arrow. Contained by its restrained exterior, the interior and fittings of this show car left a most profound impression. No effort had been spared to make every detail harmonious and of authentic craftsmanship typical of the brothers Adam in 18th Century England. The most involved part of its interior seems to have been the headliner, which was custom woven to match ancient hand weaving so that even the outline of the car's ceiling was precisely followed and a related figure woven around the dome light. To do this, 38,000 cards were cut for the Jacquard loom. These alone weighed about a ton. "There are 13,000 weft and 5,120 warp threads used in the ceiling alone," the text revealed, creating the effect of "an Adam period settee placed against the wall of a room." The three-cushion tonneau seatback of conventional construction was outlined with a carved rail of mahogany. Upholstered in a "soft warm gray with design units in silver thread, accented in Wedgewood blue," each of the three back cushions was decorated with "a medallion of Adam period design" woven into the fabric. Similar medallions were woven into the backs of the auxiliary seats and the door panels as well. Carved panels of mahogany inlaid with "genuine Wedgewood medallions" finished the back of the front seat and the doors. Special utility cases were created to match these panels. Hardware and utility case accessories were made of silver and blue enamel matching the color in the tapestry medallions. The dome light was of Belleeck china, again with matching colors. Publicity noted that the design had originated in "the factory Art Department, and both design and material used are the exclusive property of the Pierce-Arrow Motor Company." Other color ensembles were apparently offered using this design as well. A standard 48 HP Suburban retailed for $6,800 that year; the price of Adam period cars would be "furnished upon application." Clearly, the newly reorganized company was still appealing to the same exclusive sector of the market.

No major changes had been made to the line of 1917 cars, except for the higher prices due to rising inflationary pressures. There were three new models introduced, however, consisting of a Four-passenger Roadster and a smaller Convertible Roadster, available with two-passenger or three-passenger front seat and a "small auxiliary seat." These styles were offered for all three chassis. A Town Brougham body was introduced only for the 38-C-4 models. It was essentially a variation on the French Brougham style having a narrower rear seat. Additional Auto Show Pierce-Arrows were displayed at the 233 West 54th Street showroom of the Harrolds Motor Car Company that week.

Due to the reorganization of the company, great pains were taken to assure dealers at the show about its stability. Pierce-Arrow headquarters for the week were maintained in Room No. 735 of the Biltmore Hotel, where a stenographer was stationed during business hours with time off for lunch. The executives who oversaw the various activities of the sales staff, Messers Foss, Newlin, Patten, and Hodge could be reached through this office during the show.

A newly completed 48-B-4 Suburban beside body building "H" on Great Arrow. Its brightwork appears to be brass, an extra cost option (courtesy University of Michigan Special Collections).

The annual NACC auto show banquet took place on Tuesday evening at the Waldorf-Astoria. "It was," *Automobile Topics* reported in its February issue, "one of the happiest get-together affairs that this association has ever held. President, Col. Charles Clifton presided, and the only speech of the evening, aside from Col. Clifton's address of welcome, was by Job. E. Hedges, and as usual whenever this speaker is heard, was witty and entertaining, and at the same time full of much that was worthy of deep thought and consideration." For this event, "burlesque decorations" were again awarded to three of the officials present for accomplishments during the past year, and, after the keynote speech, a mock trial of important individuals in the industry written by Fred E. Dayton and Henry Caldwell was presented. Titled "Lost in Litigation," it was directed by Alfred M. Delisser, being a "4-cylinder episode" in "four acts and sixteen fire escapes." The reporter noted "This was an extremely clever and timely satire, good-naturedly hitting many of those present connected with the industry." Several pioneers of the automobile industry, such as Elwood Haynes and Alexander Winton, attended along with nearly all the current leading figures.

The anticipated Pierce-Arrow company luncheon for agents, salesmen, and other members of Pierce-Arrow organizations across the country was held at the Biltmore, beginning at 12:30 p.m. on Thursday. Every company participant had received an invitation to the gathering. Unlike the NACC event, this was clearly serious business, and there was no satirical play presented. The objective of this luncheon was to satisfy the selling staff that the changes made to the company would not result in any lowering of product standards. Two presentations were given, one by Clifton himself, the second by Henry May, company vice-president and general manager. Both speeches were printed in the next issue of *The Pierce-Arrow Salesman*.

There is no evidence that Charles Clifton felt any sense of vindication or triumph upon ascending to the summit of power at the Pierce-Arrow Motor Car Company; certainly none is reflected in his remarks at the luncheon. "Mr. Toastmaster and Gentlemen," he began. "It is a very great pleasure to see so many gathered here who have been with us from the beginning. We have not been an organization of change. The majority of the men who are here, the responsible selling factors today, are those men who started out with us, grew up with us and are still with us. This phase of it is a very great pleasure to me."

From that introduction, Clifton alluded to the changes that had been made at Pierce-Arrow. "To be elected, of course to the financial leadership of the organization is also a very great pleasure," he continued, "but one of which I am afraid I do not take full significance. My whole thought, during the past fifteen or twenty years, has been that while, in a business or organization of any sort, it is necessary to have a leader, the leadership may be more or less sentimental. I have been very much occupied with the effort to so build up this organization that, whether it had a leader or not, didn't make much difference. I feel that we have come to a point where we can be proud of the efficiency and character of our organization." He stressed again the importance he placed on character. "I want to say to you gentlemen," he remarked, "that I am proud of this organization because I believe that the human character here is the counterpart of our product." He went on to note that, for the first time, members of the selling agencies along the Pacific Coast were attending the show. "Like all men out in the West," he declared, "they have had to depend on themselves; and to have these men mingle with you is an advantage for both sides. I regard it as a distinct subject for congratulation."

Clifton then brought his short address to a close with a deft twist. "I was told," he noted, "that Mr. May was going to make a few remarks, and that when Mr. May was asked to talk, he said, 'I always come after the Colonel and the Colonel doesn't leave me anything to say.' (Laughter.) That is one of the greatest compliments ever paid to a public speaker. I take that compliment home and I am very much gratified if I have been so comprehensive in my talks, but I can't help feeling that I am occupying valuable time, so I am going to leave Mr. May to give you the substance of my speech. (Prolonged applause)."

When Henry May took the podium he declared it his purpose to summarize "the policy of the company and the maintenance of the quality of the product." Having been a part of the George N. Pierce Company from its inception, May could attest that its original policy, carried on into the current lines of automobiles and trucks, was to "engage the services of the most efficient engineers, employ highly skilled workmen, purchase the best quality of materials and equip the plant with the most up-to-date machinery and tools" to turn out the best possible product. "That it has been a wise policy is shown," he went on, "by the continual growth of the plant. At the time the new buildings were erected in 1906–07, they contained a floor space of about 330,000 square feet, which has now been increased until the total floor area is approximately 1,250,000." He noted that the plant had shipped as many vehicles in 1916 as it had in record-setting 1915, despite a three-week machinists' strike in the spring of the year. This total amounted to 4,500 vehicles. That this policy would be maintained was guaranteed by the continuity in factory organization. Only Charles Sheppy's role had been enlarged to "a position where we feel he will be of more value to the company." Sheppy had been part of the Pierce operation since at least 1899 and was chief experimental engineer, but his duties would now be expanded to appointing inspectors, a vital part of the Pierce policy. Intense monitoring was also demanded for materials put into the vehicles. The company was finding inspection and testing of raw materials to rigid specifications was of increasing importance. So was testing and inspection of various purchased parts. The inspection department had recently been moved into its new building to help facilitate this work. Machines in the plant were the "newest and best that can be made" installed in the most modern type of factory buildings, while methods were continually being advanced. "The various departments," May explained, "such as Gear Cutting, Cylinder, Crank-case, Transmission, Milling, Drilling, Grinding, etc. are specialized more than in the past, each being under the supervision of an expert foreman who has charge of all operations under his control." Inspection still followed every operation upon the parts, producing perfect parts at close tolerances. Each sub-assembly was tested before being applied to the chassis. Assembly was not speeded up by piece work or "mechanical means such as moving chains, etc." May stressed that it was a "Quality First" operation throughout. Even so, the factory planned to increase pleasure car output by 40 percent in 1917, "which our plant is quite capable of producing." May's speech also evoked supportive applause from the audience.

Back in Buffalo, while this was going on, the Pierce-Arrow engineering department had been mulling over organizational issues. David Fergusson and John Younger, the chief car engineer and chief truck engineer, respectively, had been visiting the engineering departments at Cadillac, Dodge, and the White company to get a sense of how engineering routines worked at each. It appears that the stimulus for the visits was to streamline the process at Pierce-Arrow for turning out successful new designs. The two men had compiled a report on their observations that had been submitted in November, just before the financial reorganization.

Their conclusion was that other engineering organizations had better communication with the manufacturing departments, which allowed greater speed in transforming designs into finished parts successfully. They believed that this process also was assisted by reducing what they described as "many intermediaries" and by giving greater control and responsibility to the engineers themselves. They made recommendations that included setting up direct lines of authority: "Mr. Fergusson and Mr. Younger to be in direct charge of all designers, detailers and tracers on pleasure car and truck work, respectively; Mr. Way to be in direct charge of all designing and drafting room detail relating to pleasure car bodies; Mr. Pleuthner having charge of all production drawings, details and tracings, including the checking." They also called for the engineers to supervise experimental work directly instead of through "intermediaries." One of these last was said to be someone who communicated between the engineers and H.M. Blaufuss, who supervised the manufacture of experimental designs. Benefit from this change had recently been seen in "the speed of getting aeroplane forgings directly by engineers." They also suggested closer contact between the engineering department and production engineering, blue printing and the tool drafting room. Their overall recommendation for the two divisions was that David Fergusson remain chief engineer for automobiles, assisted by Mr. E. Harris, who would also supervise experimental car design, and John Younger continue as chief truck engineer, assisted by Mr. F.W. Davis, who would also supervise experimental truck design. These men would supervise all related testing and drafting as well. Pleasure car body development would be headed by Mr. Way with a separate responsibility to management; so also would planning and tools, experimental mechanical, mathematical research, chemical and metallurgy, as well as the responsibilities of someone named Foley, who apparently supervised the keeping of files and records. Various other suggestions were also made regarding the way certain manufacturing and testing operations were carried out. Among these were changes in tolerances for machining parts, increasing the speed of engines being run-in after assembly, and trying out the "chain belt scheme of manufacture" for moving engines to and from block test. This last was unlikely to please Mr. May. They also observed that Park Drop Forge Company had such resources that it should be an alternative source of such parts as crankshafts to Wyman and Gordon.

Whether or not all these suggestions were adopted, by March the department had made a definite change in their approach to developing improved pleasure car engines. The new experimental motor designs being discussed all had double intake and exhaust valves. The valve-in-head approach, by contrast, was heard of no more. At this time, Stutz was racing overhead cam engines, but had put dual valve T-head engines in its production cars. Whatever Pierce-Arrow's inspiration, Mr. Magoffin had submitted on March 20 a "preliminary report on the four-valve motor" that was said to be "highly satisfactory." In April, suggestions were made on intake passages for the "#7 experimental motor." By May 1, "present designs were OK'ed for production." These included four-valve cylinders in both 38 HP and 48 HP sizes. This was a truly prophetic development. Concurrently, interest in electronic gear boxes continued. This time The Elma Magnetic Gear Box design was chosen for investigation, and Fergusson asked during the March 30 meeting that it be redesigned. The design had been "submitted by Mr. Burkhardt," according to notes from engineering meetings, and the new version was ready in April. Further efforts to improve the Elma electronic gearbox continued into June.

In the February *Pierce-Arrow Salesman*, the company announced that "Mr. Arthur E.

Killinger has succeeded Mr. Herbert M. Dawley as manager of our Art Department. Killinger had been for five years "in charge of all leathers, cloths and other upholstery materials as head of our Trimming Stock Department." The article went on to detail Dawley's joining the Laidlaw Company, Inc. adding, "It is not our intention to lose the benefit of his excellent good taste in future designs and selections for Pierce-Arrow cars."

This year Charles Clifton made his first gift to the permanent collection of the Buffalo Fine Arts Academy. It was a portrait by American painter Florence Julia Bach. Clifton's later support financed many more additions to the collection.

Meanwhile, trouble had arisen with the reassembly of trucks exported in "knocked-down" form to France for army use. Complaints suggested that the factory assistant general manager, H. Kerr Thomas himself, needed to investigate the problems on site in France. Thereafter, Kerr Thomas sent for Ted Selman, his own assistant, who had delivered the very first French Army trucks back in 1915. In his memoirs written in 1953, Selman noted that by this time the Pierce-Arrow operation in France had grown to giant size. Depots for unloading, assembling, and repairing Pierce-Arrow trucks for the French Army had multiplied from the original one at Le Havre to include Brest, St. Nazaire, Nantes, La Rochelle, La Pallice, and Bordeaux. Occasionally Marseilles was also employed. The complaint concerned lack of company support for the uncrating and assembling of trucks at these ports. When Selman arrived to investigate at Bordeaux in January 1917, he wrote, "I found the quay-side depot, where Pierce-Arrow trucks were being worked on, without help from us. Two men should have been there at the moment." Further investigation disclosed that the designated supervisor and his assistant "had let women and wine capture them." The guilty parties were repatriated to Buffalo and their successors proved to be "a splendid crew who worked exceedingly hard during the following two and a half years." Selman would remain in charge and reckoned that the French Army eventually absorbed some 9,000 Pierce-Arrow trucks and "the equivalent of 20% in major units" for repair and replacement of parts.

A second prolific Allied customer for Pierce-Arrow trucks during the war was Imperial Russia. Tom McArtney, another highly skilled workman, was sent by Pierce-Arrow to Petrograd (renamed from St. Petersburg during the war because of its German-sounding name) to help ready and repair the Pierce-Arrow trucks for Russia in a similar fashion to that employed by Selman in France and England. According to a story McArtney sent to the July 1916 *Pierce-Arrow Salesman*, the ignorance of the Russian "muzhik" about mechanical matters was hard to overcome. "It is very difficult to get the drivers to do what we want," he wrote, concerning the maintenance of 38-C-3 touring cars used by Russian Army generals. "They will alter an adjustment five minutes after we have made it." The challenges of this endeavor had only just begun.

The ultimate deterioration in the relations between the neutral United States and the Imperial German Empire began when the latter resumed unrestricted submarine warfare on Thursday, February 1, 1917. Even the ships of neutrals would now be sunk without warning in the war zones. On Saturday that week, President Wilson broke off diplomatic relations with Germany and sent her ambassador home. Hoping to be a mediator between combatants, Wilson still did not yet ask for a declaration of war. However, the danger to U.S. shipping prompted him to ask Congress to arm American merchant ships. Meanwhile, the attempt to find the bandit Villa in Mexico had ended on January 25, and all U.S. troops were home by February 5.

A work crew in France undertakes to open wooden boxes, each of which contains a knocked-down Pierce-Arrow truck ready to assemble (courtesy University of Michigan Special Collections).

Under a New York dateline of April 3, reported in the April 5 issue, *The Automobile* revealed that the NACC had taken charge of the Technical School for Automobile Draftsmen and Mechanics "to meet the need for more and better draftsmen in automobile body factories." The school had been conducted in New York City for 37 years and was open to all employees of automobile or body manufacturing plants. Daniel T. Wilson chaired the committee in charge of the school. Charles Clifton, president of the NACC; H.H. Rice, treasurer of General Motors; and NACC general manager Alfred Reeves had been added to the governing committee. Plans were under way to double the size of the school by accepting an offer of larger quarters at 20 West 44th Street. According to the story, graduates of the school "are now connected with practically all the prominent automobile and body building plants in the country." Studies in both the day and evening classes and its three-term correspondence course were detailed in the story.

Within weeks of the resumption of the German U-boat threat, American ships had been torpedoed, and American lives lost. The astounding revelation in the so called "Zimmermann Telegram" of the German proposal to help Mexico regain its former territories, including all of Texas, New Mexico and Arizona, proved to be the last straw, and the United States declared war on Imperial Germany on April 6. This step suddenly put the whole U.S. economy on a war footing. A universal military draft was quickly enacted. It was almost instantly apparent that the automobile business would be affected by the need for a large number of trucks as the army was quickly enlarged. *The Automobile* in its April 12 issue expected an army of nearly 800,000 men. The current total of 2,600 army trucks would have to be increased, but actual contracts for trucks were not going to be written until the anticipated military units were actually mobilized. Another well-known necessity was fighting aircraft and the motors to power them. This, too, was where the automobile industry could contribute to the war effort.

At the Pierce-Arrow plant in Buffalo, the first days after the declaration of war saw an outbreak of patriotic zeal. Flags were affixed to the rafters of work spaces and several departments put on shows of patriotic songs and speeches. This culminated in a great factory-wide meeting after work one April evening in First Assembly that featured a band, military units, and speeches. Charles Clifton was among the speakers. "Fellow Americans," he began, "I want to assure you that it gives me very great pleasure indeed to be with you this evening and to see the patriotic spirit which prevails among our employees. The terrible war in which this country is engaged will call, and is calling, for the best there is in every one of us. We may not be called to go and fight for the flag; but we can still show our patriotism by being loyal to our duties, our President and our flag. The day of racial distinction is past," he continued, well aware of the German and Irish minorities in the Buffalo area. "We are no longer pro-this or pro-that, but today, answering to the call of our President, we are one people, one nation, under one flag—Americans!" This was a widely-endorsed sentiment all over the United States, that previous controversies be pushed aside to support the war. The Colonel's words were published in next issue of *The Pierce-Arrow Salesman*.

By late spring it was becoming more and more apparent to American leaders just how desperate the situation was with the Allied powers that had been fighting the war for nearly three years. The Czar had abdicated the Russian throne, and the succeeding Provisional Government was unstable and weak. The French Army was practically exhausted, and an actual revolt by its soldiers was soon to take place. The British Empire had run out of both money and borrowing power to finance its fighting. Winston Churchill, previously First Lord of the Admiralty, described the approach to Ireland from North America now as "a veritable graveyard of British shipping." This resulted in Great Britain having a mere six weeks of food supplies. The opposing Central Powers were in equally bad shape. Austria-Hungary had already nearly collapsed, as had Turkey. The German people were under great strain, blockaded of raw materials and food. The war, in fact, had become a race. Would German submarines destroy Allied supply lines and starve them to surrender, or would the United States arm itself quickly enough to turn the tide against the Germans?

This alarming situation led to a very energetic buildup of the American armed forces and their industrial and agricultural supplies. Because automobile factories could easily be converted to build armaments, there was tension between their customary operations and the newly-required ones. There were continuing efforts to work out these conflicts. One of them was covered in the May 1 issue of *Horseless Age* in an article titled "Clifton and Willys on Industrial Conference Board." The board in question had been organized in May 1916, according to *The Automobile* of April 12, 1917, "guided by sound economic principle, high conception of human relationships, and the belief that only upon this basis can enduring national prosperity be built." By the summer of 1917 the board, "composed of national organizations of manufacturers," considered "matters affecting industrial development, with a view of presenting to the public and legislative bodies the business-man's side of important questions." Clearly, American business intended to organize support for their points of view when large issues of procurement came up for discussion. Clifton was in a particularly strong position to explain the attitudes among the automobile manufacturers, with most of whom he was in close contact.

Motor Age for May 24 noted that "the Pierce-Arrow Motor Car Co. has elected the following officers: president, Charles J. [*sic*] Clifton; vice-presidents Henry May and W.J. Foss; secretary, L.H. Gardner, and treasurer, W.C. Wrye." These all, of course, were experienced from many years with the firm, mostly in those very positions, although Laurence Gardner would soon rejoin the Army. He eventually became a lieutenant colonel in the Inspector General's department.

Saturday of that same week, the Clifton family witnessed Gorham's marriage to 24-year-old Margaret Frances Keenan. This was doubtless seen as a hopeful sign that Gorham had begun to settle down and become more than just a playboy.

A story in the May 31 *Motor Age* announced the formation of what the periodical headlined as "Another War Committee," noting that some automobile men had been chosen "to Advise." This Council of National Defense had on May 26 employed K.W. Zimmerschied to manage its office in Washington, D.C., as one member of an automotive committee to serve as a "co-operative committee under the leadership of Howard E. Coffin, chairman of the committee on munitions of the advisory commission," to advise and assist the government departments on "all matters involving the use of internal combustion engines, including the production of motor cars, trucks, and ambulances, tractors, motor boats and airplanes." This was a high-powered group: "Chairman, Charles Clifton, president of the National Automobile Chamber of Commerce; C.W. Stiger, president of the Motor and Accessory Manufacturers; Coker F. Clarkson, general manager of the Society of Automotive Engineers; Frank H. Russell, president of the Aircraft Manufacturers Association; H.L. Hanning, chairman, tractor standards division of the S.A.E.; K.W. Zimmerschied, past chairman, standards committee of the S.A.E." These were some of the arbiters between these industries and the national defense planners.

On June 8, the National Automobile Chamber of Commerce elected officers for the new term. As reported in *The Horseless Age* for June 15, it was "a record meeting." More than 90 companies were represented, and they elected Clifton as president again, with Wilfred C. Leland (Cadillac) as vice-president. Division vice presidents included Hugh Chalmers (Chalmers), Windsor T. White (White), and Herbert H. Rice (Oakland). R.D. Chapin (Hudson) was elected secretary and George Pope the treasurer. Alfred Reeves remained general manager. John F. Dodge of Dodge Brothers, Detroit, was added to the board of directors. Others on the board were Hugh Chalmers (Chalmers), R.D. Chapin (Hudson), C.W. Churchill (Winton), Charles Clifton (Pierce), J. Walter Drake (Hupp), C.C. Hanch (Studebaker), Wilfred C. Leland (Cadillac), Alvan Macauley (Packard), Wm. E. Metzger (Columbia), R.E. Olds (Reo), Carl H. Pelton (Maxwell), H.H. Rice (Oakland), Windsor T. White (White), and John N. Willys (Overland). At the general meeting, the members voted to purchase $30,000 worth of Liberty Bonds using the organization's treasury, and to carry bonds for "all employees who wish to subscribe." They also formed a committee that would convince manufactures to make it necessary to go to a shop to open or close a muffler cutout. This plan was necessitated by "the failure of some motorists to respect ordinances against the use of muffler cutouts." The organization also clearly expected a rising foreign market for exports and had set up an export committee chaired by Harry Ford (Saxon) to supply "information on shipping, embargoes, new tariffs, foreign dealers, trade opportunities and service for motor cars in foreign countries."

Faced with suggestions that Buffalo General Hospital was extravagantly run under his guidance, Clifton retorted that during the previous year, while Massachusetts General cost $3.31 per patient per day, and Rhode Island General $1.98 per day, Buffalo General cost $1.77. Construction of Memorial Hall continued with its completion expected in a matter of months. Hospital trustees had contributed an additional $400,000 for buildings over the last two years as well. The hospital's reputation continued to rise.

As mid-summer 1917 approached, no announcement of new models was made by the Pierce-Arrow Motor Car Co. because there were only minor running changes made in the Series 4 chassis, and no new bodies had been created. To some degree this had been the plan all along, but the sudden rise in demand from the Allies for trucks coupled with the expanded use of trucks in domestic freight hauling had resulted in attention at the plant being focused more on producing trucks than producing cars. At the same time, it was not clear what impact on automobile production the war effort would have. Pierce-Arrow staunchly maintained their intention to produce automobiles, but their output of trucks was overwhelming their output of cars. The improvements made in the car line first appeared on the upcoming "third run" of the 48-B-4 model, its most popular offering. The engineering committee also took some time to look over "drawings of Jesse Vincent's aviation motor." This last, of course, was what became known as the "Liberty" aircraft engine.

48 HP Series 4 touring car in service. Note the painted radiator shell (courtesy Pierce-Arrow Society).

The factory was on its way to producing over 5,000 trucks during the calendar year. Such figures had never been imagined before at Pierce-Arrow. Stashes of truck parts were piled all around the extensive grounds. Trucks were also being improved as demand grew. The 2-ton Model X already had full pressure lubrication. At the engineering meeting on August 17, Mr. Sheppy argued the urgent necessity to upgrade the 5-ton R-8 to the R-9 because the new model incorporated that improvement along with an improved carburetor, "both of which details," Sheppy noted, "are giving trouble on R-8's in commercial use." It was also apparent that truck production was more likely to be in line with the wishes of the Council on National Defense.

At an engineering discussion on September 11, chief engineer David Fergusson "pointed out that in a few years' time much smaller engines would be used" in motor cars. He then suggested that the 24-valve six cylinder with cylinder dimensions of the present 38 HP model, a design already under development, would give the same power as the Packard "Twin-Six" motor. Clearly, automobile engines were already beginning to develop more horsepower per cubic inch displacement. Airplane engines would lead this improvement as the war continued.

Interest in automobiles continued unabated, however, as was apparent when NACC met in New York City on October 4. *Motor Age* estimated that over 200 companies were represented. Turnout was encouraged because it was the occasion for the drawing of show space for the New York and Chicago automobile shows in January 1918. "Sam Miles, the veteran manager of the two national exhibitions," *Motor Age* noted, "came from his summer home at Christmas Cove, Me., to handle the work, and Colonel Charles Clifton, the perpetual president of the association, and Alfred Reeves, the general manager, were there also." This event indicated that numbers of exhibitors of automobiles "would be larger than for any previous show." All four floors of the Grand Central Place would be filled "to overflowing" as would the Coliseum and Armory in Chicago. Again, this year, first company to draw space was Willys-Overland, with more sales than any other NACC member. Following were Buick, Dodge Brothers, Studebaker, Maxwell, Chevrolet, Cadillac, and Hudson, in that order. The magazine noted that some 20 makes shown at the start of 1917 would not be at the 1918 show, including Cunningham, Barley, Lozier, Metz, Pullman, Pathfinder, Sun, and Sterling. Five electrics would be shown, including Baker-R&L, at whose stand the unconventional Owen Magnetic would be on display as well. The Stanley Steamer would be shown for the first time at the Chicago show. Meeting two days later, the NACC board voted unanimously that the elimination of exhaust "cutouts" should go into effect on January 1. Hugh Chalmers was elected first vice president of the Chamber and H.H. Rice vice president of the gasoline car division.

Buffalo General Hospital opened Memorial Hall, Charles Clifton's personal gift to the institution, on October 23. Among its other facilities, it contained 60 rooms for "private service." In this way, it advanced the scope of hospital services to meet the changing demands of its patients.

The notes of the Engineering Meetings at Pierce-Arrow toward the end of 1917 showed clearly that passenger car development concentrated on dual-valve engine technology. In fact, by the November 20 meeting the decision had been made to use the current 48 HP carburetor on the new 48 HP 24-valve car and to "go ahead with [that carburetor] for the one thousand cars for 1918." The 24-valve test car at Pekin Hill that month ascended the hill in

34 seconds. Starting at a speed of 10 miles per hour it reached the top traveling 39 mph. Acceleration from 10 to 60 mph in high gear took 25 seconds. At 30 mph, gasoline consumption was 10.3 miles per gallon. This new model would go into production by June or July 1918. In addition, an entirely new 24-valve six-cylinder engine with a 4 in. bore and 6 in. stroke, cylinders cast in a single block with two-part detachable heads, was under development for future models. Plans to make up such an engine for testing with enclosed valves and oil pump inside the crankcase had been approved in October.

On October 1, 1917, Miss Anna L. Cowen, the factory dining room manager, closed the facility on the second floor of the Administration Building due to the increasing number of employees, according to an article in *The Arrow*, the company magazine. Its function was taken over by 18 lunch counters throughout the plant where sandwiches, pie, and coffee could be purchased for 3¢ each, a price that was soon increased to a nickel. As time went on, the lunch counters offered a different hot dish every day, including such meals as baked beans, macaroni and cheese, sauerkraut and wieners and escalloped potatoes or soup. The "Club Lunch Room" on the first floor remained open for officers, heads of departments, and their assistants. Some 200 meals were served in this facility every day.

As the year drew to a close, the losses from the German U-boat campaign had been reduced by improved convoy tactics. The United States Army was growing as fast as possible, and enormous quantities of war material were rolling out of U.S. factories. When the NACC met on the morning of November 30, chaired by Charles Clifton, however, there was much uncertainty and even despair within the membership. Automobile manufacturers and dealers, as well as other supporting entities, were having trouble dealing with the implications of living in a war economy. Many feared automobile production was going to be largely curtailed, supplanted by production of war related products. Some smaller concerns were afraid such a restriction would mean their having to leave the business entirely. These worries had been building up ever since war was declared and had the potential to undercut the war effort and the industries that supplied its materiel.

At the meeting, to counter the concerns, Alfred Reeves read out statistics that illustrated how large and successful the automobile and truck business and its suppliers had been so far in 1917. By June 30, 1,806,194 motor vehicles had been produced by 230 makers of passenger cars and 372 truck builders. A work force of 280,000 had been paid wages and salaries totaling $275,000,000 annually. The total capital investment of the industry totaled $736 million. Then followed the statistics related to manufacturers of bodies, parts, and accessories, culminating with the figures showing the economic impact of some 27,800 automobile dealers and another 25,500 automobile service garages. Four and a half million vehicles were registered in the U.S.; 400,000 of those were trucks that transported six billion ton-miles of freight, "relieving," to quote the *Motor Age* coverage of the gathering in its December 6 issue, "the railroad to a great extent in short-haul traffic." These statistics still did not quell the negativity among some members. It was Hugh Chalmers who turned the temper of the meeting around. After a proposal that had the effect of placing the whole industry into the hands of the government, as *Motor Age* reported, Chalmers assured the gathering that he would not go back to Washington and allow "the third industry of the country to be torn to pieces and legislated out of business." Chalmers, with John R. Lee and A.W. Copeland, represented the automobile industry on the Automotive Products Section of the Council of National Defense. From his position, Chalmers had command of the facts necessary to reassure the automakers that, while some reduction in production numbers might have to occur, it would not be so great as to jeopardize the industry. In the end, the meeting coalesced, agreeing to send a telegram of support to Daniel Willard, chairman of the War Industries Board in Washington, "expressing their willingness to turn their facilities over to the Government as fast as the Government can make use of them." In the meantime, they hoped to keep their "organizations intact so as to conserve the greatest potential strength to the present and future war plans of the Government." The Great War continued to alter the patterns of not only business but also daily life in the United States. Even in Buffalo, with a large population of German descent, sauerkraut was now being called "Liberty Cabbage" as increasing anti–German sentiment appeared. Workers at Pierce-Arrow and other local companies were leaving to join the armed services. Steadily, a national will to "Defeat the Hun" was being forged. By year's end it was estimated it would take perhaps two years to successfully defeat the Central Powers.

It was also noted that the spirit of cooperation had been shown by manufacturers "giving their best men to the Government at great sacrifice to themselves and their plants." Everyone agreed that business as usual could not be expected to continue as long as the principal business was fighting the war. Therefore, production of civilian goods by the industry could not be expected to continue to increase as it had in the past. A.W. Copeland, John R. Lee and Hugh Chalmers of the Automobile Industries Board had been given the responsibility of coordinating war requirements with available industry facilities. Having noted a need for additional engineers, the three were pleased when nine manufacturers at the meeting volunteered engineers to work with them in Washington for the duration of the conflict.

Supplying transportation by means of "the modern motor car and truck" partially met the War Railroad Board's request that the overtaxed railroads' short haul traffic be assisted. The motor industry, "now rated as third among those of the United States," was playing an ever-increasing role in the nation's transportation system. The automobile dealers of the country also indicated their willingness to rearrange their organizations to meet new situations as they developed. While the manufacturers expected to make cars "to as near a normal number as materials and the coal situation permit," it was acknowledged that "there will be some decrease in the number of passenger cars produced, making them harder to get and higher in price." All these expectations would be demonstrated in the New Year.

The year 1918 began with the customary New York Automobile Show opening on January 5 and continuing until the 12th. The realities of the war situation caused the whole feel of the show to be very different from those before. For one thing, compared with 1917, the situation of the Allies in Europe was very much more difficult. The *Bolsheviki* under Lenin had taken power in Russia, and consented to the Treaty of Brest-Litovsk, ending Russia's entire participation with the Allied armies. This freed extensive German Imperial armies previously deployed on the Eastern Front for use against Allied armies in France and Belgium. Pierce-Arrow operatives, such as Tom McCartney, caught up in the turmoil as Russia slid into civil war were now unaccounted for amid a flood of refugees. On the Western Front, the French Army was slowly being rebuilt after a widespread, if suppressed, mutiny in July, but would never again be the force it had been. British forces were also stretched thin. Everyone anxiously awaited arrival of the American armies to turn the tide. On the Italian Front, a disastrous defeat of Italian armies at Caporetto that fall had relieved the pressure on the fading Austro-Hungarian armies of the Central Powers, allowing further German reinforcements in the west. American forces were certainly being amassed, but months of experience and training were still needed before they would be ready to make a large contribution. While the submarine situation had improved Allied supply, present distribution of forces on the ground now favored the Central Powers. Everyone knew that if Germany was going to launch an offensive, the time was favorable at the start of 1918.

These stark facts shadowed the mood at the Auto Show. The "1918 Show Instructions" booklet given to Pierce-Arrow salesmen, for example, emphasized the importance of making "the same presentation on all matters concerning Pierce-Arrow product." This year, that presentation consisted of de-emphasizing the luxury inherent in a Pierce-Arrow and emphasis on "the ultimate economy of the Pierce-Arrow car." This encouraged an expectation for many years of dependable service and discouraged the idea that the automobile was among the "non-essentials." It also allowed an emphasis on its high standard of "comfort, dependability and safety, with a reasonable outlay for gasoline and tires." Additionally, the company stressed that the "interruption" in production of 38 and 66 horsepower models, no longer produced at the time, was only temporary and due to "Government needs." Four hundred numbers were left open for the current, and final, run of 48-B-4 models in early 1918. It was quite clear that "Government needs" were already impacting Pierce-Arrow production. The company's declared plan envisioned production of about one-fifth the number of automobiles produced in 1917. Despite the fact that no new bodies were introduced in the line for the new year, the company stressed that 135 changes had been made. In addition to adopting Goodrich "Silvertown" Cord tires and brakes from the 66 HP, the new cars incorporated a longer hot water jacket for heating the low-volatility gasoline available at the time, a thermostatic cutoff for the radiator to speed engine warmup and an improved oil pressure gauge. The rear axle drive had also been improved so that, while manufacture was more complicated, assembly was much more trouble free. Steering column braces were strengthened on the Runabout, Coupe and Four-passenger bodies. Perhaps most noticeably, a new, more convenient, spring-loaded hood catch for the engine hood was adopted. The dashboard clock would now be hand-wound, and those cars carrying the option of spare tires at the rear would have them mounted on a Johnson rim instead of by means of mere "clips and straps" as before. In addition, body interiors were upgraded with a new instrument mounting to improve visibility in the sportier runabouts and touring cars with open sides. Other bodies still had the earlier style. Side curtains on touring car models now opened with the doors, a definite convenience. As for the price, wartime inflation had certainly set in. The seven-passenger touring car was now priced at $5,500 f.o.b., the seven-passenger Suburban at $6,800. Just the increase itself would buy a new Ford runabout. Four Pierce-Arrows were on display at the show; seven more were displayed at the Harrolds Motor Car Company showrooms. Despite the "interruption" of their production, two 38 HP models were among these display cars, suggesting their production was expected to resume when possible. Pierce-Arrow headquarters during the show were again at the Biltmore Hotel. The company itself appeared to be doing well.

Efforts to remedy the increasing congestion of railroad freight traffic had grown more intense as the war effort continued. On Tuesday, January 8, "representatives of practically all of the truck making companies of the country—the really big men and those who are next to them—assembled in convention," wrote *Horseless Age* for its January 15 issue, "in the rooms of the National Automobile Chamber of Commerce in New York at the invitation of the Chamber's Commercial Vehicle Committee for the purpose of picking up and putting together all obtainable ideas as to how and in what ways the industry can best help the Government

The popular vision of Pierce-Arrow motoring: a catalog illustration from 1917 (courtesy Pierce-Arrow Society).

in the business of winning the war." This was a tall order. Charles Clifton opened the meeting with an address. He was followed by Pierce-Arrow's assistant commercial manager, George M. Graham, speaking on "Maintaining a Record of Unselfish Co-operation." Maj. Edward Orton of the Quartermaster's Department, U.S. Army then discussed "Delivering Army Trucks by Highway," followed by Hugh Chalmers (Automobile Industries Committee), Christian Girl (Director of Production, Military Truck Division, Quartermaster's Department). Then, Roy D. Chapin, chairman of the Highways Transport Committee, spoke on that committee's work. After that, topics such as use of motor trucks for short haul work, legislation affecting the use of motor trucks and the impact of heavy loads on highways were covered by other authoritative speakers. The meeting passed one resolution pledging full cooperation

8. War Work (1917–1918)

in "developing ways and means for increasing the effectiveness of the motor truck and delivery wagon as aids in moving merchandise and other freight and express matter. Another resolution they passed tendered the U.S. motor truck manufacturers' "services and co-operation in meeting the transportation needs of the Government and the country and offer the facilities of their factories to aid in the prosecution of hostilities against the Governments of countries with which the United States is at war." They also appointed a committee of five representatives from the manufacturers to help organize and develop highway freight transportation to relieve "railroad freight congestion and to facilitate the movement of military trucks and transportation of the mails." As a part of the latter efforts, the magazine suggested that motor truck dealers could assist the process by organizing local "clean-up days" using their own trucks and cars along with those of "all his patrons" to pick up and deliver "the freight matter waiting at the station or on railroad cars to be moved away." How much of this suggestion actually was put into effect is not clear, but the proposal shows how difficult freight transportation had become.

At the January 22 engineering meeting in Buffalo, "The question of the desirability of designing a 4 × 6 inch six-cylinder engine with overhead valves and single overhead cam shaft was discussed." This was an unexpected development, indeed, especially with the factory's concentration on trucks at the time. During the ensuing discussion, the efficiency of the proposed design was recognized, but the drawback of its noise was also acknowledged. "It was thought," the notes conclude, "that if time permitted after we had finished the new 4 × 6 engine 'T' head design 244-valve [must mean 24-valve!] engine, we should design an overhead valve engine so as to have our own comparison of the two types." There appears to be no follow-up on this project in later reports. It would have produced an engine very much like Hispano-Suiza and Bentley used in the 1920s.

On the Pierce-Arrow factory floor, the production of motor trucks dwarfed automobile production that spring. Both the 5-ton R-8 models and 2-ton X-4 models were in full production, and parts of the plant were being set up to assemble sizeable numbers of the standardized "Liberty" trucks from components supplied from outside. Employment at the plant was climbing toward 10,000 workers. Wear and tear on the factory increased. The company magazine, *The Arrow*, noted that replacement of broken window glass in the plant had cost $105.21 in just the week between February 25 and March 2. This was an annual rate of $5,486.52. The expense was probably higher than usual, provoking its mention.

By the February 12 engineering meeting, David Fergusson submitted his latest design of a three-speed transmission "for the new touring car we are working on, in connection with the 4 × 6 in. 24-valve engine." Clearly, that experimental *en bloc* "T" head six-cylinder design was being seriously refined even as the war continued. At the same time it was looking like Pierce-Arrow was doing well this wartime. David Fergusson's diary noted that the company raised his salary to a whopping $15,000 a year on February 15. He had already been awarded a $1,650 bonus on January 7. There was, however, the little matter of a patent suit against Pierce-Arrow using the worm gear rear axle. David Fergusson wrote to Charles Clifton about the matter on February 1, in reply to the latter's letter of January 12. The suit apparently alleged that Pierce-Arrow was infringing patent No. 14398 of November 27, 1917, "a re-issue," in Fergusson's words, "of patent No. 1036660, dated August 27, 1912, and No. 684,575 filed March 18, 1912." Fergusson countered that the Pierce-Arrow worm-drive axles used on its trucks were designed in 1910, "incorporating the recommendations of the David Brown Company, Huddersfield, England, shown in their drawings dated July 27th, 1910—almost two years ahead of the earliest application date of above patent." The first truck with the axle in question was completed on December 24, 1910. In conclusion, Fergusson wrote, "I have taken this matter up with Mr. Thomas and Mr. Younger—they suggest that this be investigated by the Automobile Chamber of Commerce." The matter seems to have ended there. Pierce-Arrow continued using the worm drive axles, apparently without penalty.

George Kingsley Birge, the visionary capitalist who had developed the Pierce-Arrow Motor Car Co. from the George N. Pierce Co. and then served as its president, died on Saturday, February 16, 1918, "after a brief illness," according to the February 18 Buffalo *Evening News*. An obituary in the March *Pierce-Arrow Salesman* called him "a great citizen, a leading business figure and a patron of Art whose loss is deeply felt, not only in the community in which he lived, but in many quarters of the country." The success of Birge's 20-year management of the Pierce enterprise cannot be denied. Yet, in less than a year after his retirement, Birge's Pierce-Arrow company had been transformed into a war industry preoccupied with producing trucks, and the transformation was not finished, either.

Near the end of March, the German armies on the Western Front launched a terrific attempt to break through Allied lines and win the war before American armies had reached full strength. The German success was greater than the Allies had imagined it would be, but less than the Germans hoped. Although it was a near thing, the Allies managed to stem the thrust that again put even Paris in danger. The Allies hurriedly reorganized their whole command structure in ways that sped up responses to future attacks. Nonetheless, strong German attacks continued, although with less conspicuous success.

The Pierce-Arrow Motor Car Company released the report on its first complete year in business on April 2, 1918. Sales figures for the firm in 1917 were larger than ever before, and the report revealed how the balance of operations had been shifted by the entrance of the United States into the Great War. Gross sales had increased by 75 percent in 1917 over 1916 totaling $32,565,908. Col. Clifton speaking as president of the company attributed most of this gain to war orders from both the U.S. Government and other Allied governments in the war. The net profit, after payment of dividends on the preferred stock, was $3,598,748, compared with over $4 million the year before, when dividends were paid only on operations after December 6, when the new company started business. Assets had grown from $18,408,889 to $26,084,913. Net profit per share, after preferred dividends, totaled $11.19. This compared to earnings of $13.08 per share in 1916, when preferred dividends were, again, only paid on operations after the new company began business. Preferred dividends for 1917 totaled $800,000. Common shares received $625,000. Predictions of success for the new public company seemed fulfilled. Unfilled orders for vehicles totaled 5,098 on January 1, 1918, as compared to 1,343 at the start of 1917. David Fergusson recorded that he had his bonus raised on March 31 to $2250 per quarter.

The impact of war work on the company and its growing size suggested that security be strengthened at the factory. Steps were taken on January 20, by Chief Lewis W. Henafelt, who had led the plant police since 1907. His officers were now responsible for guarding "[$]10,000,000 worth of property," according to a story in the June 1 issue of *The Arrow*. The uniformed plant police officers had to be "under 45 years of age, in good physical condition, with good character and habits." They were equipped with a revolver, a police whistle, and a Billy-club. They were also sworn in as special officers of the Buffalo city police. Officers kept an eye out for problems in the plant, such as holes and dangerous places, broken doors, locks, windows, and fire doors. They also reported "loafing or improper conduct on the part of employees." Their most important responsibility, however, was to make sure that no one entered the plant unless they were authorized to do so. Staff were issued an employee name tag, or "button" indicating that person's responsibility. All those leaving the plant were checked as were their bundles, tools, and packages. Most employees arrived by means of the newly enlarged street car terminal south of the plant, but automobiles being parked were also checked in and out. (Employee bicycles were kept in the basement of the Administration Building near employee lockers.) The most obvious concern was protection of "the large number of newly finished trucks parked in the open along Great Arrow Avenue. "At times there has been $200,000 worth of trucks stored in this manner and yet not one part has been stolen or tampered with," the story averred. The story about the factory police also illustrates their enlarged duties growing from the entry of the United States into the World War. As special officers for the city, they looked for "suspicious behavior" off duty as well as on and could bring charges against "anyone who speaks in disrespectful manner of the President or manner unpatriotic or disloyal, which may discourage recruitment or cause trouble." Behaving in ways someone considered unpatriotic could get a person arrested during this time.

With Col. Clifton chairing, the NACC held its monthly meeting in New York on April 3, vexed with transportation difficulties stemming from the press of war and legal issues that confounded manufacturers' and dealers' expectations, according to the April 4 issue of *Automotive Industries*. The shipment of motor car and truck engines had been affected in a new ruling by the Classification Committee of the Railroad War Board that no longer permitted them to be shipped in "open crates." Regulations now required "the boxing of engines." The Chamber had heard arguments by J.B. Marvin of its own Traffic Committee opposing the change. The response to its protest to the Railroad War Board was eagerly awaited. Additionally, Mr. Wm. G. McAdoo, director general of the railroads, which had been nationalized until the end of the war by President Wilson on December 26, 1917, because of traffic congestion, notified the NACC that theft of parts from cars in transit over the railroads "would come under the federal law instead of state laws." This would impose a 10 year maximum sentence in federal prison for violators. The NACC also opposed a recent ruling from the Treasury Department that automobile sales outlets, known as "branch houses," would be treated "as factories, so that when a branch house sells an automobile it will have to pay the 3 per cent tax on the retail price." This ruling changed what the NACC had previously understood the law to require, and the Chamber therefore protested this new ruling.

To assist the reduction of railroad freight demands, automobile makers were driving new cars from the factory for delivery to dealers. In some cases, makers had delivered 20 to 30 percent of their production over the roads, according to a report to the NACC by its Traffic Committee. As a result, rail shipments of new cars had declined the first quarter of 1918 as compared with the year before. At this meeting, the NACC also chose its representatives to two associated organizations. J. Walter Drake, who chaired the export committee, and John N. Willys would attend the meeting of the National Foreign Trade Council in Cincinnati, April 18–20. There, they would present a paper "showing the importance of automobile exports to the country at large during the war as well as after it." The NACC also selected Col. Clifton and Herbert H. Rice of General Motors to represent the Chamber at the U.S. Chamber of Commerce meeting in Chicago, April 10–12. The war seemed to be confusing several issues that had apparently been settled before, and new decisions were made all the time to cope with war-related problems. The Chamber was making sure its views would be heard.

On May 21, Pierce-Arrow released its earnings report for the first quarter of 1918. Net profits had totaled $1,231,887. This rate of earnings, if sustained for the whole year, would net a profit of nearly $5 million, the highest in company history. The release made it clear that "official circles," as the story in the May 23 issue of *Automotive Industries* noted, did not expect such high profits by the end of the year. As it was, the company reported, 500 passenger cars were to be produced in the first half of the year, carried over from 1917. Further production of 1,000 cars during the last half of 1918 was then scheduled. Truck production was expected to total 5,000. The numbers for 1917 had been 2,600 cars and 5,000 trucks, according to the story. Company rescension tables suggest that 1917 truck production had been somewhat less than that. Whatever the true totals were, the company retained a quarterly surplus of $719,367 after dividends were paid on preferred and common stock. Investors in Pierce-Arrow preferred stock were now used to seeing quarterly notices that read: "The Board of Directors has declared the regular quarterly dividend of Two Percent (2%) on the preferred shares of the company (month, day, year) to stockholders of record at the close of business (month, day, year) [fifteen days before]. Walter C. Wrye, Treasurer." Similar notices declaring a "a dividend of $1.25 on the common stock of this Company," were regularly sent out as well. Pierce-Arrow was a moneymaking concern.

By this time the company had begun the changeover of the passenger car line to the new 24-valve 48-B-5 model that would go into production in June. The engine was the important change to the car. It amounted to the same 48 HP chassis with a new dual-valve engine with the same dimensions and detachable cylinder heads. The company noted that the Series 5 motor produced 40 percent more horsepower and gained 30 percent in efficiency from these changes. Maximum speed and gasoline economy had both increased by 11 percent. On the road, it was more powerful and more flexible than the Series 4, according to the company press releases and accounts from dealers. Acceleration was noticeably better. During the next 12 months the company planned to produce 1,000 of the new 48s. Prices of its 19 models ranged from $6,400 to $8,200, and a beautiful 41-page catalogue was issued, with scenic pastel plates and detailed engravings of the cars and their features. The Great War clearly was having two effects on Pierce-Arrow cars: fewer of them were going to be made, and they would be markedly more expensive. Of course, everyone already noticed the steady wartime inflation (known at the time as the HCL or "high cost of living"). In addition to the 48-B-5, the company produced a very few, perhaps less than a half-dozen, 24-valve experimental 66-A-5 cars, of which one still survives. Although these were company test cars, some apparently were sold to dealers where their performance was dangerously attractive, given their two-wheel brakes. Purportedly, one dealer's son was killed in a 66-A-5. Another managed to find its way into the hands of the Vanderbilt family.

Charles Sheppy, the consulting experimental engineer, who also supervised tests, announced in the May 1 issue of *The Arrow* that the plant had installed a sunken dynamometer in the plant for testing cars and trucks. It consisted of a fan "of the proper size" connected to a five-ton truck worm-drive axle with special wide wheels, anchored in a cement pit, the top of the wheels at floor height from underneath. The vehicle was driven onto the unit and anchored. As it ran, a Warner instrument showed the speed achieved. Using this apparatus,

8. War Work (1917–1918)

all adjustments could be made indoors and only the final test needed to be done on actual roads. The previous winter had been bitter in Buffalo, and this innovation would be welcomed by the testing staff. By this time, Charles Sheppy, was in charge of an extensive team of inspectors. His assistant, according to a company organization chart, dated first 1-28-18 and renewed 3-4-18 and 9-26-19, was C.B. Brooks. Foreman of inspectors was W.C. Schultze, who supervised a list of 14 inspectors spread over production and assembly spaces. Mr. Ulrich supervised passenger car dynamometer, road tests and engine test out of "Building E and sheds #1 & #2."

Inlet side of the Series 5 Dual-Valve Six Pierce-Arrow motor (courtesy Pierce-Arrow Society).

L.G. Williams supervised truck dynamometer and road tests and final truck inspection out of shed #1, #2 & #3. L.R. Loder watched body fitting-painting, final assembly-trimming of passenger cars in Buildings G and H, 3rd and 4th floors. W. Youngert had authority in Building B over "first assembly." Truck "first assembly" was also inspected in Building B by J. Ochtman. Me.[sic] C. Mayback was the engineering inspector in the balcony of Building B covering passenger cars-small fittings "first assembly." E.G. Marquardt and B.E. Torkelson were on the third floor of Building C for engine assembly fitting. Also working on the third floor of Building C, covering engine assembly before and after lap and engine tests, was M.M. Hart, while R. Wray inspected engine assembly, carburetors, water and oil pumps, and small parts in Building C, 3rd and 4th floors. For the Transmission Department, A.F. Zimmerman covered transmission fittings and steering columns in Building C, 4th floor. S. Lee was responsible in the same place for inspecting transmissions. Up on that 4th floor, S.J. Hewitt inspected front and rear axles, "universals-hoist" in the transmission department. As production at the plant increased it required more employees, and 1918 was a high production year at Pierce-Arrow.

The annual meeting of the National Automobile Chamber of Commerce was held at its New York headquarters on Monday, June 6, and was covered in an article in the June 13 issue of *Motor Age*. Charles Clifton and all the other officers were re-elected. The board was also unchanged except for the election of H.H. Rice of Chevrolet Motor Co. to take the place of the late Colonel George Pope. Thirteen new manufacturers of motor trucks were admitted to membership, including: Acme Motor Truck Co., Cadillac, Michigan; Bethlehem Motor Corp, Allentown, Pennsylvania; Brockway Motor Truck Co., Clyde, Ohio; Diamond-T Motor Car Co., Chicago, Illinois; Dorris Motor Car Co., St. Louis, Missouri; Republic Truck Co., Alma, Michigan; Sanford Motor Truck Co., Syracuse, New York; Schacht Motor Truck Co., Cincinnati, Ohio; Service Truck Co., Wabash, Indiana; Standard Motor Truck Co., Detroit; Stewart Motor Corp., Buffalo, New York; United Motors Co., Grand Rapids, Michigan; and Ward Motor Vehicle Co., Mount Vernon, New York. The production of motor trucks, it was noted, had increased 100 percent over the previous six months compared to that period in 1917. Standardization of rear axle widths for trucks, return loads issues, and establishment of rural express routes were also discussed. The Traffic Committee estimated in its report that the anticipated 25 percent increase in railroad freight rates would raise the cost of transportation by $6 million on automobile industry shipments equal to those of 1917. The cost of a standard 36 ft. boxcar load would increase $19.25 between Detroit and New York and $77.50 between Detroit and San Francisco. Doubtless aware of this, some companies had devised new loading techniques that increased the capacity of such cars for their shipments by 50 to 100 percent. The earlier plan to accept shipments of motors only in boxes had, thankfully, been abandoned due to protests, and motors could now be shipped in "racked" cars. Proposed consolidation of separate Western, Eastern, and Southern railroad classifications into a single standard was expected to ease some shipping problems as well. Some reluctance was evident in the sense of the meeting that participation in the Chicago truck and tractor show, scheduled for the fall, be left up to individual members. Many seemed to feel the time was not opportune for such a show. Perhaps the most important decision by the Chamber, however, was to form a committee that would "delve deeply into standardization and conservation matters with a view to co-operating more closely with the Government in saving materials." This was certainly a useful way to head off suggestions that passenger car production used materials that were "in great demand for war work." This especially included chromium, steel, and tin. There being a war, the board decided it would be better "to substitute more common materials for those that are in great demand for war work." In June, the engineering department at Pierce-Arrow welcomed a new engineer into the truck department, according to *The Arrow*. He was Stanley W. Mills, who "will act in an assisting capacity to Mr. [Francis] Davis." Mills had a fine reputation, having previously worked for American Fiat in Poughkeepsie, New York, Detroit Axle and Cadillac Motor Car Co. Meanwhile, truck production was continuing under great demand, with some unexpected complications.

These complications were well covered in an address that Assistant General Manager and General Superintendent H. Kerr Thomas gave to the assembled general foremen of the plant on Monday, June 17, 1918. The address was titled "Must Meet War Conditions," and it was doubtless something of a shock to those present, because it described a whole new set of expectations that needed to be adopted to match the changed conditions prevailing at the time. At the opening, Kerr Thomas recounted how a scene he witnessed on his way to the meeting typified the situation: Being packed in the back of a Hudson touring car for shipment to Harrolds Motor Car Co. in New York City was a motor for a five-ton truck. Improvisation was the order of this day of blockaded railroads and strained motor carriage. Kerr Thomas went on to point out that changed conditions meant production at the factory had "fallen off very much." The plant was short of men, and many of the men employed were not good men. "It isn't possible to get as many men as we want and have the quality we're used to—and the situation is not going to improve," he insisted. "The old conditions are gone and they will never come back." It was Kerr Thomas' contention that, when the war was over, the whole industrial world would be bankrupt and everyone would have to do more than they ever did before. He still had good contacts in England, and he used the experience at Rolls-Royce as an illustration of this situation. Rolls officials had recently told him that at the start of the war in 1914 Rolls-Royce employed 3,000 workmen. Within the first few weeks of battle that number was down to 1,000, of whom many were of draft age. By the summer of 1918, Rolls employees totaled 8,000, building "only R-R aircraft engines. Now, a third of the work force was women, another third partially-disabled soldiers and the remainder older people. These unexpected employees were turning out engines "of the highest quality" at an enormous rate.

Kerr Thomas went on to explain that conversion to these new manufacturing circumstances involved a change in expectations about qualified employees. Where it had been reasonable to expect technical expertise on the factory floor, shortages of qualified people meant that the technical men who remained now had to be elevated to positions of "foremen, setters-up and change hands" for the less-skilled workers. "This is going on all over Europe," Kerr Thomas emphasized. "Nothing is being done the old way." They now had to assume "that the old methods, which you and I and all of us, practiced before the war are as dead as the dodo and are never coming back." Foremen would have to take more of the responsibilities, achieve closer supervision, make decisions more rapidly and build up resourcefulness on the factory floor. Steps to bring about the necessary adjustments at the plant would start with establishing a training school in order to teach basics to these new, unskilled employees. "They are going to have to be taught that the machine will set the pace, and they have got to learn to follow it in such a way that it isn't kept waiting." Attitudes at the foreman's level, too, would have to change. "In the first place," Kerr Thomas declared, foremen should "realize that you are going to have worse and worse and worse help right along. Secondly, we are going to ask you to deliver more and more and more stuff until the war ends—and after. Thirdly, how you can fit those two possibilities into one another and make them dovetail so they will be going along smoothly." He foresaw that the plant would hire mostly women amid a shortage of toolmakers. The instruction department at the plant would provide preliminary instruction, and the foremen would complete the training. This meant that "you have got to constitute yourselves as schoolmasters, and decide first what you want to teach your people and how to go about it." In conclusion, Kerr Thomas insisted the conditions meant the factory personnel "have got to make an entirely fresh start with our method of running the factory. In all probability," he then warned the foremen, "we shall have to increase the size of the factory very materially in the near future." Within three or four months Kerr Thomas anticipated the arrival of many new machines, and machinists had to be trained to use them when they arrived. His lecture to the foremen, recounted in the July 1 issue of *The Arrow*, must have had approximately the effect of a cold shower on his listeners.

Charles Clifton became president in 1918 of the Buffalo Fine Arts Academy, an organization that he had been associated with for some years and would generously support for many more. Over the years he aided the academy "by direct gifts of works of art, by gifts of moneys which were to be spent in principal, and moneys which were to be set up as an endowment for a picture fund," according to the organization.

In an article in the August 1 issue of the company magazine, the extent of the Pierce plant's electrical operations showed how a growing, modern, industrial complex functioned in the summer of 1918. Headlined "Enormous Power Consumption," the survey began by explaining that the factory utilized both "Niagara power and Pierce power" to drive various electrical motors of from ½ to 200 horse power that did work "30–50% above their rating." This was possible only because they were well-maintained by a skilled group of nine men. In addition, the blueprint machine in the Office Building had 1,600 candlepower in each lamp, fed by a generator in the basement. Factory offices were lit by arc and carbon Mazda nitrogen lamps, giving them a steady light. Working spaces were lit so as to duplicate

1919 48-B-5 Roadster, seating four (courtesy Pierce-Arrow Society).

daylight. Outside the plant, buildings, alleyways, and open yards were illuminated by 1,000-watt nitrogen and flood lamps producing 87,000 candlepower. Exits and hydrants were lit by red lamps. Alarm boxes had their numbers lit for identification. The plant had two passenger and eleven freight elevators. The First Assembly space in Building B had two three-ton cranes and one five-ton crane. There were also three yard hoists, used to lift tester's weights of two and five tons onto completed trucks being tested. They also lifted crated trucks and cars onto railroad flat cars for shipment. Some of these loads weighed seven tons. Materials loaded on and off rail cars were lifted by these hoists also.

The factory had a pneumatic tube communication system that enabled quick dispatch of work cards and reports between offices. An elaborate time-keeping system involved 55 job clocks, 76 card time recorders, 8 time stamps, and 130 wall clocks, all controlled by a master clock in the Clock Room of the Office Building basement. The master clock blew the factory whistle and rang bells in the various departments at the times the office and the factory itself opened and closed during the day. Its record of time determined the pay of hourly employees. At the switchboard, an Auto Call system used bells in the departments to alert individuals on call. The plant fire alarm system was controlled by electric switches in the Engine Room of the Power House. In the offices, buzzers and bells with push buttons called from office to office. Electric horns in the factory spaces called people from one place to another. The Japan Room had nine electric ovens to furnish even drying heat. Electric air fans and 200 electric heaters for winter helped maintain temperatures in the plant. The plant kitchen used electric grinders, cutters, and washers as well. Lunch stands used electricity, too. Altogether the plant contained 1,000 miles of cable and 12,000 lamps to provide these services.

The August 15 issue of *The Arrow* covered the Pierce-Arrow Benevolent Association Field Day, at the annual company picnic on Erie Beach the week before. A full day of games was enjoyed amid good summer weather.

8. War Work (1917–1918)

The number of employees serving directly in the war itself had already suggested that some sort of memorial for them should be considered. In the spring, a committee had been formed to plan such a memorial. It was chaired by Frank C. Brown, with S.O. Fellows, F.B. Hubbard, L.W. Henafelt, E.F. Himmele, Robert Coleman, Walter Newsome, Robert Gerlach, and Arthur E. Killinger. After some considerable discussion, a design was agreed upon and laid out by none other than Herbert M. Dawley, previously of the Art Department at Pierce-Arrow. The highly symbolic design incorporated a bronze tablet with room for inscriptions, showing a youth who "personifies the skilled automobile mechanic laying aside his tools and personal ambition, and grasping the sword of Justice which has been thrust into his hands by the figure of Liberty." The tablet, about 54 inches square, was expected to be completed early in October for mounting somewhere on the plant grounds. More than 1,000 Pierce-Arrow employees were serving at the time in the U.S. armed forces. The cost of the memorial was expected to total some $1,000, to be raised by popular subscription among Pierce-Arrow employees in amounts not to exceed 20¢ per subscriber. Dawley was described as "particularly fitted for this work, not only because of his artistic sense, but because his long association with Pierce-Arrow men and methods enabled him to catch the spirit of our organization...."

Also in this issue of *The Arrow* was a letter to Walter M. Ladd of the company from Tom McArtney, dated March 27, 1918, from Harbin, Manchuria, where McArtney had managed to end up after a successful dash from Petrograd to escape the violence currently sweeping

Herbert M. Dawley's sketch for the World War Memorial, 1918 (courtesy Pierce-Arrow Society).

through the collapsed Russian Empire. It was rightly headed "Tells Vivid Story." McArtney's journey had taken 22 days from Sunday, February 24. Things had become so dangerous in the capital that he was about to try to leave by sledge in the dead of winter despite lack of food and "the excited conditions among the peasants who were on the watch for any rich Russians who tried to escape from Petrograd." Good fortune intervened and he was ordered to leave by the American Consul on a train that left Petrograd just an hour and a half later. McArtney departed essentially with only the clothes on his back for a journey across European and Asian Russia to Mongolia. "I was forced," he wrote, "to leave behind most all of my personal belongings, tool chest and tools (with the exception of a few small wrenches), all factory letters and blue prints, also 'dope' that I have been collecting for years." During the long journey he and the others on the train had to be constantly on guard because "the soldiers (who were fleeing from Petrograd and the front by the thousands) and workmen and also gangs of robbers are the boss now and do just what they like." Even this was an improvement over conditions in the old Russian capital itself where unburied bodies lay in the streets and food supplies were mostly a matter of luck. Money from his pay was not obtainable except in tiny amounts due to bank restrictions. The running battles between factions striving for control of the city broke out constantly. "I have lain [on the street] for hours at a time," McArtney wrote, "afraid to move while the bullets from the machine guns passed over my head within a few feet." This was the sad end of the Pierce-Arrow supply mission to Russia, but McArtney was at last in friendly hands and on his way home.

An article in the August 15 *Automotive Industries*, datelined August 10 at Buffalo, noted, "The Pierce-Arrow Motor Car Co. has made arrangements with the Wright-Martin Aircraft Corp. whereby it will manufacture Hispano-Suiza airplane engines. These will be produced at the rate of 30 per day by Jan. 1 [1919], and it is expected that the rate of production will be increased to 50 per day by April next." This was a major displacement by "Government needs" at the Pierce-Arrow company. Hispano-Suiza was a Spanish engineering company organized in 1904 to build automobiles in Barcelona. Its greatest asset was not Damian Mateu, the capitalist who financed it (the *Hispano*), but Marc Birkigt, the engineer who was its chief designer (and the *Suiza*). After the World War started, in late 1914, Birkigt designed a 200 HP 120 mm. × 130 mm. V-8 airplane engine at the new subsidiary factory in Paris. This aircraft engine greatly impressed the French military. In the end, some 50,000 of these engines were manufactured by various companies under license for the Allies to use in a variety of combat aircraft and had an enormous impact on future engine designs. They performed beautifully but were, due to the precision required in their manufacture, challenging to make. These water-cooled engines had separate steel cylinders threaded into an aluminum head and water jacket casting, its overhead valves driven directly by a single overhead, gear-driven camshaft. In April 1917, Wright-Martin had imported French machinists to build these engines at the Simplex factory in New Brunswick, New Jersey, and had completed the first of them by August of that year. As American production of warplanes built up in advance of the expected spring offensive to end the war in 1919, Wright-Martin had purchased the General Vehicle Co. plant on Long Island where an Abner Doble-designed steam car was to have been built, converting it for aircraft construction. Wright-Martin needed another engine supplier and chose Pierce-Arrow. Ernest Hamilton, who was hired to work in the Pierce-Arrow tool design department by Mr. R.W. Appleton in 1909, recalled these war years for author Marc Ralston in 1981. The tool design department in 1918 was located in the Pierce-Arrow office building just under the cafeteria, across from chief engineer David Fergusson's office. The press of war work required some 70 employees in the drafting office. Appleton himself noted in an article in the September 15 issue of *The Arrow* that the blueprint shop between July 1, 1917, and July 1, 1918, had made 78,000 prints of new parts, 172,000 change prints, 20,000 tool draft prints, and 90,000 replacements, plant engineering and miscellaneous prints. There were also 13,000 photostats concurrently made. During the summer and fall of 1918, the factory was energetically setting up the plant to produce these Hispano-Suiza engines. This involved many new machines, rearranged and enlarged production spaces. By the middle of September, *The Arrow* even noted the razing of the factory power plant's old section to clear space for six new boilers to be installed to increase its power output.

At this time, a significant advertisement began appearing in national publications. Simple and dignified and with only text, its heading read "War and the Pierce-Arrow." It was clearly meant to alert the public to the changes that the war was bringing to the firm's operations. The heart of the text began, "The Pierce-Arrow Motor Car Company is cheerfully replacing passenger car production with war work. When we complete and sell the present limited number of Dual Valve Six cars, material for which was ordered prior to April, 1917, there will be no more until labor and steel are available without detriment to the military program." Noting that Pierce-Arrow had dropped two popular models to concentrate on one in order to rapidly divert capacity to war work, the ad concluded that "practical patriotism demands that we should now make only Pierce-Arrow trucks for essential uses and such other products as the War Department may require." The "other products" clearly referred to the airplane engine program then in the final stages of preparation.

In its October 1 issue, *The Arrow* reported that John D. Nuskoy, foreman of the Service Department, took a two-ton Pierce-Arrow truck with pneumatic tires on a quick trip from Baltimore to Buffalo in just 37 hours. "At camp Holabird," he wrote, "where thousands of army trucks were quartered, we saw Capt. Bowen, Lt. Bigelow, Gorham Clifton and Eddie Greiner." These were all men associated with Pierce-Arrow. Gorham Clifton was, of course, Charles Clifton's son.

By October the worldwide influenza epidemic had reached Buffalo, which noticed an increased absence in the workforce due to illness. At the time, "as many as one hundred were cared for at a time" in Buffalo General Hospital, "by a depleted staff and personnel and volunteers" according to author Evelyn Hawes. "Hot mustard chest plasters and foot baths, bed rest and plenty of liquids brought relief." Surgery was avoided for fear of contagion and influenza patients crowded the hospital's treatment spaces.

In the second week of the month, Pierce-Arrow was deep in the promotion of the Fourth Liberty Loan among its employees through mass meetings at the plant regardless of the epidemic. By this time nine Pierce-Arrow employees who enlisted had fallen in battle. That fact, and the difficulties American troops faced, formed the bulk of a bond selling campaign speech that George M. Graham of the sales staff gave to employees in the plant's assembly space. It was in the course of his speech that the two most recent casualties were first disclosed, as an inducement for everyone to raise their bond purchases so that the plant total could rise to $1 million, exceeding the $596,000 raised during the previous Third Liberty Loan campaign. "Make It a Million" was the motto this time. It was, Graham declared, "Our plain duty!" He pointed out the breadth of sacrifice already exacted from those at Pierce-Arrow, running from the lowest laborers to the sons of the management. Sons and sons-in-law of military age in service included those of "Colonel Clifton, Mr. May, Mr. Foss, Mr. Thomas, Mr. Guider, Mr. Sheppy, everyone...." Graham noted that the previous Liberty Loan campaigns had each been followed by battlefield successes by the American Expeditionary Force. "For the first they gave us Chateau Thierry, which stopped the Germans at the point of their most dangerous advance on Paris. The next was the Saint Mihiel Salient. For the third they gave us the victory of the Argonne Woods. Now, ladies and gentlemen, the forth loan is the greatest of all. I do not know what its dividends will be, but I'm not sure but what they may send us Berlin itself."

In the November 1 issue, *The Arrow* was able to declare that the Fourth Liberty Loan drive had indeed netted double the subscription over the Third. The impact of the flu epidemic on production, however, was alarming. Articles in the issue stressed the need for proper treatment and rest to avoid pneumonia. Such mass meetings as had been part of the Liberty Loan campaigns were being discouraged. On the war front, however, the climax of the struggle was clearly at hand. One by one, the lesser members of the Central Powers sought terms to end the fighting. As for Germany itself, public unrest and battlefield losses, evoked fears in the high command of actual Allied invasion and possible civil war such as Russia faced. Hoping that President Wilson's Fourteen Points would guide the victors to an understanding peace, a new German government reached an agreement with the Allies for an Armistice that began at 11:00 a.m., November 11, 1918: "the Eleventh Hour of the Eleventh Day of the Eleventh Month."

News of the armistice arrived in Buffalo unanticipated. The length and uncertainty of the struggle that began four years before made its end seem especially sudden. It was also warmly received. At Pierce-Arrow Ernest Hamilton, who with his crew had been working overtime, evenings, and weekends to retool for airplane engine production to begin, remembered that draftsman Willie DeChend picked up his piccolo at the news, playing "Yankee Doodle." He then "marched through the shop with many men falling into line behind, and out the door and down to Buffalo. Some didn't come back to work for several days!" Coverage of the event in *The Arrow* was headed "Pierce-Arrow Opens Buffalo's Peace Celebration Amid Cheers." Crowds of celebrants marched excitedly down Main Street to Niagara Square.

The transition back to a peacetime basis proved to be every bit as complicated for the Pierce-Arrow company as the conversion to war work had been. To begin with, the elaborate facilities to produce Hispano-Suiza airplane engines had to be dismantled before a single engine had been completed. That meant a project which consumed some five months of preparation, according to Ernest Hamilton, never paid off. Its end was marked by a tiny entry in the December 11 issue of *The Arrow* that read, "In sad but loving memory of the Aircraft Department. Gone but not forgotten by those that loved it best." By contrast, production of Pierce-Arrow trucks continued apace. Over 3,500 of models R8 and X4 were yet to be completed. In addition, the company had an area on the third floor of Building I, "just below the Tin Shop," where they assembled United States Standardized "Liberty" or Class B military trucks from parts supplied from "[s]ome two hundred purveyors of manufactured parts," according to the October 15 issue of *The Arrow*. These were assembled at the rate of about eight per workday, on average, and had been for "the past five or six months," according to the story. The article, entitled "Liberty Trucks," presented an extensive look into the divisions and supervision of truck production at Pierce-Arrow. H. Kerr Thomas was assistant general manager supervising the whole truck department. George W. Cooke was general superintendent, and Robert Gerlach superintendent of assembling. The Liberty trucks had their own Assembly Department, managed by Clarence Fields and assisted by the floor inspectors, George McDermand and George Kraetz. Bench work was in the charge of Elmer Hornburkle, and Robert McLernon was stock clerk. The truck operations turned out some 7,450 Pierce-Arrow trucks and another 700 to 900 Liberty Trucks in 1918. Stocks of parts were piled in almost every vacant space in and around the 45-acre plant. The article mentioned that a space called "Liberty Park" had been set up outside "next to Camp Dix" to store larger Liberty Truck assemblies. The names copied those of important military installations. "Sills and frames," the article went on, "are stored next to the Pierce-Arrow Skating Rink which used to be the Grand Canal during the Pan-American Exposition." With war's end, much of this activity declined rapidly. Still, David Fergusson recorded in his dairy on December 24, "Received a bonus from Mr. May of $2,250."

The uncertainties that dogged the transition from war to a peace basis had to be worked out with dispatch. A week after the armistice went into effect, members of the NACC met in Washington, D.C., Col. Clifton chairing. Actual representatives were sent by "practically every large motor car company," according to the November 21 issue of *Automotive Industries*. This included Packard, Pierce-Arrow, Locomobile, Paige-Detroit, Studebaker, Cadillac, Buick, Chevrolet, Chalmers, Peerless, Overland, Cole, Hudson, Hupmobile, Maxwell, Kissel, Reo, Mitchell, Briscoe, Liberty, Premier, Lexington, Oldsmobile, and Stutz. The Chamber was said to represent more than 100 makers. Ford Motor Company was still not among them.

One effect of war production was to reduce automobile output by half in 1918. The first government curtailment had been 30 percent in March. This was followed by a 50 percent cut in July. Even truck production was curtailed to 1917 levels during the last half of the year. The industry now hoped to return to a peace basis by May 1920. Casualties of the war in 1918 were the National Automobile shows mounted by the NACC in New York City and Chicago. At this meeting, the manufacturers determined they could not prepare a suitable show in the time remaining before January that would "do justice to the industry and fittingly celebrate the military victory." Dealer sentiment seemed to be that local shows could be held, according to President Vesper of the National Automobile Dealers Association.

The larger concern was over government policies regarding the cancellation of wartime contracts and reduction of "possible labor troubles." That these should be decided with fullest cooperation suggested that a committee of manufacturers meet with Chairman Bernard M. Baruch of the War Industries Board to advise about such matters. Automobile makers' representatives named were "Hugh Chalmers (Chalmers); Alvan Macauley (Packard); H.B. Jewett (Paige-Detroit); Roy D. Chapin (Hudson); Charles Clifton (Pierce-Arrow). Motor truck makers representatives were George M. Graham (Pierce-Arrow); Windsor White (White); L.H. Boylston (Service); S.M. Williams (Garford) and A.C. Burch (Clydsdale)." It was the announced intent of the government to cancel only contracts where the vehicles were not in actual production. At the time of the meeting, orders for some 81,000 trucks and other vehicles had been cancelled, and orders for trucks in actual production had been reduced by about 50 percent. Pierce-Arrow had an order for 1,100 2-ton trucks reduced to 700. The contracts for 25,000 "Liberty Trucks" together with major service units had been cancelled altogether. Windsor White complained that an order for 8,000 "A" trucks placed with White had been cancelled with 1,000 delivered and another 1,000 in production. The makers stressed that as much as possible, enough orders should remain to keep workers at the plants employed until peacetime production could begin. It was necessary for the American Expeditionary Force to commandeer German trucks for occupation duty, so some additional trucks were still needed even though the war itself was over. It was agreed that trucks shipped abroad would not be returned but sold abroad. Those that remained useful in the U.S. would be used by the Post Office. An arrangement between the War Department, War Industries Board and the U.S. Employment Service had successfully managed labor problems during the war and had recently shown positive results with displaced airplane workers in Dayton, Ohio. This was an indication that employment could be found for released workers. Resolutions of thanks from the Chamber to Hugh Chalmers and C.C. Hanch of Studebaker were passed for their wartime work on behalf of both the government and the industry. While not all the current issues had been resolved, everyone seemed pleased that the policy was to promote cooperation as a way to foster "a quick return to commercial practice."

The war was over, but the peace had yet to be engineered. On December 4, President Wilson left New York on the *S.S. George Washington* to negotiate settlement of the World War at the historic peace conference in Paris.

In Buffalo, the Pierce-Arrow company faced a greatly altered postwar reality.

~ 9 ~

Esprit de Corps (Early 1919)

> Col. Clifton always felt that his financial success was largely happenstance. As such, he felt that money in his hands was a public trust, to be spread about in benefactions. He was in modest circumstances before Pierce-Arrow made him wealthy. He was a freight clerk on the Erie. Then he was in the coal business. That went bad when he was a middle-aged man. He looked around for a couple of years, to find something to do when Pierce and Birge took him into the company down on Hanover Street. His first job was assistant treasurer—just a clerkship.
> —Hilton Hornaday, *Buffalo Evening News*, May 7, 1938

As 1919 began, Charles Clifton occupied a position of extensive power in his native city, as well as in the second largest industry in the country. Beside the commercial enterprises he led, Clifton was president of the Buffalo Fine Arts Academy and the Buffalo General Hospital Board of Trustees and had been president of the Allied War Relief of Buffalo and of the Buffalo Chapter of the Fatherless Children of France, for which he was made a *Chevalier* in the French Legion of Honor. Clifton was a director of the Marine Trust Company, a leading Buffalo Bank, and was an active member of the Buffalo Club, Buffalo Country Club, and the Saturn Club in Buffalo, the Engineers' Club of New York City and the Detroit Athletic Club. He was also widely recognized as a patron of the arts. The stresses of war had dislocated all those entities in important ways. Readjustment to peacetime conditions was only beginning, and all Clifton's skills would be tested while negotiating its challenges.

Because the NACC did not mount the usual New York and Chicago automobile shows in 1919 due to wartime limitations, such shows as were held were sponsored locally, with varying success. The Pierce-Arrow Motor Car Co. at this time was still completing wartime orders for 1,500 Model R-9 and 850 X-2 trucks. The cancellation of the Hispano-Suiza aircraft engine program freed more space to assemble the last of the 1,000 48-B-5 cars scheduled for the 1919 season. Engineering Department discussions at the beginning of 1919 showed a concentration on developing the forthcoming models of Pierce-Arrow automobiles, while trying to assimilate the advances in manufacturing and production technology developed across the industry during the war. At the engineering discussion of Tuesday, January 7, David Fergusson reviewed plans for improved Pierce-Arrows in 1920. Francis Davis submitted detail drawings of a $4\frac{1}{2} \times 6\frac{3}{4}$ inch overhead valve truck engine for consideration as well. Passenger car improvements were based on the Series 5, referred to during the meeting as the "present

No. 19 car": cylinders were improved, a lower bevel gear ratio adopted and free-wheel second and third speed gears for easier shifting incorporated, In addition, a further improved model was envisioned, based on the "No. 57 car which is No. 19 car lengthened to take our 48-B-6 engine." This second experimental model incorporated *en bloc* cylinders, "possibly enlarged to 4½ × 6 instead of 4½ × 5½—Delco ignition and possibly Delco generator and starting motor." Free wheel transmission and "improved location for the gear and hand brake levers," were also considered. The engineers decided to evaluate using "Alemite grease pump and connections" to replace the current chassis grease cups, along with other detail changes. Developing these features would take months in some cases.

The impact of war work was still felt. Pierce-Arrow was proud to promise employees who left for the war that "Your Job Is Permanent," as the advertising cards in the trolley cars of the International Railway said. Pierce seemed confident that the postwar demand for trucks would be especially strong. Employee publication *The Arrow* printed articles welcoming those who were returning. Pierce-Arrow's wartime experience mirrored that of many other automakers. *Automotive Industries* published an account about the industry's role in its January 30 issue titled "Automotive Industry of Great Aid in Winning War." C.C. Hanch, heading the Automotive Products Section of the War Industries Board, had released a report on its activities from Washington that noted some of the achievements by the industry during the conflict. Details of the limits on automobile manufacture put into place back in 1918 made interesting reading: "During the last 6 months of 1918, when reduction of passenger cars was limited to 50 per cent of 1917," read his report, "manufacturers requested permits for production of 295,468 cars, which was allowed." A total of 186,178 cars were assembled during the third quarter; 109,290 were scheduled the last quarter. More important from a wartime standpoint were the billion dollars' worth of trucks built for the military. Cooperation between the government and the automotive industry through the Automotive Products Section was seen as a great success.

Ted Selman, Pierce-Arrow's service representative with the French army, visited the factory early that spring. At the time, Selman believed that the Pierce operation in France was largely a costly, non-productive service despite the high regard in which French officials held their vehicles. Selman himself was the principal reason that their favorable opinion was sustained. He had worked very determinedly to deliver good service. Learning that the cars had been withdrawn from French Army service on orders of the transportation officer at the *Grande Quartier Generale*, who considered their demountable rims unsafe, Selman had obtained permission to discuss the matter at GQG. While the matter was being hashed out, who should appear but Marshal Foch, the supreme Allied commander, who liked his Pierce but expressed disappointment that they were "bad cars." In the heat of the argument and knowing such problems had never been encountered in service, Selman suggested that the cars be tested with partially deflated and even flat tires, over the worst roads at hand. The Marshal ordered the transportation officer to accept whatever findings the tests uncovered. Selman did the driving for the test, in the process scaring "the wits out of that [officer] chap (as well as myself)." Nothing else happened, except the Pierce-Arrows went back on the road. The Marshal then asked Selman to drive him to Paris and back. Selman found Foch "an extremely kind, very old, gentleman, who delighted in such things as the lovely countryside and the delectable lunch whipped up for him, his staff officers and me—amid wild confusion (occasioned by his unexpected presence) at a restaurant along the way." While in France, Selman was sometimes summoned by opera diva Mary Garden to her home in Monte Carlo "to attend to the ailments of her Pierce-Arrow." The car was likely the one that was first to sport an Archer radiator ornament, designed by Herbert Dawley at Miss Garden's request, and fashioned of sterling silver. Since Robert D. Garden, the singer's father, owned the New York Pierce-Arrow agency, the factory was always anxious that she be pleased. Selman observed that the opera singer was always accompanied by one or another young Frenchman on her travels.

Selman was only the best-known success story for Pierce-Arrow in the export market. Other successes had been made by Tom McCartney in Russia, George Schuster in China, W.J. Fox in the Balkans, and Faye W. Hillbert in Spain. Successes they had turned company attention to them and the markets they had served. While in Buffalo, Ted Selman was a celebrity, treated to a dinner in the Club Dining Room at the factory. Lawrence Corcoran, the new passenger car sales manager, was toastmaster. Expanding possibilities seemed to be opening up for Pierce-Arrow all over the world.

Concerns about the Engine Test Room arose during the March 4 Engineering Department meeting. Producing airplane engines during the war had demanded precision assembly and more durability in service. A letter was drafted at the meeting to alert general manager Henry May about problems with the current motor test system, expounding the advantages of adopting a newly-developed electric dynamometer motor test system. A description of shortcomings in the current system began with the letter's first sentence: "The present system is unsatisfactory—we use a fan attached to the engine flywheel to absorb the power of the engine when running." The method exhibited several failures. First, it took high speed before the fan absorbed the engine's power effectively. Second, the noise of the fan made it difficult to hear engine noises that could signal problems. Third, many engines suffered damage from being run with pistons and bearings assembled too tightly, which the tests did not expose. Last, the bad condition of the air in the Testing Room made it "impossible to get good men to stay there." As a result, the factory was finding that some 70 percent of engines installed in chassis

A Series 5 French Brougham, the apex of social *hauteur* at the time (courtesy Pierce-Arrow Society).

for final tests were being rejected. The conclusion was that the "present system is not satisfactory—it is very expensive as a great deal of unnecessary handling of engines is required." The proposed electronic system would overcome these problems while saving gasoline and water during the tests. Using electricity from the dynamos to break in engines at the beginning allowed the same dynamos later to produce "a big surplus of electric current generated that can be used in the factory." At length, the decision was made to install the new system.

The Pierce-Arrow Motor Car Co. released its annual report for 1918 on April 7, 1919, the day before its annual meeting. Its contents revealed the effects of the tumultuous year just passed on the company's finances. Net operating profit for 1918 totaled $4,273,171, as compared with $4,791,274 for the year before, according to the *Wall Street Journal*. Gross sales were up 27 percent ($41.4 million in 1918 compared to $37.5 million the previous year). Some 8,635 vehicles had been made in 1918 (1,168 passenger cars, 7,467 trucks). In 1917 2,532 cars were assembled and 5,161 trucks. The day the report was made public, Pierce-Arrow preferred stock sold for around $103 a share, the common at $46. The firm calculated that its war business in 1918 totaled some $26 million. Like the rest of the industry, Pierce-Arrow hoped to finish up its war work by the end of May so it could offer a complete line of new Pierce-Arrow cars to what it expected would be an eager market. Dual-Valve experimental cars of 38, 48 and even 66 HP sizes were undergoing tests to prepare for that happy occasion. Surviving documents from the Pierce-Arrow engineering department suggest that all these cars had T-head motors. Earlier interest in overhead valves, such as that shown by Francis Davis, apparently had not led to production designs.

In *The Arrow* of April 1, the company revealed that employment at the plant totaled 6,776, of which 769 were women. This indicated a decline of more than 1,000 employees since the height of the war the previous fall. Of those remaining, 4,224 had been employed at Pierce-Arrow for more than a year. The longest serving employee, in fact, had been with the firm since 1883. The ambitious project to enlarge and improve the factory power plant continued. *The Arrow*, in its February 15 issue, carried an article describing construction of the new concrete smoke stack that would eventually tower 220 feet above the factory floor and 165 feet above its elevated, 20 ft. square, 4½ ft. thick, reinforced concrete pad, the steel columns of which also supported the big new boilers. Later that year, photographer Charlie Estabrook would climb the stack to get a panoramic picture of the office building from its vantage point. In the same issue, the magazine described the work of the plant janitors. Fourteen were employed by day in the Administration Building alone. Two of them swept the basement and took "care of the 800 bowls [probably wash basins] there." Polishing 100 brass doorknobs along with "about 100 brass plates on office doors" and cleaning "about two hundred windows inside and out" were also among their duties.

An article at the beginning of March described the more spectacular operations in "First Assembly" that visitors especially enjoyed. Some 20,000 guests from all over the world had toured the plant during the previous two years, according to Chief Henafelt's register in the factory reception room. First Assembly activities involved "Big Electric Cranes," as the article titled them. Two were of three-ton capacity and one of five, and they lifted heavy parts for assembly up twenty-five feet and across a space of fifty feet by one hundred feet above the assembly floor. One young woman evidently wanted to ride in "that cage" attached to the crane for the operator to use. When asked why by John W. Wilson, the general foreman of First Assembly, she explained that she wanted to see if the operator used an opera glass to assist setting down accurately "one of those big engines into its bed so neatly without being up close to it." Other work by the cranes included placing rear and front axles, motors and transmissions, and heavy truck wheels on the truck frame. Frames themselves were also placed on the assembly floor by the cranes. The Pierce-Arrow style of assembly was obviously quite different from the assembly-line methods used in the Detroit factories of Ford Motor Company and other large-scale producers at the time. However, the Pierce plant still processed some 11 million pounds of materials every month in its Receiving Department, according to its foreman J.F. Burlingame, quoted in the April 1 issue. Railroad siding tracks along the north side of the plant contained space for loading and unloading about 60 cars. Materials were then carried to the appropriate testing and storage areas by a fleet of four 5-ton trucks and three 2-ton trucks. Three rebuilt passenger cars, known around the plant as "canoe wagons," were used for delivery of "hurry up orders." Within the plant, an "Electric Tractor," capable of pulling a load of 10,000 pounds, along with five large and three small electric trucks, distributed materials and assemblies for operations and inspection.

Among the amenities to which plant workers were accustomed included a lunch hour concert in the First Assembly on Tuesdays and Thursdays by the forty-member Pierce-Arrow employee band, directed by George Peck of the Inspection Department. From time to time "sing along" sessions were presented consisting of popular songs. Granger Morley directed the singing on those days.

Perhaps the most impressive event of the whole year at the Pierce-Arrow factory took place on the late afternoon of May 29, 1919, when the entire staff and work force gathered on Elmwood Avenue in front of the office building to participate in the unveiling of the bronze memorial tablet "erected by the employees of the company as a tribute to the men who answered the country's call," to quote *The Arrow* in its issue of two weeks before. The tablet was now mounted on the building's front façade. Careful instructions were given to veterans to wear their military uniform and appear "in the alley behind the main office building at 4:45 p.m." They would then march under the direction of Major S.W. Reichard, behind the Pierce-Arrow Band, to the street, where the ceremony would begin at 4:50. By previous arrangement the street was cleared of even streetcar traffic. The Buffalo *Evening News* the following day estimated that the crowd had been made up of 8,000 employees plus "several thousand relatives and friends." More than 900 soldiers and sailors in uniform took part. The dedication was attended by Mayor Buck of Buffalo and the board of councilmen, as noted in the following issue of *The Arrow*. The dignitaries were "escorted to the platform by President Clifton, Vice-President May, Second Vice-President Foss and other officials of the company." An aerial bomb announced the opening of the ceremonies. Selections by the band were followed by an invocation by Chaplain John C. Ward, introduced by George M. Graham, who presided. Graham's opening speech remembered the thirty-two Pierce-Arrow employees who died in the Great War. "No tablet," Graham remarked, "be its art ever so perfect, no music, be it ever so thrilling, no flags, flutter gloriously as they will, no throng, cheer so madly as they may, or word of eloquence, no matter how burning its import, can add to the glory of our 32." His thoughts were followed with an oration by the Rev. Henry A. Mooney of Buffalo. The 480-pound monument's sculptor, former employee, now Major, Herbert M. Dawley, was present for the dedication of the tablet, already embedded in the office building's façade. Fifty-one years later Dawley recalled for the Pierce-Arrow Society's editor, Bernard Weis, that the dedication was "A never-to-be forgotten day in my memory, for, in addition to my personal pride, it brought forth the esprit-de-corps that existed in the Pierce-Arrow Motor Car Company, from the highest to the lowest."

As summer approached, the automobile industry was thinking about the upcoming models for 1920 and the organization of the customary shows to publicize them. The *Automobile Trade Journal* for May published a story about a prospective truck show, entitled "Pulcher Heads Committee on National Truck Shows," datelined New York City, April 12. "Martin L. Pulcher, vice-president of the Federal Motor Truck Co.," the story began, "has been appointed by President Clifton of the National Automobile Chamber of Commerce, as chairman of the Motor Truck Show Committee to arrange for proposed exhibitions of motor trucks in New York and Chicago next winter during the same weeks as the national passenger car shows." The other committee members were A.J. Whipple, general sales manager of the Diamond T Motor Car Co., Chicago, and David L. Ludlum, the president of the Autocar Co., Ardmore, Pennsylvania. It was reported in the June issue of the same magazine that Clifton had selected members for the committee organizing the 1920 passenger car shows on May 5. Its members were John N. Willys, chairman, from Willys-Overland, H.G. Root of Westcott and H.M. Jewett of Paige. There would be a more customary start to next year's selling season for automobiles and trucks.

During that spring and early summer, a series of unusual articles appeared in *The Arrow*. Rather than describing operations at the Pierce-Arrow plant or news items about the employees, these articles attempted to explain to the readers some of the more complicated aspects of operating a profitable manufacturing business. One result of wartime pressures had been the development of science-based practices to improve precision and efficiency all across industry. The *Arrow* began explaining some of these practices for its workers, perhaps in hopes of building support for attempts to incorporate such innovations on the factory floor at Pierce. The first of these articles had appeared in the May 1 issue and concerned the Production Engineering Department. It was written by W.K. Gaffke, the assistant production engineer. The object was to emphasize the importance of the proper development and use of what were called "operation cards" that guided completion of the parts of an assembly to the blueprint specifications "whether they are made of leather, glass, fiber, tubing, wood, fabrics, castings of all metals, forgings, bar or sheet stock." Each such card was the product of collaboration between engineers and machinists or other workers and covered all aspects of the production of any given part. "These operations cards," Gaffke wrote, "are for the use of all employees and are accessible at all times. To obtain the best results with the least effort, consult the operation cards before starting a job. This should be done to keep up with the progress of manufacturing methods. No matter how many years the job has been done one certain way it does not signify that improvement cannot be made."

The second article in the series appeared in the June 1 issue. It was written by A.R. O'Neil, and was titled "Body Experimental: As the Types of Bodies Have Increased This Department Becomes Very Essential." The article explained the complexity involved in developing and producing Pierce-Arrow automobile body pieces. Body Experimental did all the planning for construction steps such as body mill, body file, body assembly, body trim, and body fitting, developing templates for the various body part operations. They also furnished specifications for wood parts. Templates for the Body Filing Department, for example, included maple forms for shaping the body castings "to their proper turn-unders and frames to hold these castings in position while they are being riveted." The author remarked on the success of the "new card system" used to keep records of body parts and templates. The system had "saved the company hundreds of dollars in both time and materials."

By far the most complex of the series of articles, however, appeared in the next issue of *The Arrow* on June 15. An unsigned contribution titled "Cost of Production: Reduction of Overhead Expenses Means Greater Prosperity and More People Employed," it explained in a series of examples how improved methods of production increased the profits to factory and workers by making more efficient use of "burden costs" involved in operation of the factory. This complicated idea was part of the economic concept known later as "productivity." What all these articles suggest is that Pierce-Arrow was deeply involved in improving the methods and approaches used in its plant. Some disquieting signs already had appeared. The recorded surplus for the first quarter of 1919 had totaled $567,884 or a mere $1.47 a share. While the war work had yet to be completed, it was clearly not furnishing the income Pierce-Arrow needed to cover the dividends it was expected to pay.

Meanwhile, Charles Clifton was also involved with the NACC. The annual meeting of the Chamber took place the first week in June, but coverage focused on Clifton's annual address, the text of which was released on June 16. *Automotive Industries* in its June 19 issue highlighted several aspects of his report covering the organization's activities.

An important issue the Chamber considered was a response to a suit by Locomobile against its cross-licensing agreement. The Locomobile Company and its president, Andrew L. Riker, maintained, according to the April 14 issue of *Automotive Industries*, that the agreement discouraged inventive genius and obstructed and prevented the natural development of the automobile by securing for the NACC "a virtual monopoly in and the control of the patent field of the industry, thereby increasing its power and influence therein and giving it the authority to dispose of property of incalculable value." In response, the Chamber placed the matter into the "hands of Mr. Fredrick P. Fish, who drew up the original Cross-Licensing Agreement."

Clifton noted that the agreement had been "operating successfully for four years," and was "generally looked upon as a broad piece of co-operative work, with no objection from any other source." Some 600 patents were part of the agreement at the time, while 117,000 more were in its Patent Department files, brought from Washington to the office in New York. So successful had the agreement been up to that time that it furnished the pattern for a similar cross-licensing agreement among the aircraft manufacturers as an attempt to lessen litigation there. A motion to dismiss the present suit was passed, "setting forth that the Locomobile suit should be directed against the other firms in the agreement and not against the Chamber."

To assist the time-payment sale of automobiles the NACC made a presentation to the Federal Reserve Board to "have motor cars and motor trucks classed as marketable staples and the bankers' acceptances in connection to them acceptable to the Federal Reserve Banks for rediscount, thus saving one-half to one percent." While the board decided to put the vehicles in the same class with cotton, coffee, wheat, and similar commodities, it gave a "definite statement that the ruling did not detract from the worthiness of motor cars as security." Time payment sales of automobiles would increase in importance in the future. The interactions of the NACC with other "associations in our line," as Clifton put it, were cultivated with contributions to such other entities as the AAA, the SAE, the National Industrial Conference Board, Associated Advertising Clubs, the Highways Industry Foundation, the National Association of Credit Men and a $700 membership in the U.S. Chamber of Commerce. The NACC also cooperatively worked with "a score or more of other organizations, all having interest in the making, selling or using of motor cars."

Several legislative issues were part of the Chamber's concern because they affected the six million owners of motor vehicles. Especially threatening in its view was "singling out of our industry for taxes not placed on other users of the highway." Approving increased registration fees "when the money is put on roads," and "limitations as to weights and sizes of vehicles for use on the road, together with proper sizes and tires and speeds," the chamber was also agreeable to "taxes not in excess of 25¢ per horsepower and 25¢ per hundred pounds in weight." It also willingly supplied assistance, literature, and experts for legislators in the states, but no financial contributions for road construction. Every year the activities of the organization had grown as the automobile industry had done. In its account of the meeting, the July issue of the *Automobile Trade Journal* summarized Clifton's assessment that, while production in the industry was, as yet, "far from normal," it was able to "supply the needs of the nation with its regular lines" more successfully than any other industry that had converted so much capacity to war work. Membership in the organization had reached 117 members, and "finances are in excellent condition." He did note problems experienced with the quality of the gasoline available at the time, adding that "due notice will be given so such changes as may be contemplated in the fuels they are able to supply." A major proportion of the Chamber's work during the next year, according to Clifton, "will be in connection with the manufacture, sale and use of trucks."

Deliveries of the new Pierce-Arrow models for 1920 began in June. As one catalogue for the year put it, "The interval between the signing of the armistice and the present time has enabled us to get into production in both the 38 H.P. and 48 H.P. models. Each car will carry the new dual valve six motor, which was introduced to the public in July 1918." Indeed, the new Model 48s were quite similar to those of the year before. The engine castings had been beefed up, and some changes calculated to make the cars easier to drive had been incorporated, but for the most part they were alike, even in appearance. Only two new body styles had been added among the 32 offered. Each of the two was a glimpse into the way Pierce-Arrow foresaw the future. One was a four-passenger sedan on the smaller model chassis, the other a six-passenger touring car on the larger. At this time, the designers believed that the width of rear seats for three disturbed the flow of body lines and were attempting to shrink tonneau width. In addition, the little sedan displayed a new approach to an owner driven closed car. Rather than removing the partition from a chauffeur driven formal car, stretching the left front door and adding a longer side glass in front, this new sedan had four doors each with window lifts and a more compact body length, in line with current styles. Even in Pierce-Arrow's rarefied market, informality was entering closed car offerings.

Two noticeable mechanical changes had been incorporated also. Rather than the previous dual ignition with distributor and magneto, its ignition system used dual distributors, developed in collaboration with the Delco Company. This followed the practice used in the Liberty airplane motor. The instrument, asserted Pierce-Arrow, "represents a perfection not yet attained in any similar device." Indeed, driving ease had noticeably increased, with much less need to reset the spark lever. In addition, the overrunning gears in second and third speeds of the transmission improved the ease of shifting at speed, without the need to double clutch. This ease, admittedly, was at the sacrifice of engine braking in the intermediate gears.

9. Esprit de Corps (Early 1919)

The superiorities already seen in the earlier Series 5 were apparent also in this new line. The 48 HP cars represented the fifty-first model developed at Pierce and was dubbed Series 51. (The Engineering Department still referred to these new models as Series 6.) In parallel, the 38 HP was labeled Series 31. For reasons of economy or, perhaps, time, the usual lavish sales brochures did not accompany this lineup of cars into the market. Simple, smaller and rather plain booklets with photographs of the cars were used instead. Magazine advertising, however, continued the previous tradition of full-color artists' illustrations in large format and compact text copy.

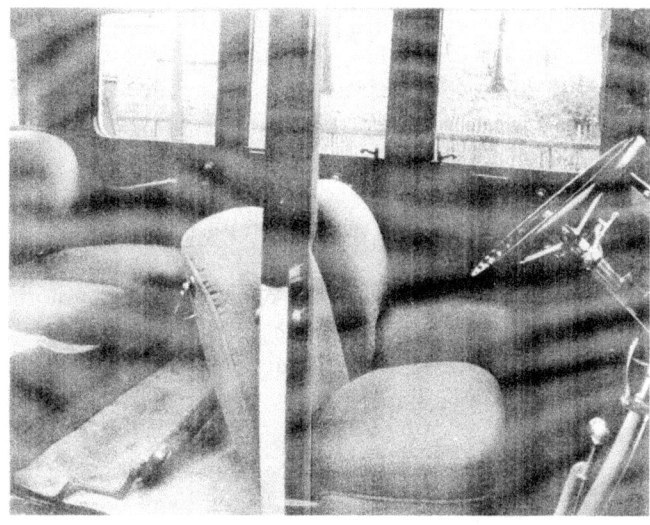

The first Pierce-Arrow four door sedan interior on a 1920 Series 31 (courtesy Pierce-Arrow Society).

The first postwar Pierce-Arrow offerings were now on the market. Accordingly, 48 HP Car Number 511121, the 121st built, was delivered to President Wilson under the ongoing lease agreement with the government. On July 9, 1919, this Vestibule Suburban, probably wearing its alternative touring car body, met President and Mrs. Wilson at Washington Union Station to return them from the recently completed Versailles Peace Conference to the White House. Despite the evidence of continuity, however, postwar complications were already engulfing Pierce.

The Pierce-Arrow Motor Car Co. had always taken pride in the contribution it made to the life of the growing city of Buffalo. Any acknowledgment of its superiority in product and organization was assumed to be an honor to the city as well. Its reputation there was jealously cultivated. So it was a particular point of pride when on June 20, 1919, the Buffalo *Times* ran what the company considered a "tribute" to the way the "Company Promotes Health and Happiness of Workers." The article began with an acknowledgment that "it seems a difficult matter to reach every one of the more than 9,000 employees," but that the company enjoyed "marked success." The award of the highest rating by the New York State Compensation Insurance Board was seen as "the highest possible commendation of the methods employed to protect the health and lives of its workers." Within the factory, the lighting system provided "almost daylight" with a million panes of glass; a "nearly ideal ventilation system" supplied pure air, thorough, effective, sanitation methods. Safety within the plant was overseen by a safety department that systematically inspected machine guards to protect workers from injury and first aid rooms to immediately dress injuries, avoiding contamination. "Every employee," the article noted, "is provided with free individual cakes of soap, individual towels and an individual washbowl with hot and cold water." Well-ventilated individual lockers were provided as well as lunch counters around the plant to offer food and refreshments. A special dining room was available for the many women employed in the business offices. A steam laundry washed the table linen, napkins, and "thousands of towels" daily. The Pierce-Arrow Employees' Benevolent Association, which had assisted employees for many years, was also mentioned as an important part of the company's welfare work, along with various sports leagues and *The Arrow*, the company's bi-monthly magazine. The whole organization was gratified by this local attention and publicized it widely.

This year the Charles Clifton Fund was established at the Buffalo Fine Arts Academy, of which the Colonel was president. He initiated it with a gift of securities valued at $100,000, the income from which was to be used for the purchase of pictures. "By means of this income," the Academy wrote, "the Academy has been and will be enabled to add to its collections periodically."

While this accolade was being published, unforeseen activity was seen in the trading of Pierce-Arrow shares in the stock market. Rumors explaining this trend were reported in the press. Among them was the suggestion that the Pierce-Arrow Company was about to be sold. Col. Clifton and Treasurer Walter C. Wrye, in fact, felt it necessary to officially deny that rumor in a *New York Times* story datelined Buffalo, June 30. "The officials declared they knew of no foundations for the report," the story insisted, "though they admitted that control of the corporation might be obtained by stock purchases on the market."

This news story marked the beginning of a period of unprecedented turmoil within the management of the Pierce-Arrow Motor Car Co. Three days later, on the eve of the Independence Day holiday, *The Wall Street Journal* carried a story headlined "Pierce-Arrow Passes Its Common Dividend." This announcement, following a directors' meeting, revealed that, while earnings for the fiscal year had been more than $5 a share on the common stock, during the remainder of the year the Pierce-Arrow board foresaw "need for a considerable amount for contemplated capital expenditures for the purpose of maintaining the high standard of quality and meeting competition." On July 1, bank loans by the company totaled $2,150,000 and cash on hand exceeded this sum. All the same, the board concluded, "net earnings cannot be expected to continue as in the past until the transition to a peace basis has been accomplished."

Clearly, the Pierce-Arrow board meeting earlier that week had been eventful. The board of directors consisted of nine members. Four of them, Clifton, Henry May, W.J. Foss and Joseph G. Dudley, the firm's attorney, were connected with the operation of the business itself. Of the other five, J.F. Alford and C.H. McCullough represented local businesses, while W.S. Cox, C.J. Schmidlapp and Frederick Strauss represented the Seligman and Chase banks of Wall Street. Precipitating the decision to pass the scheduled dividend on the common stock was doubtless the disappointing earnings for the first six months of 1919. The exact figure would eventually prove to be $3.17 per share after preferred dividends were paid, well below what had been earned in comparable periods of 1917 and 1918. Adding to their concern was the fact that Pierce-Arrow was only just completing the war work previously contracted for. There can be little doubt that anxiety was rising within the investment community about Pierce-Arrow's future. Activity in the stock market involving Pierce-Arrow shares was probably a sign of this. At this moment the postwar market for automobiles still looked strong, but Pierce-Arrow itself did not appear to be performing well. Already, once-confident truck manufacturers feared the large production during the war would reduce postwar sales, and trucks were supposed to be Pierce-Arrow's big moneymaker. July looked like it was going to be a bumpy month on Elmwood Avenue.

~ 10 ~

Finding a Peace Basis (Late 1919)

> Of a suave and benign manner, "The Colonel," as he was known among his brother executives, was invariably cool and collected: the true diplomat. Few recognized the evidences of the great authority that he wielded for he was outwardly the calm and unemotional chairman on all occasions. Few knew the fires of righteous wrath that could flare up on occasion, for he was as strict a disciplinarian of himself as he was of his associates.
> —*Automobile Topics*, 1928

In the *Wall Street Journal* for Tuesday, July 8, 1919, an impressive advertisement appeared touting the Marine Trust Company, an influential Buffalo bank. The ad was complete with a drawing of its tall office building on Main Street at Seneca. The bank's resources then totaled over $100 million, an increase of some 25 percent over those of a year before. The names of its 23 directors were listed. These included "Charles Clifton, President, Pierce-Arrow Motor Co."; George F. Rand, the bank's president; John J. Albright, builder of the Lackawanna Steel Company on Lake Erie; Jacob F. Schoellkopf, chairman of the Niagara Falls Power Co.; William H. Truesdale, president of the Delaware, Lackawanna & Western Railroad; and Walter P. Cooke, an important local capitalist who would figure significantly in Pierce-Arrow affairs as time passed. Among the remaining 18 members were other important Buffalonians. It will be no surprise, then, to find that Pierce-Arrow's bank was the Marine Trust Co.

On Wednesday morning, the *Journal* carried a startling story headlined "Pierce-Arrow Will Be Managed by Goethals & Co." The first sentence of this story revealed that the Pierce-Arrow board at some point had made a revolutionary change in the top management. It read: "The fact that John C. Jay Jr., has been elected president of the Pierce-Arrow Motor Car Corporation means that Geo. W. Goethals & Co., Inc. will manage the affairs of that corporation. Mr. Jay is a member of the Goethals firm and is regarded as one of the most experienced organizers in the country." This meant, in simple terms, that for the first time since before the incorporation of the Pierce-Arrow Motor Car Company in 1909, Charles Clifton would not be its operational head. It would later become clear that he had been moved into the more ceremonial job of board chairman, a post he would hold for the rest of his life. No enlightening details surrounding this unexpected change have survived. Did Charles Clifton want to shed some of his duties as his sixty-sixth birthday approached? Were some board members dissatisfied with the performance of his presidency, marked as it was by declining profits? Did the man stand in the way of the ambition of someone important? We will doubtless never know the answers to these questions. What is certain is that the Colonel remained from that time on still a ponderable figure in the Pierce-Arrow organization and an important minority stockholder until his death.

John C. Jay, Clifton's designated successor as president of Pierce-Arrow, was a New Yorker, "a member of the Goethals firm," according to the story. Frequently at that time, dignified advertisements appeared in the *Wall Street Journal* promoting "George W. Goethals & Co., Inc., Consulting Engineers, 40 Wall Street, New York." John C. Jay, Jr., was among the several associates listed in the ad. He had an impressive heritage. His namesake ancestor John Jay was one of the diplomats authorized by the Continental Congress to negotiate the treaty of peace with Great Britain that ended the Revolutionary War. He was the author of several of the "Federalist Papers" supporting adoption of the Constitution of the United States, and he was the first Chief Justice of the U.S. Supreme Court. The firm with which his descendant was associated was headed by the man who took over a stalled Panama Canal construction in 1907 and brought it to a successful conclusion in August 1914, just as the World War began. Later, during the war, Gen. Goethals was put in overall charge of procurement and transport of supplies for the U.S. Army. His postwar career was that of consulting engineer, a vocation he followed until his death in 1928. "It will be recalled," the *Wall Street Journal* continued, "that George W. Goethals & Co. managed the Wright-Martin Aircraft Corporation during the war." Wright-Martin, as we have seen, contracted for Pierce-Arrow to build Hispano-Suiza airplane engines for them in 1918, although the contract was cancelled before any were ever completed. It may have been this connection which led to Goethals being employed to assist, through Jay, the Pierce-Arrow management. One assumption, at least by the *Wall Street Journal*, that seemed to underlie the choice was that "new financing will be necessary." Its purpose was not stated, but the demand for Pierce-Arrow cars was supposed to be twice their current production, and demand for trucks was seen to be extending to "foreign fields as well." The passing of the dividends on the common stock was seen as "preliminary to new financing and switching of the management to the Goethals company." These moves may have been in the planning stage for some time. Further enlargement of the Pierce-Arrow plant to increase output was clearly a goal, and the change of top management indicated that other changes would follow.

At the end of the week, *The Wall Street Journal* could report "Pierce-Arrow Has Upturn," pointing out that the share price had risen 12 points in the week since the dividend was passed. The paper pointed out that there were reasons why "the Durant-du Pont interests" might be interested in Pierce-Arrow rather than Willys or Maxwell. While G.M. had a "dominating position" in the market for low-priced cars, they had no high-priced car, "that is a car selling for over $5,000, so that the acquisition of the Pierce-Arrow Co. might easily fit in well." By July 26, the paper, after consulting some of the people involved, learned that General Motors would not be interested in buying into either Pierce-Arrow or Stutz. One G.M. spokesman emphasized that point, noting, "A good deal of hand work enters into the construction of Stutz and Pierce-Arrow automobiles, and it would be impracticable to attempt to build such cars in large numbers. Quantity production necessarily means machine work entirely." Pierce-Arrow production was estimated to be "considerably less" than the yearly Stutz production of 3,000 cars. These facts were also apparent in Buffalo at the Pierce-Arrow factory.

Henry May convened a meeting of the Engineering Department on Friday, July 18, to "obtain suggestions in regard to any improvements on #71 car before ordering material for production." It is likely that this car number refers to the previous 4 × 5½–inch six-cylinder dual-valve single-bloc design, but that is not certain. Experimental chassis and engines with varying numbers and assorted components were being tested at the time. In any case, it appears that the company intended to have a new model to introduce at the usual time in the summer of 1920. The single decision the group made at this meeting seems to have been to eliminate the magneto in the upcoming model, already the case with current production. The next week, Charles Sheppy brought the group a question from "Major Gilbreth's Department" about the possibility of bolting spring hangers to the frame instead of riveting them "in order to accommodate the system of assembly which they were recommending." This shows that Pierce-Arrow had hired the Gilbreth time and motion study experts, featured in the popular memoir *Cheaper by the Dozen*, to look over assembly procedures at the plant. Perhaps this was an early part of John Jay's organizing efforts.

As these events were taking place in Buffalo, an NACC press release dated at New York City, July 17, was published in the *Automotive Industries* issue of July 24. "Charles Clifton, president, and other officers," it began, "were re-elected at the directors' meeting in Buffalo yesterday." Apparently, the NACC board still held their summer meeting in Buffalo. "Aside from Mr. Clifton, who is with the Pierce-Arrow organization," the story continued, "the officers are: First vice-president, Hugh Chalmers, Chalmers Motor Co.: second vice-president (Passenger Car Division) R.D. Chapin, Hudson Motor Car Co.; second vice-president (Motor Truck Division) Windsor T. White, White Motor Co.; secretary, C.C. Hanch, Maxwell Motor Co.; treasurer, H.H. Rice, Chevrolet Motor Co. The Cleveland Automobile Co., Cleveland, Ohio and the Holmes Automobile Co., Canton, Ohio, were elected to membership." The exact position that Charles Clifton now held at Pierce-Arrow was apparently not clear when the directors met. His impact on the operations at the NACC was, nonetheless, prominent. As seen when, in its August 7 issue, *Automotive Industries* published the membership of NACC standing committees "appointed by Charles Clifton, president of the organization, to serve during the coming year." The extent of the organization's reach is clear from the committee names: Passenger Car Show Committee, Patents, Legislative, Highways, Traffic, Electric Vehicle, Membership, Foreign Trade, Conservation, Motor Truck, Rural Motor Express, Truck Standards, Hand Book, Truck Committee on Standard Repair Parts and Service Policies.

On July 30, the *Wall Street Journal* at last revealed that "Charles Clifton has been elected chairman of the board of the Pierce-Arrow Motor Car Co., and John Jay was elected president." The company also released its second quarter earnings statement. The surplus for the period totaled $625,804 or $1.70 per share of common stock, slightly better than the preceding quarter, but still well below the year before. By now, observers noted weakness in Pierce-Arrow share prices.

Beyond doubt, the previous two weeks had been eventful at the Pierce-Arrow Motor Car Co. Turmoil is inevitable whenever long-established ways of doing things are altered, and that is what the new leadership was clearly employed to do. Changes in systems presently used at the plant to produce cars and trucks were under careful assessment. The systems in place were of long standing, in some ways dating clear back to the old George N. Pierce Co. That is because their devising was under the supervision of the general manager, Henry May, who had begun his association with Pierce as a 12-year-old errand boy in 1873 for the firm of Heintz, Pierce & Munschauer. He had left with George N. Pierce when the latter started his namesake company in 1878. May grew with the firm, taking night school courses to advance his knowledge. Over time, he rose within the company and was eventually rewarded by George N. Pierce with a partnership. He was greatly respected by everyone who worked with him. Laurence H. Gardner, the company secretary after 1896, called May "the sheet anchor" of the business: "He was the brains of the Pierce-Arrow factory," Gardner asserted. After considerable research, including a 1905 European trip with chief engineer David Fergusson, May supervised the development of the new plant on Elmwood Avenue. He had many years of experience, understood operations very thoroughly, and knew how to develop a skilled work force.

John C. Jay, Jr., had apparently been hired to introduce the most efficient methods possible at Pierce-Arrow to produce in quantity the finest vehicles possible. Beginning as an apprentice at the Pennsylvania Steel Co. after graduating from Williams College, Jay had risen through the management. Following that, he eventually became chairman of the board at the Maxwell Motor Co. a leader in production innovations. During the World War he headed the Republic Truck Co., and served on the board of the Savage Arms Co. From his own experience Jay knew modern plant operations, and the Pierce plant, built to allow flexibility of use, offered a likely place to employ them. Judging from what we know now, it is safe to assume that Henry May did not welcome this new direction. Working through the resulting conflict between the ambitious reformer and the respected general manager took some time. The outcome of the encounter began to become apparent on Tuesday, August 5, when Pierce-Arrow's general manager gave what *The Arrow* called a "Lawn Party" with refreshments at his Crescent Beach, Ontario, summer home. Guests included "100 friends of Mr. May along the Lake Shore." A "number of Pierce-Arrow department chiefs" were also recorded as attending the fete. The party "refreshments" probably included alcoholic drinks, no longer legal in the United States after the Prohibition laws had gone into effect on July 1. The Pierce-Arrow band provided music and "young people danced." As the next few weeks passed, it became quite clear that this event was what would under more usual circumstances have been considered a retirement party for Henry May. Although his actual departure from the factory would not take place for months, May probably stopped being the actual general manager at about the time of the party. He also held a sizeable investment in Pierce-Arrow stock. His secretary at the plant, Edna Forbush, retired in October, and that may well represent the effective end of May's direct involvement with the company.

At the start of 1919, the two most powerful men at the Pierce-Arrow Motor Car Co. were President Charles Clifton and Vice-President and General Manager Henry May. By September, both had been displaced to make way for new managers associated with George W. Goethals Co. The response in the case of each man illuminated his individual character. Charles Clifton quietly became chairman of the Pierce-Arrow board and served there in a very public way for his remaining years. Henry May simply retired for good and took no further part in Pierce-Arrow affairs "although the company needed him, and needed him badly in later years," according to Hilton Hornaday, writing in the Buffalo *Evening News* of May 7, 1938. May might well have reacted to the proposals to rethink operations in the plant as a repudiation of him personally because he was so largely responsible for them. Such a hurt may have proved impossible to overlook even with the passage of time. May, however, resolutely declined public comment on his old company. Indeed, he only gave a single interview on the subject for the rest of his life. Charles Clifton also had a very deep connection with the company from 1897 onward, but he seemed to accept the idea that a new approach was desirable. The fact that he served the whole industry as president of the NACC and had wide knowledge of its operations may well have given him a perspective that May did not have in his more parochial situation. Whatever the reason, these August 1919 changes marked the end of the old Pierce-Arrow Motor Car Co. as it was developed and guided by George N. Pierce, George K. Birge, and Charles Clifton.

Once Henry May stepped down, operations at the Pierce-Arrow plant were open for thorough examination, and consequences would be felt among personnel. Edward J. Weiser had already resigned as general foreman to join Hudson in Detroit. The company gave him a gold Howard watch at his retirement party. As the month of September began the scope of the changes at Pierce-Arrow began to be disclosed to the public. "John Jay Heads Pierce-Arrow" headlined one description in the first September issue of *Automotive Industries*:

Henry May in retirement (courtesy Henry May IV).

> Buffalo, NY, August 30—John C. Jay, Jr., was elected president of the Pierce-Arrow Motor Car Co. to succeed Col. Charles Clifton, chairman of the board. George W. Mixter was appointed vice-president and general manager, in place of Henry May, resigned. M.E. Forbes was elected treasurer to succeed W.C. Wrye, who resigned as secretary and treasurer. S.O. Fellows as comptroller will assist Mr. Forbes. E.C. Pearson, formerly assistant secretary was made secretary, and J.F. Guider succeeds G.W. Cooke as general superintendent.

In his careful fashion, chief engineer David Fergusson made himself a new organization chart dated September 2, 1919, with the longhand note "Pierce new management started Aug. 18, 1919." Even then, he could not keep up. On his chart, the assistant general manager under Mixter was still H. Kerr Thomas. Under that box his August departure is noted in Fergusson's tight script. These seismic changes reverberated out into the Buffalo community and beyond. Years later, Herbert Dawley told historian Maurice D. Hendry, "This new lot fired executives like Truman fired five-star generals." In the Kerr Thomas case, Dawley recalled, he was told, "We need your office." Litigation was threatened should he claim the three years left of his contract. In the end, Kerr Thomas accepted the offered settlement and departed. Hilton Hornaday, in his *Evening News* account already mentioned, declared the new officers "fired everybody right and left, including George Cooke, the last man in the world Birge, Clifton or May would have let go." On the other hand, chief engineer David Fergusson had an increase of his salary beginning the first of September to $18,000.

For the benefit of the employees at Pierce-Arrow an explanation of the August changes at the top level of the company was written by Charles Clifton on August 26, 1919, and appeared in the September 1 issue of *The Arrow*. "For over twenty years," he wrote, "I have been actively connected with the up-building and management of this Company, and during the last three years, as its President. I will continue at the head of the business, as Chairman of the Board of Directors, being succeeded as President by John C. Jay, Jr., who will as President, take over the active executive management." Clifton then proceeded to list the names of officials now at the top of the company management, together with their background and experience. Of the six officers he named as part of the management team, only half were associated with Pierce-Arrow previous to the Goethals association. "The policy of the new management," Clifton continued, "first and above all else is based on quality. The reputation of our product rests on Pierce Quality, the best in the world and this great reputation must be improved if all of us together can find a way." After noting the "great strength and marked individual ability of the Pierce-Arrow Organization," he urged study of the "problems of the business" in order to "meet the new problems of today," and indicated his willingness along with that of Jay and Mixter to discuss these concerns personally. Finally, Clifton stressed the importance of co-operation with officers and foremen as the restructuring of the company continued. "The problems arising from the World War are tremendous," he ended, "and of vast consequences to the future. We must produce and sell in order to survive. We must have the most economical and scientific production consistent with our high quality. We must also seek wide markets. To accomplish these things calls for everyone to co-operate to the limit!"

With all this change within the company, Pierce-Arrow remained the object of speculative rumors. An article in the October 11 issue of *Automotive Industries* carried the company's denial of any intent of merging with General Motors Corp. to produce a "small, medium-priced car." New president Jay explained, "The directors and officers of the Pierce-Arrow Motor Car Co. have no knowledge of any change in the control of the company, nor of the purchase on the open market of the controlling interest in this stock by any other automobile company." He also specifically denied any plans to produce a medium-priced car, stressing the company would "continue to build a line of products of the highest quality, and of the same type upon which its reputation and success has been established."

As fall slipped toward winter, and Henry May wrapped up his affairs at the factory to retire into private life, mementos of his association with Pierce-Arrow accumulated. A short article appeared in the October 15 issue of *The Arrow* that began, "When Mr. Henry May returned from a recent fishing trip, he found a very pleasant surprise in the shape of two handsome sterling silver vases, which were on the table of his office when he walked in." One of the 24-inch high vases was shown in a photograph. Engraved around the base of each was "HENRY MAY, SEPTEMBER, 1919. FROM THE EMPLOYEES OF THE PIERCE-ARROW MOTOR CAR COMPANY" in Gothic type. Along with the vases "a very handsome punch bowl" was presented to Mr. May by the Pierce-Arrow Agents' Efficiency Association. A more personal gift came from the Pierce-Arrow Employees' Benevolent Association, the factory charity of which May was the long-time head. From that appreciative organization Mr. May was presented "some very fine cigars." Amid his departure, his subordinates were also depart-

The Pierce-Arrow factory in 1920, greatly enlarged by war demand (courtesy Buffalo and Erie County Historical Society).

ing. F.H. Egan, assistant superintendent of manufacturing, resigned and headed for Hudson. Frank Brown, superintendent of the Body Division, also resigned, with uncertain prospects. The Body Division faced changes in the basic structure of Pierce-Arrow bodies. Mr. Brown at his retirement party, reported in *The Arrow*, wished "the present management the best of success in their undertaking." Brown was succeeded by his former assistant, John Squelch. The foreman of the Broach Division, Roy Mickle, was leaving. The assistant manufacturing engineer, G.C. Huff, also resigned and was replaced by a man named Cooke. Some of those departing were replaced by subordinates, others by successors who were brought in from outside for their special skills. Among the latter was C.M. Tichenor, who was named to replace Kerr Thomas as assistant general manager. Tichenor had experience in automobile production and engineering "with a number of prominent automobile concerns," according to the November 1 issue of *The Arrow*. All the same, these changes took place only at the upper levels of plant operations. The vast bulk of the work force remained.

Efforts to bring more "economical and scientific production" into the factory were now well underway. *The Arrow* would presently run a sequence of articles describing the operations of various departments around the plant, and the improvements adopted for their work. The Carpenter Shop, located on the third floor of Building J and highlighted in September, was one example. Its operations had since August 1918 filled 900 factory orders for crates, motor stands, trucks for materials transport inside the factory, desks, tables, doors, floors and other wood parts. The Tool Room on the fourth floor of Building C was written up in October. The toolmakers made production tools for nearly every factory department and had use of the famous Johansson Gauge Blocks for precision measurements. The same month, John Miller of the Metallurgical Department explained the importance of the heat treating done in Building F. On another page Albert Stettenbenz, who designed covers and title pages for company booklets, was profiled. A music enthusiast, he was known as "Stet" around the plant and his tastes are summed up by the title: "'Stet' Spurns Jazz." Another interesting profile appeared in the November 15 issue, when Charlie Brenner, who supervised shipping at the plant, recalled his long association with the company that stretched back to 1883. He remembered when the original Hanover Street plant, built as a wheel works, had burned. Operations were moved temporarily to the nearby J.T. Noye building, which was the eventual site of the Lehigh Valley passenger station. After the factory was rebuilt, Charlie recalled shipping "fifteen carloads of refrigerators to the freight house in four days." During that period of success tricycles were tried, followed by bicycles which came to be a popular product—a hundred were made a day. Sometimes Charlie worked almost until midnight preparing them for shipment. Charlie was in charge at the time of the move to the new Elmwood Avenue plant. "I received orders to sell the horses and wagons; and it was then that I was given the first four-cylinder car built by the Pierce Company. It is hard to believe, but it was only a matter of a few months ago that the motor was given to the scrap heap after having been driven approximately six hundred thousand miles or twenty times around the world."

The success Pierce-Arrow had experienced in France prompted marketing vice-president Foss to expand the Pierce-Arrow organization there. Having consulted with Ted Selman, who believed the chance for growth in the French market was unpromising, Foss appointed H.J. Sturdevant of the Rochester, New York, agency to head the French organization. *The Arrow* reported in July that Sturdevant had sold his interest in the Rochester Pierce-Arrow distributorship to his brother and left for France, having concurred in a plan to sell 1,000 trucks in France the following year. Selman remembered that Ansley W. Sawyer of Dudley, Stowe & Sawyer then went to France to set up the reorganized Pierce operation to be known as *Société Anomyme des Automobiles Pierce-Arrow*. While the operation in France was being expanded, Ted Selman was dismissed and returned to the United States.

An important step to improve the process of completing Pierce-Arrow engines was announced in an *Automotive Industries* article datelined Buffalo, NY, November 19: "The Pierce-Arrow Motor Car Co. has completed the installation of an extensive electric test system for its passenger-car and motor-truck engines. The installation includes a large number of electric block test stands for lapping-in and 'firing' and a set of five individual silent rooms, each containing an electric cradle dynamometer, where the finish tests are run. By the method of testing used a large amount of electrical energy will be saved for utilization in the shop system." The electric equipment, including rotary converter and electric hoists, was built and installed by the Sprague Electric Works. This system, located on the third floor of Building C, was in use from then on to assemble and test new motors. There would be no more bad air and noise to distract testers.

Another advance in method, this time in the selling of trucks, was announced in November. Francis W. Davis had left his position as assistant chief engineer of the Truck Department to become "Consulting Truck Engineer." His new position made good use of Davis' years of practical experience in design, manufacture, sale and operation of Pierce-Arrow trucks. He would be available to agents and owners as well as the factory in solving specific problems involving trucks, "with a view to broadening the field of truck operation," according to *The Arrow* of December 1.

Still considered a leader in the industry, the plant had been visited by over 12,000 people from all over the world during 1919. Among them were King Albert and Queen Elizabeth of Belgium. A considerable celebration was mounted by the city for their October visit in Buffalo, and a Pierce-Arrow transported them. The king's leadership during the Great War had made him a hero.

During this eventful year, Pierce-Arrow had launched its postwar line of cars and trucks and begun to reorganize its operations to take advantage of improvements discovered in the rush to improve production during the conflict. The company's recovery from the impact of the Great War was under way, but by no means complete.

~ 11 ~

Toward Quantity and Profit (1920)

> [George H.] Day and Charles Clifton, president of the A.L.A.M., were in the lobby of a Detroit hotel when [Henry] Ford and [James] Couzens entered. All four were startled when Ford put out a hand and the enemies chatted until he asked, "How'd you like to look over our plant?"
>
> "We'd be delighted," responded Day and Clifton, and the four, entering a Ford, whirled away to the factory.
>
> —*Motor World*, August 9, 1906

The first national automobile show of the postwar era opened amid great excitement at two o'clock Saturday afternoon, January 3, 1920, in the Grand Central Palace in New York City. Simultaneously a motor truck show opened in the Eighth Coast Armory in the Bronx at 194th Street and Jerome Avenue. Eighty-four makes of automobiles were on display in the Palace, according to the *New York Times* story that appeared the next morning. Of those eighty-four, the Milburn was an electric and the Stanley was steam-powered. "In addition to these cars," the story went on, "the Lafayette, the first brand-new 1920 creation, will be exhibited in the lobby of the Hotel Commodore." Coverage of the show emphasized the eagerness of the various manufactures to display their post-war models. However, the ones on the floor showed little change from those marketed the year before. This was certainly the case with Pierce-Arrow, and the company apparently prepared no special show models. As usual, a number of upper-level executives were in attendance at the Pierce-Arrow space near the front entrance. Charles Clifton may well have been among them. He certainly was among the officers of the National Automobile Chamber of Commerce, whose banquet was held the following Tuesday. The *Times* was impressed by the dominance of six-cylinder models at the show. The number of makes offering a six, already the most common engine configuration, had grown by 20 percent over 1919. Closed cars were also more popular than ever before, a sign that automobiles were more frequently used in winter. Body styling was not much changed from 1919. The most common characteristic was that the height of the hood was customarily the same height as that of the beltline of the touring car body, showing a single unifying highlight that ran from the radiator all the way to the rear of the car. Prices had risen noticeably for 1920, just as had the prices of everything else. This was another result of the war. The price of the least complicated Pierce-Arrow touring car on the 38 HP chassis, for instance, was now a whopping $7,250 at the factory. The 48 HP seven-passenger touring car of the type that had listed for $5,000 in 1915 now cost $7,750. The Vestibule Suburban model like the White House car was all the way up to $9,450. At the other end of the price pyramid, a new Model T Ford touring listed at $525. The Ford, of course, was not to be seen at this NACC event.

The New York Auto Show would continue for a week and was the locus for meetings and parties that made it the signal event of the whole automobile industry. Just weeks prior to the show, the Automobile Salon had been held at the Hotel Astor off Times Square. This earlier show was held for makers of custom automobile bodies to exhibit their wares to the public. Members of the NACC were not allowed to display their cars at the Salon, but many cars built by them carried custom bodies and were displayed. The Salon would become very important for the industry and Pierce-Arrow as the new decade wore on, especially after it moved to the second-floor ballroom of the Hotel Commodore in the fall of 1920. Pierce-Arrows shown at the Salon became the most expensive, exclusive, and spectacular to be seen.

The Annual Banquet of the National Automobile Chamber of Commerce took place on the evening of January 6 at the Commodore Hotel and was covered in the *Automobile Trade Journal* for February. They described the occasion as a "banner night" for the members present and the largest ever held. The 800 guests seemed excited to see the revival of the traditional activities around the New York show. At the speaker's table Col. Clifton presided, "in his usual kindly manner," the article noted, and introduced George M. Graham, the orator for the evening, and he "held the audience entranced by his wonderful flow of wit, humor and hard facts concerning the industry." Also at the head table were such luminaries as Alvan

1920 Series 51 6-passenger touring car, its sides sportingly low (courtesy Pierce-Arrow Society).

Macauley of Packard, R.E. Olds of Reo, war ace Eddie Rickenbacker, John N. Willys of Willys Overland, Roy D. Chapin of Hudson and F.W.A. Vesper, president of the National Automobile Dealers Association. The burlesque, another tradition, was presented at the end of the evening, billed as the "Twentieth Annual Musical Skid." This takeoff of the industry had a set that mimicked the Maxfield Parrish painting of King Cole's Court in the Hotel Knickerbocker and what General Manager Alfred Reeves described as "twenty-one rotten actors." The *Trade Journal* described the "usual hits in regard to the country going dry, but the real feature of the evening was the awarding of certain prizes to Col. Clifton, C.C. Hanch, and D.D. Dort by the Chancellor of the Court, alias Alfred Reeves."

Back in Buffalo at the Pierce-Arrow plant, employees were noting changes and adapting to them. The January issue of *The Arrow* boasted a new editor, George E. Morgan, a revamped format and the reduction to a single issue per month. Covering the entire first page and part of the second was a lengthy dissertation entitled "President Jay Tells How Each Has Task to Share in Company's 1920 Prosperity." This opening was expanded in a subtext below which noted the chief executive's thesis that the members of the company family could prosper only if the company prospered and that, to meet the competition, all had to join in efforts to increase production and eliminate waste and duplication. From now on there would be no more ambitious talk about enlarging the plant, quite the reverse, in fact. John C. Jay's text itself began with a summary of the history of the Pierce-Arrow enterprise extending from its beginnings with George N. Pierce himself nearly a half century before. The crux of the argument was built around the postwar conditions facing the company. "Today, therefore," Jay argued, "our problems are those growing out of the war. We have a plant much larger than is needed for our normal production. The costs of everything have gone up forcing us to increase our own selling price. We have had to practice rigid economy. The dividend on our Common Stock has been suspended; our force has been reduced; our night shift eliminated. Wherever possible, waste, lost motion and duplication is being eradicated. These things are necessary to enable us to save money." More importantly, Jay continued, "only by greater output can we fill our surplus buildings, keep everyone employed, expand our business and show the healthy growth that we need so that we all may prosper." The conclusion of Jay's argument was that to accomplish these results it would be necessary to make a better arrangement of machinery "and more of it," improve routing of materials within the shop, practice "intelligent" purchasing and follow-up for material, provide a good system for accounting, and conduct wise engineering and forceful selling. "Most of all," he wrote, "a determination on the part of all of us to PULL TOGETHER." It is perhaps an insight into the then current state of affairs on the plant floor to note that an article about plant safety on the magazine's second page stressed the need to keep plant work space aisles clear. "Aisles," the admonition ran, "must not be blocked or obstructed in anyway [*sic*]. Safety requires safe walkways." Pictures of the newly completed factory Power House were printed in the same issue. It was the final accomplishment of wartime factory enlargement.

On the sales front, the company was touting the response of the new Dual-Valve models on the road. Ignition and transmission changes made driving the cars much less complicated, and the increased power could be applied much more quickly than ever before. "The Pierce-Arrow is a car that can be driven with a facile hand," the company wrote in one newspaper advertisement during the New York show. "No brute force is needed to start, guide or stop it; boundless power is in leash waiting the word to be off, but checked, changed or stopped with equal ease." It may have been during a demonstration of those responses that an important Pierce-Arrow salesman at the Harrolds Motor Car Co. was killed in an accident on Fort George Hill in New York City as reported in the January 15 *Automotive Industries*. Robert C. Reid, the 44-year-old secretary of the agency, was driving two passengers down the steep hill toward Dykman Street when he turned sharply to avoid a stalled car ahead of him. The resulting skid caused his car to topple over a 25 ft. embankment. His two passengers, one of whom was the St. Louis Pierce-Arrow agent Sam Breadon, managed to jump out successfully, but the car landed on Reid and killed him. Mr. Reid was a very popular figure, not only in New York City, but at the factory in Buffalo, where he commonly penned articles on truck salesmanship for *The Pierce-Arrow Salesman*. News stories of his death appeared in the next day's papers on Monday, January 12. The auto show had just ended that weekend.

As the systems of the Pierce-Arrow plant were undergoing careful revision, a Motor Transportation Department to direct the fleet of trucks serving productive departments of the plant had been organized. According to an article in the same issue of *The Arrow* as Jay's editorial, its headquarters were "in the end of building D on street 3." From that point it dispatched the 18 large Pierce-Arrow trucks and 12 "small cars" that moved about one-third of the six million pounds of material which entered the plant each month. They also transported outgoing material. To coordinate this operation the department head, A.C. Ostiguy, had divided the city into three delivery zones to cover the freight stations and switching yards of some dozen steam railroads that served the city. Each day trucks left the factory yard at 7:30 in the morning and 12:30 in the afternoon with outgoing material to deliver and then receive incoming material to transport back to the factory. There was a Black Rock zone to the northwest of the plant, a City zone for those to the south and a North Elmwood-East Buffalo zone to the north and east of the plant. In addition, smaller items around the city were picked up by "a light 'skidoo' truck" leaving at 8 and 1 o'clock.

All day trucks within the plant grounds moved a variety of material from department to department, and there were nearly 300 departments at the factory, according to *The Arrow*. Paper, other office supplies and printed forms were dispatched by the Stationery Department in the Office Building basement. A factory messenger service staffed by 22 teenage boys dressed in jacket and tie distributed some five to six thousand pieces of mail sent within the plant every day. The group had two offices, one in the basement of the Office Building (Building O) and another on the first floor of the Sub-Assembly Building (Building C). Every morning, the article explains, "the boys line up for inspection, which includes 'general appearance, shoes shined and hair combed.'" Fred Weaver was the head messenger.

In January, according to *The Arrow*, the factory telephone number was changed from the previous North 1261 to Bidwell 3240.

The reorganization of the Pierce plant, surprisingly, even involved Ted Selman, whose intent upon leaving France was to look into opportunities in Detroit. He made arrangements to interview at Hudson, but had stopped at Harrolds Motor Car Co., on West 54th Street New York City, for a simple social call. Robert D. Garden, as we have seen, owned the entire Pierce-Arrow operation around the city, including the main showroom, several outlets in the suburbs and an elaborate Pierce-Arrow service garage, doubtless the best in the country, in Long Island City. This involved many millions of investment dollars, and Garden was happy to see Selman because he had concerns that the new managers at Pierce-Arrow, being relative newcomers to the industry, might not be entirely suitable to guide forward progress for the company. This important dealer was well aware that the decisions they made had a profound effect on his investment. After telling Selman of his concerns, Garden passed along a message from someone Selman described as "an old timer" at Pierce, "urging me to come and meet the new General Manager." In subsequent conversations with Col. George W. Mixter, Selman found the latter agreed with his own assessment of present affairs in France, but also felt it was management policy to leave such decisions to the active sales head, still W.J. Foss, Selman's old adversary. However, Mixter unexpectedly then asked Selman to take up a whole new effort at Pierce-Arrow by "becoming a member of his planning staff, which I did." Selman's extensive experience as assistant to H. Kerr Thomas gave him wide insight into factory operations as well as marketing and service issues in France. From his comments, it appears that Selman came to have some important influence on Mixter's plant staffing decisions.

Efforts to facilitate co-operation among the upper level of Pierce-Arrow executives were furthered by what was called a "Get Together Dinner" at the Ellicott Club downtown, attended by 512 heads of various factory departments Saturday evening, January 17, 1920. It was sponsored by "the Management," according to coverage in *The Arrow* for February. The occasion involved "merriment, music, speeches, songs, excellent menu and all around good fellowship," according to the coverage. The Speaker's table was occupied by the very upper level executives: President John C. Jay, Jr., Vice-President and General Manager Col. George W. Mixter, Vice-President in Charge of Sales W.J. Foss, Treasurer M.E. Forbes, General Sales Manager George M. Graham and General Superintendent John F. Guider. President Jay acted as toastmaster and extolled the virtues of cooperation in the process of achieving the company's goals. General Manager Mixter also spoke, advising among other things to "listen attentively to what they [the employees] say," and noting, "The man worth while is the man with a smile when everything goes dead wrong." The final speech was "a flow of wit and good natured satire" by George M. Graham. At the end of the dinner all joined in singing "The Star-Spangled Banner," the way they had sung "America" at its start. All the signs pointed toward an effort to build up support for the new management's production goals.

As February began, an article in *The Arrow* illustrated a corollary to the emphasis on increased production. Written by Vice-President in Charge of Sales W.J. Foss, himself, the piece was titled grandly "Distribution of the Pierce-Arrow Product." Its main thought was that "all in the organization assist in the marketing of our product by careful and intelligent attention to the quality of workmanship in their particular jobs." Ways to help such merchandising seemed, in Foss' article, to boil down to care and cooperation among all the levels of the firm. "I am very optimistic as to the great future in store for this Company," Foss declared. "We are constantly establishing new distributors, and during the past eighteen months forty-one new distributing points have been added to our list in this country. We are just beginning to develop our market for foreign trade," he continued. "We now have distributors in Japan, China, India, Balkan States, Spain, Portugal, Russia, Great Britain, Cuba, Mexico, Puerto Rico, Argentina and Uruguay, and we are only starting." Foss expressed his confidence that the output of the plant would more than double within the next three years, "and I know the product will be better in quality, design and workmanship than it has ever been before." It read like yet another morale builder from the new managers.

Several articles in that month's issue show some interesting aspects of automobile construction processes at the time. Among them were steps described by the Gisholt Department concerning the attachment of rear axle tubes to their differential cases. Key to the process was a tank "full of Sodium Nitrate" heated to a temperature of 800° Fahrenheit. By means of a factory crane the gear case was submerged at one side in the tank "for several minutes." With the opening enlarged .015" to .020", the case was removed and the axle tube "which is .004" larger than the bore in the case" installed and allowed to cool. After that the process was repeated for the other side. Photos showed Emanuel Jones ("one of the faithful employees of the Pierce-Arrow Motor Car Co.") performing these operations. The article notes that the general foreman of the Gisholt Department was Joseph Waldorf, assisted by Ralph Bortree, Al Obenauer, Charles Gertis, Victor Seeley, and Fred Grambow. Another doubtless "faithful employee" of the plant had retired. This was John Zangerle, oldest man in the factory at age 83, who worked in Final Assembly. He had been hired on the first of January 1887 by the old George N. Pierce Co.

The routine used to feed employees at the factory was explained in another article. Young women paid at the factory rate served at the 18 lunch counters throughout the plant. They also got a lunch for their work. Miss Anna L. Cowan, manager of the lunch counters, noted, "We are now serving one hot dish at each counter each day—at five cents an order." Another 200 officers of the company ate a table d'hote meal in the Club Lunch Room on the Administration Building's first floor.

An important improvement to increase factory output addressed both the speed and the quality of engine testing. This new system was explained in detail in *Automotive Industries* for February 19. After assembly on the third floor of Building C, engines were "run-in" with an electric motor. After that, the engine was hooked up to fuel, water, and exhaust pipes to run under its own power for several hours at different speeds and outputs. "Throughout this run the engine is under observation as to internal friction, speed and horsepower developed," the story explained. After this test, the engines were each disassembled and the parts inspected, necessary corrections made, and then reassembled. The final test was run in the "Silent Room," coupled to an electric dynamometer, which captured complete data on power output, gasoline consumption, internal friction, and other aspects. Simultaneously, the tester adjusted ignition, carburetion, and valve lift. This procedure remained in effect for many years to come.

It may well be that Charles Clifton no longer had as active a part in decision making for day-to-day operations at Pierce-Arrow as he had before. However, he unquestionably a played a powerful role as chairman of the trustees at Buffalo General Hospital. According to hospital historian Evelyn Hawes, he was convinced that the public now demanded "100 percent efficiency," a repeated Clifton descriptor at the time, and, moreover, was willing to pay for it. Feeling that it was desirable "to lessen the hospital stay of a patient," he decided that high standards in personnel "were apt to accomplish such a goal" and noted that "psychological factors," a developing field of treatment, were important. "A sweet, amiable temperament," Clifton pointed out, "is often made irritable, peevish and sometimes uncontrollable by suffering." He felt reaching these goals implied the need to invest in new facilities, a course he supported directly himself. This involved expansion of Memorial Hall with an additional two stories. Clifton envisioned that part of the space would be used for maternity care.

The next Pierce-Arrow executive explaining the efforts of the company was George W. Mixter, vice-president and general manager, who wrote an article for *The Arrow* for March entitled "Problems We Must Solve in 1920." Mixter held a crucial place in the company structure. Being the general manager meant that he made the decisions about overall operations

Series 51 French Suburban (courtesy Pierce-Arrow Society).

within the plant. Its output would be directly affected by every one of them, and the success of the enterprise would rest primarily on that. The intent of the management was to increase production by multiples, develop new production methods allowing yet higher volume and create new models that would take full advantage of the production methods developed. "We are building more passenger cars than we have ever built before," Mixter wrote. "A large number of the cars now being worked on have already been sold to customers. For next fall we will have many new designs. It is a big job to get the tools ready, and rearrange the shop for this new work. During this rearrangement you may find your own work upset. Talk to your foreman about your problems, always bearing in mind, 'the man worth while is the man with a smile when everything goes dead wrong.'"

Col. Mixter was an 1895 graduate of the Sheffield School at Yale University, who had worked for years for Deere & Company, manufacturing agricultural machinery. Eventually he was placed in charge of 12 Deere manufacturing plants and was a company vice-president. During the First World War, Mixter had served as an officer in the U.S. Army. His background impressed upon him the importance of coordinating the various efforts in a manufacturing enterprise. He began his remarks with the observation that there were "about four thousand stockholders, who have, in effect, loaned the Company the money with which to do business." Also part of the "Pierce-Arrow family" were about 7,000 employees at the plant making "about twenty-five thousand people in this city" directly dependent on the company as a source of income. Mixter clearly took the broad view of his position and encouraged such an attitude on the part of employees. "Evidently," he insisted, "the family cannot prosper unless money, men and customers all pull together. It is the job of Management to take care of all these interests, see that they do pull together, and that every one gets a square deal." He also stressed the important role *The Arrow* played by informing employees of management's intentions. In addition, Mixter's presentation furnished evidences of the stress arising from turmoil across the world as the effects of the war continued even after the peace was signed. Governments had been overthrown in Germany, Russia, the Austro-Hungarian Empire, and Turkey. George Mixter concluded his talk by urging all his readers to become familiar with the Constitution of the United States. "Each one of you," he admonished," can give to those with whom you come into contact a better understanding of some of the efforts of today to overthrow our institutions, largely through the radical agitator who is taking advantage of organized labor to bore from within and force the principles of anarchy upon the American people." The great "Red Scare" was well underway in America.

By this time, the development of new Pierce-Arrow car and truck models for the 1921 model year was nearly complete under the direction of Chief Engineer David Fergusson. The designs could properly be considered improved versions of current Pierce-Arrow vehicles, although greatly changed. While the new managers were determined to make radical changes in plant operation, they did not insist upon radical revision of the engineering staff's conceptions for future offerings. The designs were very thoroughly refined, however, and incorporated many advances. Among them was the adoption of Alemite grease fittings. These vehicles were all developed from research with engines having a $4 \times 5\frac{1}{2}$ in. bore and stroke designed for production in the reorganized plant. Features of these car and truck models were:

1. *En bloc* cylinder castings
2. T-Head motors
3. Dual enclosed valves, inclined to the head
4. Full-pressure lubrication from cast-in delivery pipes
5. Dual ignition
6. Heated intake air passed through cylinder block from the exhaust manifold
7. Water-jacketed intake manifold
8. Disc clutch
9. Transmission counter shaft below main shaft
10. Left drive with center control

Preproduction dual-valve cars and trucks of the new designs were already on the road in the South, where roads were clear for continuous operation. Start of production was set for late summer, when factory changes were expected to be complete.

The Pierce-Arrow Motor Car Co. released its annual report for 1919 on March 24. Net earnings of $3,161,122 compared with $4,273,172 in 1918. Net profit was $2,491,070 or $6.75 per share of common stock, compared to $7.86 the year before. Federal taxes paid had fallen by half and dividends by about $1.25 million. Surplus for the year totaled $1,378,570. On December 31, 1919, the total company retained surplus had been $3,571,570. President Jay was quoted in the March 25 *Automotive Industries* saying "necessary war expenditures in buildings and machinery have left the company with facilities in excess of normal requirements. Plans for the present contemplate increased production in passenger cars and trucks which should result in a reduction of overhead expenses and lower costs." The company seemed confident that this program would reverse the declines in profits seen over the previous three years.

More details about the rearrangements under way at the factory were spelled out in the April issue of *The Arrow*. The article, titled "Sidelights on Our Production Problems," was written by Assistant General Manager C.H. Tichenor. From his remarks, it was clear that he was the actual factory manager because he focused entirely on successfully completing scheduled output. Schedules were built from agents' orders and determined the "types to be manufactured, the quantity and the definite month in which these deliveries must be made." The thrust of Tichenor's paper was that schedules must be fulfilled completely, accurately, and on time by the 7,250 employees in the 1.5 million sq. ft. factory. He emphasized the importance of rapidly processing available materials, an inventory which averaged about 12 million dollars, so as to consume them methodically in a balanced manner. He also pointed out the vital importance of handling materials and performing operations properly to make each part as perfect as possible. This was absolutely necessary to support the planned scale of production. At the time, the ambitious schedule for the year was 200 vehicles behind, according to Tichenor, but "all previous records have been broken in certain departments throughout the plant in the past two weeks and General Superintendent John Guider reports that all departments are out to do their very best and that the month of April is going to be a record breaker from start to finish." This was despite another outbreak of flu at the time.

The company was clearly intent to accelerate its output. There was, however, a complication: "From now until July," Tichenor noted, "certain rearrangements will be made in certain portions of the factory in order that our work will progress through the plant in a more orderly manner and enable us to get out a greater production with the same amount of floor space, at the same time eliminating excessive handling of materials." Beyond the inevitable confusion such changes were bound to provoke while being carried out in the midst of the projected production increases, they also would drastically alter the way Pierce-Arrow would build its cars and trucks in the future. The days of overhead cranes lifting heavy assemblies to stationary chassis were going to end. A moving assembly line was being installed on the ground floor of Buildings H and J, the southernmost buildings along Great Arrow Avenue. Chassis assembly would occur in building J and final assembly in H. In the body factory (Buildings G, H, I, and J) the work would be greatly changed because the unique Pierce-Arrow cast aluminum body was being supplanted by a more conventional one of pressed aluminum panels attached to a hardwood ash structure. Body finish and interior would be largely the same. This less-costly coachwork was called a "composite body" in the trade. Its development prompted employing custom body builder Leon Rubay to assist James R. Way and lay out a more contemporary style for the new line.

Several pages of this same issue of *The Arrow* featured experiences of long time employees, who contrasted the firm they first went to work for and the current industrial giant. John Erith was manager of the company cigar stand in the basement of the Office Building. He recalled his position at the turn from the previous century as a timekeeper in the Hanover Street plant. At the time, the company had facilities on Main Street, another on Lloyd Street, and the last on Court Street as well as the main Hanover Street operation. Making up the payroll then was a challenge. The factory week ended on Thursday. On Friday the payroll was assembled, the work data and pay were calculated by hand, and envelopes, pay slips, etc., were prepared. Saturday was payday, and Erith accompanied the cashier on his trips to the several sites to pay off the workers.

Chan Cowles, general foreman of the Pierce-Arrow parts department, had been hired in 1895, when the company had just ended the production of household goods to concentrate on bicycles. The parts office on Hanover Street was housed next to the stable for the horse Charlie Brenner employed to transport the finished bicycles from factory to the shipper. "Charlie, his horse and I became fast friends," Cowles wrote. At the time this story was written Cowles needed about 60 assistants on Elmwood Avenue to handle the worldwide demand for parts.

Another article described the operations at the Store Department, located in a recently completed single story building labeled "Building W." This department processed a monthly delivery of nearly 650,000 numbered forgings, stampings, steel and malleable iron castings, brass, magnesium and aluminum castings, along with 15,000 ft. or so of steel tubing and 16,676 lbs. of brass, not to mention some 205,000 feet of rolled steel.

Amenities at the plant continued. A published schedule for each noontime concert by the Pierce-Arrow Band on Tuesdays and Thursdays in April included four or five selections for each concert, among which were usually a waltz and fox trot as well as a march or some descriptive selection. Every concert ended with the Star-Spangled Banner.

The Pierce-Arrow board of directors met on Saturday, April 24, Charles Clifton chairing the meeting. One topic on the agenda was the election of someone to fill a vacancy. Charles H. McCulloch, president of Lackawanna Steel Co. in Buffalo, had died, but the board did not yet fill his seat. Asked by the press if any action had been taken by the board relative to the rumored acquisition of Pierce-Arrow Motor Car Co. by General Motors Corp., Clifton replied, according to the account in *Automotive Industries*, "Our answer is that we elected the old board of directors."

Clifton contributed the lead feature in the May issue of *The Arrow*. It was unrelated to company matters and titled "Success May Be Acquired from Careful Study of Human Nature and Reading of Good Books." It read like a grandfatherly appraisal of his lifetime of experience. "If a man with a busy, active business life of near to 50 years cannot tell something from the experience that is worth while," Clifton wrote, "he is 'a poor stick.'" His reflections amounted to a personal endorsement of the importance of a continuing education, and the title is its very thesis. The realities of his life limited Charles Clifton's opportunities to receive a formal education. "It was a keen disappointment to me," he admitted, "that I could not have had a college education but stern necessity compelled me to become a bread winner at 17." What Clifton used for an education were his experience and a thoughtful selection of reading material. He described the process as "the Public Grammar School with a Post-Graduate course in Human Nature." Clifton argued against wasting time on current best-sellers or transitory entertainment that go "nowhere and give nothing." His preference was for biography out of a wide field of literature for every taste, because "it is so full of human nature." It is, he maintained, the most interesting various and useful subject there is. He advocated reading each word aloud, "thereby learning new words, absorbing literary style as well as wit and wisdom." Reading the masters was, he averred, the way he rescued his thinking when "harassed with mental problems and difficulties." Among the books in Clifton's library at 789 West Ferry was a prized first folio of Shakespeare. Walls of the residence displayed his discerning collection of original art. That year, Charles Clifton was also the chairman of the Art Committee

Charles Clifton, now chairman at Pierce-Arrow, stands beside his Series 51 6-passenger touring car, about 1920. His interests then extended into philanthropic work, which included presidency of the Buffalo General Hospital (courtesy University of Michigan Special Collections).

at the Buffalo Club. According to that year's U.S. Census, his household on West Ferry was made up of Charles, occupation "auto industry," Grace Clifton, wife (64 years of age), Alice S. Clifton, student at a private school (16 years old), Margaret Calman, a 46-year-old Irish cook, Margaret Neeson, the maid and a Scot, and Rose Simmons, a 50-year-old Irish servant. Charles seems to have preferred being chauffeured to driving himself, but no chauffeur is listed. Perhaps the company provided one.

The Clifton family was expanded by a grandson in 1920. He was Gorham Clifton, Jr., who for various reasons eventually came to be known as Mark, born to Gorham and Margaret Clifton. His father Gorham, according to Mark many years later, did not stabilize his life after his marriage as was hoped. While he served in the World War, his drinking and lack of control brought him into conflict with his superiors, and in the end, Charles Clifton had to intervene in some way to extricate Gorham from his predicament. The younger Cliftons had settled in Philadelphia, Gorham having been a golf champion there before the war. They rented a house at 6946 Roach. Gorham had somehow secured a job with the Foss-Hughes Co., the Pierce-Arrow distributor for the region, and attended Pierce-Arrow sales conventions at the New York shows from at least 1916. This was, Mark insists, the only job his father ever had. Even then, Gorham became steadily less and less controlled. Cycles of binge drinking would climax with one or two days to sober up, followed by a week or so of work until the cycle began again. The existence of Prohibition did not discourage this cycle. A particular barber, Mark noted, was able to bring Gorham back to a somewhat serviceable condition Saturday morning after a bibulous evening. The barber remembered Gorham as a charming man. This is also how he often seemed to affect the ladies.

One impact of redesigning the entire lineup for 1921 was that the Tracing Room was turning out their precise line drawings in ink on linen cloth as fast as possible in sizes from "B" to "O." The total number of tracings for the month of March alone totaled 549. It took a staff of nine working constantly, according to Miss A. Estelle Aldrich, a supervisor of the department. Her description was contained in the May issue of *The Arrow*. There were also continual tracings made of running design changes. "The Pierce-Arrow Motor Car Company was the first firm in Buffalo to employ girls for the work," she wrote. "The experiment was so successful that girl tracers are here to stay." The war had ushered in a new era. Women would now gain the right to vote.

The Annual Meeting of the NACC was held in New York the first week of June. It would be their last at the old Transit Building on 42nd Street. Plans to move over to the Marlin Rockwell Building at 46th and Madison Avenue were well advanced. The NACC offices on the 14th and 15th floors would open July 12. In its coverage of the annual meeting *The Automobile Trade Journal* remarked that the automobile industry "now produced eighty-five per cent of the world's output," which had increased its interest in foreign trade. Also noted was the fact that the "truck business is booming," and that "the present output of plants is estimated as being seventy-five percent of the normal rate of the first quarter of the year." The election of officers retained Clifton as president. Roy D. Chapin was elected vice-president. Windsor T. White remained the second vice-president representing the truck members; C.C. Hanch became second vice-president for the passenger car division. A.J. Brosseau of the International Motor Truck Co. replaced Hanch as secretary. H.H. Rice was re-elected treasurer. Harry M. Jewett of Page-Detroit was added to the board as was W.C. Sills of Chevrolet.

In Buffalo, the economic condition of the country was having a destructive impact on some carefully prepared plans. In a June article in *The Arrow*, Floyd H. Smith, the manager of purchases, explained what he said was a widespread concern of Pierce-Arrow employees, namely "the shortage of materials." As the article continued it revealed the increasing difficulty of bringing into the factory all the materials that were vital to sustain the level of production called for in the company plans. The most obvious problem was obtaining sufficient quantities of steel, although there were also shortages of purchased parts. The problem had begun the previous fall when several steel plants were shut down by worker strikes. This was followed by railroad strikes that not only left the Pierce-Arrow factory short of fuel but slowed the production of steel in even the reactivated steel plants. Winter storms that slowed all traffic aggravated the situation. Then, as spring arrived, switchmen went on strike. When the article was written, Smith maintained, "For ten days no carload of freight moved either in or out of our factory, and this happened right at the peak of production." The shortages had been addressed by the Follow Up and Traffic divisions sending trucks out to fetch short materials in such places as Cleveland, Pittsburgh, Newark, and Worcester at added cost. The plant remained in operation, but it had been a struggle.

Another glimpse onto the factory operations published in June was about the production departments at Pierce-Arrow. These were made up of the Routing Office, Machine Shop Clerks, In Process, Shortage, Schedule, Stock Chasing, and Messenger departments. All these were supervised by George O'Day, H.A. Kolb assisting. For tracking purposes, all material was accompanied to each operation by a card: from Specification to Store to Machine Shop to Pay Roll to Process department, which kept record of all material received and finished. This way the location of all material would be known to the Shortage Department. When shortages turned up, Stock Chasing was given the task of providing them. On Schedule Charts, supervised by foreman J.J. Danaher, the details from the cards enabled the production department to "see at a glance the exact number of cars which can be built" at any given time.

On Wednesday, June 2, the Pierce-Arrow board of directors released their account of the annual meeting, which was published by *Automotive Industries* under a New York dateline in the June 3 issue. A substantial change was made at the top of the management, John C. Jay, Jr., having been elected chairman of the executive committee, and George W. Mixter elected to succeed him as president. Col. Clifton was reelected as board chairman. Other officers elected were W.J. Foss in charge of commercial matters; W.C. Pearson, secretary, and M.E. Forbes, treasurer. Walter P. Cooke, now chairman of the board at Buffalo's Marine Trust Co., was elected a member of the Pierce-Arrow board and the executive committee. Both Jay and Cooke would retain close connections with Pierce-Arrow for many years. "Pierce-Arrow has maintained substantial production and is showing satisfactory earnings," the story continued. Reported earnings totaled $717,265 for the first quarter. Inventories had been reduced and loans were being liquidated "at a rate faster than called for by due dates, the officers said."

This new management of the Pierce-Arrow Motor Car Company was graphically laid out in a beautiful hand-lettered organization chart dated June 15, 1920. At its crest were "The Pierce-Arrow Motor Car Company Stockholders," represented inside a neat box. Directly below that was the box for the "Board of Directors, Charles Clifton, Chairman." Two boxes occupied parallel levels below that. On the left was the "Executive Committee, John C. Jay, Jr. Chairman" and "Finance Committee, Chas. Clifton Chairman" to the right. The next layer was that of the new "President and General Manager, G.W. Mixter." To the right of that a small box connected to "General Counsel, J.G. Dudley." Below that were two parallel boxes, one for the Planning staff under W.H. Ladd, the other, company secretary, E.C. Pearson. Below that and connected to the six major departments in parallel trains of boxes below was the Assistant General Manager C.M. Tichenor. The departments he coordinated into an interdependent whole were Finance, Purchase, Distribution, Engineering, Manufacturing, and Industrial Relations. Altogether 50 discrete positions were listed within its neat pattern. The chart suggested that the major steps to reorganize Pierce-Arrow operations were now complete. The description along with it in *The Arrow* for July gave the impression that the complex maneuvers to remake Pierce-Arrow were moving successfully toward the anticipated postwar goals.

That same month a story about the general foreman of assembly at Pierce-Arrow was published. Robert "Bob" Conn had worked at Pierce for 25 years, beginning as a machinist. He had previously worked as a machinist at Brooks Locomotive Works in Dunkirk and learned the trade on their locomotive erection shop floor. He had joined Pierce during the bicycle days and was the foreman of their wheel department. It would now be his task to move the factory into the new higher level of production as part of the management's plans. His approach seemed to be summarized in these observations: "I believe in encouraging the men. I never ask a man to do something that I wouldn't do myself. My men work with me—not for me."

This impression of unimpeded progress toward company goals guided by the organization chart would soon prove to be premature. Pierce-Arrow tradition expected new models to be unveiled in mid-summer when they hosted members of the national dealer network for the occasion. Despite the confident tenor of Treasurer Myron Forbes' explanation of the vital importance of "Printed Forms and Their Uses" to start the July issue, the executives surely had concerns about the ability to actually go into production of the new models whose design alone had taken years to complete. Forbes, in his meticulous way, had pointed out the importance of accuracy in the recording of information. "The operations of the Company are guided by its records," Forbes wrote "and without them it could not properly exist." This obvious truth was accompanied by some further observations about the need to make use of existing forms when appropriate, rather than devise new ones because of the expense involved just stocking them. This was the first time the somewhat retiring treasurer had been encouraged to pen an article about the details of his work since he joined the firm in the fall of 1919. Previously an accountant with Haskins & Sells, later employed by a number of industrial corporations as auditor, he had been works manager of an armaments manufacturer during the World War. Expressing his opinion in a clear and careful style, Forbes left the impression that he could be counted on.

In the plant itself, however, the extensive reworking of factory operations was taking longer than planned. The new truck models were introduced to sales cohorts at the usual season, even if circumstances delayed such timely introduction of the passenger car line. Festivities began in Buffalo on Monday, July 19. In the *Convention Salesman* for the day (Price: A Smile; Weather Today: Very, Very Dry) an ambitious program was laid out for the sales forces. Conventioneers, having stayed at hotels downtown, hurried to Shelton Square to catch special street cars leaving for the trip to the factory at 9:30 a.m. Opening events began at 10:30 on the first floor of Building J, the easternmost giant four-story body building beside Great Arrow Avenue. "Enthusiasm marked the convention's proceedings from the start," opined the next day's issue of the *Salesman*. "Chairman Robert O. Patten and General Sales Manager George M. Graham were roundly cheered when they appeared. Then came a spontaneous tribute to Col. Charles Clifton, Chairman of the Board of Directors, which was profoundly impressive. In a body the delegates "rose to their feet as Col. Clifton ascended to the speakers' platform." Clifton began his welcome address with these words: "Gentlemen, I thank you for that spontaneous outburst of enthusiasm. You have nearly taken my breath away. A part of that, however, was due to hitting a long trail to get up here. I thought it was about the longest golf hole I had ever tackled."

In his prepared remarks, Clifton conveyed the uncertainty and challenge which was, no doubt, broadly felt among the members of the new management, employed as they clearly had been to build up earnings for the company's stockholders. The contrasts between the way the old company had operated and the expectations of the present were reflected in the Colonel's speech. "I am glad to welcome you here at this time," he began, "because I consider it one of the most critical times in the history of this business." He then gave a short reference to the company's early truck history: "The purpose of the Company in developing this [first] worm-drive truck was to provide for the expansion of the Company's business along new lines," he noted. "The passenger car business, built to the standard which we had set, necessarily did not lend itself to large expansion, and consequently the Pierce-Arrow truck business was created." He described the early results as "a disappointment." But "with the war came a very large development in our production. We were obliged to produce for war purposes, and when started on that program it was impossible to change in any particular the line of trucks which was produced at that time." This had been due to pressures from the French government not to complicate their stocking of service parts. With the end of the war and with the efforts of the engineering and manufacturing departments, "We are now able to present to you the very latest developments, and I believe the superior of anything produced anywhere in the line of trucks."

Moving to the sales challenge, Clifton noted the downturn in the economy that faced the company. "We have come to a time when expansion in business enterprises has come to a halt and is beginning to recede," he said. He then made a most unusual digression into a metaphor taken from the old proverb about killing the goose that laid the golden egg. "And I want to refer to this Company, if you please, as that old Mother Goose. We have never come to you with our troubles (and we have had them); we have never come to you and said we have got to make more money out of you in price or in commission. We have carried the bag for a good many years and today we must have a lot of co-operation carrying that bag."

This amounted to a succinct summary of the change of circumstances that had occurred over a year's time. One factor was reflected in the raised expectations now placed on the network of agents over the country and the world. "We have," Clifton emphasized, "set up the fairest prices on the smallest margins for this Company that safety will permit. The whole problem has been set up on the idea of quantity, consequently, our profit and quantity go hand in hand.... Go at this problem loyally and enthusiastically and forget about extra discounts, forget about all that kind of thing, forget about prodding up old Mother Goose and trust us to see the matter through. Your own efforts will determine whether you get profits or whether you don't."

Conditions now altered interactions between factory and dealers. "Since I last addressed you," he reminded them, "a new crew has come to the floor. That crew has my, and I hope it has your, entire confidence.... This crew has definitely placed upon the market a line of new trucks re-designed from the ground up and produced under modern manufacturing conditions. At the same time they have produced a new passenger car, and that also absolutely up to date and modern in every sense. It has been a Herculean task; it has been a task that older men would shrink at, and I think it is a wonderful tribute to the organization which is operating this factory."

Clifton now went on to describe unexpected and disappointing developments following the World War. Material prices had continued to rapidly rise, rather than fall. Those increased costs meant that "in spite of a price raise in passenger cars in June 1919, we ended last year's business with the smallest fraction of one per cent of profit on the turnover of $12,000,000 of passenger cars." He then upbraided "misapprehension [that] the margin of profit for this company on its product was something extraordinary," citing financial statements "that are public property" as proof. He again stressed the importance of quantity production. "Fix this quantity idea in your minds," he concluded. "It is the key note of your success and our success—and can come only from absolute loyalty and co-operation."

Following Clifton's welcome, Truck Sales Manager Robert O. Patten, chairing the meeting, introduced President George W. Mixter, noting as he did so that "sales stimulus will be greater than ever before because in addition to durability and reliability, we have enhanced the trucks with great pulling ability equal to any demand, wonderful economy in fuel, quick accessibility when replacements are needed." Of Mixter, Mr. Patten emphasized that he had been "the man in charge of aircraft production during the war and brought out of disorder an organization which showed results." Previously Patten noted, the "vast production and management of the wealthy and prosperous Deere interests were entrusted to his care." President Mixter began his speech, "Manufacturing Pierce-Arrow Trucks," at about 10:45, taking an hour or so to lay out the overall conception of the factory alterations, culminating with the directive, "Much has been done here in Buffalo; much remains to be done here and by you, and we expect you to do your part and immediately double your truck business."

Following Col. Mixter, Chief Engineer David Fergusson spoke on "The Advantages of Design," in which he described the development of the dual valve truck line, and its superior performance over previous models. At the end of his talk, scheduled to end at 12:30, luncheon was served in the factory before the next meeting began at 2 o'clock. Service Department manager Fred J. Wells then spoke about "Accessibility for Repair." The following talk about the vital "Stock of Parts for Service" by C.D. Cowles, manager of the Parts Division, was scheduled during a half hour after 3:00 p.m. The introduc-

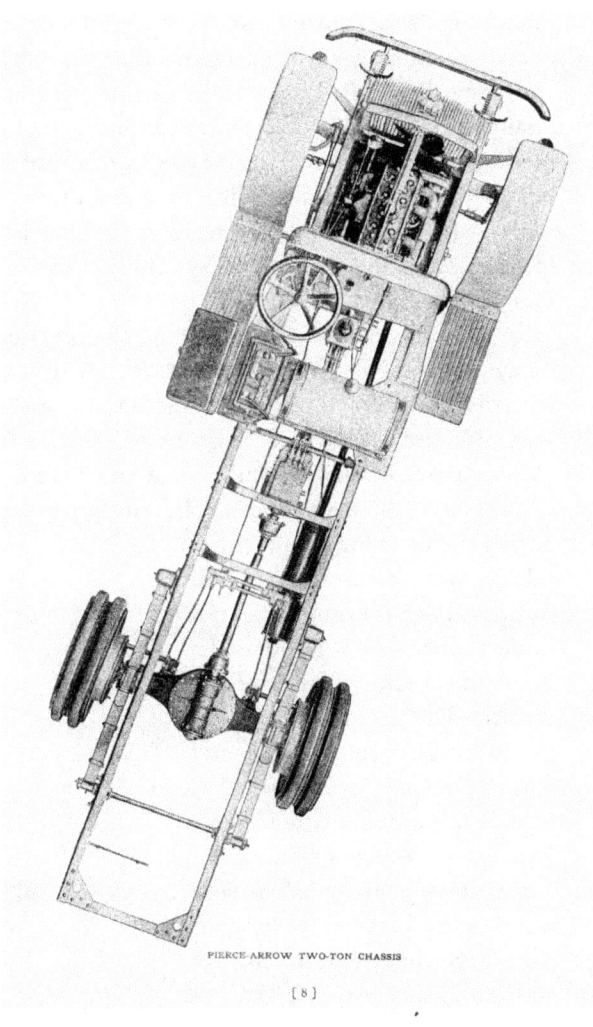

The postwar Pierce-Arrow truck: Chassis of the 2-ton model with dual-valve 4 × 5½-inch, 4-cylinder engine (courtesy Pierce-Arrow Society).

tion of the 2-ton Model X-5, on either solid or pneumatic tires, occurred at 3:30. After inspection of the trucks, sales literature about them was distributed. This event lasted for an hour and a half before the street cars took the participants back to their hotels for time to relax after a long day.

The old outlets for relaxation had been somewhat curtailed this year when involving alcoholic beverages. However, the city of Buffalo was never known for very determined adherence to the strictures of the Volstead Act. Perhaps some of the conventioneers took the time to read over Assistant General Manager C.M. Tichenor's article about the increased production made possible by improvements at the Pierce-Arrow factory that had appeared in that day's issue of *The Convention Salesman*. It was as good as its title: "Here Are Brass Tack Reasons Why Volume and Quality Are Now Achieved in Our Factory." The great advances centered on improved machine tools, now working at faster speeds and combining multiple operations that sped tasks markedly and improved "progressive operations" to reduce unnecessary movement of materials during processing. Most spectacularly, as Col. Tichenor explained, "The chassis assembling will be on a moveable trackway of the most modern type and as the chasses [*sic*] move down the trackway the various parts are assembled upon the frame work, until it finally reaches the end of the trackway and is a completed vehicle ready for the road test. This method eliminates a great deal of labor in the moving of the chassis and insures the assembling being done in a very methodical manner." Production Engineer E.A. Taylor, who had experience with production operations at Cadillac and Maxwell, was credited with layout and installation of the progressive assembly system. Assembly line production had arrived at Pierce-Arrow.

The salesmen were entertained that evening at a convention dinner in the opulent Lafayette Hotel on Washington Street downtown. On Tuesday the whole race began again with the catching of the street cars at Shelton Square to arrive at the plant by 10:00 a.m. Talks on the second day covered "Salient Competition Features" (Engineer Frances W. Davis) and "Motor Truck Markets" (Carl H. Bowen), before the introduction of the 3½-ton Model W-2 trucks at 11:30. Again both solid and pneumatic tires were displayed on examples, and during the hour-long inspection, sales literature was distributed. Luncheon was again at 12:30 under supervision of Miss K. Leonard, director of factory food services. The talk at 2:00 p.m. was by the recently promoted General Sales Manager George M. Graham and pointedly titled "Sales Expansion." Reasons behind the departure of Vice-President Foss were undisclosed, but by that time, according to Ted Selman's account, it was already clear that the expansive plan to sell a thousand Pierce-Arrow trucks in France that year was a complete failure.

The dual-valve engine of the 2-ton 1921 Pierce-Arrow truck. Larger trucks carried a 4-cyl, 4½ × 6¾-inch engine (courtesy Pierce-Arrow Society).

When Mr. Graham's talk concluded, the 5-ton Model R-10 was then introduced in the manner seen before, except that the option of pneumatic tires was, apparently, not included. When the street cars departed for town at 5:15 p.m. the salesmen had been given the night off to socialize, travel up to Niagara Falls on the interurban line, visit Crystal Beach by ferry boat or ride out onto Lake Erie. Other amusements were available in the many theaters and restaurants of the city. Many old friends were renewing their acquaintances and having a good time. It is quite likely that Charles Clifton was among them. He had known many of these men for years.

Next day's itinerary was different from Monday and Tuesday. Instead of riding up to the plant, the directive was to meet at Lafayette Square by 9:30 and from that location "March to B.R. & P. depot" for departure on the Buffalo, Rochester and Pittsburgh train south into the hilly terrain near Colden (specifically at "Ed Miller's farm"), arriving at 11:15. This was the site for the conventioneers to witness hill-climb tests of the new truck models in competition with trucks from recent production. The course was 5,500 ft. long, rising over 400 ft. from end to end. At its steepest point, the grade was 20.94 percent. Driving demonstrations and power tests were also scheduled. Performance of the new truck models was suitably impressive to everyone. After time out for luncheon "on the field," activities resumed with a baseball game and "aeroplane flights" with pilot Lee Chase in a Curtiss biplane. These entertainments were followed by refreshments. The train back to Buffalo left at 4:15 and the convention ended.

That Saturday, a big road trip for 500 factory foremen planned to the same site in Colden was rained out and postponed until the next Saturday, July 31. Truck tests, a picnic, and a baseball game were once again a great success. This second excursion was even written up in *Automotive Industries* for August 5. Improved new truck models were now officially launched into the market with high hopes for great success.

The August issue of *The Arrow* contained a lengthy article by George M. Graham titled "Keeping Product Up-to-Date Vital to Manufacturing Success." After a short history of the company and its proud reputation, Graham explained the difficulties that attended the development of the new truck and car lines. "Out of a series of conferences," he wrote, "there grew gradually this important basic fundamental in respect to change under discussion: That we must maintain the quality traditions of the past, but ally them to modern designs and progressive manufacturing methods." He then pointed out the important improvements developed for the new lines and their great superiority over their predecessors. Serious problems had arisen, however.

The week of August 2 the management took "radical steps" to rectify serious shortages of materials in the factory. The problems

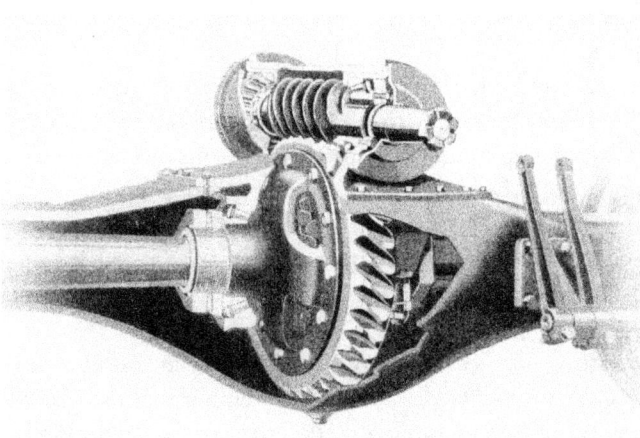

Cutaway view of the worm-drive axle gear applied to Pierce-Arrow trucks (courtesy Pierce-Arrow Society).

had been developing since May, and by early August between "25 and 30 of the ablest executives in the organization" were being sent out to chase stock. According to President Mixter, direct appeal was being made to the presidents and general managers of the companies at a cost of "between $5,000 and $10,000 per week in traveling expenses alone so as to have the best Pierce-Arrow men available right at the source of supply." A special eight-page issue of *The Arrow* addressing the situation was released later in the month to aid rebuilding the morale of some 7,000 employees coping with these handicapped factory operations. George W. Mixter himself wrote the lead article entitled "The Pierce-Arrow Situation," explaining the causes of the problems and the attempted cures. He attributed the difficulties to steel and coal strikes the previous fall and current railroad and coal mine labor difficulties that prevented fuel deliveries. As for Pierce-Arrow, he wrote, "The shipping situation may be summarized by saying that after some of the 38 HP passenger cars now in work are shipped, we will be unable to make further shipments. Shipments are the direct source of money for pay-rolls and raw materials, and evidently shipments must be resumed at the earliest possible date to make the business successful. Meanwhile expenditures must be curtailed." Unlike Detroit factories that had laid off as many as 200,000 workmen, Pierce-Arrow did not find a lack of demand and expected to be able to sell all its anticipated production. It was the lack of various supplies purchased from the East Coast to as far west as Omaha that curtailed the scheduled production of 6,000 vehicles, divided equally between cars and trucks, that had been mentioned in the March 31 *Wall Street Journal*. The company clearly expected a yearly output in the five digits when plant re-organization was complete.

Mixter noted at the end of his article: "The basic Pierce-Arrow conditions are good. We have a fine plant; most of the new tools are available now; the layout provides the doing of more work than in the past. Liberal orders are being received every day for the new trucks." He expected that the efforts to obtain supplies would bear fruit, "and within a short time we will put the plant back on a normal operating basis." The rest of the issue was filled with an explanation of the company "Policies and Aims" by Col. Tichenor, and a description of the recent truck tests on the "sun-kissed hills of Colden, N.Y." Noticeably, there was also an article extolling the advantages of remaining in Buffalo rather than seeking employment elsewhere, indicating that there may have been some unrest among the employees at this turn of events. In its August 19 issue, *Automotive Industries* noted that Pierce-Arrow had reported earnings of $1.4 million for the year up until June.

An extensive nine-page feature article by P.M. Heldt describing the new Pierce-Arrow truck line appeared in the September 9 *Automotive Industries*. The subtitle noted the radical approach taken by the company with this development. "The step taken by this pioneer manufacturer," the magazine opined, "is probably the most radical from both production and design standpoints in the history of the industry. An additional model and many changes in both engine and chassis are announced. Provisions for pneumatic tires are made by governor." The subsequent analysis was detailed and complete, covering every aspect of the design with many illustrations and drawings.

However, the selling economy continued to weaken. Layoffs continued as sales in the auto industry slipped drastically. Pierce-Arrow had to deny in late September that the plant would be "closed indefinitely." The denial appeared in *Automotive Industries* of the 23rd, along with its assertion of a "steadily increasing volume of truck business." A production increase beyond the current 66 percent was expected as "the plant gets into the swing of turning out

1921 Pierce-Arrow truck with stake body (courtesy Pierce-Arrow Society).

the new dual-valve models." Earnings for the second half of the year were estimated to be $1 million. The next week, the magazine reported a Pierce-Arrow price increase averaging $250 on its passenger car models. In response to questions Clifton was quoted as saying, "There has been no reduction in production costs." Prices for the line of touring cars now ranged from $7,500 to $8,000. The company's October 28 earnings report indicated a drop during the September quarter. According to a story in that day's issue of *Automotive Industries*, the surplus for Pierce-Arrow during the July–September quarter had totaled $355,310, compared to $705,779 for the quarter before. It amounted to 62¢ a share of common stock, compared to $1.10 for the September quarter in 1919. The first nine months of business at Pierce-Arrow had netted $1,778,354, as compared to $1,670,540 during the same period in 1919—43 cents a share more. This did not suggest the company had made great strides raising earnings. Not unexpectedly, Pierce-Arrow stock was a volatile issue for investors at this time. At the beginning of 1920 the Pierce-Arrow Motor Car Co. had 1,800 holders of its common stock and 1,720 holders of preferred shares, according to the *Buffalo Express* newspaper of February 15, 1921.

Disappointing figures at Pierce-Arrow were not atypical for the industry as a whole at the time. As the summer of 1920 slipped into fall, sales of automobiles and trucks were both lagging seriously. Financial difficulties overtook many enterprises, and interest rates were high. The sort of fear that often rose in hard times could be seen. At the NACC meeting the week of October 4, Charles Clifton warned against the effects of "idle rumors" thoughtlessly spread by those associated with the automobile industry, not just at high levels, but also salesmen and traveling men in accessory and parts supplies. "There is nothing in the general condition of the country," Clifton was quoted as saying to *Automotive Industries*, "that indicates a long period of depression. Depressions in the automobile industry in the past have been for short periods," he assured his listeners, "as clearly shown in 1907, again in 1913 and again in the early part of 1919." Clifton was a patient man who had seen several periods of hard times in his long career. He nonetheless had a determination, as he said later, to "turn the clouds around so that you do not see the black side, but that you see the silver lining, which is always on the other side of the clouds." Later that month Clifton appointed members of the NACC Service Committee to fill vacancies due to resignations. This included its chairman, A.B. Cummer of Autocar, who replaced E.T. Herbig.

The week of November 7 marked what may accurately be described as the climax of the whole year that followed the upheaval of mid–1919 at Pierce-Arrow. Sometime on Monday the 8th Charles Clifton was asked by the press to comment on activities in the stock market against shares of Pierce-Arrow. His response was to declare a favorable long-range outlook for his company. "The Pierce-Arrow Motor Car Co. has devoted recent months," he asserted, "to preparation for production of new lines of both trucks and passenger cars. During this period shipments have been limited. The company will enter upon 1921 in an unusually strong position to secure a liberal volume of business." A dramatic unveiling began the very next evening with the first viewing of the new model Pierce-Arrow car by "between four and five hundred of the plant executives," reported in the December issue of *The Arrow*. They met at six o'clock on the second floor of Building H, where the completed bodies would be collected for lowering onto chassis moving down the new assembly line below. An evening repast was laid out by Miss Leonard's commissary department on tables for guests to carry to their places. "Throughout the meal," the magazine noted, "Harry Peck's orchestra played popular tunes." After which, the customary cigars having been lit, the executives repaired to the end of the hall where chairs had been assembled for them to listen to talks by Col. Mixter, Col. Tichenor, Mr. Corcoran, and Mr. Fergusson, the general manager, assistant general manager, passenger car sales manager, and chief engineer respectively. Between them they covered the design, production, and sales efforts behind the new models. The reported extent of David Fergusson's remarks was "I've done my best, now do yours." After the speeches, the cars themselves were displayed for the first time. The next evening the same show opened for the personnel of the entire factory. "The wives of the men who build the cars," *The Arrow* wrote, "had a chance to see what their husbands were doing." The freshly completed cars were the final product of many months of hard work, not only in their design but the methods used to produce them as well. According to President Mixter, a million dollars had gone into factory rearrangement alone. The new machinery cost another three-quarters of a million. There must have been some relief felt along with the satisfaction of seeing the job's completion.

Two days later, Friday, November 12, the dealers who sold Pierce-Arrows over the whole country examined the cars at the second Pierce-Arrow sales convention of 1920. This time, instead of at the plant, the meeting place was the impressive red stone 74th Regiment Armory at Niagara and Connecticut streets. Much hoopla accompanied this important introduction, much like during the earlier truck sales convention in July. This morning was taken up with speeches by Clifton, Mixter, Fergusson, and Graham, all reprinted in the Saturday issue of *The Pierce-Arrow Salesman*. That afternoon a formal display of the cars was the climax of the day's program. In the evening the cars were viewed at close range accompanied by available factory men to answer questions. Saturday's schedule began at the factory ("8:30 a.m. Street cars leave Main Street and Shelton Square"). All day, demonstration rides in the dramatically changed cars were given every 40 minutes for eager conventioneers. Cards were issued, assigning times for each rider. While the rides went on, tours of the factory were given as well. Luncheon took place at one o'clock, after which the meeting adjourned, cars taking the participants to nearby Clarence, New York, where J.A. McCullough explained the new body construction. This aspect was perhaps the most radical change to the Pierce-Arrow concept. The convention closed with a banquet at the Buffalo Automobile Club, of which Charles Clifton was vice-president, also in Clarence.

Much of what the sales force heard at this event matched what was covered at the earlier sales convention. After all, the basic concept of both cars and trucks was quite similar, although to a different scale. Charles Clifton's welcome address at the opening was even similar, with an interesting variation. While discussing the changes seen in the industry after the war, Clifton recalled a sales convention at its start, during which he predicted the world afterwards would "never be just the same old world that it was before." Then he made this wistful digression. "Perhaps I have said 'I' a good many times, but you all realize, I am quite sure, that my life for the last 25 years has been devoted to this business and when I say 'I' when I ought to say 'we' I apologize for it, but my endeavor has been to write my character and the character of my associates into the line of cars. You all have known in the past," he mused, "the old associates. Some of those, unfortunately have had to be severed. As a man gets older in life the severing of those relations becomes like a surgical operation."

However nostalgic Clifton may have felt about the old days, he remained relentlessly upbeat at the conclusion of his remarks. "Do not forget the old concern is still on the map," he urged, "that the old concern is revivified and made more useful and more up to date. This is the crisis which we are passing, and we are passing it with surprising success. All we need, is for the selling units of this organization to get behind it with enthusiasm; to get behind it with intelligence and put the whole scheme over as one of the great events in the motor world. Gentlemen, I welcome you."

From that point, the long succession of events urged the sales staff to work very hard at quickly moving the production into customers' hands. Emphasis was on finding buyers for what was offered. Special equipment orders were discouraged. Dealers were, it was suggested, the natural providers of such conveniences because later installation avoided slowing the production line. As Col. Mixter put it, "it is to your interest and the factory's interest to keep the plant moving along smoothly and every time you ask us to introduce an apparently minor, but odd item on the equipment of a car, you slow up the procession." While the management's commitment to quality production was asserted, for clearly explained reasons the emphasis had definitely shifted toward quantity.

Press coverage of the new Pierce-Arrow car began over the next few weeks that preceded the 1921 New York Automobile Show. The specimen article from *Automotive Industries* that appeared in its November 25 issue made an interesting contrast with the extensive coverage they had given the truck models two months before. This article, titled "Pierce-Arrow Drops '48' Chassis Model," filled but a single column of the page, and contained no illustrations.

Fully half the story was about the alterations to the 38 HP size motor and the fact that its power range had risen to 3,000 rpm. Its single block construction was mentioned, as were its dual Delco ignition, its three-speed transmission, multiple dry-disk clutch, and the adoption of a Stromberg carburetor. The appearance of band brakes on the rear wheels was noted, along with the adoption of semi-elliptic rear springs. Choice of fender lamps or bracket lamps was mentioned, as were tire sizes. Unmentioned was any description of the composite wood-framed bodies on the cars, or the new 138 in. wheelbase length. Most puzzling was the lack of any mention of Pierce-Arrow's change to left-hand drive and center control of the transmission. Other publications such as *Motor Age* included illustrations of the car and its engine along with some text, but no great elaboration was provided. The cars were, evidently, on sale, but their current availability was not clear.

Vice-President George M. Graham began at once to carry out his carefully laid out plans to market the new Pierce-Arrow. Two catalogs, using two different illustrators, were printed for the agents to use. A limited number of the "Large catalogue," with Adolf Treidler color illustrations, was available. These were quite lavish. The "Smaller catalogue" with sepia prints of illustrations by Amos Northup was available "in quantity within reasonable limits," according to Mr. Graham's "Passenger Car Conference" letter of December 2. Amos Northup was now head of the Art Department at Pierce-Arrow and went on to a distinguished career as a designer of some of the advanced styling efforts for production car design on Willys, Graham, and Reo chassis.

Advertisements showing the new Pierce-Arrows would not be released until January, but important promotions were already taking place. In his letter, Graham mentioned that there had been "a considerable representation in New York for the Salon and the Harrolds Motor Car Company display" in November. After commenting on "the most astonishing number of orders, considering the almost disturbed conditions" that the cars had already generated, he touched on some especially important points for salesmen to keep in mind as they set out to sell the cars. Because of all the changes made from traditional Pierce-Arrow practice, Graham stressed the need to refer to the new car without any reference to horsepower, unlike the previous practice. In view of "the greatly increased power," he asserted, the reference to rated horsepower was "entirely without meaning." He also pointed out that the headlamp option, on the fenders or on fender cross bars, was not always understood, many show cars having headlamps on crossbars. He urged salesmen "vigorously to press home the argument that we highly value the distinctive feature of the lamps on the fender, and have no thought of any change." Likewise, the appearance of disc or wire wheels as options on show cars did not mean they were superior. He stressed "the Company's opinion that the advantage is with the wood wheel for distance touring."

He also suggested that the superiority of the new body construction be emphasized. This was described in the "Sales Pointers on the Pierce-Arrow Car" booklet, distributed to the sales staff. The new "aluminum plate" panels were touted as superior in strength, silence, ease of repair, and lightness to cast aluminum construction. In his following "Passenger Car Conference No. 110" dated December 16, Graham noted the advantages of the reduced number of body models in the new line, saying it "has greatly simplified our dealers' problem of stocking cars for the different seasons." Ten body types had been distilled from the previous 60-odd. He argued that "each is so designed ideally to fit its particular field." He then went on to describe the 10 models individually, describing the way each filled a particular use. An example of his descriptions was that written for the Landaulet and Brougham, "the two cars," he wrote, "that place Pierce-Arrow in a class entirely alone." Noting that "these new cars more than held their own at the display in New York during the week of the Salon Show," he stressed the price advantage the standard bodies had over custom bodies, maintaining the Pierce-Arrow closed cars had a smaller margin of price over the open cars "than any of the high-grade manufacturers." In addition, they were able to compete against even custom-built cars. "No comment in New York," he wrote, "was more frequent than one concerning the difference of $3,000 between our standard closed cars and the $12,000.00 representing the cost for a Pierce-Arrow chassis with body of the custom maker." The reception of the new Pierce-Arrow seemed to be quite promising.

At this point in late 1920, it appeared that Pierce-Arrow was within sight of the objectives that had brought about such fundamental changes in its leadership, operations and output over the previous year. It was now reorganized on a peace basis as required. Despite the cold economic climate there seemed to be a feeling of great achievement and a vision of great success. It would be the natural outcome of the company's long and successful reputation as the builder of the best and only the best by the best and for the best. It only remained to finish the complicated reorganization and turn out its lines at the higher volume it was confident it could merchandise profitably.

1921 Series 32 Pierce-Arrow Landaulet (courtesy Buffalo and Erie County Historical Society).

~ 12 ~

A Most Difficult Year
(1921)

> I had gotten a job offer with Laidlaw. I told the Colonel about it, and a short time later he called me into his office. He knew of impending changes and said, "Things are going to happen around here, son. We are going to have new people in who will have no truck with the way we've been doing things. You're a luxury in most places around here, son, and so, my advice to you is—take that job." I left shortly thereafter.
> —Herbert M. Dawley, Pierce-Arrow Art Department

The 1921 New York Automobile Show was held at the Grand Central Palace the second week of January, with the nearby hotels acting as supplementary sites showing some newer and less popular makes. The number of exhibitors at the show was the same as the year before—307. Eighty-nine makes of cars were on display. *Automotive Industries* in its January 13 issue headlined "Novelties Not Abundant at New York Show" over its review. It did note that "Relatively new chassis, such as Lafayette, Lincoln and Pierce-Arrow are magnetic centers." These were among the "thirty-eight polished chassis" that were on display at the show, a number that the magazine sadly noted fell below the number at earlier shows. For a 75¢ entry fee spectators could browse for hours investigating the variety of offerings. Trends were clear, but innovations were minor, and could mostly be classed as refinements. Cars were being used for a wider range of purposes and more challenging service than ever before. Comfort and reliability were seen as paramount. While changes were not spectacular, they were important. Among the most notable was the increasing popularity of the unit engine/transmission. This and the use of more powerful Alemite pressure grease fittings were both major steps forward. Pierce-Arrow featured only the latter. Of more significance, perhaps, was the obvious decline in the use of the "T-head" motor, such as Pierce-Arrow used. Nearly one-third of cars offered in 1913 had a T-head layout. They now appeared on only 4 percent of 1921 production cars, overwhelmed by the L-head engine. Closed bodies were in greater demand for their comfort in all weathers. The magazine remarked at the brighter colors with which cars at the show were painted. Pierce-Arrow felt it had an advantage with its redesigned model in a field that was largely unchanged from 1920's offerings. Its most spectacular show car would doubtless have been the 2-passenger Runabout, a low, sporty model that featured a disappearing top. A variation of this car, painted a spectacular yellow color, had been the hit on the Leon Rubay stand at the Automobile Salon weeks before, written up in *Vanity Fair*.

12. A Most Difficult Year (1921)

For comparison, there were new and advanced competitors like the eight-cylinder Lincolns and Lafayettes. Their impact on the market would not be clear until their production reached normal levels.

The customary NACC dinner at the Commodore on Friday was also covered in this show issue of *Automotive Industries* under the headline "Confidence Features 21st N.A.C.C. Dinner." The declining market for motor vehicles may have diminished the sense of celebration for many of the 700 attendees, among them "some of the most prominent automobile bankers in the city," to quote the reporter. "There was no atmosphere of gloom," he maintained, however, "but rather the reverse." Charles Clifton, the toastmaster as well as president, was quoted as saying in this context, "Things aren't so _____ bad as they have seemed." The evening's speaker, Francis H. Sisson of Guarantee Trust, opined that "the most critical of the post-war adjustments have been passed." There were hopes that this optimistic note would carry over into sales.

Concurrent with the show opening was the beginning of the Pierce-Arrow nationwide advertising campaign. The large format, high-quality magazines saw the usual full-page color advertising from Pierce-Arrow, every example of which featured an illustration of a single body style against a milky background and labeled a "portrait" by Edward A. Wilson. With that note and the name of the body style portrayed, the only copy to read was "Pierce-Arrow" in large script. It was the company's usual understatement. Although much changed, the new Pierce-Arrow was marketed with a quite familiar advertising format.

Back in Buffalo, however, uncertainties were quite evident. President Mixter, writing a New Year's greeting in the January 1921 issue of *The Arrow*, exhibited a noticeable concern. He pointed out the positive reception the new models had received, and the fact that the factory had "orders for over three months' conservative passenger car production." But selling conditions were not at all promising. "At present," he noted, "all manufacturers of trucks are experiencing serious curtailment of sales, and Pierce-Arrow is no exception to this general condition." As a result, the number of employees working at Pierce-Arrow was less than half the number working during the summer of 1919. Careful cost saving was the order of the day, although there was clear hope that the company was "in a fine position to get business when the conditions of the country make this possible." At about this time it was announced in *Automotive Industries* that Alfred Weiland, a former production engineer at Wright-Martin Co. and the Goethals partners, had been hired as an engineering assistant to President Mixter.

For some weeks there had been repeated bear raids at the New York Stock Exchange against Pierce-Arrow stock. In fact, the exchange itself was investigating a particularly serious raid on December 8 that had lowered the price from 76 to an ending price of 68 after hours of gyrations. Repeated assurances of the company's strong financial condition despite high inventory costs due to the new models and sales running some 20 percent below 1919 appeared in trade papers. *Automotive Industries* noted in its February 17 issue that, as of January 1, holders of Pierce stock numbered 2,880 for the common shares and 1,800 holding preferred. In the same issue a story titled "Pierce-Arrow Ready to Resume Schedule" announced that the reorganization of the Pierce-Arrow factory for volume production had finally been completed and that "regular schedules for its new passenger cars and trucks" had been announced the day before. "Few appreciate," President George W. Mixter was quoted as saying, "the enormous amount of detailed planning and physical work necessary to rearrange a big factory, install new machinery and produce new tools, dies, jigs, templates and other essentials required when new motor car and motor truck models are launched." Mixter anticipated that a factory force of 5,000 workers would eventually carry out his production plans.

The Arrow fulfilled its mission of publicizing the activities in the newly reorganized plant that spring. In the January issue, Production Engineer E.A. Taylor explained the benefits to body finish of the newly installed Nichols Drying System of air washers, heaters for exhaust and live steam, humidifiers, and accurate control system that brought "the *perfect* drying day into the factory every day and for all bodies." Taylor would soon leave his position at Pierce-Arrow to manage production at Liberty Motor Car Co. An adjacent page of the magazine showed the machining of a Series 32 engine block by a "new multiple drill." In the February issue, following an article about the Parts Department by the manager, Chan Cowles, was a page of photos and a description of engine testing by foreman L.H. Gates. He described in detail the process of assembling and testing the Dual-Valve Six on the third floor of Building C behind the machine shop. He noted that 20 test stands were in place, with 9 more being prepared. Assembly and testing had been carefully thought out so that the motors on their individual stands moved in only one direction during the process. Six rooms were in place for the silent test of motors with double-ended dynamometers "so that one engine may be prepared for test while the one on the other end is being run." Another page displayed photographs of the body drop in Building H on the new assembly line. Having been inspected on the second floor by "Uncle Charlie" Pfieffer, the body was lowered to the ground floor to be mounted on the chassis under the supervision of "Bob" Conn, after which the completed car was ready for inspection.

Leading the stories in the March issue was a description of the Pierce-Arrow Motor Car Co. Employees Benevolent Association and its activities by the company treasurer, Myron Forbes. His article was carefully documented with facts about the income and expenses incurred as it carried out its charitable tasks. In the same issue was a photo story about M.H. Lepine, who designed monograms and crests on Pierce-Arrow cars. The following month, a long story by H.P. Hinman about the newly completed factory power plant was published. As power plant manager, Hinman was able to completely cover the various activities in the facility such as concocting of production gasses for the factory, generation of electricity, and the transformers required to properly supply the necessary current. The plant also furnished the power that turned the shafts driving the miles of belts attached to the machine tools of the plant.

In that issue, as well, Allen Terrant contributed a description of the way the piece rate system for paying employees was developed and adapted to the work in the plant. This was Mr. Terrant's main occupation for the production engineering department at Pierce-Arrow. Sales were admittedly slow, but the tenor of these articles was that the operation of the Pierce-Arrow factory was equal to the challenge of high quality production at a competitive price.

On February 2, the Pierce-Arrow Motor Car Co. issued its annual report for the year ending December 31, 1920. It had recorded a net profit of $1,769, 914, a bit of an achievement for a year when the economy had endured such a steep decline. While earnings were just over half those of the year before at $3.88 a share, Pierce-Arrow, remarkably enough, had generated a surplus of $969,914. This added to a profit and loss surplus that now totaled $4,541, 545. Observers were impressed at these results. As the *Wall Street Journal* put it in its February 7 issue, "The company is in better all around position than ever before." Not only

Machining the Series 32 monobloc dual-valve engine at the plant (courtesy Pierce-Arrow Society).

had Pierce made a decent profit during hard times, they had used the depressed market as an opportunity to rearrange and re-equip the plant, allowing more efficient and more exact production techniques. In his comments on the report President George W. Mixter mentioned that some 80 percent of the tools and machines used in making the older models had been charged off against the previous reserve for depreciation. Loans, however, had more than doubled to $5.8 million. Part of that could well be attributed to expenses of the re-organization, but another chunk of it went to pay "merchandise creditors," according to the February 9 *Automotive Industries*. Overall, the magazine concluded in its February 17 issue, the outcome for 1920 was "satisfactory testimony as to the way Pierce-Arrow has weathered the trade cyclone."

Meanwhile production totals were inching up as adjustments within the re-organized plant were worked out. *Automotive Industries* reported in its March 31 issue that the plant was operating at "something over 50 percent capacity." They also reported that there had been "substantial improvement" in demand for passenger cars, but that "few trucks are being sold." By the April 21 issue, the magazine noted that Pierce-Arrow had shipped 280 passenger cars in March, and "April schedules call for 300." This was said to be "approximately capacity production for the passenger car plant." Truck sales remained slow, however. By this time it was taking 31 minutes to assemble a car on the conveyor, which traveled 7.7 inches per minute. Each station on the line was 20 feet long.

Unfortunately, by the spring of 1921 it had become clear that the new Pierce-Arrow car was displaying some serious problems in service. In late April, Delmar G. "Barney" Roos had been made car engineer under David Fergusson. Roos was a brilliant young engineer who had left Locomobile, now beset with problems, where he had worked under the great Andrew L. Riker. On April 28, Fergusson sent Roos a 13-page memorandum, with copies to "Mr. Mixter, Mr. Weiland, Mr. Roe and Mr. Sheppy," outlining the problems with the new car being addressed by the Pierce-Arrow experimental department "[I]n order that you may be thoroughly conversant with the development work in connection with the model 32 car." Noises from periodic vibration of the engine crankshaft and the timing gears topped the list ("the most important item," Fergusson noted). This problem demanded repairs for cars already in service and a permanent fix for future production. Other problems to be addressed included the flexing of car underframes and the new bodies in difficult road conditions, vibration of the steering column in the driver's hands, and the lack of caster action in the steering. There were other smaller issues. The interior and exterior hardware, supplied by the Sterling Bronze Co. after an exhaustive search at president Mixter's insistence, was not popular with dealers, especially the exterior closed car door handles. The front fenders, supplied by the Mullins Co., were troubled with cracking where they were attached to the frame and needed to be strengthened.

The periodic vibration from the engine was eventually controlled by application of a Lanchester damper to the crankshaft pinion on the camshaft drive train. Some cars already in service had even been experimentally retrofitted with a second flywheel at the front of the engine as a palliative, and an open version of the damper was to be applied to those. Some little time was spent developing the exact materials and assembly techniques to be used in production cars for the device, issues not completely settled until July. Concurrently, a variety of camshaft and other gears were fitted in an attempt to lessen engine gear noise. This second problem was not completely sorted out until August. As work progressed it became evident that the exhaust valves were not effectively cooled, and valves of ⅛ inch smaller diameter were designed to allow space for more cooling water around them. Tests of this new construction followed. The underframes were strengthened with side members ¹⁄₁₆ inch thicker. At some point, they were made ½ inch deeper and another cross member was added as well. The steering column was eventually relocated on the frame side members to eliminate engine vibrations traveling up from the engine to the driver's hands. All these efforts amounted to a "crash program." Mr. Roos noted in a July 5 memorandum to Mr. Weiland (copies to Mr. Fergusson, Mr. Guider, and Mr. Himmele) about the "Lanchester Dampner [sic]—Second Thousand Cars" that "There has been a good deal of confusion arising from the various experiments carried on by both the factory and the engineering [sic] Department due to the haste in which we are working out this problem." It might be added that even before all this revision the Stromberg carburetor, as originally fitted, had been replaced by a typical reed-valve Pierce-Arrow model similar to those Charles Sheppy had devised years before. Some records indicate that Sheppy himself was either let go or resigned from Pierce-Arrow around this time. If so, the separation was not long before being reversed. "Father" Sheppy remained a central figure in the Pierce-Arrow engineering department until his death in 1927.

12. A Most Difficult Year (1921)

There were other issues on the mind of President Mixter that spring of 1921. Back in January 1920 he had undertaken for Pierce-Arrow to finance the development of an advanced chassis design by Sidney Waldon of Detroit, previously employed by Packard. This was originally proposed as a four-cylinder car, seating four passengers. When this agreement was made George W. Mixter was still general manager at Pierce, and he seemed anxious to explore wider options open to the company for the future.

Before advising the agreement with Waldon, Mixter had sent chief engineer David Fergusson to Detroit to look over the plans for the new car and report back, which Fergusson did in a four-page summary, with an attached data sheet laying out estimated performance of the design. Some parts of the four-cylinder motor were then being machined for installation into a sample prototype car, and Fergusson described the car as having an engine and chassis of "rather exceptional" design. "The engine design is very clean," Fergusson wrote, "being largely a copy of the Hispano-Suiza engine except that the cylinders are a block casting of cast iron instead of being an aluminum case with steel liners. This makes a very clean and cheap cylinder casting."

At first glance, the proposed car did not suggest itself as a likely Pierce-Arrow design, having an overhead camshaft and a rear suspension system described by Fergusson as "similar to the Marmon." Waldon, however, foresaw the possibility of a six-cylinder version that would have a displacement of some 300 cubic inches, developing 110 horsepower at 3,000 rpm. This was more appropriate for a Pierce-Arrow, and Mixter went ahead with an agreement to underwrite the development, allowing Pierce-Arrow to use it if successful. The contract was signed on January 1, 1920, and extended to January 1 of the next year. It called for Pierce-Arrow to pay $41,468.16 to start the work plus periodic payments totaling another $33,531.84 (which eventually climbed to an even $50,000) while picking up expenses along the way. In 1921, Pierce-Arrow was not yet willing to contract to use the design, and, perhaps, felt it needed further development. On March 31, 1921, an extension of the contract was signed, enabling Waldon and his co-developer E.H. Sherbondy to continue their development work for another year in return for an additional $35,000 paid in installments.

Mixter was also convinced that some sort of public demonstration of the new Pierce-Arrow car was urgently needed to establish its reputation for reliability and strength on the road. Accordingly, Francis W. Davis told author Maurice D. Hendry in 1971, "On first April, Colonel Mixter called me into his office and said, 'Davis, we want to give the new car a cross-country test. We should have done this before putting the car into production. You, [experimental engineer, John] Talcott and [publicity director] Charlie Hodge will go along.'" A seven-passenger touring car was taken from the assembly line and prepared for the 10,000-mile journey from New York to California and back. The excursion took from April 7 to May 24 to complete, with visits to Pierce-Arrow agencies along the way. The route chosen was largely the Old National Trails Route through the country's mid-section, including the legendary Santa Fe Trail over New Mexico's Raton Pass, then on through Gallup and Flagstaff, Arizona, over the Cajon Pass into Southern California. Davis took 137 photographs during the journey, and a narrative of the trip for dealers appeared in "Passenger Car Conference No. 122," dated June 2, 1921.

Experienced drivers on such test runs, including Sidney Waldon, advised against making the trip in the spring because of the deep mud over roads west of the Mississippi and the likelihood of snow drifts in the high mountains out there. Both these difficulties were manifest during the trek, forcing continual repair of tire chains, off road travel in the mountains and periodically chopping collected mud out of the fender wells on the Plains. The journey was a complete success, however. On their side-trip up to San Francisco the mud-encrusted car arrived at W.F. Culberson's Pierce-Arrow Pacific Sales Company on Geary Street during the celebration of "Open Road Week" and was immediately placed on the showroom floor for publicity purposes. The only serious damage occurred after smashing into an unseen sunken spot in the road at 40 mph, which damaged two front springs. Occasionally the car had to be pulled out of deeper muddy patches with teams of horses, nothing unusual for such a trip at the time. When the trio entered the plant grounds on May 24, Davis remembered a "heroes [sic] welcome." Certainly, the car had performed very well in the Pierce-Arrow tradition.

In the April issue of *The Arrow*, a photograph of the front of the new White House limousine was printed on page 18, along with the assurance that it was on its way to serve newly inaugurated President Harding. Showing the conventional treatment of lamps on enclosed Pierce-Arrows, this car had "cheese box" headlights rather than the more conspicuous fender lamps.

However, the Pierce-Arrow Motor Car Co. faced a complicated situation that spring of 1921. The expected smooth progress toward larger and more profitable production appeared to be stalled. The truck market was very slow and the new car model was undergoing hurried revisions, despite its obvious promise. As Treasurer Forbes was well aware by that time, things were starting to look very dark for the company financially. As chairman of the Finance Committee, Charles Clifton knew this as well.

News of the situation became public when the *Wall Street Journal* for Tuesday, May 10, carried disturbing news. "Pierce-Arrow Deficit Due to Poor Truck Business," read the headline. The Pierce-Arrow Motor Car Co. had just announced that for the first time in its recorded history, it had lost money. The deficit totaled $489,502 for the first quarter, which the newspaper attributed to "the general stagnation of the company's motor truck business." Although the company had shipped over 500 cars during the period, roughly equal to the quantity shipped the year before, truck sales lagged far behind. This forced plant overhead expenses to be supported by what amounted to less than half the business. More alarming was the fact that "increasing sales resistance has been felt and demand has fallen off considerably from the April average." As a result, company plans were to "curtail operations, reduce forces and otherwise effect rigid economies wherever possible." To add to the bad news, the paper saw no indications that things would get better during the second quarter.

A news release the next day revealed the turmoil that the situation had initiated in Buffalo. The "working contract" between Pierce-Arrow and the Goethals partners had been terminated. Goethals & Co. was withdrawing from the Pierce-Arrow plant, although Pierce had invited Col. George W. Mixter to remain as president. The official story seemed to be that Goethals had suggested parting company with Pierce, the work they had been hired to do ("assist in bringing the plant back to a peace basis and revising its line of cars and trucks") having been accomplished. For his part, Col. Mixter had apparently agreed to leave his position with Goethals and relocate permanently in Buffalo. This story was widely covered. *Automotive Industries* noted in its May 12 issue that "his management has been entirely successful." The company's quarterly report did not appear to give obvious support for that conclusion.

With sales falling off and debts rising, the guidance that the Goethals partners provided to Pierce-Arrow certainly did not seem to have resulted in successful new product lines that

12. A Most Difficult Year (1921)

enlarged demand. Admittedly, the whole automobile industry was under great pressure at the time. No downturn in the market for automobiles had ever before been so severe or prolonged for the industry. Every maker was affected. Financial losses were widespread. Less secure companies were going to the wall. Pierce-Arrow's selling difficulties were commonplace. Crucial to survival was the ability to sustain losses while the downturn persisted. In this regard, Pierce-Arrow seemed fairly well protected. It had entered 1921 with retained earnings that totaled more than $4.5 million. However, the company now had debts that exceeded its nest egg. Assuredly there were also indications that the factory reorganization assisted by Goethals was successful at lowering costs.

If there was a weak spot for Pierce-Arrow it appeared to be in the product line itself. The new Goethals leadership did not appear to have impacted the approach very much. New postwar models were meticulous refinements of the previous models, laid out for efficient production and left-hand drive. No one seems to have asked if that was the most fruitful way to develop designs with a larger appeal. While the quality of the cars was very high, so was the cost to produce them. In the past, Pierce-Arrow was accustomed to being able to sell everything it made regardless of cost. Perhaps that is why some obvious questions were not debated as the new models were developed in 1919–1920. While some production costs were reduced for these vehicles, much higher demand than before was needed to sustain company profits. So far, such demand had not been seen. Indeed, truck sales, the big profit center for the company, had sharply declined. It appears in hindsight that their offerings were adequate but not trend setting. Most glaring of the shortcomings was probably the decision to retain a T-head configuration in both car and truck engines. One clear outcome of the war was an expanded knowledge, as airplane engines were quickly improved, of exactly how power was generated by gasoline engines. In fact, a substantial part of the SAE summer convention in 1920 was devoted to this very subject. One casualty of that improved understanding was Pierce-Arrow's engine configuration. The shape of its combustion chamber limited the power the engine could put out. Even to ignite all the fuel in the cylinder required costly dual ignition. The competing L-head and valve-in head engines were no secret to the Pierce-Arrow engineering staff. They even laid out such engines, and tested many more made by competitors, but the need to adopt these more powerful and less expensive layouts never seemed to occur to them. Perhaps this was due to concentration by the company on motor trucks during the war, when their competitors were involved in aircraft engine development. Their best chance to pick up some of this understanding was never fulfilled because the Hispano-Suiza aircraft engines they were contracted to build were never actually produced, despite a crash program to set up the facilities to do so at great expense.

The war period had seen a good demand for cars in the Pierce-Arrow price range, and that uncommon demand continued after the Armistice. When the new Pierce-Arrow cars were first offered in November 1920 they entered a market composed not only of the old competitors, Packard, Locomobile, Winton, Crane-Simplex, etc., but also newly-designed upstarts whose design reflected some of the wartime advances. Except for Packard, whose Twin Six in many ways inspired the V-12 Liberty aircraft motor, the old-line firms hewed to their conservative approach, as did Pierce-Arrow to some degree. Of the newcomers, two V-8 luxury cars were direct competitors in Pierce-Arrow's market. These, of course, were Henry Leland's superb Lincoln and D. McCall White's admirable Lafayette. These two and the Pierce Series 32 Dual Valve Six were each of similar size and weight, were all beautifully finished, had force-feed engine lubrication and similar drivetrain layouts and braking systems, and even shared the same tire size. Lafayette carried a 348 cubic inch engine developing 90 HP on a 132-inch wheelbase; Lincoln had a 357 cu. in. engine also of 90 HP and a long wheelbase of 136 inches; Pierce-Arrow developed 100 horsepower from its substantial 414 cu. in. motor and carried it on a 138-inch wheelbase. The two V-8s weighed less and had smaller cylinder dimensions and less complex valve gear than Pierce-Arrow. They were all high-priced cars, Pierce-Arrow's range of $6,500 to $8,500 being the priciest among them. For each of these makers, the hope likely was that sales would reach 6,000 cars that year. In the end, none of them came close. Lafayette, late to go into production, managed only 700 cars, Pierce-Arrow produced fewer than 1,500 and Lincoln built just under 2,500. All of these competitors were losing money in the vicious down market.

Facing severe financial challenges, the Pierce-Arrow board decided on June 2 to pass the quarterly dividend on its preferred shares due to be paid on July 1 to "conserve the assets of the company during the present period," according to that week's issue of *Automotive Industries*. This dividend had been paid since January 1, 1917. Three weeks later the company released figures it hoped would show that the company was in no immediate danger. According to *Automotive Industries*, the release was intended to refute Wall Street rumors that had driven both share classes to lower levels the day before. The new figures revealed that the April 30 balance sheet showed quick assets of $20,878,000 compared with current liabilities of $8,379,000. The June 23 New York release insisted that "The Pierce-Arrow Motor Car Co. is in a sound condition." The board admitted that "our business has slumped and the truck business is very poor. We sold 2,200 passenger cars last year. Our schedule this year was 1,000 passenger cars to June 1." So far, some 850 had been sold and shipped in 1921, while the company had orders for 350 more on the books. Cash on hand totaled $1,337,000, and bank loans had risen to $6,650,000. The statement made the best of this situation with the assurance that "our borrowing limit has by no means been reached." All the same, the retained earnings were obviously slipping away fast. A general reduction of 10 percent in salaries was imposed on June 15 as another way to cut overhead.

The June issue of *The Arrow* had reached Pierce-Arrow employees and included an interesting lead article by Charles G. Kaelin, who would appear to have been some sort of superintendent in the body factory at Pierce-Arrow because the title of the article was "The Development and Production of Passenger Car Bodies." It was an insider's description of the way Pierce-Arrow developed the appearance and construction of its new composite bodies. The elements Kaelin noted as necessary considerations when body designs were developed were (1) mechanical, (2) beauty, (3) general design, (4) harmony with other units and (5) comfort. The first step after receiving "instructions to proceed with a new design" was for the Engineering Department to lay out the lines of the body on a blackboard in full size. It is likely that James R. Way, longtime body engineer at Pierce-Arrow, supervised this process.

Sure enough, an illustration in the article shows the chalked lines of a sedan body on a large blackboard. What is interesting is that the drawing does not show a Pierce-Arrow body then actually being produced, but what would show up later that summer as a four-passenger sedan of a new series of bodies. This was actually a sneak peek into the future. When the design on the blackboard was approved, it was transferred to a full-size body draft on "heavy drawing paper." On this draft was a grid of 10-inch squares, something like a giant piece of graph paper. The squares were the means by which dimensions from body lines drawn on the draft could be transferred to other drawings or actual parts of the "first body," the model for finished car pieces derived from the draft. Because the very large sheet expanded and shrank from changes in temperature, dimensions were not taken off it by measurement, but by what Kaelin called "scaling." Some parts were three-dimensional objects too complicated to draw and were made by fitting those pieces into the appropriate space on the "first body" itself. Drawings were necessary for other parts because they were going to be metal castings, forgings, or constructions. The completed body draft was "turned over to the Body Experimental Department for the construction of the first body." The "first body" was a full-sized mockup. Wood parts were laid out by the "Layout Man" in the form of templates for the shaping of the wood parts. These could be very complicated three-dimensional items shaped carefully by hand, using the curves on the draft as a guide. From these patterns, each one having the size, shape, thickness and kind of wood stamped on it, the production body parts were made. The Layout Man then constructed the "first body" out of the pieces so developed. The rest of the work of constructing the first body, according to Kaelin, the "paneling, painting, trimming, etc., is done in much the same manner as in regular production, with the exception of the forming of the aluminum panels, which in an experimental body must be made without the forms that are usually used." These forms were developed by the experimental body department along with the pattern body, the machining fixtures for the wood mill, the assembling fixtures, the metal forms to shape body panels, gauges, templates and sweeps for production. When everything was finished, four or five sets were made up for each type of body to see if everything would fit together. Then corrections were made before parts were ordered for production bodies.

While these efforts to redesign Pierce-Arrow closed bodies and perfect the chassis of its automobiles went on in Buffalo, on Thursday, June 2, Colonel Charles Clifton was in New York presiding at the annual meeting of the National Automobile Chamber of Commerce at the Marlin-Rockwell Building on Madison Avenue. It was a tumultuous occasion. All year long, the NACC had tried to bolster the confidence of its members, disillusioned in the face of a relentlessly soft market for their products. By June, the ravages of the season's low sales volume had provoked a sometimes-desperate avalanche of price reductions. As *Automotive Industries* reported in its June 2 issue, an even dozen manufacturers had lowered prices that week. Among them were both Lincoln and Lafayette. Hudson and Studebaker had cut at least $150 from their prices, and the Nash factory in Kenosha was on half-time because of slack sales. The magazine's coverage of the NACC meeting was headlined "Manufacturers See Need for Decision on Prices." They looked to Clifton and the organization to "stabilize the industry." The article emphasized, "It was felt, that whatever reductions are contemplated in prices should be made at once in fairness to dealers and to the purchasing public." The magazine's deadline did not allow them to cover the afternoon session of the annual meeting, so any decision made by the members was unrecorded there. Later on the agenda were reports on business conditions in various sections of the country regarding importation of trucks exported during the war and distribution of service parts. The report made to the meeting by W.P.G. Harding, governor of the Federal Reserve Board, was covered, assuring them that "there would be no discrimination against automobile paper." The story reported his declaration that "so far as finances are concerned he can see no reason for anything but optimism in the future." His optimistic remarks may or may not have been reassuring to his listeners.

Even less publicized was the election of officers for the organization, which took place later in the meeting as well. As expected, Charles Clifton was re-elected president, making it the eleventh time he had been chosen to serve.

Clifton was also gone from Buffalo on July 11 to give a talk at the celebration in Cleveland of the 20th anniversary of the White Company's entry into the automobile business. In his talk, noted in the July 14 *Automotive Industries*, Clifton recalled his twenty-year friendship with Windsor T. White, company chairman, dating "from the days of the now famous New York-Pittsburgh Mudlark Tour in the fall of 1903." Clifton was the only representative of the whole industry present at this gathering of the White family of officers, employees, and representatives.

Later in July, Monday the 18th to be exact, Clifton was in Buffalo to chair the board meeting of the NACC. "Directors were in Buffalo," *Automotive Industries* reported in its July 21 issue, "for the monthly meeting, which has been held here once a year since Colonel Clifton became president." In honor of his election to an 11th term in office, the directors presented him with a painting for his private art collection: *Le Palais Rouge*, a scene of Venice painted by Henri Le Sidanier. In making the presentation, *Automotive Industries* reported that Packard Motor Car Co. president Alvan Macauley had said, "people usually wait until a man dies before they laud his efforts, but that in the case of Colonel Clifton his services to the industry had been so great and had extended over such a long period that it was considered a privilege to give him the painting as a token of appreciation for his valiant services." Macauley went on to summarize Clifton's place in the industry as "the father of co-operative competition."

Despite this high point in the summer of 1921, the financial toils of Clifton's company were emphasized by the end of the month when the results of the second quarter were released. *Automotive Industries* noted in its July 28 issue that Pierce-Arrow's operating loss for the April–June period had risen to an alarming $828,866. A year before the company had reaped a profit of $1,432,766. The addition of allowance for federal taxes, etc., brought the three-month total deficit to $1,400,550. There was no way to sugarcoat such results. The only salvation depended upon the market that could be developed for its product lines. Indeed, all hands were by that time occupied with the improved line of cars to be put on sale in August and designated Series 33.

The dealer convention to boost the new line opened at the factory on Tuesday, August 9. Works Manager John F. Guider reported the result in the September issue of *The Arrow*. The effect of Pierce-Arrow's troubles on plant morale was evident in his remarks. "There is no doubt but that the cars going out are the most expensive and best built cars ever turned out at the Pierce-Arrow factory," Guider wrote. "I hope every man will realize the

The Series 33 Pierce-Arrow Dual-Valve Six motor, as revised at heavy cost in 1921 (courtesy Pierce-Arrow Society).

12. A Most Difficult Year (1921)

superiority of the car and do his work in a spirit of co-operation and pride." He noted the dealers at the convention had left with the feeling that they made "a very fine car and one that will sell in great numbers." Dealers had ridden in them through the Boston Hills and looked over several "new types of bodies on the 33 chassis." Ed Retling, the supervisor of the test program, added that "She's the same old powerful dual-valve, only better." It seems to have exhibited a noticeable improvement in road behavior because of heavier frames "with the extra braces." The 19-year veteran tester wrote, "Over rough roads you won't get any weaving motion and that means no body squeaks or rattles." In summary, after covering the effect of the damper on engine vibration, new spring shackles, and driving position, he concluded "She rides like a ship in a dead sea." All efforts in the magazine were clearly aimed at making the whole factory staff boosters of the line. Admiring comments by dealers like Sam Breadon of St. Louis, Tony Ledermann of Utica, Henry Paulman of Chicago, and W.F. Culberson of San Francisco were quoted, and editor Allen Werner exhorted at the start, "Let's make it a boosting party."

By this time, everyone was aware how high the stakes were for the company. On August 15, the company reduced prices on its line by $1,000 on open models, $500 on closed cars. In addition, several new body designs were on sale, a coupe-sedan, four-passenger sedan, and a French Limousine with a stylish open chauffeur's compartment. By August 22 a new seven-passenger sedan and enclosed drive limousine were added. The new bodies were notable for the thin door and windshield pillars. Front doors of closed models now opened to the rear, and ventilation was carefully provided with adjustable windshield, door glass that lowered out of sight and "duplex" rear quarter windows. A tonneau ventilator was concealed in the dome light fixture. Most importantly, the construction of the roof structure had been changed to eliminate drumming sounds. These closed cars, along with their open counterparts, a runabout, four and seven-passenger touring cars, and convertible Landaus, would constitute the Dual-Valve Six offerings for the next five years.

To publicize the new line, its altered contours and features, the company released a new catalogue with large color illustrations of closed cars in the line by Amos Northup. Some of these illustrations were used in the few full-page color advertisements the company could still afford to run in late 1921 and early 1922.

October 1921 proved to be an eventful month at the Pierce-Arrow Motor Car Co. In the previous month or two the softness in the market for automobiles, and even trucks, began to strengthen. However, the difficulties the company had undergone began to have their inevitable negative effect, which resulted in the departure of two very important figures. David Fergusson, who had been chief engineer for essentially all of Pierce-Arrow's existence, announced on October 8 that he had "severed his connections with that organization." This unexpected announcement appeared in *Automotive Industries'* October 13 issue, along with the speculation that "It is probable that the company will not appoint a successor." Fergusson's 10 percent salary reduction in June may have been part of his reason for leaving. He soon opened a consulting practice and ended up as chief engineer at nearby James Cunningham Son & Company in Rochester, the maker of very limited production luxury cars.

The magazine assumed that car engineer Barney Roos would remain in the engineering department at Pierce, along with E.R. Friend, a former General Motors and Murray Motor Car Co. engineer who had recently been named car chassis engineer there. In the same issue, the magazine also covered the equally unexpected departure of Vice-President George M.

Graham who had decided to move over to the Chandler Motor Car Co. as vice-president, overseeing "sales, service and advertising." Starting in the newspaper business, Graham had supplied publicity, advertising, and promotion campaigns for several automobile firms, including White, Packard, and Mitchell. He had joined Pierce in 1915, and rose to become the sales head by 1920, as well as doing important jobs within the industry during the war. He was especially well known for his oratory and had a reputation as an analyst and economist. Graham remained an important figure in the automobile business for many years more. His reason for leaving Pierce-Arrow was "a desire to associate himself with a quantity production company producing popular priced and high-grade cars." The Chandler/Cleveland combination had sold over 23,000 cars in 1919 and was looking to enlarge its market share. When Graham left Pierce-Arrow a spectacular send-off was held at Buffalo's Ellicott Club on October 28, attended by virtually every high-level official at the plant, including Robert O. Patten, truck sales manager and toastmaster; Col. George W. Mixter, president; Charles Clifton; John F. Guider, production manager; Myron E. Forbes; Laurence E. Corcoran, passenger car sales manager; Robert F. Coleman; Joseph C. Dudley; Chan D. Cowles; Thomas J. O'Rourke; Fred G. Wells; E.F. Himmele; Charles Sheppy, and Walter P. Cooke.

Other, more positive, things were also happening at Pierce that October. In fact, it must have been a bit of a relief to read a story in the October 20 *Automotive Industries* headlined "Pierce-Arrow Nears Normal Conditions." Col. Clifton, from his official position as chairman of the Pierce-Arrow board, had released a statement dated the 17th noting that "production and sales activities, which have been increasing gradually for the last three months, now have reached proportions rapidly approaching normal." So promising was the situation that the Colonel said he expected the production force of 4,250 workers would continue running at full time for the next six months, with even a possibility of needing more. Both car and truck orders had seen great improvement. "In September we shipped twice as many trucks as for any other one month of the year," he wrote. "On Oct. 1 we had more orders on hand than on the first of any month this year." There was an unexpected quality to this statement, not so much due to its content as to its source. For more than a year, Charles Clifton's name had not regularly appeared on such statements from Pierce-Arrow's management. Normally the company presidents, John C. Jay, Jr., at first, then George W. Mixter, had originated them. It may be that the importance of such an improvement in the demand for Pierce-Arrow products prompted the occasion. It might also indicate that there was some disarray within top management, or a desire to use Clifton's long-developed credibility to enhance the message.

The statement released by Pierce-Arrow early the next month was not so sanguine. Its headline in the November 3 *Automotive Industries* read "Pierce-Arrow Deficit Increases Last Quarter." That deficit from the end of the July–September quarter totaled "$2,109,999 after charges, depreciation, and Federal taxes." Things had certainly not been moving in a favorable way during 1921. The previous quarter's loss was only $1.4 million. The corresponding quarter in 1920 had netted a surplus of $355,310. In fact, the first nine months of 1921 had seen a deficit that reached over $4 million. These circumstances suggested to the directors that they set up a "special reserve fund of $3,750,000" against the possible "shrinkage of inventories and other contingencies." It was a provident act but a lot of damage had already been done. Shortly after this release a substantial change in personnel took place.

In the November 10 issue, the "Men of the Industry" section of *Automotive Industries* revealed that "Myron E. Forbes, who has been treasurer of the Pierce-Arrow Motor Car Co. since August 1919, has been made vice-president of the company. He will continue to act as treasurer." A brief resume of Forbes' career followed. The November issue of company magazine *The Arrow* carried congratulations for Forbes on page 3: "In recognition of his capable management of the treasurership of the Pierce-Arrow Motor Car Company, Myron E. Forbes has been promoted to the office of vice-president of the Company." It is perhaps worth noting that one of Myron Forbes' predecessors as treasurer at Pierce-Arrow was none other than Charles Clifton.

Later in the issue, a story, "Second Truck Experimental Trip," gives a glimpse into the processes used by the company to refine its product. A crew from the experimental department had taken a truck late that fall out to Wilkes-Barre, Pennsylvania, for testing on Giants Despair Hill, which was "a good mile in length and the average grade is 14 to 20 percent" according to Mr. Gordon, the truck experimental engineer who had supervised this second trip to the site for test purposes. The company had found the site "ideal" and hoped to establish a permanent camp near Wilkes-Barre, a convenient 270 miles from Buffalo. The weather during the tests was described as wet and cold. "These tests are purely for experimental purpose," Mr. Gordon noted, adding the trucks were put through situations "which the ordinary truck never has to face." The engineers had set up a campsite by the roadside, with "sustenance and sanitation considered." The group, besides Gordon, included "Messers Kobler, Hilbert, Hutton, Kranskopf, Ortner, Newsome and Huber of the Experimental Department, and Mr. Francis Smith of the Service Department." Among the visitors to the camp as tests were carried out were Francis Davis, Harry Ward, and Stanley Mills. The Pierce-Arrow Company continued using this site for testing its products for many years to follow.

Myron E. Forbes, rising star at Pierce-Arrow, became the firm's vice-president in November 1921 (courtesy Pierce-Arrow Society).

By the December 1 issue, *Automotive Industries* was willing to make a brief analysis of Pierce-Arrow's prospects in its "Financial Notes" columns. Their prognostications, probably based on company sources, started with the suggestion that a small profit might well be achieved for the final quarter of 1921. Unlike the $4.5 million surplus with which the firm started the year, they imagined the amount would have fallen to "less than $500,000." The company had improved its prospects, in the opinion of the magazine, by adjusting its inventories down by $2 million and by "a reduction in the overhead." They expected no reduction in the $7 million in bank loans by year's end, however. They did find optimistic evidence that passenger car sales were "in fairly good volume" and "truck trade holding up." Helping the latter situation was the order for 87 heavy trucks from New York City that totaled $350,000. The order also brought the output in the truck department at Pierce-Arrow up to "about 100 percent." At least some improvement could now be seen in the company's situation, however precarious it might turn out to be.

Quite unexpectedly on December 29, George W. Mixter resigned his position as president and withdrew entirely from Pierce-Arrow. Announcing the resignation, Col. Clifton noted that Mixter had consented in May to remain president "until certain work he had inaugurated was completed." Although the work in question, which was not specified, had in fact not been completed, Mixter had asked to be relieved of his position. While Myron Forbes was the obvious choice to succeed Mixter as president, and was, in fact, so named by the magazine, some confusion surrounded that office for months to come. To move ahead from the negative news, Clifton expressed satisfaction with indicators that the company made "a product which can be manufactured with satisfactory results both to the public and to stockholders." From a low point of 1,800 workers earlier in 1921, Pierce-Arrow now needed about 3,200 to supply demand. The situation at the end of 1921 was not all negative at least.

~ 13 ~

Searching Out Safety (1922–1923)

> When I was a young man, Charles Clifton, although from a fine family, was far from wealthy. He was a member of the First Unitarian Church downtown, where he rented a sitting in a pew. Being short of funds for some time he did not pay the pew rent. He received several notices about it, and eventually was told that the sitting was rented to another who would pay. He stored up that experience in his mind and decided that one day he would get even with them.
>
> Not long afterwards, he was confined as a patient in General Hospital for expensive treatment, and inasmuch as he had not the wherewithal to pay, he received repeated notices from the hospital. This also he stored up in his mind.
>
> In 1891, he married Miss Grace Gorham, a member of Trinity Church, and they settled on Irving Place. The Cliftons had a son, Gorham, and two daughters Katherine and Alice. Katherine became very ill and died in 1902 at the age of ten years. This stroke, as it were, from the hand of God, Col. Clifton took deeply to heart.
>
> During the following years, he achieved eminence and wealth. His opportunity came to get even.
>
> He sent a large sum of money to the First Unitarian Church to endow pews on condition that they be made free.
>
> He provided funds for the erection of a new wing of the General Hospital which later on became known as the Clifton Building. This was Charles Clifton's way of getting even.
>
> —Reverend Cameron Davis, Rector, Trinity Episcopal Church

In its January 12, 1922, story with what proved to be the erroneous headline of "Fergusson Will Rejoin Pierce-Arrow Company," *Automotive Industries* behaved as if they had been chastened. "The announcement by Colonel Charles Clifton, chairman of the board, that M.C. Forbes [sic] had been placed in charge of operations was misconstrued," began the second paragraph. "Forbes' title remains that of vice-president and no one will be elected for the present to succeed George W. Mixter as president." It is difficult to ascertain just who exactly undertook the president's duties at Pierce-Arrow for the next several months. Hilton Hornaday, writing in *The Buffalo Evening News* May 7, 1938, had no doubts. "Col. Clifton stepped into the driver's seat as the big boss again," Hornaday wrote, "and had to rehire Sheppy to get out a car that would run. Around the plant, in those days, they used to call this 'Sheppyizing' the cars." Perhaps the period at issue was an example of the objective Clifton himself mentioned at New York to the company dealers in 1916. "I have been very much occupied with the effort to so build up this organization," he had said, "that, whether it had a leader or not, didn't make very much difference." This ambition seems a bit unsystematic somehow. Perhaps Myron Forbes was in fact given all the executive authority without the title for some reason. An informal committee system could even have been developed temporarily. In any case, the deciding power for the Pierce-Arrow management at that time was in the hands of banks, both in New York, especially the Seligmans, and in Buffalo. Whoever was in charge had to have their confidence. There is every reason to suppose, however, that Myron Forbes and Charles Clifton worked comfortably together at Pierce-Arrow's front offices.

Now, the firm set out to recover its former standing. The New York Automobile Show opened on Saturday, January 7, 1922, at the Grand Central Palace for automobiles and accessories, again under the sponsorship of the National Automobile Chamber of Commerce. For the occasion, Charles Clifton, as NACC president, was invited to contribute his observations for the *New York Times* show supplement the next morning. In an article entitled "Want Owner's Good Will," he presented a wide-ranging overview of the situation within the industry. "It will be a good year for the car owner," he noted at one point, "and good in certain respects for the dealer and manufacturer." His dissertation included mention of an improved export market, the expansion of long distance trucking, and the importance of public financing for and organization of a United States highway system. "Expansion," he noted in his very first sentence, "will characterize the year in 1922 in the motor industry. I do not mean necessarily that there is going to be larger production," he continued. "In fact, any one who speaks of growth simply in terms of production has a very limited conception of what the industry means. Beyond a certain point essential to carry the overhead, output of new cars is secondary to other considerations." It was the voice of experience, his optimism still apparent.

The annual dinner of the NACC was held on Thursday evening, January 8, at the Commodore Hotel grand ballroom, and was covered by both *Automotive Industries* and *Automobile Trade Journal* in subsequent issues. "Charles Clifton, president of the N.A.C.C., presided as toast master," the *Trade Journal* wrote in its account. "Eight hundred executives of automobile factories attended the banquet." First speaker that evening was Edwin Denby, the secretary of the Navy soon to be disgraced in the Teapot Dome scandal, who had served on the Detroit Board of Commerce and was well known in the industry. In what *Automotive Industries* called "a rousing reception," a United States flag was run out from the balcony and Navy signal flags over the speakers' table spelled out "Welcome" while the orchestra swung into a rendition of the National Anthem. Denby's speech itself was a personal recollection of his experiences in the Marine Corps. as a private and as a petty officer. One passage was directly related to the current industry circumstances. "It is a matter of tremendous pride, to you and to me," Denby said, "to think that through this terrible depression through which our country has been going, the automobile industry has more than won its way and held its own, and now I think we begin to see daylight. That is what we think in Washington, and that is what I think you think." Humorist Irvin S. Cobb, the "King of After-dinner Speakers," then delivered a talk titled "Gasoline, the New National Drink," in which he argued for world-wide development of roads and the cars to travel on them. O.C. Hutchinson of Dodge, chairman of a special committee "to investigate the Pirate Parts Situation," read the committee's report, which concluded that once a manufacturer had "made his parts right, distribution right and his discounts right, the rest of the job is education." And the dinner closed with distribution of the usual burlesque awards for achievement to various executives.

Pierce-Arrow had brought an impressive delegation of its executives to the automobile show. According to *Automotive Industries* of January 12, it included Clifton, as chairman, leading the group accompanied by "M.C. Forbes, vice-president; Charles Sheppy, chief engineer; L.C. Corcoran, passenger car sales manager; and R.O. Patton, truck sales manager." They would perhaps have already had copies of the new 18-page brochure showing the entire line of Pierce-Arrow "Open Car Models." This would appear for the spring selling season and featured lovely pen and ink over scratchboard illustrations by Mildred C. Green. The company continued to mount advertisements of its new offerings with the Amos Northup catalogue renderings through the early spring as well. At that point, national advertising appeared to stop. David Fergusson, by the way, never returned to Pierce-Arrow, *Automotive Industries'* report to the contrary notwithstanding. In fact, Charles Sheppy probably became chief engineer because "Barney" Roos was persuaded to return to Locomobile in 1922.

By this time, Ted Selman had rejoined Pierce-Arrow, unexpectedly enough, to conclude what had turned out to be a difficult situation in France. Selman had been quite content at Hudson, but received a letter from George W. Mixter, then still president at Pierce, asking if there was "any chance that under the present depressed conditions you would care to make a change," noting that he felt Selman's leaving had been a "distinct loss." Selman declined the offer with thanks but was then surprised to receive a return telephone call "from the man I had known as Treasurer at Pierce, saying, in effect that the Mixter management was out," and that he now was "in charge for Buffalo banks." Selman's second refusal was met with repeated calls to his office from Buffalo until they attracted the attention of Roy D. Chapin, the head

A Series 33 Enclosed Drive Limousine, practically Pierce-Arrow's bread-and-butter offering (courtesy Pierce-Arrow Society).

of Hudson Motor Car Co., who was also quite active with Clifton in the NACC. Talking the offer over with Selman, Chapin noted that indications were that Pierce-Arrow was on the way out, but he understood Selman's loyalty because of the way earlier Pierce management had treated him as an employee, especially during his very serious illness in 1915. Chapin agreed to let Selman rejoin Pierce temporarily to assist in the liquidation of its troublesome French assets, which was the job Forbes wanted him to do. That completed, Selman could rejoin Hudson. Selman then consented to a two-year contract with Pierce-Arrow, living and travel expenses paid.

Arriving in France, he found a vast supply of costly service parts with no appreciable market, due to "import duties and unfavorable exchange rate." A similar, if less extensive, situation existed in the British Isles also. Rather than dump the parts on the market for whatever they would bring, Selman and Forbes worked out a plan to go into manufacturing of parts "by arrangement with a well-known French car builder" that was also active in the market with surplus wartime trucks. A trunk load of blueprints were sent over from Buffalo to expedite this program, and hiring of employees with "marked ability" to carry out the plan went ahead.

As the selling campaign advanced in the early months of 1922, the price of shares in the Pierce-Arrow Motor Car Co. began unexpectedly to decline. A *Wall Street Journal* account mentioned that they had been "heavily sold all day" on Tuesday, February 7. Most troubling to the market appeared to be the overhang of a large debt from 1921. "Earnings of the company showed improvement in the last quarter," the publication noted, "but there are no indications that indebtedness can be reduced to any extent through earnings in the current year." *Automotive Industries* noted in a February 9 story that New York banking circles were aware of "an arrangement" allowing the company to obtain a million dollars cash "which will be used to pay all merchandise creditors." They added that the business of the company "especially in its truck department is more satisfactory than it has been for a long time." An unexpectedly strong sign of improving business in passenger cars was celebrated at the Pierce-Arrow plant on February 22 at a dinner given to honor Carl R. Osborn, the manager of the Colorado Springs branch of Denver's Kumpf Motor Car Co., the Colorado Pierce agency. Mr. Osborn had sold 13 cars in a week that month and had secured an order for 60 touring cars from the Broadmoor Hotel in Colorado Springs, according to the *Gazette Telegraph* newspaper. This last group of cars, painted "Artillery Gray with Thistle Green wheels," were to be employed for tours up Pikes Peak.

All in all, however, there seemed to be some anxiety about Pierce-Arrow's future. The $8 million the company currently owed, according to the *Journal*, was not expected to increase, but a means to pay it off had not been amassed, although some sort of bond issue was anticipated. "Pierce-Arrow's forthcoming annual report for 1921," the newspaper predicted, "will show a deficit of approximately $4,000,000," noting "a small profit" from operations in October and November. "Everything considered," they wrote, "Pierce-Arrow appears to be in fairly good all-around condition. With inventories marked down close to current raw material costs, anything approaching normal operations should permit of a satisfactory earnings showing." The catch, of course, was determining just what "normal operations" were going to look like. The expected "normal operations" anticipated in the reorganization of 1916, or even 1919, had not been achieved so far.

Amid these concerns, the Buffalo Club elected Charles Clifton as its president for that year. Rupert Warren wrote of Clifton at that post for the *Buffalo Club 125th Anniversary Book*,

Outside the Pierce-Arrow factory in the early 1920s. A Series 32 sedan with an early 6-passenger body is parked near the service area, and workmen repair the plant's plank road. In these postwar days the area is full of employees' cars (courtesy Buffalo Pierce-Arrow Museum).

"Clifton was an outstanding business leader … a vastly charitable man … but much of his charity was secret."

When the Pierce-Arrow Motor Car Co. released its annual report for 1921 at the usual time on March 1, 1922, it revealed, as expected, that the previous year had been bad. It looked, in fact, nearly catastrophic. The *Wall Street Journal* two days later put the situation very succinctly:

> The annual report of the Pierce-Arrow Motor Car Co. is just twice as bad as the quarterly reports indicated. As per quarterly reports, a deficit of between $4,000,000 and $5,000,000 was indicated. The annual report shows an actual deficit of nearly $9,000,000. Pierce-Arrow's surplus was not only wiped out, but there is a profit and loss deficit of $4,422,000. The report shows $7,150,000 owed to the banks. Since December 31 the company has borrowed an additional $1,000,000, making total loans $8,150,000. The loss last year was equal to almost $90 a share on the preferred. It is unusual to see a surplus of $4,541,547 at the close of 1920, transferred from the liabilities to the assets side of the 1921 balance sheet where it becomes a profit and loss deficit of $4,422,145.

Losses for 1921, in fact, had totaled an alarming $8,763,712. Under Chairman Charles Clifton's signature, the company offered the explanation that "The reduced volume of business caused an abnormal operating cost, which, together with the reduction made in selling prices and losses sustained through the writing down of inventories and commitments resulted in a loss as above." The March 2, 1922, *Buffalo Morning Express* headline understandably assured affected readers, "Pierce-Arrow on Upgrade Now, Directors Show."

There were still some curious aspects to ponder from the report, however. The most intriguing single entry quoted was, "Estimated losses in conjunction with inventories, adjustments in respect of obsolete parts, and in connection with changes in models." This totaled a whopping $4,197, 021.73 during the year. This certainly looks like an "abnormal operating cost," and it may well represent the actual cost connected with re-engineering the new Model 32 cars when the customers began bringing them back. The company appeared to be hanging on by the fingernails. Those closer to the situation believed that the many responses by the company to its situation during the last year had been costly, but if it survived they could pave the way for profits later. The present situation was certainly a challenge.

Another surprise appeared in the *Automotive Industries* datelined New York, April 5. The brief news item headlined "Merger Rumors Denied," and the magazine casually dropped the rumor that "management of the Pierce-Arrow Motor Car Co. would be taken over by C.W. Nash, preparatory to a merger with the Nash Motors Co." A routine company denial followed. Then, Thursday, April 13, the Pierce-Arrow board met with the board of Lafayette Motors and arrived at a tentative agreement for a merger of those two companies. A press release mentioned detailed "plans for the consolidation of the Pierce-Arrow Motor Car Co. and the Lafayette Motors Co." that were being worked out "following a conference of bankers and officers at which the plan was agreed upon in principal." As described in *Automotive Industries*, the plan was for Charles W. Nash, president of Lafayette, to become chairman of the board for the consolidated companies, "while Colonel Charles Clifton, chairman of the board of Pierce-Arrow will have charge of all operations." Nash Motors interests were not involved in the deal at all. Lafayette was a separate operation entirely. Banks said to have had a part in these discussions included J. & W. Seligman & Co., with interests in both Pierce-Arrow and Lafayette, and Lee, Higginson & Co., associated only with Lafayette. Both banks would supply board members for the consolidated company.

Following the sharp downturn just experienced by the industry, it was hardly surprising that consolidation would be sought by companies in exposed positions. However, this particular amalgamation seemed a bit odd, involving as it did two makers of expensive luxury cars, though Lafayette prices were some $1,500 lower than those at Pierce. Neither firm had reached its original postwar goals. Lafayette seemed especially disappointing. During its first year only some 700 cars had been sold. Pierce had not done all that much better, but the market for Pierce-Arrows now seemed to be improving, even in trucks, while Lafayette continued to lag. An important reason for the merger plan, according to Charlie Nash, was the capacity at the Pierce-Arrow plant to turn out good quality automobile bodies. Lafayette reportedly had been "experiencing difficulty in obtaining satisfactory bodies for its chassis," according to *Automotive Industries*. Nash, originally trained in a coach and body building factory, knew what he wanted from experience.

An April 18 scheduled meeting of Pierce-Arrow stockholders was postponed for lack of a quorum, according to an *Automotive Industries* story that week. Replying to questions, vice-president and general manager Myron Forbes, just returned to Buffalo from a visit to Lafayette in Indianapolis, insisted that there was "no announcement to be made at the present time concerning the merger and plans for the future would not be discussed." The next Monday further progress toward an agreement was reported from New York. The plan now called for an exchange of stock along with an issue expected of some $10 to $12 million worth of "notes and bonds" to pay off the Pierce-Arrow and La Fayette bank loans, "and provide working capital in addition." The plan was expected to be "submitted to stockholders in a short time," according to *Automotive Industries*.

The proposed combination abruptly collapsed on May 15, as reported in the May 18 *Automotive Industries*. The Seligman banking house that day made the announcement that the consolidation had been abandoned "because of inability to agree upon terms." No further details were given at that time. And none ever followed either, although the story reported that Charles Clifton had promised in Buffalo that "a statement of reasons would be given out in New York by committees representing both boards of directors." Rumor had it that one of the smaller banks lending to Pierce-Arrow did not go along with the agreed interest on the new securities proposed in the deal. Another rumor suggested that some Nash Motors interests did not like the involvement of C.W. Nash with this consolidation. Immediately after the announcement Lafayette production was moved from Indianapolis to Milwaukee where it languished. The end of this proposed merger meant Pierce-Arrow had to uncover some other way out of its debt problems.

An alternative path Pierce-Arrow could pursue had closed earlier that month. In a letter to Sidney D. Waldon dated May 5, 1922, Myron Forbes assured him, having received counsel from "Mr. Dudley" the company attorney, that the "rights as to patents, designs, etc." from the experimental car program that was assisted by George Mixter "revert to you." The agreement between Waldon and Pierce-Arrow had been allowed to lapse on April 1. A single experimental four-cylinder prototype from this program remains extant.

Representatives from some 100 manufacturers in the NACC membership met on Thursday, June 8 at its headquarters, and was reported in the June 15 issue of *Automotive Industries*. "The members who attended the meeting," the report noted, "were enthusiastic about business conditions and were virtually unanimous in asserting that their factories were operating at capacity." Outlook for the rest of the year was seen as very positive. Charles Clifton chaired the meeting and delivered an address somewhat at variance with the mood of the crowd. Pointing out that retail demand generally rose from two to six months in advance of production, and sales declined about the same interval ahead of production, he urged caution in the automobile industry. "Asserting that he would not sell the automotive industry short at any time or under any circumstances," *Automotive Industries* noted, "Colonel Clifton said he believed this was the time for conservative planning and thinking so that the manufacturers might not get into a position which would be harmful to themselves, their suppliers and their dealers."

Later in the meeting, still buoyed with enthusiasm, the members voted to continue "all the activities which the N.A.C.C. has carried on, notwithstanding the fact that it may mean further inroads upon the surplus in the treasury of the organization." There had been a heavy deficit the year before, but optimism was in the air. Directors whose terms had expired were re-elected, including Roy D. Chapin (Hudson), C.C. Hanch (Lexington), J. Walter Drake (Hupp), H.H. Rice (Cadillac) and John N. Willys (Willys-Overland).

Following the general meeting, an organizational meeting was held by the NACC directors, who unanimously re-elected Charles Clifton for another term as president. Also elected were Roy D. Chapin, vice-president; C.C. Hanch, second vice-president for passenger car division; Windsor T. White, vice-president for motor truck division; A.J. Brosseau, secretary; H.H. Rice, treasurer, and Alfred Reeves, general manager. At the even later meeting of motor truck members, Daniel L. Turner, the consulting engineer for the New York City Transit Commission, spoke on "The Auto Bus in the New York Transit Plan."

On Saturday, July 17, Pierce-Arrow announced a reduction of prices on its entire line of cars by $1,200 to $1,500. There was a general tendency to reduce prices at the time, especially on closed cars. The Essex coach model, introduced at the low price of $1,395 that year, had raised the popularity of closed cars. Pierce-Arrow prices now began at $5,250 for open cars, with $6,800 for the coupe being the entry point for closed models. The seven-passenger sedan listed at an even $7,000 f.o.b. This reduction could well have reflected improved productivity at the Pierce-Arrow plant as the reorganized operation was improved. That week's issue of *Automotive Industries* had, coincidentally, presented the fifth in a series of articles by Norman G. Shidle examining the automobile business in detail. This one was titled "$90,000,000 Business in High Priced Cars During 1922," and suggested that the sales of cars priced over $3,000 would "constitute about 1.5 percent of the total number of cars produced" that year. If true, this would represent a decline from 2.3 percent in 1921, but was not too far from the percentage the magazine found consistent from about 1915 on. Earlier years had seen higher percentages, even up to 6 percent in 1912. The high-priced percentage was also notably high in 1920, when it made up 3 percent of production. In 1922, seventeen makes produced cars in that price class, involving about 20 percent of the automobile manufacturers. Data in the article clearly showed the competitive market of which Pierce-Arrow was a part. Although that particular segment of the market was not as affected by price competition as others, Pierce-Arrow prices were in the higher range, even in this market.

Later that month renewed efforts to improve Pierce-Arrow's financial position were reported in *Automotive Industries*. Bank loans, they noted in the July 19 issue, had been reduced by $250,000, bringing the total down to a still hefty $7.9 million. By the July 24 issue, the magazine disclosed that a meeting of the directors that week would "discuss measures looking toward either the reorganization of the company or raising new funds." The banks involved, the article asserted, "will do everything possible to avert drastic action." The story also revealed that the price reduction earlier that month had more than doubled orders. "Additional men are being taken on," they wrote, "and production is expected to reach ten cars a day. Truck demand," they cautioned, "continues to lag and the truck output is under five a day." Apparently, the company continued to make slow progress toward stability. While there were signs of improvement, things were still disturbing enough for truck engineer Francis Davis to leave the company altogether. He had begun to feel that Pierce-Arrow was no longer keeping up with advances in the industry. His disillusionment with the company had started during the war when it decided not to pursue his design for a limited slip differential for trucks, a project that he had undertaken to cure problems trucks encountered in use around the battlefields. Davis left and set himself up as a consulting engineer for truck transportation improvements, eventually devising the power steering system now universally employed in the vehicle industry. The test bed for the latter development was his own 1921 Series 32 Pierce-Arrow runabout.

Pierce-Arrow did not announce a revised model lineup at mid-summer that year. Improvements were indeed made in its offerings, but all were minor "running changes." No new model introduction was staged, and not even national advertising appeared. Seen in a surviving engineering paper from January 1923 were schedules recording the sell-off at this time of the original closed bodies made for Series 32. These included the six passenger Sedan, Vestibule Sedan, the "old" Limousine, and the "old" French Limousine. The last two were both examples of the early style of limousine with full front roof, but touring car front doors. The "enclosed drive" limousine style with full front doors would prove more popular in the future. Later models of these types had the improved bodies with padded roofs and dome light ventilators. By 1923, all the older style bodies had been liquidated.

The August 17 *Automotive Industries* published NACC production figures which indicated that July production in the U.S. would total 246,600 cars and trucks, as compared to 288,000 in June, which had been the largest monthly figure ever recorded. The July figure did exceed the previous July figures by 39 percent, however. There was no doubt that the market was now recovering well from the 1921 downturn. Overseas, Pierce-Arrow was still trying to develop a profitable export business. Tom McArtney, who had escaped from the civil war in Russia back in 1918, was now working as a service and mechanical officer in Buenos Aires, Argentina. Ted Selman continued to work through the inventory problems in France and Britain. He was, evidently, achieving some success. In a letter later that fall, Myron Forbes remarked that he wished Selman was available to work in Buffalo, "but I will have to forgo the pleasure and benefits to be derived from your services," he wrote "with the full realization that you are saving us a great deal of money in the French situation." Selman also recalled that, at about that time, Col. Clifton entrusted him with a covert mission to personally deliver "a satchel full of important papers" from the head of Dunlop Tire & Rubber Co. (presumably in the U.S.) to his superior in England. Rumors were circulating that the rubber giant was "being fleeced to the tune of millions of dollars" in a factory project for Buffalo, and the papers allegedly pertained to the situation. Pierce-Arrow also used Selman as their

A sporting Series 33 4-passenger touring car (courtesy Pierce-Arrow Society).

agent attempting to buy "ten bodies of assorted types from leading [European] makers." Only M. Van den Plas in Belgium was interested, provided he was supplied with "dummy chassis for him to design to." The resulting $10,000 cost for each body was received with consternation in Buffalo, and that was the end of the project.

As the summer declined into fall, the actions of the Pierce-Arrow company underwent a subtle change. Some of its earlier confidence seemed to return. Most noticeable was the beginning of a nationwide advertising campaign in *The Saturday Evening Post*. From that October, through the next year and into 1924, full-page Pierce-Arrow advertisements appeared about twice each month. Their format was similar to what Pierce had used before, with large artist-rendered illustrations and evocative copy. Unlike the bulk of its earlier national advertising, however, these were not printed in expensive four-color process, but were composed of simple line drawings. These advertisements were the work of Henri, Hurst & McDonald, the current advertising agency for Pierce. The subject of the advertisements alternated between automobiles and trucks. A selection of newspaper advertisements with similar content for local dealers to use was available as well.

During a dinner on Friday, November 1, 1922, Charles Clifton was honored at the Buffalo Club with a formal ceremony to award him the Order of the Legion of Honor from the government of France "for services to France during the war," according to the next day's issue of *Automotive Industries*.

Later that month, November 28 to be exact, the Pierce-Arrow board at last named Myron E. Forbes president of the company, "thus relieving Col. Clifton of the detail work and leaving him a free hand to map out and direct the policies of Pierce-Arrow," according to a story in the November 30 issue of *Automotive Industries*. The magazine went on to describe Forbes as "prominently identified with the company as treasurer, vice-president and chief executive." S.O. Fellows succeeded him as treasurer at Pierce-Arrow. The story went on to compliment Forbes as having guided the company to "gratifying progress," suggesting that his elevation could be "interpreted to mean that Col. Clifton has completed his work of reconstruction undertaken two years ago." To further complicate the account, the article recorded that Clifton, having retired once, had at that time been called back to "the head of affairs" because the company was "in such shape" as to demand it. Having put in a busy two years, the story explained, "the Colonel feels that he can give up the presidency and remain as chairman of the board." The magazine noted Charles Clifton's great interest in "public welfare work in Buffalo." That and his continuing post as NACC president had further encouraged Forbes' advance at Pierce-Arrow.

As the year 1922 came to an end, the Automobile Salon already over, preparations for the NACC's 1923 automobile shows in New York and Chicago were disclosed. The show in New York was to be held from Sunday, January 6, to the following Sunday at the Grand Central Palace. That was the centerpiece, and many related events were scheduled also. From the 8th to the 13th the Automobile Body Builders would have their own show at the 12th Regiment Armory. The NACC Annual Dinner would be held again at the Commodore on January 9, at 6:30 p.m. The SAE dinner would be at the Hotel Pennsylvania on the 11th at a similar time. These were extended, convivial affairs not overly hampered by the theoretical existence of Prohibition. Through the week various luncheons were staged by related organizations: the Rubber Association at the Waldorf, the Motor Truck Committee on Friday, and dealer meetings for Oldsmobile, Franklin, and Hupmobile. In Chicago the NACC automobile show would be held at the Coliseum and the First Regiment Armory from January 27 to February 3. Over that same period the Chicago Automobile Salon would be held at the Drake Hotel, following its November closing in New York. Also during the week the National Automobile Dealers' Association and its board of directors would meet at the LaSalle Hotel.

An interesting project of the NACC was related to the show. It was an attempt to accumulate data about marketing, set up in the form of a contest to "feel out the public pulse as to the value of national shows," in the words of *Automotive Industries* in its December 23 issue. Essays were sought from motorists and "members of the industry" answering the following three questions about the national automobile shows: What value did they have for (1) the public, (2) my company and (3) me personally? Each of the three topics had to be covered in no more than 500 words, and the essays must reach S.A. Miles at the NACC offices by January 3. First place winner would be presented with a $200 pocket watch. Second and third places received watches worth but $150. It would be Charles Clifton's job to pick the judges who evaluated the essays. That project would be sort of a transition into the New Year from 1922, a year that witnessed the rebound of the automobile industry and progress of the Pierce-Arrow company away from corporate wastrel toward stable enterprise.

The year 1923 began with considerable confidence in the automobile industry. After all, the year before had been unexpectedly good. A *Wall Street Journal* headline for the January 11 story said it all: "Motor Industry Fared Well Throughout 1922." Among the five automobile companies analyzed to illustrate the point was Pierce-Arrow. Its recovery, although less spectacular than Chandler's and General Motors' had been, was, according to the story, a "substantial improvement." Their output had increased by only about 500 vehicles over that of 1921, but they had cut company losses to an expected $375,000 compared to the nearly $9 million the year before. Car sales had increased by 100 percent the second half of the year over the first. A revival in the truck business, the magazine concluded, "should enable Pierce-Arrow to show a real profit this year."

Reports had turned even more positive by the issue of January 19. While the nine-month figures for 1922 had shown a $376,960 loss at Pierce-Arrow, sales the last three months had been "at record figures." The New York branch had averaged more than two car sales a day during October, for example. Income had been high enough to pay off a million dollars of company debt, and it now appeared Pierce-Arrow actually broke even in 1922. The *Wall Street Journal* added that at a recent board meeting, a plan spoken of earlier to restructure its debt had been tentatively approved. By the January 26 issue, the company reportedly had "practically concluded arrangements for paying off its $7,150,000 bank loans through the sale of new securities." The February 1 issue of *Automotive Industries* reported that $7.7 million would soon be raised to pay off the current floating debt "and provide new working capital." The author of this proposal is unknown, but it was at least approved by the Pierce-Arrow Finance Committee if they did not actually author it.

The basis for restructuring the debt was in two parts. In the first part, the Pierce-Arrow Motor Car Co. would issue $3.5 million in one year 6 percent notes, backed by an issue of $6 million first mortgage gold bonds. The second part, the *Wall Street Journal* reported, would be for stockholders to subscribe to $4.2 million in 20-year, 8 percent debentures and accompanying shares of "no par value cumulative prior preference stock which is entitled to $8 a share in dividends annually." A sinking fund would retire $25,000 face value of the debentures annually, and the prior preference stock was convertible into common stock. To provide for

The 1924 Series 33 7-passenger sedan, with optional front brakes (courtesy Pierce-Arrow Society).

that conversion, 78,750 additional shares of common stock would be authorized. The securities had already been underwritten, according to *Automotive Industries*, by a syndicate that included J. & W. Seligman & Co., Hayden, Stone & Co., Chase Securities Corp., O'Brian, Potter, & Co. "and associates." The underwriters would take over any of the securities not purchased by stockholders under their subscription rights. Stockholders approved the proposal at a special meeting February 19. It took effect April 1, 1923. As Pierce-Arrow undertook this program to steady its financial ship for the future, it must have been a source of some satisfaction to Charles Clifton.

Spring advanced and Pierce-Arrow's situation seemed much more positive than it had for some time. Myron Forbes told the *Wall Street Journal* for its February 22 issue that the company had "booked more orders for trucks in January and February to date than for several years. Completion of the refinancing would give the company "in excess of $1,300,000 cash" after the bank loans had been liquidated. With the new successes, the company was now considering the future. "Management believes sufficient volume in both passenger car and truck business can be attained to carry overhead and place company in its former earning position," the article noted. There was some interest in the direction product development was headed, but the article specifically emphasized that "no plans have been considered for production of a popular priced car." The enlarged plant and its overhead had now been increased by the annual $672,000 fixed costs of the new securities. Sales continued to look good, however. In early March Forbes reported that passenger car sales were 161 percent better so far in 1923 than they had been the year before, and truck orders had increased 262 percent. At a dinner for Pierce-Arrow distributors on Monday, March 13, at the Iroquois Hotel in Buffalo, Forbes predicted "unprecedented prosperity," according a *Wall Street Journal* article. The next day a pamphlet turned up touting the manufacturing profit of $571,991 Pierce-Arrow had made in 1922.

The same day, the Annual Report for 1922 had been released. The summary from the *Wall Street Journal* that Tuesday summed it up in these sentences: "Pierce-Arrow Motor Car Co., for year ended Dec. 31, 1922 shows net income of $10,809, after taxes, depreciation and interest. This compares with net loss of $8,768,712 in 1921." In his comments on the report, President Myron Forbes clearly expected record production in 1923, although he noted that costs of materials and labor were rising and could cut into profits. He also noted that the scheduled production favored less profitable passenger cars 60 percent to 40 percent over trucks. This demonstrated, again, a failure of the market to meet the expectations of five years before. All the same, Pierce-Arrow reported on March 20 that the production of passenger cars totaled 140 in January, 160 in February, and was expected to pass 200 by the end of March. Productivity had risen from 15 men per month to build a car in 1920 to the present 10. Overhead at the factory had been reduced by $2,750,000 compared with 1921. The goal was to produce 5,500 to 6,000 vehicles by the end of the year.

Meanwhile, six new members, representatives of the syndicate underwriting the new securities, had joined the previous nine Pierce-Arrow directors on Monday, March 27. They consisted of G.M. Dahl, Lewis G. Harriman, J.H. McNulty, Roland L. O'Brian, Albert D. Sikes and Carlton M. Smith. They represented variously, Chase National Bank, Guarantee Trust Co., Irving Bank-Columbia Trust Co., Hayden, Stone & Co. and J. & W. Seligman & Co., of New York and Marine Trust Co., Fidelity Trust Co., and O'Brian, Potter & Co. of Buffalo. By the 30th, it became clear that in early 1923 the company had to produce 30 percent more trucks than cars to meet orders on hand. Over 900 vehicles had been shipped so far that year. "Banks have prophesied a substantial comeback under the operating management of M.E. Forbes," *The Wall Street Journal* noted approvingly.

Such heady news must certainly have encouraged some thinking about how the growing demand could be supported and enlarged. Accordingly, the *Saturday Evening Post* campaign was extended, and new sales promotions under the direction of Bill Henri of Henri, Hurst & McDonald were being developed. Back in the engineering and sales departments plans were under way to expand both passenger car and truck lines and take advantage of increasing opportunities in bus transportation and a strong car market. There was now a growing energy at Pierce-Arrow.

Some final details of the financial plan were reported in an *Automotive Industries* story datelined April 20 from Buffalo. Documents had been signed by Myron Forbes and E.C. Pearson, company secretary, for Pierce-Arrow and A. Ferguson, vice president, and F. Wolfe, assistant secretary for the trustees who would hold the $6 million Gold First Mortgage bonds on the "Elmwood and Great Arrow properties and the plant and machinery." These were security for the $3.5 million in 6 percent one-year notes being offered. The papers were then filed at the office of the county clerk and a mortgage tax of $21,000 paid. O'Brian, Potter & Co. issued a small brochure in May publicizing the offer of Pierce-Arrow Debenture 8s "as a businessman's investment." Part of the pitch was that sales for the year were, so far, "over 220% of those for the same period last year and unfilled orders on the company's books run over three times as large." Included as well was a reprint of a supportive editorial from the *Buffalo Courier* mentioning a postwar management that had "ignored long established policy and years of costly investigation, and started in with sweeping changes" that ended with the company "founded by George N. Pierce and so admirably built up by Col. Charles Clifton" figuratively piled up on "the rocks of financial despair." They then complimented the performance of Myron E. Forbes' "splendid psychological grasp and indefatigable energy" that had allowed the company to show a $105,000 profit for the first quarter of 1923. "We could use many more men like Myron E. Forbes," the paper concluded.

Charles Clifton made some headlines in *Automotive Industries* that June. The NACC held its annual meeting in New York beginning on Wednesday, June 6, for committee meetings. The board of directors met that morning, while the afternoon was taken up with the meetings of the legislative, motor truck, and highways committees. The Nominating Committee also had their session. Most trade conditions were seen as positive, and more cars than ever were being financed with time payments. The board discussed the gasoline tax "thoroughly" before sending it on to the general meeting the next day. The gas tax issue took up a long time and no final conclusion was reached. After that the elections were held on the nominees sent in by the committee on nominations. The result was the re-election of the entire slate. Officers and directors remained the same. "Colonel Clifton," the magazine noted, "starts in his eleventh term as president." Roy Chapin was vice-president again, as he had been since 1918. Later that month the magazine revealed that Charles Clifton had drawn attention to the growing problem with traffic that the wide adoption of automobiles had brought about. He had written letters suggesting that large cities take steps reducing the problem to mayors of such cities as Chicago, New Orleans, San Francisco, Boston, Atlanta, and Detroit plus the president of the National Conference on City Planning. In the letter, he had offered such solutions as more playgrounds to get children off the streets, improved traffic safety regulations, open boulevards paralleling crowded main thoroughfares, and providing additional parking spaces. Much discussion still continues around these same issues.

In 1923 Pierce-Arrow did not make large changes for the fall or introduce new models of either cars or trucks. Behind the scenes, however, carefully focused work was under way to develop important new Pierce-Arrows. The car engineers were in the midst of scaling down the Series 33 into a lighter and more maneuverable size to compete in price with smaller Packard and Cadillac offerings. Truck engineers were adapting a worm-drive axle for use in a purpose-built bus design that would also make use of the big dual valve six-cylinder motor. Both projects were moving along well, but neither was ready to introduce by mid-summer. Another task for car engineers was to incorporate front wheel brakes to meet the new competition already seen from Duesenberg and the foreign Hispano-Suiza and Isotta-Fraschini. In 1922, Pierce engineers had contacted Ted Selman in France, asking him to investigate the possibilities of arranging a license to use the French "Perrot" front brake system. General Motors offered a better price and obtained that license. Selman then found a promising alternative in the Isotta-Fraschini system that the respected Italian firm had been perfecting since 1908. Negotiations began with Isotta wanting a royalty of $15 a car to give Pierce-Arrow exclusive U.S. rights. This was more than Pierce wanted or was willing to pay for, and eventually Selman made a deal to secure rights for Pierce-Arrow alone to use the system for royalty of a dollar a car. The major difference between the two mechanical front braking systems was that the shoes in the Isotta system were pushed apart from the bottom by a cam turned by a rod in the front axle, whereas the Perrot system spread them at the top. Because there proved to be problems with brakes locking with the Perrot system at first, Selman described the Isotta mechanical brakes as "a perfect application." It was subsequently engineered into both the existing and the projected Pierce-Arrows.

Ted Selman later arranged the sale of all French Pierce-Arrow interests to a local man who paid Pierce royalties and served as their representative well into the 1930s. At this point Selman left Pierce-Arrow for the last time, highly praised by company officials.

By the late summer Pierce-Arrow financial news was very encouraging. The August 2 *Wall Street Journal* noted that earnings for the first half of 1923 were enough to pay all the interest charges associated with its restructured debt. The profit of $307,177 for the quarter brought the half year profits to $547,500, slightly above the needed $546,000 in interest. Production had totaled 2,157 during the period, 1,118 cars and 1,039 trucks. A $2 dividend had also been paid on the prior preference stock. At this point, company officials were expecting a higher output at Pierce-Arrow in 1923 than any previous peacetime year.

In September, the Pierce-Arrow Finance Corp. was incorporated in New York State to act as a source of credit for Pierce-Arrow distributors, dealers, and customers. Its entire $500,000 of capital stock was owned by the Pierce-Arrow Motor Car Co. and its officers and directors were active in the Pierce-Arrow company as well. Myron Forbes was president of both. The vice-president and general manager of the finance corporation was F.R. Bartlett. At the time Pierce-Arrow still owned the entire capital stock of the *Société Anonyme des Automobiles Pierce-Arrow* in Levallois Perret, France, as well as Puget Motors, Seattle, Washington. The company also had controlling interest in the Great Lakes Motor Co. of Cleveland, Ohio, which had been reorganized earlier that year. All these commitments were evidence of the company's intent to make use of time payments in their selling operations, and willingness to operate additional company retail outlets.

At the start of November, Pierce-Arrow reported operating income of $179,029 for the quarter ending September 30. Net income was $41,178. After meeting dividend requirements on the prior preference stock, there remained a balance of 9¢ a share for the 8 percent cumulative preferred stock outstanding. Dividends had last been paid on those shares the first quarter of 1921, so the company had more than two years of dividends to make up. Net income for the first nine months of 1923 had totaled $308,089.

As the year drew to a close, the automobile shows for the coming year were anticipated. In November, the Nineteenth Automobile Salon was scheduled for the 11th to the 17th at the Commodore, and there was an additional exhibition by the newly organized Foreign Automobile Association at the old Hotel Astor for November 4–10. There was no doubt that elaborate custom coachwork was in demand among the well-heeled. Occasional Pierce-Arrow chassis were sold for custom body firms to complete to customers' orders.

Charles Clifton, as president of the NACC, attended a meeting of truck representatives of the Chamber with delegates from the American Electric Railway Association on December 10 to "map out a policy on legislation, taxation and public utility commissions" that would benefit both street railways and motor bus operators. The use of motorbuses in local transportation was increasing, with even trolley operators employing them for use on some lines. The meeting agreed to form a committee, which A.J. Brosseau of the NACC would chair, to work out a frame for cooperation. Pierce-Arrow by that time had already begun selling its first Model Z buses and expected to do well in this expanding market. It was a promising finish to a year of important accomplishments at Pierce-Arrow. Not only that, Gorham and his wife Margaret had presented Charles Clifton with a namesake grandson that year as well. This all must have been a source of considerable satisfaction to the 70-year-old Colonel, and optimism about Pierce-Arrow's future seemed justified by its current gains.

~ 14 ~

New Horizons
(1924–1927)

> His most pleasing personality, complete knowledge of the industry's problems, his tolerance for all, his good and farseeing judgment as well as his always unswerving adherence to justice were a most powerful influence in establishing the high standards of business, fair play and justice that characterize the world's greatest industry.
> —Frederick J. Haynes, Dodge Bros., Inc., 1927

As the year 1924 began Charles Clifton found himself the chairman of a company filled with a buoyant optimism that it had not felt for some years. Pierce-Arrow was expanding its operations to offer two new models and anticipated wide success. The Model Z bus chassis appealed to the growing number of bus operators. Nearing production was a new automobile of high quality but less size and weight to reach a wider market than the Series 33.

The National Automobile Show, still under NACC sponsorship, opened in New York at 2:00 p.m., Saturday, January 5, 1924, up in the spacious Bronx Armory at 193rd St. and Jerome Avenue. A heavy snowstorm coupled with subway crashes hindered travel uptown that night. This unexpectedly made an unknown make displayed in midtown at the Commodore Hotel lobby the hit of the show. It was called the Chrysler.

Pierce-Arrow had just introduced the four-wheel-brake option on its cars at a price of $250. *Automotive Industries* covered the advance January 3 in an article titled "Pierce-Arrow Added to List of Cars Fitted with Front-Wheel Brakes." This option began to be applied on the Series 33 cars beginning about serial number 339000. According to the article, some modifications to the front springs and front axle were required to accommodate the front brakes. The rear brakes were modified as well, their external shoes being eliminated. Heavily ribbed drums were used, and the front brakes were slightly less powerful than the rears. Forty percent of braking effort for front brakes was the goal, similar to the weight distribution on the front axle. Unlike several other systems, Pierce-Arrow allowed front brakes to operate under all conditions. Their application was said not to interfere in any way with steering the car. The hand brake applied only the rear brake shoes by cams at the wheels, turned, as with the fronts, by bell cranks and rods. Front and rear brake pairs were separately equalized. The first advertisement of the new brakes appeared in the January 12 *Saturday Evening Post*, its illustration showing a big sedan driving through a heavy rain. The text of the two-page spread emphasized the superior control such brakes made possible. "The announcement," the copy read, "is made at the conclusion of four years of experimental development. During this period Pierce-Arrow engineers built, studied and tested every type of four-wheel brake mechanism."

Pierce-Arrow retained its usual headquarters for the New York show down at the Biltmore. A published schedule listed its "Meeting" as running there all day on Tuesday. With a new brake system and the plans for a new model later in the year, there was much to discuss. Directors of the NACC attended the Chilton Presentation at the Commodore on Tuesday afternoon, where the talk by J.H. Collins of the Chilton and Cass Journal companies was titled "Present State of Automobile Industry."

Following the great improvement in the automobile market during 1923, everyone expected another good year. Charles Clifton's annual commentary on the state of the industry appeared in the *New York Times* automobile show supplement on Sunday, January 6. "The major problem of the year," the Colonel wrote, "is not how many cars are going to be produced, but how well we are going to make use of the motor transportation which we have." After noting in his column the many new uses being met by automobiles, he concluded, "The year 1924 will be one of motor transport progress, not alone in the more efficient and safe management of our highway traffic, but also in the economic advantages and conveniences which motor vehicles afford."

Early in the year, Pierce-Arrow organized the Pierce-Arrow Truck Sales Corp. with capital of $25,000 to facilitate distribution of trucks and busses in the New England territory. Pierce-Arrow also added $375,000 in additional capital to the Pierce-Arrow Finance Corp. in 1924. Both these subsidiaries were entirely owned by the Pierce-Arrow Motor Car Co.

The Pierce-Arrow Motor Car Co. released its 1923 annual report on February 13, and

Series 33 Runabout for the man or woman "about town" (courtesy Pierce-Arrow Society).

Automotive Industries characterized it as "one of the most favorable issued in several years." Profits from operations "after deducting all expenses of the business, including experimental work" had totaled nearly $2 million. After provision for depreciation, interest and debenture payments, a net profit of $372,712 remained. A dividend of $94,500 was paid on the prior preference stock and $278,812 was added to the surplus. After paying out another $750,000 to reduce bank loans early in the year the ratio of assets to liabilities had improved from 2.7 to 1 at the end of 1922 to 4.2 to 1 by early 1924. Things were looking up.

In his report to Pierce-Arrow shareholders, President Myron E. Forbes credited these improvements to improved plant utilization, noting that the new bus models had "aroused the keenest enthusiasm among motor bus users and operators" during demonstration trips. He mentioned a "substantial number" of resulting orders, and observed it was "our opinion that the new bus chassis will soon become an important part in our volume of output." In addition, he described the work of the experimental and engineering departments to develop "a new model passenger car of a lighter type than our present model." He was not yet ready to announce it but assured his readers that "should we produce a lighter car, as a companion to the present model, its manufacture will in no way affect the present Pierce-Arrow car." By this point, experimental work on the car he described was nearly complete, and a rigorous testing program had been undertaken. A surviving expense sheet from the Foss-Hughes agency in Philadelphia shows that they conducted test runs of chassis number 800001 from February 19 to March 20, 1924. At the end, the car showed mileage of 11,772. Their request for reimbursement from the factory for expenses was noted on March 24 as "OKd by M.E.F." In the not too distant future, limited actual manufacture and assembling tests would begin. The Experimental Department policy kept experimental models on the road 24 hours a day using relief drivers in three shifts. "These tests continue," Charles Sheppy told dealers, "until some parts fail or until the mileage equals at least the equivalent of five years' service in the hands of the purchaser." For six months prior, and in preparation, "superintendents and foremen visited plants of leading motor car manufacturers and carefully compiled their observations," in the words of Works Manager John Guider. A series of meetings was then held to develop a manufacturing method for the new car to assure that it would be both easy to manufacture and reliable. The remembered problems of the early Series 32 cars were not going to be repeated.

Members of the NACC met the first week of March. Among their concerns was mounting evidence that automobile sales were not as strong as had been expected. One fear was of the recently introduced lower pressure "balloon" tires being promoted in a way that suggested cars without them were "not up to date." As reported by *Automotive Industries*, the NACC asked Charles Clifton as president to appoint a committee of three to help the rubber manufacturers and the SAE to agree to standards that were "acceptable to both tire and car manufacturers." Trying to use the new tires on older wheels was proving to be unsatisfactory in many cases due to clearance problems and hard steering. It was hoped that the new standards would limit the range of tire sizes offered in order to permit larger quantities and supply the demand. Members were not rejecting the balloon tires, but wanted the supply to quickly increase, allowing them to be used as standard equipment. Col. Clifton was expected to appoint the committee members perhaps within a week's time.

Later that month, stories in the business press focused on the condition of the Pierce-Arrow company's finances. On the 20th the *Wall Street Journal* ran a story that reported the

$3.5 million in notes had been reduced by one-half during 1923 and early 1924, just as President Forbes had planned. This reduced the annual interest charges of the company by 15 percent to 20 percent, or about $250,000. In 1923 interest had consumed 68 percent of Pierce-Arrow's net profit, making this reduction of great interest to stockholders. The net of $372,712 in 1923 "indicates substantial recovery toward an earnings basis when contrasted with net of $10,809 the preceding year and a deficit of $8,763,712 in 1921."

That conditions existed to achieve increased earnings seemed evident to the paper. They concluded that "a substantial increase in output this year" would be brought about by Pierce-Arrow offering "a specially designed six-cylinder passenger carrying bus," and, shortly, "a new model passenger car of a lighter type than the present model which may also become an important factor in 1924 production and earnings." In addition, the operations in the Pierce-Arrow plant itself had improved. "The former esprit de corps at the plant," the reporter wrote, "which made Pierce-Arrow one of the outstanding successes in the motor field, prior to the disastrous attempt to produce a quality product on a quantity basis, has been restored." Improved quality had, in fact, reduced the number of employees in the factory service department from 87 to 14.

By the end of March, the activities of the finance committee were moving to underwrite improved operations. The *Wall Street Journal* of March 26 noted in a story, datelined Buffalo, that bankers there and in New York City were "discussing the possibility of new financing in connection with the expansion plans of the Pierce-Arrow Motor Car Co." This was expected to include the refinancing of the remaining $1.75 million in 6 percent notes due on April 16. The speculation was that "a new issue of notes or bonds totaling approximately $3,000,000 to $3,500,000 will be made, a portion of which will refund present outstanding notes and the balance to be used for additional working capital." The additional funds would enable "introducing a new car in the moderate priced field."

By April it was becoming clear that automobile sales were slower than had been expected, and Pierce-Arrow was no exception. When the company released its quarterly earnings ending March 31, it showed that net income was $78,729, only 47¢ a share for the 8 percent cumulative preferred stock and far less than the $105,058 earned in the first quarter of 1923. The figure fortunately was still 63 percent above fixed charges. The *Wall Street Journal* optimistically suggested in its May 12 issue that "the company should have no difficulty in covering interest requirements this year and continuing the 8% dividend on the preferred stock." Quarterly interest on the $4.2 million of 8 percent debentures totaled $84,000, and dividend payment on the 15,750 prior preference shares consumed another $31,500. With these developments, the price of Pierce-Arrow shares had, not surprisingly, declined to new lows for the year. The common was one-eighth of a point below its 6¼ low in 1923, although the preferred was still nearly five points above its 13½ low the year before. By this time arrangements had been made to renew $1.75 million in notes, but no new funds for expansion had been obtained. Still, President Forbes was quoted as saying business in April had been the best so far in 1924. Because the number of cars in distributors' hands was low, the company expected good business in May and June. "The company will introduce a popular priced six-cylinder model this summer," the story went on, "and plans are now going forward to place this car on a quantity production basis." Substantial new tooling and rearrangement of the plant was involved for this project, which promised to "materially increase Pierce-Arrow's earnings and prospects."

A program this year by the Buffalo Fine Arts Academy to purchase a marble sculpture by Edward McCartan entitled *The Kiss* led Charles Clifton as president to institute a Special Sculpture Fund with a gift of $25,000. "The principal of this fund," the Academy wrote, "was to be and has been used for the purpose of developing an interest in the acquisition of sculpture."

The annual meeting of the National Automobile Chamber of Commerce was held in New York the first week of June. Discussions centered on the state of the automobile market for the summer, often a slow period as manufacturers retooled for the next year's season. While the spring sales had been slower than expected, there was some confidence that June would be "a good month," according to a story in the June 12 *Automotive Industries*. That outcome was said to be somewhat governed by "the results of the political conventions." The chamber decided to authorize holding a second World Motor Transport Congress "at such time as may be selected by the Foreign Trade Committee." They also approved a budget of $12,000 for the fourth "National Safety Essay and Lesson contest," paying expenses and obtaining prizes for the winners. Continued funding for the United States Bureau of Standards to study improvement of motor fuels was authorized by the board as well. The next day the NACC board met and re-elected all its current officers. Colonel Clifton was thereby elected president of the Chamber and its antecedents for the 20th time. A special June 25 directors' meeting was scheduled in Detroit to consider "renewal of the cross-licensing agreement among members of the Chamber." The agreement was in fact renewed at that meeting.

That year the city of Buffalo seemed to follow Col. Clifton's 1923 advice to mayors of large cities about expediting automobile traffic. A "new boulevard" of the sort he suggested was planned for Delaware Avenue., a main artery out from the center of town. As a preparation for the widening of the street "hundreds of stately elms," in the words of one writer, were removed, creating a storm of protest. Local artist Charles Burchfield, who was also employed as a designer at the Birge wallpaper company, painted a widely admired watercolor titled "Civic Improvement" in protest. Charles Clifton himself did not make a recorded comment on the issue, even though he lived only a block or so west of Delaware.

By its July 10 issue, *Automotive Industries* confidently predicted that production schedules for the industry would pick up "the latter part of this month as manufacturers complete their inventory taking and swing into production of new models." An estimated 265,000 cars had been produced in June, definitely a slowdown from the 312,813 completed in May. "The June decline was not unexpected," the magazine noted, "in view of the gradual slowing up in the preceding months." *The Wall Street Journal* reported in its July 21 issue that Pierce-Arrow had probably made about $450,000 in the first six months of 1924 and speculated that pending developments "in the immediate future may completely change the outlook for the company next year." They complimented the "present management" for making "good progress in strengthening its present line of cars, trucks and buses." Sales of the Dual Valve Six models were said to be "the largest in the history of the company." On August 1, the company planned to announce its greatly anticipated line of "moderate priced cars."

And that Friday, the new Series 80 Pierce-Arrow car was displayed across the country, available for "thorough demonstration," according to introductory advertising. It was, as seen in the August 12 issue of *The Saturday Evening Post*, advertised as "A New Car—A New Size—A New Price." In the July 30 *Automotive Industries* an extensive technical description of the car appeared, authored by Donald Blanchard. The feature article's title, "Lighter Six with L-

Head Engine," was followed by a neat summary of the car in the sub-heading: "Piston displacement and weight are 30 percent less than that of the larger model which is continued. Four-wheel brakes, balloon tires and torque bar are features." Blanchard noted the cylinder head design of its L-head motor secured "high turbulence of the mixture" producing 72 developed horsepower from its 289 cubic inches displacement. Considerable advancement was seen in the unit engine/clutch/transmission arrangement and 7½ inch deep 0.30 carbon steel channel section frame members of ⅛ in. stock. To minimize wear on shackles, frame ends were bent parallel to the direction of travel. *Automobile Topics* ran similar coverage, noting that the price "assures it a strong position in the field."

In this model Pierce-Arrow had designed an engine so it could be assembled on an assembly line, the crankcases being pushed along "rails" from station to station as assembly progressed. A complete line of seven body styles was announced, but it seems certain that no more than two were offered in quantity at first. The company thereby arranged to have a good supply of the new car to start with. The early advertising showed only the seven-passenger touring car (with permanent top and side curtains) at $2,895 f.o.b. and the five-passenger sedan at $3,895. The touring car would be available "in either of two shades of blue with wheels to match and gray striping," according to Blanchard. Upholstery would be of "pebble grained black leather." The sedan was, given market trends, likely to outsell the touring car. It was also available in two colors, "Royal blue and Brewster green with gray striping." Mohair to match the exterior body color upholstered the sedan, and silk roller shades, a vanity case and smoking case were all standard. Fenders, upper body, splash aprons and body moldings were all black enamel. These limited colors were a dramatic alteration to the approach Pierce-Arrow had previously taken with its offerings, but they reveal a determination to simplify the production process and foster a more rapid worker understanding of this unfamiliar "quantity production basis." Judging from remaining cars, only the sedan bodies of these two offerings were actually constructed by Pierce-Arrow in its body plant. The touring car bodies appear to have been subcontracted from outside suppliers and constructed of steel panels. Again, the effort to simplify start-up of this important new model is clear. This may also explain the contracting with Brown-Lipe to build the transmissions and the use of a Borg & Beck clutch. Rear axles were supplied by Timken, and its artillery wheels were also purchased from Hoopes Bros. All in all, the Series 80 Pierce-Arrow was a carefully thought

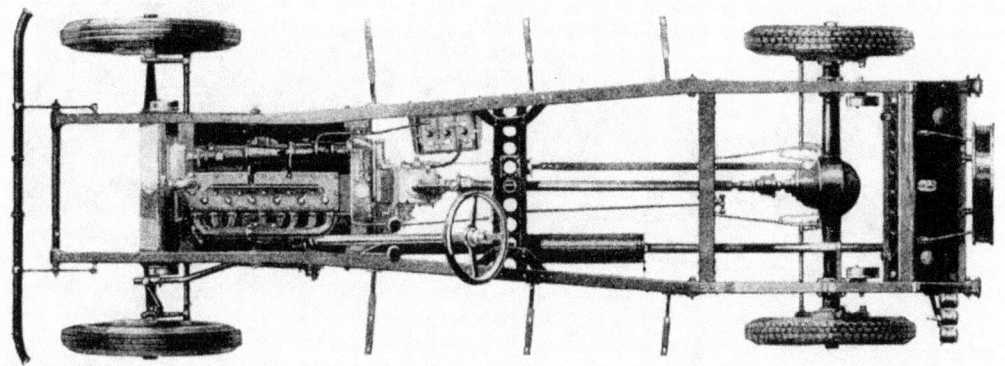

Chassis of a lighter, more easily assembled Pierce-Arrow car: the 1924 Series 80 (courtesy Pierce-Arrow Society).

out offering that, perhaps for the first time for the company, was solidly in the mainstream of automotive fashion.

Pierce-Arrow still played its part in headline-producing events of the 1920s. One of those took place in Washington, D.C., that August. The newsreel cameras captured the image of the gleaming Dual Valve French Landau with the Presidential seals on her tonneau doors leaving the Union Station carrying the visiting Prince of Wales up to the White House for dinner with President and Grace Coolidge.

Subsequently, on September 6, two seven-passenger closed cars were brought out as Series 80 offerings, a sedan at $3,995 and a $4,045 enclosed drive limousine. The popularity of closed cars in the winter was, by now, clearly evident. Early series 80 promotional materials included just these four models. Sport model open cars would wait until the spring. *Automotive Industries* had noted in summer that "The whole attitude of the industry is that conditions are now on the mend, that the worst the year has in store has happened and that from now on business will get steadily better." It seemed that the new Pierce-Arrow car was being introduced into a solidly rising market.

Possibly as recognition of his business prowess, Myron E. Forbes soon became a director of the Buffalo Trust Company. George F. Rand announced his election in the September 10 Buffalo *Commercial*. "Although young in years," Mr. Rand was quoted as saying, "he is a man who has had a broad experience not only in financing and accounting but in the sales and production phases of industry as well. The loyalty and spirit of cooperation which pervades the 5,000 employees of the Pierce-Arrow Motor Car Company today is proof of his genius for organization."

The company released its second quarter earnings report in late July showing an increased net income of $138,144. This was less than the corresponding quarter in the previous two years, but still good, considering the circumstances. In its August 20 issue, the *Wall Street Journal* recorded that Series 33 passenger car sales had totaled 285 in the first quarter and risen to 400 in the second. Pierce-Arrow had accumulated a comfortable $153,373 surplus

The Series 80 7-passenger touring car: permanent top and side-curtains, $2,895 at Buffalo. Its larger sibling cost $5,250, still with front brakes a $250 option (courtesy Pierce-Arrow Society).

14. New Horizons (1924–1927)

in the first half of 1924, and chances appeared good for even better results as the year continued. By August 21, the paper revealed that it was "particularly bullish" about Pierce-Arrow shares "because of the enthusiasm resulting from its early sales of its new model."

Sales growth continued during the fall months. On November 1, 1924, the Series 80 four-passenger coupe model appeared. Arranged in the fashion of the time, it had a driver's seat in front and a narrow rear seat with a storage compartment. An occasional seat folded down in front for the fourth passenger. Its price was a reasonable $3,695 f.o.b. This completed the Series 80 line of closed cars. Apparently "first sculpted in clay," to quote company statements, their bodies all displayed a somewhat different aspect from the larger Series 33 cars, having noticeably curved window reveals, especially at the rear quarters. Roofs were slightly domed but had no dome light ventilator in the tonneau like the Series 33. It is likely that James R. Way fashioned the clay models as chief of body design. The sharper edges of the bodies designed earlier in the decade were noticeably softened in the new model. A greatly expanded advertising program to promote the Series 80 was undertaken that fall. Attractive black and white illustrations with evocative copy in full-page advertisements appeared in the big glossy magazines like *Country Life, Vogue, House & Garden,* and *Life.*

Pierce-Arrow's surplus rose to $137,281 during the third quarter, leading the *Wall Street Journal* to remark that Pierce-Arrow "seems to be staging a comeback." In the November 22 issue, a further advance was recorded with the news that October had produced a monthly

Series 80 7-passenger sedan for 1926 (courtesy Pierce-Arrow Society).

net income at Pierce-Arrow of $144,299. "Shipments in November," the paper advised, "are expected to be the largest in the company's history, due to the heavy demand for the new Series 80 car." Outlets selling the company's products had grown from 75 in January to more than 225 "and new applications are steadily reaching the factory." An extensive summary of these satisfying developments appeared in the *Wall Street Journal* Thursday, November 17, in a story headlined "Pierce-Arrow Improving Position." It noted that profits for the year already had outstripped those of the full year in 1923, reaching nearly a half-million dollars. Money available for dividends on Pierce-Arrow cumulative preferred shares was climbing, although no sign of plans for actual payment was seen as yet. The analysis stressed the "expanding operations following introduction of the new medium priced car this summer." Estimating Pierce-Arrow factory capacity at 7,500 to 10,000 vehicles a year, the writer noted "a comparably limited field for its high-priced products." With the introduction of the Series 80 "the company more than trebled its output." Production of 5,000 vehicles annually was now likely. Already the total for 1924 approached 3,000. Given these developments, "prospects for substantial earnings on the old preferred stock are bright." By the Saturday issue of the next week, the periodical noted that "Maxwell and Pierce-Arrow preferred have doubled their low prices of the year." In both cases new models had sparked the recovery: Success of the Chrysler buoyed up Maxwell and the Series 80 did the same for Pierce. Pierce-Arrow preferred shares closed at 36⅛ that week.

When the Automobile Salon opened at the Commodore to run from November 9 to 15, Pierce-Arrows with custom bodies were among the makes "Exhibited by Coachmakers." Hugo Pfau, who worked at LeBaron, Inc., later remembered the occasion as the first appearance of the Series 80 Pierce-Arrow as a show car.

The December 10 *Wall Street Journal* discussed the Pierce-Arrow financial situation from the standpoint of its borrowings. Company debt total now had risen to at least $2.2 million because of borrowing "to finance introduction of the new light six models." Whether the half million or so of those new borrowings would be paid off at the April due date or funded had not been decided. Much depended on how strong demand for the new car proved to be. This, in turn, depended upon the number of sales outlets. The selling organization that had been set up to distribute 1,500 or so of the Series 33 a year was insufficient to handle the demand for the Series 80, which was currently running about 500 cars a month. The plan was to expand the outlets further "to take care of the full factory capacity of 10,000." The demand for trucks had been increased by production of the Model Z bus to some 2,000 vehicles a year. Large expenses for further creation of new models continued. October's results gave a $16 return on each share of preferred stock.

The 3½" × 5" Series 80 engine; aluminum crankcase, iron block, unit transmission (courtesy Pierce-Arrow Society).

"Dividends have been accumulating on this issue since June, 1921," the article noted, "and will amount to $30 a share in January, 1925." Pierce-Arrow had not yet demonstrated a continuing ability to generate profits of that size, although things had improved substantially.

Automobile Trade Journal published a "Silver Anniversary Issue" in December, anticipating the year-long celebration the industry mounted in 1925. The issue featured a number of stories tracing aspects of the growth of the infant automobile industry into the giant it had become in a mere 25 years. One of the stories, titled "National Automobile Chamber of Commerce," reviewed the functions of industry associations to work "jointly on those matters in which everyone had an interest, such as shows and good roads, subjects of concern to the industry as a whole rather than any one company." Charles Clifton's election to the presidency of the Association of Licensed Automobile Manufacturers in 1904 was described as "most important to the industry." As the industry developed "from a novelty into a vast transportation business, Colonel Clifton with diplomacy and vision has guided the manufacturers." The magazine designated the cross-licensing agreement as the most important achievement of the NACC. "Through it," they wrote, "all manufacturers pooled their patents, thereby eliminating the most of the vast amount of litigation which hampered the early days of the business." The patent pool now contained some 1,000 patents. "On practically every motor car," they concluded, "there are ten or twelve patents that the use of has been granted by some company in the pool." C.C. Hanch and R.A. Brannigan managed the patent pool, which the *Trade Journal* credited with encouraging standardization of parts, lowering prices, and facilitating mass production.

Transformational successes in 1924 built confidence at the Pierce-Arrow Motor Car Co. and reflected well on its leadership. Charles Clifton, likely still its most widely-known executive, enjoyed widespread admiration and approval among the whole automobile industry, and, indeed, the country. It had been a good year.

The 1925 New York Automobile Show, again mounted by the NACC at the Armory in the Bronx, opened Saturday, January 3. It was the "Silver Jubilee" of these particular shows and was marketed as a celebration of the industry's astonishing growth. Preliminary figures from the NACC indicated that production of cars and trucks had totaled some 3,650,000 vehicles in 1924, a healthy ten percent growth over profitable 1923. Charles Clifton's observations of the industry's situation from his perspective as NACC president appeared in Sunday's *New York Times* special automobile show supplement. The strong assertion from his pen was the great positive impact the motor car had on society as a whole and that such progress could now spread around the whole globe. A freedom that the private car gave an individual was its most important outcome, from Clifton's point of view. "This service, I feel," he wrote as a summary of his opinions, "is worth even more than what we may call the commercial economic values, because it is a manifestation of one of the chief impulses which have built up this country; it contributes to the preservation of one of the finest qualities of mankind."

The supplement also revealed many activities that surrounded the show itself. The city's great hotels, both downtown and beyond, were hosting meetings for automobile companies, and in many cases displaying additional cars. Maxwells and Chryslers, for example, were on display at the Commodore, as were Auburn and Sterling-Knight. Dodge Brothers preferred the Hotel Pennsylvania for its setting. Studebaker had showings at the Plaza. The Astor was another traditional meeting place. Several dinners there were sponsored by participants. The

SAE sponsored one and the Cadillac Old Guard gave another. Special events were held at many hotels for the wives marooned in the city by show participants that employed their husbands. A sign of things to come was the Hotel Alamo sending a radio broadcast to each booth of the show itself, passing along the latest news dispatches from the industry.

Pierce-Arrow had an attractive new sporty model to highlight at the show. It was the Series 80 runabout, priced at $2,895. An equally sporting four-passenger touring car, also with a fold-down top, had also joined the Series 80 line, carrying two additional passengers for just $200 more.

Automotive Industries covered the NACC Silver Jubilee Dinner at the Commodore on Thursday evening. More than 1,000 attended to hear Dwight W. Morrow, a J.P. Morgan partner, give the featured address which described business conditions, and how to accommodate thinking to their changes. "During the dinner," the magazine wrote, "a testimonial was presented to Samuel A. Miles by President Charles Clifton for his work as show manager during the quarter of a century and medals were bestowed upon 11 pioneers of the industry by the Smithsonian Institution." The toastmaster was Roy D. Chapin, president of the Hudson Motor Car Co., and humorous remarks were supplied by Neal O'Hara. Ten of the pioneers awarded medals were pictured with their awards. Ransom Olds apparently had left early.

The Pierce-Arrow Motor Car Co. released its eighth annual report the second week in February 1925. The net profit of $751,060 was no surprise and greatly appreciated. The company not only doubled its net over that of the year before, it had reduced notes payable by $299,500 from the $2.5 million owed in 1923. All the while it had managed to bring out the Series 80 at a cost of around $1 million and increased its investment in the finance corporation as well as the truck sales operation in New England. These were looking more and more like steps toward a profitable future. In his report to stockholders, President Forbes stated, "We are convinced that the broadening of our distributing organization with the marketing of our Series 80 Passenger Car, will have a decided effect in increasing the demand for our entire line of products," noting that "the benefits obtained from this new addition to our line of products during the last quarter of the year are very gratifying." The number of Pierce-Arrow sales outlets had now grown to 306. At the end of his message, the president voiced the com-

Spring offering: Series 80 Runabout, with rumble seat (courtesy Pierce-Arrow Society).

pany's pleasure "in expressing to both Employees and the Distributing organization our appreciation for their loyalty and excellent spirit of co-operation displayed during the year."

Very real progress had been made, and Pierce-Arrow was apparently approaching the point where it could fulfill its promise of consistent dividends. Three difficulties needed to be overcome for that to happen. First, the burden of debt had to be eliminated; second, the prior-preference stock needed to be wiped out and, lastly, the arrears in cumulative preferred share dividends had to be paid off. Each of these had its challenges.

Nevertheless, the spring of 1925 proved to be a portentous time at Pierce-Arrow. On April 15, according to a story in *Automotive Industries*, M.E. Forbes arranged to "set up a factory branch in Chicago," by purchasing the facilities of H. Paulman & Co., the long-time Pierce-Arrow outlet there. In an April 20 article, the *Wall Street Journal* reported that "March shipments of Pierce-Arrow Motor Car Co. were the largest since May, 1920. The outlook is April business will exceed the record established in March." The report described sales of the Series 80 models as "steadily increasing" since its introduction. Every bit as promising, truck production for the quarter was said to be 55 percent better than sales the first quarter of 1923. A sizeable portion of that increase was in sales of the Model Z bus model. These sales successes had built up company cash to about $2 million. Speculatively the newspaper mused, "It is likely the company will be able to pay off a large part if not all of the bank debt before the end of the year."

The very next day Pierce-Arrow paid $500,000 to the banks, reducing the indebtedness to $1.7 million. Not only that, the mortgage bonds used as security for the debt were then returned to the company treasury, and the remaining bank loans were carried on straight credit lines, "a condition which the company has not enjoyed since 1921." Immediately, Pierce-Arrow preferred stock rose in the market, giving what the financial newspaper called "indications of important accumulations based on satisfactory outlook for the company's business."

Model Z bus: dual-valve six-cylinder engine, worm-drive, and body by the Lang company of Cleveland (courtesy Pierce-Arrow Society).

Output of Series 80 cars was expected to reach 500 in April, the exact target figure hoped for when the model was under development, and bus production was "sold into mid-summer." The quarterly statement from the company was released that week, showing a net profit of $200,416, two dollars per preferred share. A brand-new color catalogue showing the seven Series 80 styles was being distributed to dealers across the country, and an ambitious new advertising campaign launched. National coverage was now entirely in high-prestige magazines. Series 80 advertising, in black and white, showed cars in distinguished settings surrounded by a circular border, and short text beneath. Stylish color renderings of the Dual Valve Six were again used to advertise the luxurious senior line with almost no copy at all. Looking toward the future, the company was working on a Series 80 model aimed to expand the market even more. Having seen the success the style had for Hudson and Essex, Pierce-Arrow was readying a coach body for introduction in the summer.

Meanwhile, some substantial improvements had been made to the Dual Valve Six. Crankshafts now had oval webs, rods had rifle drilled oil passages and valve seats were greatly improved to eliminate their tendency for cracking. Other detail changes were made to brakes and dimmer switch construction, and a triple tail light arrangement like that on the Series 80 was added. Body offerings were unchanged. Serial numbers began with 340001. Some of the engine improvements were soon applied to Series 80 motors as well.

On May 8 in a story "special to *The Wall Street Journal*," Pierce-Arrow's payment of another $500,000 to the banks was revealed. This reduced the debt total to $1.2 million. "Under President M.E. Forbes' management," the article enthused, "the company not only has reduced its loans to the present low mark, but has expended more than $1,000,000 in machinery and tool equipment for the production of the moderately priced car that was introduced last year." Pierce-Arrow was said to be operating its Buffalo factory "on a full schedule to meet the demand." That Friday afternoon Pierce-Arrow 8 percent debenture bonds reached a price of 99½, up 1½ points for the day. It was turning into a heady spring in Buffalo.

On May 29, Charles Clifton was part of a special occasion at Indianapolis the night before the Memorial Day race. The Indiana Section of the Society of Automotive Engineers gave an "Anniversary and Welcoming Dinner" for visiting SAE members and leaders in the automotive industry, according to a story in *Automotive Industries*. The event took place in the main dining room of the Indianapolis Athletic Club. The Indianapolis Chamber of Commerce was another sponsoring organization. Along with Clifton other special guests were Edgar Apperson; Orville Wright; Harry Horning, president of the SAE; Alfred Reeves, general manager of the NACC; Maj. Gen. Dwight E. Aultman, Commander of the 5th Corps. U.S.A., with other officers from Ft. Benjamin Harrison; and Henry and Edsel Ford. Speakers described phases of progress in the automotive industry over the previous 25 years. Fred E. Moskovics, president of Stutz, assisted with the dinner and the speakers. A special block of seats at the 500-mile race was reserved for these and other guests.

That same year the city of Buffalo, reacting to an obvious demand, began construction of an automobile bridge over the Niagara River at Black Rock to the Ontario, Canada, shore opposite. This plan to facilitate international motor traffic would be called the Peace Bridge. Charles Clifton was a part of the effort and was named a vice-president of the Peace Bridge Company.

By June 19, the *Wall Street Journal* was impressed enough with Pierce-Arrow's financial performance that they published an examination to detail the accomplishments and difficulties the management encountered. It was provocatively titled "Pierce Dividend Unlikely Soon." Reviewing the performance of the company, it noted that earnings on the preferred stock had risen from 11¢ a share in 1922 gradually, step by step, to $6.25 in 1924. All the same, preceding payment of dividends on the preferred stock was paying off (1) six million dollars of 7 percent first mortgage bonds (now held in the company treasury), (2) twenty-year 8 percent debenture bonds totaling $4.2 million, and (3) eight-dollar prior preference stock totaling 15,750 shares. Should all this be accomplished, the company still owed accumulations totaling 32 percent on the preferred shares themselves, amassed since suspension of dividend payments in April 1921. The current prices of the debentures, prior preference, preferred and common shares had risen to a total of $20 million. This compared with a value of $7.6 million the year before. The next day a small follow-up story appeared that featured the reaction of President Myron Forbes to the achievements he had overseen at Pierce-Arrow. An associate reported the executive had recalled, "I told you when we were trying out our new bus line on the Buffalo roads a year ago last February that some day someone with patience would make a lot of money in Pierce-Arrow stocks. If I had followed my own prediction I might have made a great deal without working so hard for it. But I happen to be an automobile manufacturer, not a speculator, and the rewards seem to come more slowly in that field."

The NACC board met to elect officers, that month, and re-elected Charles Clifton as president for the 21st time, reported in the *New York Times* of June 14. The story also traced his presidency of predecessor automobile associations. Roy D. Chapin of Hudson and Alvan Macauley were elected vice-presidents. Other officers elected were A.J. Brosseau of Mack trucks as secretary, H.H. Rice of General Motors as treasurer, and Alfred Reeves as general manager. Elected for three-year terms as board members were Roy D. Chapin, George M. Graham, Charles D. Hastings, H.H. Rice, and John N. Willys.

On June 28, Myron Forbes reported that Pierce-Arrow had made yet another payment to reduce its loan totals. This time it was for $225,000, reducing the loan total outstanding to $975,000. Cash on hand remained $1,841,283.

The Series 80 Coach went on sale late in June. It was a significant Pierce-Arrow in a number of ways. Unlike earlier Series 80 body styles that were more luxurious in interior fitments than the trade had anticipated, this was a body built to meet a price. The concept of the so-called "coach" automobile body was the development and the promotion of the Hudson Motor Car Co. in 1921. The goal was to narrow the great price differential between the open touring car and the closed sedan. After the end of the Great War it became clear that the closed car was the car of the future. The sooner its price was reduced the sooner that would happen. Hudson decided to offer a closed car at a price competitive to the touring car, a difficult task because the body was so much more complex to build. So, the company asked two automobile body specialist companies for their help. Budd was consulted about how to make the metal parts of the body with the least expense. Briggs was asked for advice on how to efficiently shape the individual wood pieces in the body frame structure. At the end of the process Essex, the lower-priced companion car to Hudson, announced a two-door closed car at a price of $1,495, just $300 more than the touring car model. They called it a Coach, perhaps as a reference to the carriages in which royalty rode, and it was an immediate success. In fact, the name became a generic term in the 1920s for a no-frills entry level five-passenger,

2-door sedan body with folding front seats to allow entrance to the back seat. The connotation of the name, however, did not harmonize with the image Pierce-Arrow had been cultivating for over 20 years.

Consequently, Pierce-Arrow went to considerable lengths to reorient the implications of the name in its promotion of this new car. The introductory advertising contained a good deal of text under the attractive rendering of the new car. The first line of copy suggested the message: "HAND BUILT!" A virtual rhapsody of high-toned allusions followed about doors, entry, seating area, upholstery, trim, and body construction. "A coach?" the conclusion read, "In design, yes. But, in fact, a Pierce-Arrow *closed car*. A new standard of fine car value, and a new low level of motoring economy." A separate folder about the new 2-door Coach was released that followed the same pattern, stressing the body construction to the extent of including a photograph of the complete chassis and ash wood body frame before paneling to show its beautiful cabinetry.

The recovery at Pierce-Arrow attracted the attention of another financial publication in July. *The Magazine of Wall Street* compiled a story entitled "Pierce-Arrow Comes Back" that took up a full page of its July 18 issue. The focus was on the prior preference stock's "spectacular rise," and the reasons behind it. A nice graph of aspects of the company's performance back to 1916 was a part of the coverage. The magazine's conclusion was succinct: "At prevailing prices around 105, the stock has ceased to be attractive on an investment basis." The fact that the prior preferred could be converted to common stock shares made it attractive "for those

Series 80 Coach, introduced in June 1925 to expand the market for the model as a reasonably priced closed car (Buffalo and Erie County Historical Society).

who care to entertain a long range speculation." By July 25, Pierce-Arrow had announced that it had paid off all remaining bank loans and was now free of such debt "for the first time since the deflation of 1920," according to the *Wall Street Journal*. The earnings report for the June quarter revealed the source of funds to close out the bank debt because Pierce-Arrow had net earnings of $364,714. Forbes also reported a cash balance of $1.6 million. That same day, the Pierce-Arrow board of directors ordered the redemption of all prior preference shares for $100 each on October 1, 1925. Since this issue was convertible with the common stock at five shares of common for one prior preference, and the common stock was then trading at over $30 a share, investors would certainly convert them rather than take the cover price. The company was paying off obligations as quickly as possible. Eliminating the dividend payments on the prior preference stock and interest payments on the debt would save Pierce-Arrow $250,000 a year. In an article published by the *Wall Street Journal* on July 31 Pierce-Arrow was reported to have had the largest July business "of any month in the company's history, not excepting the highly prosperous war period." Orders in hand guaranteed high output during August and September. Output had already surpassed that for all of 1924. As the price of Pierce shares rose, unsubstantiated rumors began to surface of accumulation of shares with the object of eventual control. Both American Car & Foundry and Dodge Bros. were speculated as having an interest.

On Wednesday, September 2, there was considerable ceremony at the Engineering Club, 32 W. 40th St. in New York, where a farewell luncheon sponsored by the NACC was held for the eight official delegates from the United States to the Pan-American Road Congress in Buenos Aires, Argentina. According to a story in the *New York Times*, they would depart on the Grace Line steamer *Santiago* on Thursday, starting an extensive tour of "the principal ports of Panama, Peru and Chile" before their arrival in Buenos Aires for the opening of the congress on October 3. Charles Clifton presided at the luncheon and stressed "the importance of cooperation by the United States with the South American states in their highway construction." H.H. Rice of General Motors, the chairman of the delegation, remarked that the visit was not a "commercial enterprise," but rather "to lay the pavements in the highways of friendship which will unite the North and South American continents."

On Tuesday morning, September 15, the *Wall Street Journal* ran a story titled "Reasons for Rise in Pierce-Arrow," attributed to the *Boston News Bureau*, which may well have meant that Clarence Barron himself was the source. The story described the progress the company had made in overcoming the difficulties that had set them back after the end of the war. "Pierce-Arrow just now," the author wrote, "is enjoying the greatest prosperity it has had since the early days of its present corporate career, which dates from 1916." He predicted the net for the third quarter would be "well over $400,000" following $364,000 and $200,000 in the second and first quarters of 1925. The yearly earnings were predicted to be about $1,250,000. The most hopeful sign noted was the steadily improving market for the company's products. July and August had seen 500 Series 80 cars assembled, a pace expected to continue in September. Monthly production of the Dual Valve Six added another 75 to 100 cars each month. "As for buses," he wrote, "the surface of the market has only been scratched.... In August 35 buses were shipped out and the same schedule prevails for September. This amounts to an annual rate of 420 buses." The fact that the buses used the same motor as the large passenger car "pulls down unit manufacturing costs tremendously. At the same time it absorbs a tremendous overhead." While substantial problems still stood in the way of regular dividend payments even on the preferred shares, "another year or two of current prosperity may tell a different story." By this time Pierce-Arrow common stock traded in the low 40s, the preferred at over 90 and the prior preferred, now just short of its redemption date, traded around 210. Debentures traded at around 106.

The September quarter was reported out in late October. Net income had totaled $405,777. In nine months Pierce-Arrow had earned $970,908. Rumors abounded. One of them published in the *Wall Street Journal* of October 29, noted that the bankers "who have been identified with Pierce-Arrow after its introduction to Wall Street" were "understood to have sold a majority of their stock on the recent advance believing that it has discounted possibilities for a long time ahead." That being the case, questions about who actually controlled Pierce-Arrow "are puzzling the Street." And Pierce share prices continued to climb.

As the year wound down, plans were under way for 1926. Shipments declined a bit at the end. For October, 780 units were shipped; in November, 595. December was expected to see 400 more. This gave Pierce-Arrow a year's total of 7,000 units. Of these, about 2,000 were trucks. About 20 percent of the commercial shipments were buses. Hopes were for a 50 percent gain in bus production in 1926. The year had seen an almost startling improvement in Pierce-Arrow's financial condition and a much simpler path to the resumption of dividend payments on preferred and even common stock. The long awaited yearly production of 6,000 vehicles had at last been achieved.

The New York Automobile Show returned to the Grand Central Palace in mid-town for 1926. It opened on Saturday, January 9, to run a week from 10:00 a.m. to 11:00 p.m. Fifty makes of gasoline-powered cars were on display and eight taxicabs. The Sunday *New York Times* published its customary Automobile Show supplement the next day, and it also included the now customary assessment of the state of the automobile world by Charles Clifton. The Colonel's observations this year concentrated on how the success of the automobile in America was exportable all around the world. "Our foreign market," he wrote, "will prove to be just as sound, just as extensive and just as permanent as the motor trade in the United States. Both are established upon a basic need."

One of the week's big events took place on Monday at the Hotel Roosevelt, where 200 delegates from all over the world had gathered for the second World Motor Transport Congress. In his welcoming speech, Col. Clifton emphasized that the basis of any program involving motor transportation was the "recognition of the automobile as a utility." It was not the purpose of the meeting to "urge you to buy American cars," he pointed out. "Our aim is to sell transportation regardless of the country of origin, and the object of the congress is to discuss methods whereby the highway transportation facilities in all parts of the world may be increased with benefit to the inhabitants."

The NACC annual dinner was held the next evening at the Commodore for 1,000 guests. Some were delegates to the World Transportation Congress. All heard a speech from Commerce Secretary Herbert Hoover entitled "Why Americans Should Oppose Government Control of Rubber and Other Raw Material Imports." His heavy sentiments were offset by "Senator" Edward H. Ford, the "humorous speaker." Customary burlesque awards for achievement were also part of the program, which had been put together by Alfred P. Sloan, who chaired the dinner committee.

Some good news for Pierce-Arrow's exposure to the public was revealed that month in the *Wall Street Journal*. Ten Series 33 Pierce-Arrows had been purchased by the Pikes Peak

Auto Highway, "associated with the Broadmoor Hotel at Colorado Springs, Col." It was, the newspaper informed its readers, "one of the largest fleets of Pierce-Arrows in the world." It was also a step in the Pikes Peak Company's plan to replace earlier two-wheel brake Series 33 touring cars on the rigorous Pikes Peak climb.

Rumors persisted through the month that American Car & Foundry was purchasing Pierce-Arrow stock in order to obtain control. This was denied by ACF and unsubstantiated by any actual facts. The apparent success of Pierce-Arrow over the last year evidently attracted some speculative interest in its stock.

Further inducements to speculation were apparent the second week of February when Pierce-Arrow Motor Car Co. released its Annual Report for 1925. Its net had reached a surprising $1,629,781, equal to $15.46 a share on the cumulative preferred stock, according to the *Wall Street Journal*. Should its dividends of $200,000 be paid, $2.26 a share remained for dividends on the common stock. This last eventuality was not possible, however, until $40 per share of arrears on the cumulative preferred stock was paid off, and the available money did not stretch that far. At the end of 1925, Pierce-Arrow current assets totaled $12,781,671, of which some $2 million was cash. Working capital totaled $6.6 million more than the outstanding 8 percent debentures. The company had enlarged its investment in the Pierce-Arrow Finance Corp. to $875,000. It looked like a golden opportunity to extend Pierce-Arrow's market penetration, and the company had the money to do it.

Meanwhile, Charles Clifton, as president of the NACC, had appointed Walter Schmidt as field representative of the organization to work with other countries to develop motor transportation. Clifton promised, according to a February 2 *New York Times* story, to soon name an additional three people to assist this effort. These steps were an outcome of the World Motor Transport Congress held the month before in New York. Mr. Schmidt was going to visit Australia at the invitation of the Australian Motor Convention, after which he would spent the next nine months visiting Hawaii, New Zealand, British Malay States, Burma, India, Ceylon, Persia, Syria, East Africa, and South Africa.

"Automobile leaders and in many cases Government officials are alive to the fact that the spread of motor transportation to the point where every family has a car is an ideal which will spell economic well-being and more satisfying life for the individual," Col. Clifton was quoted as saying. This appointment was an effort to coordinate local motor transport efforts all over the globe. The experience of the American automotive industry was transferrable to other countries, and these appointees would facilitate the process. "This international movement," Clifton noted, "recognizes that the automobile is a democratic institution, that it makes available national resources, creating wealth so that the masses of the people can afford their own motor transportation."

Pierce-Arrow was poised for success this spring, and the company staged a sales convention for some 600 salesmen at Buffalo to prepare for a big push. The motto of the gathering that began on Monday, February 15, in the Ballroom of the new Statler Hotel on Niagara Square was "10,000 Series 80's." That was the sales goal. If successful, this would effectively double sales over those of 1925. It was ambitious and means had been prepared to help the agents reach that total. It began with expansion of the "coach" line. On display at the convention were three new coach-derived bodies: a 5-passenger 4-Door Coach ($3,250), a 7-passenger 4-Door-Coach ($3,350), and a Limousine Coach ($3,450). For the original line of Series 80 bodies, now referred to as the "Deluxe" line, the range of colors on body finishes had been expanded, new fabrics offered for upholstery along with "luxurious new appointments, including a vanity case with a high-grade clock." The reputation of the Series 33 Dual Valve Six as the ultimate luxury car was touted as well.

Every facet of the sales program was explained in detail during the afternoon session, by Chief Engineer Charles Sheppy, Passenger Car Sales Manager T.J. O'Rourke, Pierce-Arrow Sales Corp. Vice-president W.R. Bartlett, Advertising Manager W.M. Baldwin, Works Manager John Guider, Territorial Manager William Shortal, Service Manager F.J. Wells, Advertising Councilor William B. Henri, President M.E. Forbes, and General Sales Manager L.E. Corcoran. Speaking for the salesmen were W.F Culberson, president of the Pierce-Arrow Pacific Sales Company, C.W. Cady of the Harrolds Motor Car Company, and Joseph C. O'Rourke of the Pierce-Arrow Sales Company in Buffalo. The effects of the program were quickly promising. By April 12, the *Wall Street Journal* reported from Boston that the number of "Series 80 cars shipped during the month of March, 1926, as compared with March, 1925, represents an increase of 73%, the largest shipments in the history of the Pierce-Arrow Motor Car Co." Shipments of all Pierce-Arrow vehicles from the factory during the first quarter topped the same period in 1925 by 30 percent—822 units. Series 80 shipments would total 1,100 for the quarter. Myron Forbes, returning from a trip through the west, was optimistic about business conditions and the likelihood of increased dealer orders.

The first quarter financial report, released by Pierce-Arrow in late April, showed a net profit of $328,982, over $100,000 above the 1925 figures. Now the talk in financial circles was about how the company would tackle the problem of dividends as profits increased. And, not too surprisingly, on Monday June 7, the Pierce-Arrow board voted to pay the $2 quarterly dividend a share of preferred stock on July 1 to holders of record on June 18. This was a neat place to start because it held the arrears on the stock at a convenient $40 a share. Now the problem was how to contrive to pay off all the $4 million in arrears so that dividends on the

In the expanded Series 80 line this 4-door, 5-passenger Coach was part of the push to sell 10,000 Series 80 cars in 1926 (courtesy Pierce-Arrow Society).

common stock might be resumed. Financial commentators chimed in with suggestions as to methods. The preferred dividend was duly paid on July 1.

Charles Clifton was elected to another term as president of the National Automobile Chamber of Commerce in a meeting of its board of directors on Monday, June 7, 1926. All the other officers were likewise re-elected. *The New York Times* reported the next day that Colonel Clifton had pronounced the automobile industry to be "in excellent condition and that credits are on a sound basis" in his annual message to the Chamber. It was his opinion that conservative practices were being followed in the matter of time payments for automobile purchases with more companies insisting on the one-third down payment and no more than 12 monthly payments. These were the methods that Pierce-Arrow itself was using to build sales toward the target level.

On July 13 in the *Wall Street Journal*, an interesting engineering project was revealed under the headline "Automobile Producers Turn from Aluminum." The article pointed out the increased production cost of using aluminum to save automobile body weight. This situation had resulted in high-production cars abandoning aluminum for body construction to make body panels out of pressed steel. The exceptions seemed to be "the highest priced cars." Pierce-Arrow automobile bodies, as one example, still had aluminum cladding over hardwood frames. Not only that, the article mentioned that Pierce-Arrow had built four experimental automobiles for the Aluminum Company of America that were "made entirely of aluminum except for a few parts, such as springs, to which it was impossible to adapt aluminum." The expected savings in gasoline and tires did not materialize, however, and "the experiment was not successful."

A report on these four cars later submitted to Roy A. Hunt of the Aluminum Company of America was dated October 5, 1926, and detailed the differences between the experimental cars, which carried a 249 cu. in. six-cylinder engine in a 133 in. wheelbase, with the Series 80 Pierce-Arrow on a 130 in. wheelbase and 289 cu. in. six. Tests found that the ALCOA engine developed 75 horsepower compared with the 65 developed by the Series 80 motor. Other differences favored the experimental in ride, handling and stopping. Three ALCOA executives owned examples of the cars made with Pierce-Arrow. Two were seven-passenger sedans and were owned by Andrew W. Mellon, U.S. Secretary of the Treasury at the time, and his brother Richard B. Mellon. A five-passenger sedan version was driven for a number of years by A.V. Davis. This last is the single survivor, now in the possession of the Henry Ford Museum in Dearborn, Michigan.

Charles L. Sheppy, a Pierce veteran from the very early days, finished up as Chief Engineer (courtesy Pierce-Arrow Society).

Pierce-Arrow was already working on ways to build on the experience they had obtained working on these aluminum experimental cars. Chief Engineer Charles Sheppy, his Assistant Chief Engineer John Talcott and Passenger Car Engineer Charles Pleuthner were working on ways to incorporate aluminum into production Series

80 engines. Not only would weight be saved, but greater power could be extracted as well. Aluminum piston rods and pistons were designed along with an aluminum cylinder head and compression raised to 4.65:1 from 4.45:1. A heavier crankshaft was employed to handle the increased power. Tests of these changes during the summer proved the new engine to be "a remarkable piece of engineering," in the words of Myron Forbes.

Later in July, the second quarter earnings by the Pierce-Arrow Motor Car Co. were released, showing a net of $474,861. After paying the preferred dividend, the remaining earnings would equal 83¢ a share on the 328,750 shares of Pierce-Arrow common stock. This was a nice return, bringing the total earnings for the first half of 1926 up to $803,843, compared to $502,131 for the same period the year before.

There had now been 15 straight quarters of improved financial performance by the Pierce-Arrow Motor Car Co. For at least a year, earnings had been produced in what now looked to be a normal pattern. Although the truck and bus business had not yet reached the level expected during the 1917 reorganization, profits were being made regularly. The board of directors and the finance committee of Pierce-Arrow, both chaired by Charles Clifton, had been working out a plan to ask the stockholders' authorization for an increase in the number of shares of Pierce-Arrow common stock, and the creation of a class of Second Preferred Stock to fund the payment of the arrears owed the holders of cumulative preferred stock and the retirement of the 8 percent debentures. The proposal was made on August 19, calling for a special meeting of Pierce-Arrow Motor Car Co. stockholders on September 10 in Buffalo to ratify the proposal. Details of the plan were published in the *Wall Street Journal* of August 21, under the headline "Pierce-Arrow Plans."

On July 27, the *Wall Street Journal* carried an advertisement announcing that the facilities of the Harrolds Motor Car Co. in New York City and its suburbs had been taken over by the Pierce-Arrow Sales Corporation. It would now be a "Direct Factory Branch." This may have been brought about by Robert Garden, the former owner, wanting to retire, or a determination by the company to be more assertive in the New York metropolis. In any case, it was expected to be a benefit to both patrons and Pierce-Arrow for the factory to be in direct control of its largest outlet.

Gorham Clifton and his wife delivered a third grandson, Peter, in 1926. In 1924 Charles had built a new home for his son and family to replace rented Philadelphia quarters at 6846 Roach. The new house was an impressive structure of gray fieldstone in a fashionable Colonial style at 6446 Greenhill Road, just off the Main Line. Mark Clifton, who grew up there, recalled that it had a great central hall with wings arching up over it on either side. The house also had four fireplaces. Turmoil, unfortunately, had continued within Gorham's family, stemming from his alcohol dependence. Those problems became so worrisome they induced Charles Clifton to set up individual trusts for his son Gorham, Margaret Keenan Clifton, and each of their sons.

Mark remembers a trip to his grandparents, Charles and Grace Clifton, at their home in Buffalo for "ten days or two weeks" when he was five or six years old. He found it not a pretentiously large house, although it did have a *porte cochere* over the driveway on its west side. Bedrooms were on the upper floors. The levels of the house, he recalled, were "like interrupted layers, each rather like a frieze, "overhanging like tiers with wood supports." It had a front footage of perhaps a hundred feet, with a "not terribly big" front lawn. The Colonel's commanding presence was something Mark clearly felt, but no emotional closeness. His grandmother, he described as a "really cold fish." Some years later, he remembered, she corrected him for referring to a washrag. "My dear," she said, "it is a wash *cloth*!" Mark does not recall any signs of affection between his grandparents. Each seemed to have clearly defined and separate roles. Mark considered the library of the house to be his grandfather's refuge, surrounded by his collection of books and fine art.

On September 17, the *Wall Street Journal* reported an announcement by Pierce-Arrow president Myron Forbes that a new Dual Valve Six line would be called the Series 36, starting at a price of $5,875. This offering amounted to an upgraded Series 33. It was made up of the same engine, modified to improve performance, on the same chassis, lowered and widened to permit a slightly lower and larger body. Four-wheel brakes and balloon tires would now be standard equipment. Body lines were brought up to date, still imposing, but lowered with deeper, more enclosing fenders. A Bragg-Kliesrath vacuum booster was added to the brakes of this heavy car, along with a rather complicated oil filter using a stack of felt discs. An array of 15 lavish body styles was offered for the model, with the promise of extensive custom alterations, should the buyer desire. The Series 36 incorporated nitrocellulose lacquer finish, which was now adopted throughout the Pierce-Arrow line. It allowed both a greater color choice and faster body completion. Interiors boasted "Roman Gold" fittings. Needlepoint medallions on the seat backs in the tonneau were an option. By this time, it could be reasonably wondered why the company chose to put money into improving this already obsolescent T-head-engined car instead of building a more fashionable eight-in-line motor by adding two cylinders to the successful Series 80 six. The answer may be that Charles Sheppy, the chief engineer, did not want that. It could also have been the realization that doing so would be seen as copying the strategy that produced the popular Packard Single Eight. Most importantly, perhaps, the company was still trying to erase the debts incurred from the disaster in 1921, and simply could not afford the development costs of a brand-new engine. Myron E. Forbes was very optimistic about this new luxury chassis, however. He set out with Sheppy aboard the *USS Leviathan* to introduce the model at the Paris automobile salon in October. This little trip would have unexpected consequences.

The Series 36 Dual Valve Six, introduced in late summer 1926 with four-wheel-brakes standard, refined motor, and richly appointed bodies, and priced to sell (courtesy Pierce-Arrow Society).

A decision about issuing the second preferred stock to pay the arrears owed the cumulative preferred stock would be put off, Mr. Forbes made clear at his departure, until his return from Europe, although he supposed at that time it would "probably be issued." He also seemed confident that the 171,250 shares of common stock authorized by the stockholders would be offered not long after. "Our prospects for the fourth quarter," he opined at dockside, "are better than they have been at any time in the past five years due to the introduction of our new Series 36 dual valve car." A price cut on the enclosed drive limousine model to $5,875 from the $7,205 of the comparable Series 33 model gave it a competitive edge, made possible by "operating economies and increased volume." Production was to be five of these cars a day. Assembly of the Series 80 would continue at six times that pace. Forbes was the very picture of confidence as he left for the Continent.

Interior of the Series 36 Landau, seatback embroidery optional, "Roman Gold" hardware standard. Bodied at the factory (courtesy Pierce-Arrow Society).

Upon his return on November 10, Forbes seemed equally upbeat with the press. "The outlook for Pierce-Arrow is very bright for next year," he was quoted as saying. "October shipments were up to schedule and November is running very satisfactorily," he continued, showing how well informed he was despite having been out of the country for some weeks. In less than a week, the results at Pierce-Arrow for the third quarter of 1926 were released. Net was a disappointing $176,247. Introduction of the Series 36 had not been quite the shot in the arm expected, although the nine-month net was still ten thousand dollars above that total in 1925 at $980,090. In any case, the regular quarterly dividend was paid on January 1 to holders of the preferred stock.

Charles Sheppy had told Forbes during their European trip that the experimental aluminum Series 80 engine was ready for production. With his usual caution, Forbes urged that more extensive tests be made before large scale production began. Accordingly, one hundred Series 80 production cars were built incorporating the changes during late 1926 and early 1927. The everyday performance of these cars was tracked carefully for problems. Pierce-Arrow was still anxious that the difficulties of early 1921 would not be repeated.

The Pierce-Arrow News for the 12th of December alerted distributors to "an opportunity to secure for your prospects who are on the market for a high-grade custom body the identical cars shown at the Salon for immediate delivery." What followed was a detailed description of four custom bodies by renowned body designers on the Series 80 that had been exhibited at the 22nd Annual Automobile Salon in New York. They were all formal chauffeur-driven cars, designed for convenient use around town, but with bespoke coachwork. They included a Cabriolet by Holbrook of Utica, New York; a Landaulet by LeBaron Inc. of New York City; a Brougham by J.B. Judkins Company of Amesbury, Massachusetts; and a Landaulet by Brunn & Co., of Buffalo. Extensive details of the paint combinations, striping, upholstery and fittings were carefully described. Clearly the factory believed that the Series 80 had the potential to be a magnet for custom bodies.

Unfortunately, the good earnings at Pierce-Arrow, so evident at the start of 1926, seemed to be fading as the year ended. The efforts, underway in late summer, to pay down obligations and commence paying dividends on the common stock were now on hold.

And 1927 dawned with an evident slowdown in the industry as a whole. Pierce-Arrow added no new models, the Series 36 having been introduced during the previous summer. Charles Clifton's portrait was on the masthead page of *Motor Age* for the January 6 issue, heralding the opening of the New York Automobile Show at the Grand Central Palace on Saturday the 8th. The Colonel was not a contributor to the publication, but he did head the sponsoring organization of the show. Fewer makes of cars would be on display than in 1926. There were now 40 manufacturers represented. Studebaker's smaller companion car, the Erskine, was the single new nameplate on the floor. A separate truck show was added. Nineteen makers took spaces for that. There was also an area for showing shop equipment, open only to the trade before 3:00 p.m., and factory tools would be demonstrated. Another space contained some 150 accessory and parts manufacturers displaying their wares. The show would continue through January 16. While the NACC annual banquet was held as usual during the show, it is not certain that Charles Clifton was present. What is known is that Vice-president Roy Chapin was the toastmaster, and that attendance was so popular that some had to be turned away for lack of seating space.

Clifton penned his annual appreciation of the automobile industry for the Sunday *New York Times* of January 9. In it he pointed out the growing number of families who owned multiple cars arising from the fact that owning a motor car "has advanced from the stage of being a general convenience to a point where living conditions are predicated on having this mode of travel for every one in the family." He clearly felt that the number of cars manufactured was not the important thing. It was this motivation for multiple car ownership that supplied one reason for his optimism about the future of the industry.

"I think it is worthwhile to stress particularly the importance of the domestic market," Clifton wrote, "because there is frequently the tendency to think that because we now have 22,000,000 motor vehicles in the country, progress in the local field must be at an end. History of the last ten years has shown that the greatest guarantee of business is a large volume of motor vehicle registrations. Why are these families owning more than one car? Because the very structure of business and society is based on the assumption that every one has an automobile. Suburbs are built radiating from the towns and from the railroads on the presumption that a motor car will always be available for those living in such homes." The sociological impact of car ownership was quite apparent to him.

That week, Pierce-Arrow ran large advertisements in the metropolitan newspapers extolling the great bargains represented in the Pierce-Arrow line, with closed cars now offered on the Series 80 chassis for as low as $2,995. However, the most emphatic pitch touted the lofty Series 36, and it was written by Myron Forbes. After telling his experience bringing a

Series 36, "the finest motor car Pierce-Arrow has ever produced," to the Paris show, he described the efforts he and Charles Sheppy made to uncover superior engines, chassis, and bodies there. "We were prepared to find the superior to our cars," he wrote "but we were disillusioned. After viewing the cars at the Paris Salon and the Olympia Show in England I firmly believe 'the 36' is the finest of them all." The advertisement concluded with Forbes' prediction that Pierce-Arrow was entering its "greatest year," when production was sure to fall behind demand. For 1927, Pierce-Arrow also offered a "Limousine Coach Taxi" model. This Series 80 model had a Limousine Coach body with some special fittings, such as a taxi meter in front, easily removable upholstery panels on the doors and rear quarter and Budd Michelin disc wheels. It listed for $3,450 f.o.b. Buffalo.

Myron Forbes gave a prepared statement to the newsmen of Dow Jones & Co. in mid–January that apparently was prompted by rumors swirling around a persistent decline in the price of Pierce-Arrow preferred stock. The statement was published in the January 19 *Wall Street Journal*. He first assured the reporters that he could see no reason why the Pierce-Arrow board would not declare the $2 quarterly dividend when they considered the matter late in February. There was a "good surplus over the amount required to take care of the dividend," he insisted. The company was not borrowing from banks and had "not done so for some time." Cash on hand at the end of the year totaled between $1 and $1.5 million. "Recent business has held up remarkably well," he went on, "considering the set-back in the automobile and truck business during the latter part of last year." In fact, Pierce-Arrow had shipped 7,246 vehicles in 1926, compared to 7,522 the year before. It was true that truck and bus business had fallen off due to the "uncertainty over installment terms" that had affected all manufacturers. "I believe this situation has been materially improved and look forward with confidence to continued good business." That day, Pierce-Arrow preferred closed at 93. The newspaper had reported two days before that in sales among the high-priced cars, Cadillac had gained 41 percent in 1926, Lincoln 12 percent, Packard 12 percent and Pierce-Arrow 4 percent. Perhaps that story encouraged Forbes to respond.

February was the month when Charles and Grace Clifton customarily took up residence at their winter home in the South. This year they stayed at the Court Inn in Camden, South Carolina, a pleasant winter resort conveniently available by means of Pullman cars on the Seaboard Airline Railway. Capitalist Bernard Baruch was fond of the place, too, as it was his birthplace. Such a holiday gave the Colonel a chance to relax, play a little golf, and renew himself.

The 1926 Pierce-Arrow Motor Car Co. annual report, released in early March, showed net income of $1,267,695 as compared to $1,629,781 in 1925. Preferred per share earnings had fallen to $12.67. Myron Forbes, in his overview, stressed the investments the company had made during the year to prepare for the future with the purchase by the Pierce-Arrow Sales Corp. of the Harrolds Motor Car Co. operation around New York City. This gave them good Manhattan facilities and "an ideal service station" located in Long Island City. An agreement had been reached whereby $972,000 of the purchase price would be paid in installments over 10 years. In addition, the automobile agency in Boston had been acquired by the Boston branch of the Pierce-Arrow Sales Corp. A $137,500 plot of land had been purchased to use for the erection of "a permanent sales and service station in Boston." Forbes also mentioned the plan to reorganize the debts of the corporation by issuing stock, which had been approved by stockholders. "Directors have not felt that the time was opportune," he wrote, "for putting

14. New Horizons (1924–1927)

A late Pierce-Arrow dual valve truck with dump body and pneumatic tires beside the plant (courtesy Pierce-Arrow Society).

into effect any part of this plan." The financial situation at Pierce-Arrow, from this evidence, clearly felt much less secure than it had the year before. Substantial obligations had been made by the company, and sales were apparently not increasing to meet them.

On Wednesday, March 2, the board of the NACC convened its regular meeting at the headquarters on New York's Madison Avenue in some disarray. Roy Chapin, its vice-president, was in the chair. Charles Clifton was still in South Carolina. And the agenda was in turmoil because the Colonel had made it clear that he was submitting his resignation as president, effective immediately. Great reluctance to abide by his wishes was immediately apparent. Telegrams were exchanged with him in Camden to make sure his mind was finally made up. It took until four in the afternoon for the board members to finally accept his decision.

From the cache of correspondence surrounding the event preserved at the Buffalo and Erie County Historical Society through the generosity of the Colonel's grandsons, David and Malcolm Strachan, it is evident that Charles Clifton's intention to resign was not sprung on the board at the last minute. It was, apparently, not even the first time he had proposed resigning. In typical fashion, he had ahead of time carefully laid out the path for his replacement to be Roy D. Chapin, the vice president. Alvan Macauley would then succeed Chapin as vice-president and Alfred H. Swayne move into the vacant position of vice-president of the passenger car division. It was all set.

Correspondence from Roy Chapin to Clifton, dated February 12 from The Nautilus in

Miami Beach, makes it clear that the Colonel had disclosed to his long-time associate his determination to retire. "If you have definitely concluded that you wish to retire from the Presidency," Chapin wrote, "I know the keenness of the regret we all shall feel." Chapin voiced his hope that Clifton would attend the March meeting "so we may discuss this matter beforehand." William E. Metzger, an important pioneer in the industry and chairman of the Federal Truck Co., wrote Clifton on February 21 from the Detroit Athletic Club, "It doesn't seem possible that you will be permitted to resign. You mean so much to the organization and have handled situations which I doubt anyone else would or could have handled. I do hope the directors will delay action and it may be that your eyes will be better."

Alfred Reeves, the NACC General Manager released the announcement of the board's acceptance by telegram from New York at 4:00 o'clock p.m.: "BOARD DID NOT WANT TO ACCEPT BUT KNOWING HIS WISHES DID SO...." Laudatory telegrams from 31 leading executives in the industry followed. The board then composed a written tribute to Clifton on his service. A committee was appointed to secure what Reeves in another telegram described as "a proper token for presentation to you in appreciation of the leadership of a great industry." The next day Reeves wrote to Clifton describing the response to a telegram the Colonel had sent the day before to the board. "Under the instructions of the board we had a hard time putting together the fine things that we all wanted to say about you." After much work, a resolution was completed for the NACC to adopt expressing its gratitude to Clifton. "Sam Miles lost a lot of sleep last night," Reeves wrote, "revising the draft which was presented and unanimously adopted." The resolution itself was published in the *Automotive Industries* of March 12. A suitably mounted copy was prepared for the Cliftons, as Alfred Reeves wrote, "to view with pride for years to come."

Col. Clifton indicated that he wanted autographed photographs from those with whom he had worked. Letters, beneath letterheads from the important corporations associated with the industry, accompanied photographic portraits from twenty-two associates in the NACC and still exist. The photographs themselves have apparently disappeared. These letters testify to the great respect and affection Charles Clifton inspired among those working with him. Even James Couzens, once the close associate of Henry Ford, sent wishes for Clifton's enjoyable retirement, although no other Ford executive, present or former, felt obliged to do so.

Among the carefully typed correspondence were two particularly touching handwritten letters from an executive at the Oakland division of General Motors. There is no signature on either letter, only initials, which are particularly difficult to decipher. They may read N.D. but are possibly R.D. The first letter was composed on stationery of the New Colonial Hotel, the Bahamas, on February 20, and discloses nothing that would indicate that the gentleman is aware of Charles Clifton's intent to retire. It gives Clifton a simple recounting of this man's continuing southern sojourn, the climate, people he's seen, golf scores, etc., all very relaxed and direct. He vows to "return tomorrow." Cablegrams have come to him bearing the sad news of the passing of four of his friends. They include George Woods, vice-president of Consolidated Gas, "one of the most popular men of Oakland, who was, like yourself and Ralph Holden a *real* friend." After which he signs off, hoping "you and Lady Grace are well and happy."

When this associate writes again, Clifton's retirement has been published and provokes the response that "they" (evidently the board of the NACC) "will miss the judgment and cogent reasoning of the 'Elder Statesman' as the Japanese call it. And they will miss your happy soothing influence in dealing with the factional disagreements and personal differences which must always crop up in the councils of strong, deliberate men." After intimating that Roy Chapin, with all his excellences, may find the job a challenge, the writer closes with these sentiments. "And please let me add dear old pal that during all that time [20 years of association] altho [sic] I have never believed in *any* man's infallibility, it was often a comfort and solace to feel sure of *one* man's integrity and that's that." At the letter's end, this associate treats the impending changes with all the sympathy of a close friend. "When I return [from a projected trip to Scotland] we must get together and celebrate in a reminiscent reunion with perhaps a few libations of proscribed tonic to gladden our hearts and refresh our memories."

It is impossible not to speculate on the proximate cause or causes that reinforced Col. Clifton's determination to leave his position at the NACC when he did. Two possible factors emerge from the many letters surrounding his retirement. The first is the already cited hope from William Metzger "that your eyes will be better." The second is found in a March 15 letter from John N. Willys, who worked with Charles Clifton from the very earliest days. "I note," Willys writes, "in your letter to Al [Reeves] you say pen writing is so painful." Anyone who has read Charles Clifton's impeccable longhand, with its beautifully formed, symmetrical letters, can easily imagine how dismaying such a condition would be to him.

The NACC board's recognition of Clifton's long service to the organization went beyond resolutions and gifts for the household he shared with Grace Clifton. Judging from Albert Reeves' telegram sent at the end of the board meeting, almost immediately they voted to elect Clifton as a perpetual honorary board member and honorary president. They were also determined to mount a special dinner in his honor. The event was planned for the board meeting in Detroit on May 12. Apparently, Charles Clifton was moved to join the board at its July meeting in Buffalo as well. In a letter to the Colonel dated March 3, his successor Roy Chapin assured him of a willingness to extend the celebration into the summer. "There will be no question," he wrote, "of our joining you at Buffalo in July if you wish it, for that is always a great party and I know the directors will be delighted to accept your invitation." The Detroit celebration was unfortunately delayed due to Clifton's "temporary indisposition." That event finally took place in New York on Wednesday, the first of June.

It appears that Colonel and Grace Clifton had perhaps already arrived in New York for the event by May 21. That day a letter was sent from the Cunard Steam Ship Company, Ltd. to "admit yourself and Mrs. Clifton within the Custom Lines upon the arrival of our S.S. 'Berengaria,' due to arrive at Pier 54, North River, Foot of West 14th Street, New York City, next Friday, June 3rd." This letter, addressed "c/o Hotel Biltmore, Madison Av. & 43rd Street, New York City" remains among the family correspondence now at the Buffalo and Erie County Historical Society. The arrangements for these customs passes had been requested by the Manufacturers & Traders Trust Company of Buffalo. Whatever it was that the Cliftons were to greet at the liner's arrival is now a mystery.

In the midst of this drama, the *New York Times* noted in its book section on March 6 the gift from Charles Clifton of four folios of Shakespeare to the Buffalo Public Library. They were apparently given some time before, and were variously printed in 1623, 1632, 1664 and 1685. The first had been traded with the Folger collection for another copy "which Colonel Clifton then owned, which contained some contemporary autographs." Along with these was a 1640 printing of the Poems, marred by some missing pages that were "supplied in facsimile."

Meanwhile, life went on at Pierce-Arrow. Still extant is a notebook handwritten by a Pierce-Arrow test driver named Garrett Fitzgerald. One section of the book concerns instructions to him for test drives beginning March 27, 1927, of the initial Series 36 Dual Valve Six, #360001, evidently still a test chassis at the plant. It begins with the note, "Not pat[ented]. Hood locked at all times." Fitzgerald's task was a night run on a circuit from Buffalo south to Bradford, across the Pennsylvania border, from there to Kane, Pennsylvania, and back to Buffalo. Of primary concern was the reading from the vacuum gauge when climbing hills. Other details concern setting the reed valves of the carburetor, setting distributor points, and attending to the experimental "Fedders" radiator. From what is written here it is profoundly clear how much impact Charles Clifton still had on the attitudes of people working at Pierce-Arrow. "This car turned over to me," Fitzgerald recorded, "on Mar. 27, 1927 at 11:45 P.M. Will run to Bradford, to Kane to Buffalo, only at night and by me for a total of 80,000 miles by order of Pres. Clifton and will be serviced only in Experimental Dept. by D. Jewell, Head of Dept." Further refinement of the Dual Valve Six was still apparently under consideration.

The first week of April Pierce-Arrow reduced the prices of its Series 80 models. They were now the lowest in company history. The Runabout and Brougham models were listed at $2,495. Prices of the Series 36 cars were unchanged. The *Wall Street Journal* noted on April 7 that the company had retired $250,000 of its 8 percent notes on April 1. "This makes $500,000 of the original issue retired," they wrote, "and leaves outstanding $3,700,000 of the notes." *Motor Age* reported that on April 23, that the Pierce-Arrow Motor Car Co. stockholders had re-elected all directors "excepting Walter P. Cooke, who was succeeded by William R. Huntley." Officers remained the same. The board, along with Mr. Huntley, consisted of Charles Clifton, Myron E. Forbes, Joseph G. Dudley, Lewis G. Harriman, E.H. Letchworth, Roland O'Brien, George F. Rand, Ansley W. Sawyer, Albert D. Sikes, Gorhard M. Dahl, John C. Jay, Albert Strauss, Carl J. Schmidlapp, and Lester Watson.

The first quarter earnings report for 1927 were released on April 26 disclosing a disappointing net of $43,774, quite a contrast with the $328,750 earned the corresponding quarter of 1926. As Forbes anticipated, the earnings were less than the $200,000 quarterly dividend scheduled to be paid on the preferred stock. The *Wall Street Journal* noted that Pierce-Arrow shares "were heavily sold, the preferred breaking to new ground for the year at $64." The cause of the decline in first quarter earnings "reflected keen competition and price reductions by other manufacturers." While lowering prices on the Series 80 line made the cars more competitive, it also reduced the profit on each car sold. "Several important firms," the newspaper noted on the 29th, "have been advising clients to liquidate long holdings in so-called low-priced independent motor stocks on theory that strenuous competition is being reflected in earnings of these companies." Not surprisingly, Pierce-Arrow was singled out as an example.

This development suggested that Pierce-Arrow cars were losing their competitive edge. One cause was clearly the fact that the body lines of the Series 80 cars were largely unchanged since their introduction in the summer of 1924. While additional styles had been added, the general appearance of the cars was still the same. This particular attribute was also of increasing importance. As K.W. Stillman had noted in the New York Show issue of *Automotive Industries* back in January, "The very great influence of body design upon sales is well evidenced by the important place it has been given during the past year in the improvement programs of manufacturers. While major improvements in engine and chassis designs have been relatively few, a great many body details have undergone alteration during the past year." The sit-

The swank Club Sedan Landau was offered on the Series 80 chassis in early 1927. In this promotional photograph taken at the plant, the standard Winterfront is mounted on the radiator (courtesy Pierce-Arrow Society).

uation was also well known in the design offices at Pierce-Arrow and among the management. In fact, President Myron Forbes had plans underway to produce a more competitive Pierce-Arrow to meet the challenge.

Unfortunately, some parts of this effort were likely affected by the death of Chief Engineer Charles Sheppy at Summerville, South Carolina, on May 2. His assistant, John C. Talcott, succeeded him. At the same time, there were encouraging signs that recently reduced prices were encouraging better sales numbers. In the June 3 *Wall Street Journal*, Myron Forbes was quoted as saying that Pierce-Arrow passenger car shipments for May were the greatest in the history of the company. "Reports from our distributors in principal marketing centers throughout the United States," he continued, "confirm our belief that there will be no let-up in the increased business which our company is now enjoying." The gains continued through June, showing a $33\tfrac{2}{3}$ percent increase over 1926. By now, the period of price lowering in the industry appeared to have ended. However, as the *Wall Street Journal* put it in a May 21 story, "A few dollars difference in the price of a car has little effect on the purchaser, if the car meets his ideas of up-to-dateness and style."

A curious development involving the Pierce-Arrow Motor Car Co. began on June 8 when Paris coachbuilder Jacques Saoutchik boarded the White Star liner *Olympic* at Cherbourg for New York. In the 1920s, the center of trend-setting automotive style was France. Wealthy, fashionable sophisticates from all over the world routinely experienced the Paris

Salon the way wealthy Americans went to the Automobile Salon in New York every fall. A multitude of automobile body-builders in England, Belgium, Italy, and Germany as well as France showed their wares in Paris. Taking a chassis from a reputable maker, these firms would design and mount unique and stylish coachwork to customer order, using rare and sometimes exotic materials with no regard to cost. Of them, none had a higher reputation than *Carrosserie de Luxe, J. Saoutchik*, established by a cabinetmaker who immigrated to France from Belarus at the turn of the century. According to his biographer, Peter Larsen, Pierce-Arrow paid for Jacques Saoutchik's trip and funded several weeks' stay to employ him at the plant in Buffalo.

How did it happen that this European cosmopolite came to be hired by the Pierce-Arrow Motor Car Co.? In an article published in the French automobile body journal *La Carrosserie* later in 1927, Soutchik was interviewed about his American trip. The origins of this sojourn were described this way: "The beautiful automobile designs that M. Saoutchik showed last year at the Grand Palais [Paris automobile show] had in fact not failed to generate Yankee admiration, and the realistic overseas manufacturers did not hesitate to contact him to come and teach them the art of French coachbuilding."

This account places the origin of the association with Pierce-Arrow at the Paris Salon of October 1926, when Myron Forbes and Charles Sheppy brought the Series 36 Pierce-Arrow to display and spent time looking over the European makes shown there. Writing years later, Jacques Saoutchik's son Pierre added further details to the story, albeit of uncertain validity. "The manager of Pierce-Arrow came to Paris and got in touch with Jacques," Pierre wrote, "to offer him to come, design and draw up the plans for new bodies, where the style must shake America." The agreement between Pierce-Arrow and Saoutchik was apparently visualized as a stay of 60 days for a price of "120,000 dollars, with travel and *de luxe* expenses paid." An interpreter would be included in the "expenses." It is no longer possible to determine the exact amount that Forbes arranged for Pierce-Arrow to pay in order to obtain the coach maker's services. That it did not match Pierre's inflated figure is virtually certain. Such stories tend to get enlarged as time passes. Forbes told a dealer meeting that fall that the Frenchman's stay lasted three weeks rather than two months. However long it was, the experience left a life-long impression on the French *carrossier*. It was his one encounter with real, big-time, volume automobile production, and he never forgot it. From available evidence Larsen estimates that Saoutchik's stay in America probably lasted about six weeks.

Pierce-Arrow by that time was hard at work on a new model, aiming to reach the marketability shown by the Series 80 at its introduction. The motor and chassis were being upgraded and an especially stylish body was seen as essential. The matter was of such importance that Forbes was willing to spend some considerable sums to import a French body designer to help.

It was probably a surprise to him when Jacques Saoutchik showed up in Buffalo with a 1:5 scale model of his latest brainchild—a patented convertible sedan body he called the *transformable*. At the Paris show Forbes had seen this carefully crafted miniature whose top could also be pulled back exposing the chauffeur *en limousine*, or completely lowered to make an open touring car. It was an ingenious and complicated creation, and the height of European fashion at the time, but a very expensive and delicate item for an American producer. On top of this, customs officials in the Port of New York had managed to drop it on the concrete floor, damaging its moving parts. It took more than a week, according to Pierre's account, to find capable workers in the Pierce plant to repair the damage, leaving skepticism in Jacques' mind about the capability of American auto workers. Repairs completed, there then was, according to Pierre Saoutchik's account, a full-size body of the design built "in the white" that incorporated a completely disappearing top and a turtle deck. No other source mentions this project, nor does any photo or blueprint documentation seem to exist. Certainly, Pierce-Arrow never offered anything of the kind for either display or sale.

So, what did Jacques Saoutchik accomplish with his trip? It is, honestly, impossible to say with any certainty. At its introduction, Myron Forbes told dealers that during the design phase of the Series 81's body, "I brought a man from Paris who stands at the top in French body designing and French custom body building—that man spent a period of three weeks in this plant—the greater part of his time checking, studying and suggesting minor details which would improve the appearance of this car and give it that everlasting touch of style appeal." Early in 1928, a full-color advertisement for the Series 81 was run in *Vogue, The New Yorker, Harper's Bazaar, Country Life*, and other high-toned publications displaying a facsimile copy of a letter written to Forbes by Jacques Saoutchik after his return to Paris, extolling the beauty and construction of the Pierce-Arrow body as being "worthy of its world renown, and merits its place at the head of American body builders." This appears to have been one of the most expensive endorsements ever obtained by Pierce-Arrow.

Pierce-Arrow's report on second quarter 1927 operations was released in late July. Having already warned on July 9 that earnings would probably be below the dividend requirements

The 1928 Series 81 2-door, 5-passenger Brougham (courtesy Pierce-Arrow Society).

on its preferred stock, the July 26 *Wall Street Journal* noted the net had surpassed that of the first quarter but still did not reach the preferred dividend amount. Quarterly profits reached $71,609. The six-month total was only $115,383 when something over $350,000 was required to meet the dividend. Car sales for the first six months of 1927 were "about equal" to those of 1926. Truck sales had fallen off substantially, as they had for most truck makers. At the start of July, Pierce-Arrow held cash reserves of $2 million to $2.5 million. There was some optimism that the cash position of the company and the expectation of improving sales would allow the dividend to be paid, and the preferred quarterly dividend was eventually approved by the board at its August meeting.

Two new "sport type" body styles were announced in late July on the Series 80, according to the *Wall Street Journal*, a "five passenger Sedan listed at $3,025 and a convertible coupe at $2,350." The new offerings did not seem to stimulate sales to any great degree. Stories in the press were seen advising investors to divest long holdings of motor stocks "on theory this industry is entering now entering a quiet period which might be reflected in these shares." The new Pierce-Arrow was not yet ready to introduce at the customary time in late summer.

Late that summer, John M. Dundon, assistant works manager, suddenly died of a heart attack at his summer home "on the lake shore," according to a newspaper account. He had worked at Pierce beginning in 1907, and in the Great War had been "chief of the aircraft work in which the factory was engaged," after which he was promoted first to superintendent of manufacturing, and then his final position. Dundon was 48 years old.

November 2, 1927, proved to be a significant day at the Pierce-Arrow Motor Car Co. in several ways. For one thing, two new faces were elected to the board of directors, according to that day's *Wall Street Journal*. Colonel John R. Simpson of New York and Randolph B. Flershem of Buffalo were the new board members. Flershem was a vice-president of the Marine Trust Co., having been formerly vice-president and general manager of sales for the American Radiator Co. Col. Simpson was associated with Sinclair Oil's foreign business. That same day in Buffalo at the Pierce-Arrow factory a convention of agents was held to unveil the new Series 81 "line of moderately priced cars," to use the description from the newspaper.

In view of the disappointing earnings performance, a good deal was riding on the introduction of this new model. President Myron E. Forbes himself delivered the sales pitch, touting the features of the car and the methods used to develop it. After a preface insisting that "I believe we make our own opportunities and they are measured by the way we see them—grasp them and back them up with hard work." He launched into a description of the objectives that motivated him and those designing the car: "To give you [the dealers] an automobile, the best in the world, at the lowest possible price consistent with quality; to give one that is easily sold; one that increases your volume of business and gives you a handsome profit commensurate with your own hard and intelligent work has been one of my visions for years, and I think I can safely say that in presenting the Series 81 today my vision is to be realized."

Forbes then explained that the mechanical details of the new model had been developed carefully and tested fully, mentioning also that the last 500 Series 80 cars had been built with the same engineering changes, "and it is a source of satisfaction to hear from the owners and from our dealers and distributors who have reported on these cars, that they did not believe it was possible to so materially improve the performance of the '80' and at the same time give the quietness and smoothness that is shown in these motors." The adoption of aluminum head, rods, and pistons had reduced reciprocating weight by 1.48 lbs. per cylinder, allowing smoother running, more rapid acceleration, and the elimination of the vibration dampener. The intake manifold had been redesigned to get better economy and better power, and a new carburetor with thermostatic accelerating well, designed in conjunction with Stromberg, had been adopted. Horsepower had increased by nearly 10 percent. Performance on the road was noticeably improved over the Series 80, especially on hills. A chassis lubrication system by Bowen, operated from the driver's seat, was incorporated. The new Marles-type steering column reduced driver effort in turning. The chassis had been lowered and widened and 20-inch wheels adopted.

Describing the body used for the Series 81, Forbes remarked that the design had been the assignment of James R. Way, whom he described as "the man who has given Pierce-Arrow its body styles." Way had been "given a free hand—he was not tied to any bumpers, radiators, fenders, lamps or anything else—he was given the wheelbase of the chassis and told to go to the job." Forbes' conclusion was that Way had turned out "a design of beauty, and it is drastic." There was no doubt that Way changed the aspect of the 130 in. wheelbase cars with his design for the Series 81. The result was more unified and less angular, with sweeping fenders and higher belt line with no molding. Forbes was especially pleased with the way the tail of the car over the fuel tank had been streamlined. The instrument panel had been ingeniously laid out with indirect lighting and contained a dashboard thermometer and fuel gauge. Interior detailing had been carefully executed, and the seating was more comfortable. The fender headlamps had been lifted higher up the fender and their diameter reduced. Standing "helmet" headlamps of an entirely new design were optional. An adaptation of Herbert Dawley's helmeted archer ornament for the hood of Mary Garden's car from a decade before was put into production for the new car, while a Pierce family heraldic crest was adopted to adorn the radiator. Unfortunately, this turned out to be the crest of a different Pierce family than that of George N.

After Forbes' presentation, the usual display of models was opened for the dealers to see. That afternoon, Forbes again took the lectern to counter negative press reports about Pierce-Arrow's financial condition. "At the present time," he revealed, "the Company has no bank loans, has cash assets in excess of $1,800,000 and has current assets of $12,000,000 against liabilities of $960,000. In addition we have recently purchased and paid for in cash $350,000 of the company's

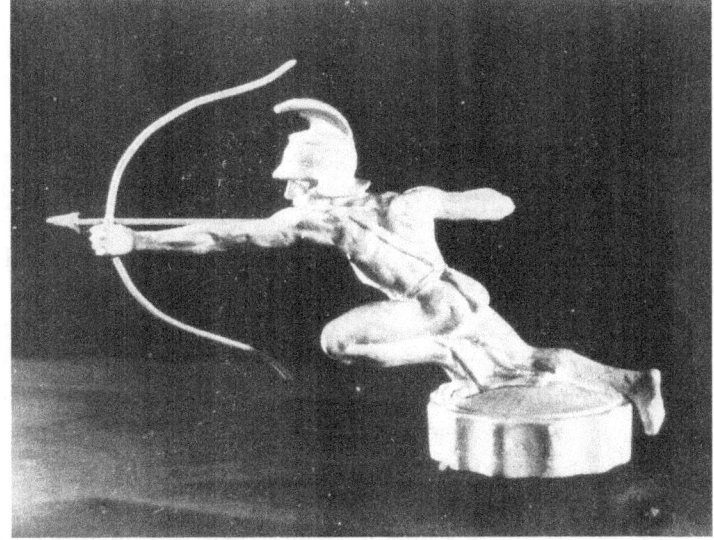

Herbert Dawley's plaster model used for the radiator ornament (cast in silver, no less!) for opera star Mary Garden's special Pierce-Arrow in the late 1910s. Housed in Paris, the car was carried off by the Germans during World War II. The figure was the basis for the 1928 chromed archer radiator ornament on Pierce-Arrows (courtesy Pierce-Arrow Society).

Twenty-year Eight per cent Debentures. These are now held in the treasury in anticipation of sinking fund requirements for 1928 and 1929." He also stressed the investment of $1.5 million in the Pierce-Arrow Finance Corp. and selling branches. If Charles Clifton attended this convention, his role was not significant enough for anyone to mention.

The crucial importance the introduction of the new Series 81 had for Pierce-Arrow was evident from reading the third quarter earnings statement released by the company the same day and covered in the next day's *Wall Street Journal*. It showed a net loss of $373,999 for the September quarter, thus wiping out any profits earned during the year and leaving a nine-month loss of $258,616. An analysis was made by the Saturday *Wall Street Journal* in an article titled "New Model May Help Pierce-Arrow." Acknowledging that the company would probably record a net loss for 1927, the reporter noted the development of the new model had adversely affected the output and sales at Pierce-Arrow while consuming development costs out of the company's stretched financial resources. All the same, the story made clear the optimism felt by Pierce-Arrow officials about the likely success of the new model, with its range of 13 body choices. Allowing that the factory prices of the Series 81 were some $150 to $200 above equivalent models of its predecessor, the newspaper pointed out they were still "substantially below" those of the Series 80 when first introduced in 1924. They cautioned expecting results before 1928, because the introduction took place "out of season." The story concluded that Pierce-Arrow now was "in a better position to prosecute active development of the new models than it was when the Series 80 was added to the line," on the evidence that since then it had managed to "pay off a large proportion of the indebtedness contracted during the postwar deflation which all but forced the company into receivership."

Production figures for its passenger cars told the story:

1923: 1,997
1924: 3,056
1925: 5,665
1926: 5,824

This had extended into 1927 as well. The nine-month figure for passenger car production at Pierce-Arrow was 4,700, actually 500 units higher than at that point the year before. By contrast, the output of trucks and busses was around 650 compared to the 1,150 completed by the third quarter in 1926. After condensing the financial achievements during the period, the article noted the additional Pierce-Arrow offerings in the high-priced passenger car field along with trucks and buses. "These phases of the company's activities," the story concluded, "which were formerly most important, have barely held their own for some years. Any improvement in the company's position in the industry, therefore, is dependent upon its success in the medium-priced field." This was the challenge the Series 81 faced in 1928.

Three weeks later, the same publication did a notable analysis from its Detroit Bureau of the Packard Motor Car Co., Pierce-Arrow's competitor. It makes an instructive comparison with Pierce-Arrow's situation. The article was titled "Packard Earnings Invested in Plant." This was an attempt to explain Packard's "strong position" in the industry. Its most compelling insight attributed Packard's great profits and ever-larger penetration of the market to its continual investment in and subsequent rapid depreciation of production facilities. "This," the article concluded, "has resulted in reduced manufacturing costs, enabling the company to lower prices and at the same time increase earnings, for although prices have been at the

A 1928 Series 36 cabriolet with several custom features, photographed at the Pierce plant. It has the lines typical of a factory body with special accessories (courtesy Pierce-Arrow Society).

lowest levels in company history, earnings have shown unusual gains." The key to Packard success was what the author called the "quantity production unit," officially the Packard Six, first brought out in the summer of 1920, and still in production, albeit much improved, for 1928. Introduced at a price of $4,950, 1,042 had been produced in the remaining five months of 1920. Now listed at a starting price of $2,285, shipments of the model ran at a monthly rate of "three and a half times" the five-month 1920 total. Profits soared also. In the nine years before 1925 profits at Packard averaged $4.4 million. In the three years since, they averaged $13.3 million a year. During those three last years, investment in plant and property were over $7 million each year. By the same token, depreciation charges totaled more than one-half of those figures each year. It was a stunning success story.

For all its earnest efforts, by the end of 1927 Pierce-Arrow had still not expunged its postwar debts and had struggled to scrape up funds to develop new models. Its lowest priced car, the two-passenger runabout with rumble seat, was priced at $2,900. By late in November, happily, market reports noted a rise in Pierce-Arrow securities, anticipating better sales of its newly-introduced models.

During 1927 Charles Clifton had seen his impact decline along with his activity. Now feeling the limitations of age, he had retired from his NACC position and was much less the guiding force at the Pierce-Arrow Motor Car Co. Still, he was the Pierce-Arrow chairman, and also the driving intelligence of the General Hospital. His standing remained undiminished everywhere. "Colonel Clifton is proud of Buffalo," one Buffalonian is quoted as saying in a press account, "and Buffalo is proud of him."

~ 15 ~

Passing (1928)

> I charge my wife and children with the care of what I have created, especially the Memorial in Trinity Chapel to my beloved daughter, now deceased. I also charge them, from their personal estates to be helpful in all good works, to remember those in trouble or distress, especially their kin and kind, and to lend their aid to the city of Buffalo towards higher ideals in civic virtue; to be patriotic Americans, constant Christians, and so to bring up their children that they may be a credit to themselves, their city, our beloved country, and the cause of Jesus Christ, our only Lord and Savior.
> —From Col. Charles Clifton's will

The year 1928 opened amid an uncertain economic situation. While the 1920–21 depression evolved rather quickly into a great expansion that had lasted six years, a noticeable slowdown began in the summer of 1926, and it was not certain that the expansion would continue. Sales at Pierce-Arrow were still good, but, with reduced prices, at the cost of its profits. There also had been a serious decline in sales of Pierce-Arrow heavy trucks and buses. Understandable alarm preoccupied the management over these unwelcome developments. The newly developed Series 81 was viewed as its crucial offering in this time of uncertainty, and it was still unclear how the new line would fare in the market. Anticipation gripped everyone as the year started, the factory poised to go into high gear if demand warranted.

"Change, Change, Change...!" screamed the headline above Norman Shidle's editorial in the January 14 *Automotive Industries*. "Throbbing through the whole picturesque panorama of people and products," he wrote, "like the recurring motif in a grand symphony, the idea of change and progress was dominant in the twenty-eighth annual New York Automobile Show which opened at the Grand Central Place on Saturday, Jan. 7." In general, the change he described, while widespread, concentrated on refinements of construction details rather than major technological advancements. Considerable attention was paid to styling efforts that altered the appearance on refined, but not radically changed, chassis. Offerings on the floor suggested that manufacturers were rethinking their competitive approach to the still-enormous automobile market. "Change," Sidle remarked at one point, "seems to have become a regular part of the routine for the automobile business; success seems to be dependent more and more on the ability to change intelligently, steadily and consistently." This was a stark contrast with the traditional approach at Pierce-Arrow.

The January 9 *Wall Street Journal* carried a series of quotes from the show under the heading "Motor Executives Predict Good Year." The publication could even suggest "Record

Output Looked For in 1928" in the title. Myron Forbes had been consulted, and he opined that conditions in key industries had changed "decidedly for the better" during the previous several weeks and foretold "a substantial business expansion." More precise insight into the viewpoint of the Pierce-Arrow Motor Car Company at the start of 1928 was seen in a story further on in the paper which quoted Mr. Forbes' assistant, one George C. Hubbs. His view was that buyers would forever strive for "better things." Proof of this trend in the automobile market was seen in the tendency for replacement models to be "a little better, a little finer, than the car they now own." Hubbs saw Pierce-Arrow as a likely beneficiary of this situation. "Speak of a Pierce-Arrow a few years ago," he asserted, "and the average man would think of $8,000 or $10,000. Today increasing numbers are learning that a Pierce-Arrow can be purchased for about $3,000. The same is true of other makers who during the early days required at least twice as much to build a car which did not possess the inherent value of today's product." He expected very large sales of cars in the "high-priced" car market, which obviously included Pierce-Arrow.

Change was also noted at the National Automobile Chamber of Commerce Banquet, held at the Commodore on Tuesday evening, beginning at 6:30. *Motor Age* noted breathlessly in its show coverage that "Two Fords Attend Dinner of NACC." Henry Ford had not graced this event since 1912, the year after the overturn of the Selden Patent. He and Edsel were both present this year "as representatives of the Lincoln Motor Car Co." The Ford Motor Co. itself had staged a show at the Madison Square Garden of its new Model A that week, at which a "Fordor" sedan body was introduced. It is perhaps coincidental to note that this NACC banquet was the first ever at which Charles Clifton was not scheduled to preside. Clifton did attend the occasion. He joined some 1,300 others, according to the magazine. Roy D. Chapin acted as the toastmaster this year, advancing an optimistic outlook. Harry G. Weaver of General Motors then spoke to the attendees about sales methods in an amusing way. His talk was followed by a humorous "roast" of various attendees by "Senator" Edward Ford, after which, Wm. M. Jardine, the secretary of agriculture, spoke about increasing mechanization seen in farming.

On the floor of the show itself, Pierce-Arrow displayed the Series 81 with some confidence. In hand were beautiful full-color catalogs titled "Pierce-Arrow Presents Series 81" illustrating seven body styles with brightly colored watercolors of the cars in stylish settings. Advertising of the new model had begun the month before with full page color advertisements rendering a head-on view of the radiator and separate helmet headlamps that included exact details of the front axle and the ribbed front brake drums. February would see ads with the same illustration in smaller size and the Saoutchik endorsement letter. Prices ran from $2,900 for the Runabout with rumble seat to a $3,550 enclosed Drive Limousine. Club Sedan, Club Sedan Landau, and Sport Sedan bodies, the last ones developed for the Series 80 in 1927, were still listed as available on the new chassis, although their roofs looked a bit square against the new fenders, engine hood, and cowl. Publicity hand-outs quoted sentences from an evaluation of the model by Niran Bates Pope published in the November 5, 1927, issue of *Automotive Industries*. The comments extolled the long tradition of excellence that fostered the high reputation of the Pierce-Arrow and its current, relatively lower, purchase cost. Among the plaudits was one praising the car as displaying a "conversational seventy" miles an hour.

Several car lines in the same price class as the Series 81 could be seen at the show. Outstanding among them was the new Cadillac, freshly restyled by Harley Earl in the manner of his greatly admired La Salle of the year before. It was a beautifully sleek array with long, swept front fenders, and a brand new 341 cubic-inch V-8 on a re-engineered and longer chassis. Beginning with a $3,350 Roadster the line extended to a 140-inch wheelbase "Imperial 7 Sedan" at $3,895. A prestige line of Fisher-Fleetwood customs continued on to a lofty $5,500.

Another greatly refined competitor was the slightly-enlarged, six-cylinder, 112 horsepower Chrysler Imperial "80" offered at $2,795 for the Roadster to a $3,495 Sedan Limousine. These, too, exhibited a much lower and freshly stylish appearance. Introduced in late 1925, this Chrysler model, then with identical cylinder dimensions to those of the Series 80, offered advanced hydraulic brakes and consistently undersold the Pierce-Arrow. Plus, as the advertisements never tired of repeating, "Chrysler model numbers mean miles per hour."

The Packard Six was also newly restyled to a very contemporary fashion for 1928, being noticeably lower, and now incorporated a hypoid rear axle. Its model 526 Runabout listed for $2,275, a $75 reduction from the year before. The model 533 Sedan Limousine now cost $2,785. At the time, the Packard was the largest selling car in this range of the market.

These were all daunting competition for the Series 81 Pierce-Arrow. There were others, too.

To help offset the worrisome decline in commercial vehicle sales, Pierce-Arrow had developed a light delivery truck based on the Series 80 mechanicals called the Fleet Arrow Wagon, which was introduced that year. Unlike larger Pierce-Arrow trucks, it had a bevel gear rear axle. Available in wheelbase lengths up to 180 inches, the Fleet Arrows sold for around $2,500. This new commercial model also made possible more use of production spaces at Elmwood Avenue.

Friday, February 18, 1928, revealed just how threatening the financial situation at Pierce-Arrow had become. The Annual Report revealing a loss that totaled $783,201 for 1927 was released. Operations had netted a profit of $202,279 to which profits from the Pierce-Arrow Finance Corp. added another $78,930. Interest charges alone had overwhelmed that, with additional depreciation charges of $605,776 adding to the net loss. Remaining costs of Series 80 development along with the development costs of its Series 81 successor and the Fleet Arrow Wagon had all been absorbed in these figures. In his explanation to stockholders, Myron Forbes stressed that no bank loans had been added and $350,000 of debenture bonds were purchased. The installment on the plant mortgage of $12,000 had been paid, as had a $97,000 payment against the acquisition of the New York City distributor. Cash reserves on December 31 still totaled $1.5 million. A repetition of such a year in 1928, however, would clearly be disastrous.

As the spring selling season approached, Pierce-Arrow appeared to be hard at work exploring new approaches to selling Series 81 cars. A revised catalog was issued with "Photographic Studies" replacing the earlier, colored renderings. The company photographer Albert Johns and his "junior" Joseph Koperski had staged an attractive series of settings for the cars "along the Lake Shore Drive or in the exclusive sections of Buffalo," according to Koperski in 1981. It also unveiled a wider range of body styles. To the lineup in the earlier catalog had been added images of a four-passenger Coupe, a body left over from the earlier Series 80, as was the blind quarter Club Sedan pictured. Unexpected additions were two open-front, formal models: an All-Weather Landau and a French Opera Brougham, the latter displaying razor-edge lines and a distinctive lantern mounted on the tonneau roof. These custom-looking cars demonstrated that Pierce-Arrow was projecting the Series 81 into the upper ranges of the market, even though the larger Series 36 was still available. Since no credit is given to another builder, it can be assumed that the factory body shop designed and built these exclusive models, which doubtless bore the little "Body by Pierce-Arrow" tags at the firewall. Newspaper advertising at this time stressed the reduced outlay to buy a Pierce-Arrow. This, evidently, extended even to the Town Car market.

Two bodies had been restyled for this later catalog. Both the two-passenger Coupe and the Convertible Coupe models showed deck lines smoothed out to a softer, almost seductive curved shape, especially along the belt. The doors and windows were reshaped to reduce height as well. These lines reflected some of Jacques Saoutchik's Paris customs of the time. Perhaps the coachbuilder had contributed more to Pierce-Arrow than an endorsement letter.

The fact that Pierce-Arrow had the ability to design and build its own bodies had always been seen as an advantage, allowing for greater customer choice and reducing outside supplier expense. The late Hugo Pfau, employed by LeBaron at the time, however, told Pierce-Arrow Society editor Bernard Weis in 1971 that "Some early Series 80 bodies (especially open ones) came from American Body Co. in Buffalo," and that "The convertible coupes were built by Phillips Custom Body Co. in Warren, Ohio." A Series 81 convertible coupe with front opening doors and bearing a Phillips body tag still exists.

By this time there were cost disadvantages from using the factory body department.

The revised version of the Series 81 coupe was introduced late, showing cowl, belt, roof and deck contours that have a very Continental look to them. Was this Jacques Saoutchik's contribution? (courtesy University of Michigan Special Collections).

Unlike most of its competitors, Pierce-Arrow body panels were not steel, but aluminum. While there were definite weight-saving advantages from using aluminum, the material required more handwork to obtain a standard part. Without the capacity to press out whole body panels in steel using the newly available massive tools, Pierce-Arrow employees punched out small pieces from 2-S-6 gray plate, half-hard aluminum stock. The pieces were then welded together to make the doors, body sides and other panels. The whole process was described at some length in the May 7, 1927, *Automotive Industries* by P.M. Heldt. Panels were then attached to the ash cabinetwork of the body frame. The result was quite satisfactory in service but expensive to produce.

Both Ford and Chevrolet had operations in Buffalo, and both had increased production schedules this spring. A story about those plans appeared in the *Wall Street Journal* of April 17. No such announcement came from Pierce-Arrow, however. Hoped-for demand for the new Series 81 had not materialized.

Charles Clifton found the bustling city of Buffalo much changed from the place had known as a boy. It had grown into a steel and manufacturing center of national importance, while keeping its prominence as an inland port and railroad hub. The new Liberty Bank towered over Lafayette Square. Express trains on the New York Central with luxurious Pullman cars still arrived and departed from east and west at the rambling, timeworn station on Exchange Street that Clifton knew well, but they were now pulled by giant "Hudson" class passenger engines of great power and speed. Now under construction was a monumental new passenger station for the line, out east of Fillmore Avenue near the stockyards, that would replace Exchange Street for Chicago-bound trains. Automobile traffic was more congested in Buffalo, but streets and roads had improved greatly. The now-completed Peace Bridge brought Canada closer than it seemed to be before. Clifton could take considerable pride in his own civic contributions. Even yet he had responsible positions, although he was officially retired. Speaking of Clifton, a younger executive in the automobile industry was heard to remark admiringly, "He has lived a perfect life, and his memory will remain green for a long, long time. Having a business ability that amounts to sheer genius, he has earned in his life a comfortable competence. Yet he lives simply and gives to charity and to the finer arts that excess which most men of means choose to spend upon themselves and their families."

Indeed, on Hospital Day, May 12, 1928, the new Renwick R. Ross Memorial X-ray Laboratory, a gift from Charles Clifton to the Buffalo General Hospital, was dedicated to the memory of Dr. Ross, a friend of Clifton's and hospital superintendent for 35 years. The facility was, according to hospital historian Evelyn Hawes, "one of the most modern and fully equipped laboratories in the country." Dr. Renwick had died the previous November. His successor, Acting Superintendent Dr. Fraser D. Mooney, recalled on other occasions Charles Clifton's concern with the lack of participation on the part of many citizens. In a conversation with him, Clifton had remarked, "Probably long before you are as old as I am, you will have learned there are very few people trained in the art of giving." The Colonel planned for his giving to extend even beyond the span of his own life. Provisions of his will furnished the means for his survivors to live in comfort for the balance of their lives and also awarded bequests to the Buffalo General Hospital, Buffalo Fine Arts Academy and the Charity Organization Society of Buffalo.

Clifton was still enough of a public figure to warrant mention in a *New York Times* story in the April 8, 1928, Sunday Automobile Pages titled "Industry Losing Early Pioneers." After tracing his long, significant career with those of his early compatriots, the paper concluded: "Colonel Charles Clifton is nearly 75. He is chairman of the Board of the Pierce-Arrow Motor Car Company and has practically retired from active service."

The first quarter of 1928 proved calamitous for the Pierce-Arrow Motor Car Co. Its quarterly report released on May 2 revealed a loss of $359,763 as of March 31. This compared with the small profit of $43,774 for that quarter in 1927. The difficulties the company had faced the year before had increased. It was now clearly in what looked to be a death spiral. Expenses had to be drastically reduced. Advertisements in the big, national magazines ceased, hardly an inducement to buyers. Myron Forbes and the other executives were mulling over ways to bring life-saving capital into the business. Newspaper advertising was drastically cut. This crisis extended far beyond Buffalo. Late that month, a Pierce-Arrow sales manager at the Chicago sales room on Broadway admitted in a letter to his brother, "I sure am worried.... Chrysler has taken over Dodge and it is practically certain that Pierce-Arrow will be taken over also. I have no doubt but that the President, Mr. M.E. Forbes will be let out and that will mean a complete change."

For some weeks, it had been obvious that Walter Chrysler was determined to purchase Dodge Brothers Incorporated from its owner Dillon, Read & Co., who clearly indicated they would sell at the right price. In a June 1 article about stock trading during the previous session, the *Wall Street Journal* reported the Street "was full of reports of consolidations in the motor field in the wake of the Chrysler-Dodge announcement [of talks]. Simultaneous strength in Studebaker and Packard gave rise to rumors of negotiations between these two companies. Various stories were also afloat regarding Jordan, Pierce-Arrow and Chandler."

That same day, Myron Forbes was quoted as admitting that the possibility of a merger between Pierce-Arrow and Jordan "has been under discussion for several days but nothing can be announced." He also categorically denied any merger plans with Reo. Clearly, the weeks of June were filled with frantic activity to save the Pierce-Arrow Motor Car Co.

On Thursday the 14th in the *Wall Street Journal*, Albert R. Erskine of Studebaker Corp. admitted at South Bend to having had "some informal conversations" with Myron Forbes about a possible merger, "but nothing definite has developed." In the same story, the newspaper's Buffalo Bureau reported Forbes himself had confirmed that the company had been negotiating with Studebaker officials concerning such a merger but gave no further details. It also revealed that the negotiations with Jordan Motor Car Co. and Pierce-Arrow were "definitely abandoned." The crisis was not yet resolved despite ongoing efforts, although the Pierce-Arrow board had met the day before, reportedly to discuss "preliminary merger plans" with Studebaker. Such negotiations take time, and the plan would not be ready to send to stockholders for another two weeks.

It is very unlikely that Charles Clifton had any part at all in these negotiations, or, in fact, many of the efforts. For one thing, at this same time the Clifton family was occupied with preparations for the wedding of 25-year-old Alice on June 28 to Kenneth Strachan of New York, who would later play an active role at the Pierce-Arrow company. But mostly, Charles Clifton himself was gravely ill. The very day of the *Journal* article he was confined to his bed at 789 West Ferry and died there in the early evening a week later, Thursday, June 21, 1928.

The papers of June 22 all across the country reported Col. Clifton's unexpected passing, noting the funeral would take place the following afternoon at three. The *Buffalo Times* reported Clifton's death as being "a shock to many who knew him." The paper recalled Clifton as having been in "poor health for weeks, but it was not until last Thursday that he was confined to his bed. Even then it was thought he would recover, but he never emerged from the relapse that set in Thursday night."

The industry press was equally surprised by Clifton's passing. "For the past two or three years," one account read, "his age had been bearing down upon him, though his general health was not impaired, and his mind was quicker and keener than ever. It was, however, a frail and somewhat enfeebled figure who rose and silently bowed acknowledgement to the applause that greeted him at the banquet of the Chamber last January. It was his final appearance before the audience that ever accorded him its highest honors."

The Clifton family physician, Dr. Dewitt Sherman, a neighbor at 680 W. Ferry St., prepared Charles Clifton's death certificate, which was received by Gorham Clifton at the family home on June 22. Dr. Sherman had treated Charles Clifton for his condition from June 15 until his death, and apparently witnessed his passing, recorded as "6:50 p.m." Cause of death was given as "stone in common bile duct."

Charles Clifton's funeral service was conducted at his home on Saturday, June 23, by his close friend Rector Cameron Davis of the Trinity Episcopal Church in Buffalo. The Buffalo *Times* that evening described the event as "a simple ceremony, consistent with his unostentatious, unaffected life, a life of service to the automobile industry in which he blazed a trail for present greatness; to a wide circle of devoted friends and to the community at large." The house, with Alice's wedding less than a week away, was decorated with "a profusion of flowers" sent in condolence from "individuals and organizations almost without number" that included all the groups with which the Colonel had been affiliated and beyond. Employees and associates supplied more as did friends and relations. A flood of telegrams in sympathy also arrived from all around the country. Albert Erskine of Studebaker sent one, naturally enough, as did W.F. Culberson of the San Francisco Pierce-Arrow agency. Other automobile companies telegraphed condolences, so did the Detroit Division of the NACC.

Friends and associates crowded the ceremony as did members of the automobile industry, although none sent official representatives. At the end, his remains were carried by representatives of E.L. Brady & Son, the undertakers on Franklin St., to the graveside service and interment at Forest Hills Cemetery. Photographs of Pierce-Arrow vehicles in the service of Buffalo funeral homes at the time suggest that Charles Clifton's body may well have ridden to its final resting place in a Dual Valve Six. Pall bearers at these services were all longtime associates of Clifton's: Ansley W. Sawyer, Shepard Kimberley, Theodore Keating, Langdon Albright, Frederick H. Williams, S.V.R. Spaulding, Edmund Pearson and, William Warren Smith.

A simple stone cross rises above the sloping expanse of lawn under which Charles Clifton's body is buried beside that of his daughter Katherine Gould Clifton and, after her death in 1940, that of his wife Grace Gorham Clifton.

Sources

Some Notes on Sources

The narrative of this book depends for its detail on periodical publications, Pierce-Arrow Motor Car Company materials and Clifton family sources. Specific references have deliberately been included in the text itself. The documents themselves reside among four library collections.

Aside from the author's notes of interviews with Charles Clifton's grandson, the late Mark Clifton (February 21, 2005), and Michele Clifton (July 10, 2004, and December 5, 2004), family references can be found in the "Charles Clifton" files at the Buffalo and Erie County Historical Society, whose staff was always most helpful during my visits to their collection.

Buffalo newspaper stories were largely accessed from microfilm collections at the Buffalo Public Library Grosvenor Collection, which also made available volumes on the history of Buffalo General Hospital, the Buffalo Club and the Pierce-Arrow Motor Car Company employee magazine *The Arrow* (1918–1922).

Pierce-Arrow Motor Car Company materials can be accessed in the Pierce-Arrow Society Collection at the Antique Automobile Club of America Library and Research Center at Hershey, Pennsylvania, which also contains the Pierce-Arrow Society quarterly magazine *The Arrow* (1957–present).

A large collection of early automobile periodicals can be accessed at the Automotive Research Library of the Horseless Carriage Foundation, La Mesa, California, and proved invaluable for uncovering important issues in the developing automobile industry.

In addition, the following published sources furnished extensive background information about the early automobile industry and people in it:

Books

Brierley, Brooks T. *There Is No Mistaking a Pierce-Arrow*. Coconut Grove: Garrett & Stringer, Inc. 1986.
Hendry, Maurice D. *Pierce-Arrow, First Among America's Finest*. New York: Ballantine, 1971.
Kimes, Beverly Rae. *Pioneers, Engineers and Scoundrels: The Dawn of the Automobile in America*. Warrendale: SAE, 2005.
Kollins, Michael J. *Pioneers of the U.S. Automobile Industry*. Warrendale: SAE, 2002.
Nevins, Allan. *Ford: The Times, the Man, the Company*. New York: Scribner's, 1954.
Rae, John B. *American Automobile Manufacturers: A History of the Automobile Industry*. Philadelphia: Chilton, 1959.
Ralston, Marc. *Pierce-Arrow*. San Diego: A. S. Barnes, 1980.

Magazine Articles

Dawley, Herbert M. "My Happy Days at Pierce-Arrow." *The Arrow* (Pierce-Arrow Society quarterly magazine), 68, no. 4 (1968 4th quarter): 2–13.
Selman, E.C. "Ted." "Tending to Trucks in World War I" *The Arrow* (Pierce-Arrow Society quarterly magazine), 08 no. 1 (2008 1st quarter): 17–23; 08 no. 2 (2008 2nd quarter): 15–21; 08 no. 4 (2008 4th quarter): 20–23; 09 no. 1 (2009 1st quarter): 15–20; 09-2 (2009 2nd quarter): 17–22.

Index

Numbers in ***bold italics*** indicate pages with illustrations

AAA *see* American Automobile Association
Aberthaw Construction Co. 56, 79
Adkins, L.D. 108
Albright, Langdon 278
Aldrich, A. Estelle 189
Alford, J.F. 128, 168
Allied War Relief 159
Aluminum Castings Co. 69, 101
American Automobile Association 43, 53, 59,74, 81, 165
American Motor Car Manufacturers Association (AMCMA) 24, 31, 43, 48, 51–53, 55
Apperson, Edgar 244
Appleton, R.W. 154
Arnold, Horace L. 28
Association of Carriage & Automobile Workers 67
Association of Licensed Automobile Manufacturers (ALAM) 23–24, 26–27, 31, 32, 35, 37, 43, 47, 49, 51–52, 57, 59, 63, 65, 74
Association Patents Committee 63, 74
Automobile Board of Trade 66–67, 70, 73–75, 81
Automobile Salon 179, 202, 231, 240, 255

Baldwin, William M. 107, 250
Bartlett, F.R. 231
Bartlett, W.R. 250
Baruch, Bernard M. 157, 256
Batchelder, A.G. 124
Bell, Lewis & Yates Coal Mining Co. 2, 11
Bennett, George W. 75, 81
Benson, E.R. 94, 110
Birge, George K. 3, 10, **16**, 33–**34**, 37–38, 44, 48, 53–54, 66, 72, 88, 108, 114, 127,146

Birkigt, Marc 154
Blakner, Carl 82
Blaufuss, H.M. 134
Borein, Edward 72
Bowan, Carl H. 194
Braley, Berton 94
Brannigan, R.A. 241
Breadon, Sam 79, 181, 213
Brenner, Charlie 71, 176
Brisbane, Arthur 60
Brock, M.I. 27, 32, 38
Brooks, C.B. 149
Brosseau, A.J. 189, 223, 231,245
Brown, Frank C. 153, 175
Buerk, Hans 98
Buffalo Club 11,13, 27, 68, 159, 188, 220
Buffalo Fine Arts Academy 135, 159, 168, 236
Buffalo General Hospital 63, 71, 114, 123, 138–40, 183, 267, 272
Buffalo Grape Sugar Co. 10
Burkhardt, Otto M. 121, 134

Cady, C.W. 250
Calkins & Holden Agency 42, 107
Calman, Margaret 188
car models: Arrow 25; body changes 68; Great Arrow 26, 33; last 4's 48; Motorette 19; Series 1 77; Series 2 87; Series 3 96; Series 4 118, 139; Series 5 148; Series 31/51 166; Series 32 200, 202, 206; Series 33 212, 224, 230, 232, 244; Series 36 253; Series 80 236, 245, 249; Series 81 264, 270; Six-cylinder (65Q) 37; Stanhope 24; three sixes 54, 62
Carey, George 33
Carriage and Bodybuilders National Association Technical School 74, 80, 136

Chalfant, E.P. 47, 50
Chalmers, Hugh 63, 66, 74, 90, 123, 138, 142, 157–58, 171
Chapin, Roy D. 75, 79, 81, 90–91, 94, 123, 138, 144, 157, 171, 180, 189, 214, 219, 242, 255, 257–59, 210, 212, 222, 235
Chase National Bank 228–29
Christmas Cove, Maine 78, 84, 103, 115, 117, 124
Clarke, James Alfred "Rene" 91
Clarkson, Coker F. 116
Clifton, Alice 8, 10, 13
Clifton, Alice S. 12, 22, 188–89, 273
Clifton, Charles II 231
Clifton, Elizabeth Dorsheimer 5, 8, **9**, 10, 11, **13**, 68, 113
Clifton, Gorham 12, 20, 114, 138, 155, 189, 231, 252
Clifton, Grace Gorham 11, 12, **13**, ***114***, 188, 252–53, 256, 258, 259, 274
Clifton, Henry 5, 7–**9**
Clifton, Henry II 8, **9**, 10, **13**
Clifton, Jeanie 7, 8, **13**, 19
Clifton, Katherine Gould 12, 21, 83, 274
Clifton, Margaret Keenan 116, 231, 252
Clifton, Mark 8, 67
Clifton, Peter 252
Clifton, Philip 8, 10, 11, **13**
Clifton, Sarah 8, 10, 11, **13**
Cobb, Irwin 113, 218
Coffin, Howard 138
Coleman, Robert F. 153, 214
Colgate & Gilbert Starch Co. 10
Conn, Robert "Bob" 191,204
Cooke, George W. 97, 156, 173
Cooke, Walter P. 190, 214, 260
Copeland, A.W. 141
Corcoran, Lawrence E. 161, 198, 214, 219, 250

277

Council of National Defense 138, 141
Couzens, James 258
Cowan, Anna L. 141, 183
Cowles, Chan 187, 193, 204, 214
Cox, W.S. 128, 168
cross-licensing agreement 111, 165, 241
Culberson, William F. 70, 83, 208, 213, 250, 274
Cuntz, Herman 26
Cutler, Elihu 23, 34

Dahl, Gorhard M. 229, 260
Danaher, J.J. 190
Davis, Arthur V. 251
Davis, Francis W. 62, 134, 150, 159, 176, 194, 207, 215, 224
Davis, Samuel T., Jr. 52, 66, 75, 117
Dawley, Herbert M. 35, 38, 53, 68–69, 78, 81–83, 100–01, 128, 153, 163, 265
Day, F.S. 36, 44
Day, George H. 23, 26, 42
DeChend, Willie 156
Dolnar, Hugh *see* Arnold, Horace L.
Dormer, James 8
Dorsheimer, Philip 5, **6**, 8
Dorsheimer, Sarah Gorgas 5, **6**, 8
Dorsheimer, William 6, 7, 8
Doyle, Brig. Gen. Peter C. 10, 11
Drake, J. Walter 223
Dudley, Joseph G. 128, 168, 190, 214, 223, 260
Dundon, John N. 264

Earl, Harley J. 270
Edge, S.F. 100
Egan, F.H. 175
Electric Vehicle Co. (ECV) 22, 23, 41, 42, 52
Elma Magnetic Gear Box 134
Eltinge, Julian D. 83
Entz, Electro-Magnetic Transmission 121
Erith, John 186
Erskine, Albert R. 273, 274
Estabrook, Charlie 108

Fassitt, J.H. "Jack" 105
Fatherless Children of France 159
Fellows, S.O. 153, 173
Ferguson, A., 229
Fergusson, David 18, **19**, 20, 24, 28, 32, 61, 79, 99, 100, 106, 121, 123, 125, 133–34, 140, 145, 155, 173, 185, 193, 198, 206, 207, 213
Fields, Clarence 157
Fitzgerald, Garrett 260

Flershem, Randolph B. 264
Forbes, Myron E. 173, 182, 190, 191, 204, 208, **215**, 217, 219–20, 222, 226, 228, 231, 234, 235, 238, 242, 243, 244, 245, 250, 253–54, 255–256, 260–61, 263, 264, 269, 270, 273
Forbush, Edna 172
Ford, Edsel 244, 269
Ford, Henry 43, 51, 57, 65, 120, 244, 269
Ford Motor Co. 23, 41, 57, 65, 120, 244, 269
Foss, W.J. 117, 128, 131, 138, 156, 163, 168, 176, 182, 190
Fox, W.J. 161
Friend, E.R. 213

Gaffke, W.K. 164
Garden, Mary 161, 252, 265
Garden, Robert D. 44, 45, 115, 181
Gardner, Laurence H. 13, **34**, 118, 123, 138
Gardner, William H. 13, 15, **34**, 39, 108, 118
Gaston, Williams & Wigmore 116
Gates, L.H. 204
George N. Pierce Co. 2, 12, 13, 15, 44, 48
George W. Goethals & Co. 169, 170, 208
Gerlatch, Robert 97, 125, 153, 157
Gertis, Charles 183
Gilbreth, Frank (and Lillian) 171
Glidden Tour 30, 32, 35, 42, 44–45, 49
Goodhue, Bertram 83
Gorham, George 10, 11, 13, 44
Graham, George M. 144, 155, 163, 179, 182, 191, 195, 200, 213–14, 245
Granbow, Fred 183
Green, Mildred C. 219
Green & Wicks 67
Guarantee Trust Co. 229
Guider, J.F. 97, 156, 173, 182, 186, 212, 214, 234, 250

Hamilton, Ernest 154, 156
Hanch, C.C. 65, 75, 158, 180, 189, 223, 241
Harriman, Lewis G. 229, 260
Harrolds Motor Car Co. 83, 252
Hart, M.M. 149
Hayden, Stone & Co. 229
Hedges, Joe 50–60, 132
Henafelt, Lewis W. 146, 153, 162
Henderson, Thomas 47, 66, 67
Henri, Bill 226, 229, 250
Herkomer Cup 35

Hewitt, S.J. 149
Highland Military Academy 8
Himmele, E.F. 214
Hinman, H.P. 204
Hodge, Charlie 131, 207
Holland, Frank 101
Hoover, Herbert 248
Horning, Harry 244
Hough, Judge Charles M. 49
Hower Tour 45
Hoyt, William B. **34**, 39, 108, 114
Hubbard, F.B. 153
Huff, George C. 175, 269
Hunt, Roy A. 251
Huntley, William R. 260
Hutchinson, O.C. 218

Importers Salon 43
Interstate Commerce Commission (ICC) 93, 128
Irving Bank, Columbia Trust Co. 229

J & W Seligman & Co. 129, 222, 228, 229
Jay, John C., Jr. 169, 170, 172, 174, 180, 181, 185, 190, 260
Jewell, D. 260
Jewett, Harry M. 189
Johns, Albert 220
Johnson, Andrew F. 74
Jones, Emanuel 183
Joy, Henry 22, 66, 110, 113

Kaelin, Charles G. 210
Kahn, Albert H. 33
Kalb, L.P. 115
Kardo Company 91, 95, **103**, 108, 109, 110
Keating, Theodore 274
Kettering, Charles 78
Killinger, Arthur E. 135, 153
Kimberley, Shepard 274
Kittredge, Lewis H. 47, 52, 75, 93
Kolb, H.A. 190
Koperski, Joseph 270
Kreatz, George 157
Kumpf, Arthur 45, 92

Ladd, Walter M. 153, 190
Lake Shore & Michigan Southern Ry. 5
Ledermann, A.A. "Tony" 86, 213
Lee, John R. 141
Lee, S. 149
Legion of Honor 159, 226
Leland, Henry 209
Leland, Wilfred C. 67, 75, 85, 93
Leonard, K. 194, 198
Lepine, M.H. 204
Le Sidanier, Henri 212

Letchworth, E.H. 260
Lind, Jenny 7
Lockwood, Thomas B. 114
Lockwood, Green & Co. 33
Loder, L.R. 149
Lozier, H.A. 35

Macauley, Alvan **92**, 93, 110, 179, 212, 245, 258
Magoffin, Charles F. 125, 134
Maguire, J.W. 45, 79, 80
Mansion House 5
Marine Trust Co. 159, 169
May, Henry 15, 17, 18, 30, 32, **34**, 38, **39**, 79, 104, 122, 128, 133, 138, 156, 163, 168, 171–**173**, 174
Maybeck, Me. C. 146
McAdoo, W.G. 147
McArtney, Tom 135, 153, 161, 225
McCullough, C.H. 128, 168, 189
McDurmand, George 157
McKinnon, A. 107, 119
McLaughlin, "Mister Mac" 101
McLernon, Robert 157
McNulty, J.H. 229
Medwedeff, M.H. 97
Mellon, Andrew W. 251
Mellon, Richard B. 251
Metzger, William E. 47, 75, 258
Mickle, Roy 175
Miles, Samuel A. 75, 78, 84, 88, 91, 103, 112, 115, 124, 140, 242, 258
Miller, John 176
Mills, Stanley W. 150, 215
Mixter, George W. 173, 182, 184–85, 190, 193, 196, 198, 199, 203, 205, 207, 208, 214, 216
Mooney, Dr. Frasier D. 272
Morgan, George E. 180
Moskovics, Fred E. 244
Motor and Accessories Manufacturers Association 74

Nash, Charles W. 222, 223
National Association of Automobile Manufacturers (NAAM) 21, 43, 52, 73, 80, 84
National Automobile Chamber of Commerce 81, 84–85, 88, 94, 103, 108–10, 113, 115, 116, 118, 123, 124, 125, 128, 132, 136, 138, 140, 141, 143, 147, 157, 165, 171, 179, 211, 218, 223, 226, 230, 232, 234, 236, 241–42, 245, 248, 251, 255, 257–59
National Automobile Dealers Association 74, 157
Neeson, Margaret 188

Newlin, W.B. 105, 106, 131
Newsome, Walter 97, 153
Nickerson, F.A. 115
Northup, Amos 200, 213, 219
Noyes, Judge Walter Chadwick 63
Nuskoy, John D. 155

Obenauer, Al 183
O'Brian, Roland L. 228, 229, 260
O'Brian, Potter & Co. 229
Ochtman, J. 149
O'Day, George 190
Olds, R.E. 51, 179
O'Neil, A.R. 164
O'Rourke, Joseph C. 250
O'Rourke, Thomas J. 214, 250
Osborn, Carl R. 220
Ostiguy, A.C. 181

Park Drop Forge Co. 134
Patten, Robert O. 131, 191, 193, 214, 219
Paulman, Henry 106, 213, 243
Peace Bridge Co. 244
Pearson, E.C. 173, 190, 229, 274
Peck, George 163, 198
Penfield, Edward 42
Perley, Myron 116
Perry, Norris 113
Pfau, Hugo 240, 271
Pfeiffer, Charles "Uncle Charlie" 204
Phillips Custom Body Co. 271
Pierce, George N. 15, **34**, 36, 44
Pierce, Percy P. 15, **19**, 20, **34**, 35, 36
Pierce-Arrow Finance Corp. 231, 233
Pierce-Arrow Truck Sales Corp. 233, 270
Pierce Cycle Co. 36
Pleuthner, Charles 79, 134, 251
Pope, Col. Albert 22, 75
Pope, Col. George 52, 70, 75, 85

Quinby & Company 30, 32

Rand, George F. 169
Rand, George F., Jr. 238, 260
Reeves, Alfred 56, 57, 75, 90, 93, 108, 110, 113, 117, 136, 141, 180, 223, 244, 245, 258
Reid, Robert C. 181
Retling, Edward 79, 213
Rice, Herbert H. 75, 88, 136, 147, 189, 223, 245, 247
Richardson, Henry Hobsen 7
Rickenbacker, Eddie 180
Riker, Andrew L. 165
Roos, Delmar G. "Barney" 206
Ross, Dr. Renwick R. 272

Rounds, E.H. **34**, 107
Rubay, Leon 186

Saoutchik, Jacques 261–63, 271
Sawyer, Ansley W. 176, 260, 274
Schmidlapp, Carl J. 128, 168, 260
Schmidt, Waller 249
Schuster, George 161
Selden Patent 22, 23, 41, 49–51, 57–59, 65
Selman, E.C. "Ted" 108, 113, 135, 160, 176, 181, 219–20, 225, 230
Sheppy, Charles 18, 20, **25**, 27, 79, 106, 121, 125, 133, 148, 156, 206, 214, 217, 219, 250, 251, 254, 261
Sherbondy, E.H. 207
Sherman, Dr. Dewitt 274
Shortal, William 250
Sidney Shepard & Co. 9
Sikes, Albert D. 229, 260
Sills, W.C. 189
Simpson, Col. John R. 264
Sloan, Alfred P. 246
Smith, Carlton M. 229
Smith, Floyd H. 189
Smith, Fred 22
Smith, H.O. 51, 75
Smith, William Warren 274
Société Anomyme des Pierce-Arrow 231
Society of Automotive Engineers (SAE) 27, 33, 35, 36, 117, 244
Souther, Henry 35
Spaulding, S.V.R. 274
Spooner, F. Ed. 44
Squelch, John 150
Stettenbenz, Albert 176
Stoddard, C.G. 51
Strachan, Kenneth L 273
Strauss, Albert 128, 260
Strauss, Frederick 168
Sturdevant, H.J. 176
Swayne, Alfred H. 258

Talcott, John 207, 251, 261
Taylor, E.A. 194, 204
Terrant, Allen 204
Thomas, H. Kerr 61, 79, 97, 105, 119, 135, 150–51, 156, 173
Tibbets, Milton, **92**, 93
Tichenor, Charles M. 175, 186, 190, 194, 198
Torkelson, B.E. 149
Treidler, Adolf 107, 200
Trimble, R.J. 128
Trinity Episcopal Church 11, 12
truck models: five-ton (R1-R9) 64, 66; Fleet Arrow 270; Model R10 195, 196; Model W2 194, 196; Model X5 193,

196; Model Z bus 231, 243; two-ton (X1-X4) 88
Turner Construction Co. 53

Ulrich, George 79, 149
Unitarian Society of Buffalo 6, 11, 46

Van den Plas 226
Vanderbilt, W.K., Jr. 76

Waldon, Sidney D. 49, 66, 75, 207, 223
Waldorf, Joseph 183
War Industries Board 158, 160
Watson, Lester 260
Way, James R. 46, 68, 101, **102**, 134, 186, 210, 239, 265
Weaver, Fred 181
Weiland, Alfred 203
Weiser, Edward J. 173
Wells, Fred J. 193, 214, 250
White, D. McCall 209
White, Windsor 33, 88, 93, 189
Whitney, William Collins 22
Williams, Frederick H. 274
Williams, L.G. 149
Willys, John N. 21, 147, 180, 223, 245, 259
Wilson, Edward A. 203
Wilson, John W. 162
Winton, Alexander 15, 22, 132

Wray, R. 149
Wright, Orville 244
Wright-Martin Aircraft Corp. 154, 170
Wrye, Walter C. 129, 138, 148, 168, 173
Wyman & Gordon 134

Younger, John 79, 125, 133–34
Youngert, W. 149

Zangerlee, John 183
Zimmerman, A.F. 140
Zimmerscheid, K.W. 138

www.ingramcontent.com/pod-product-compliance
Lightning Source LLC
Chambersburg PA
CBHW080801300426
44114CB00020B/2791